REA's Test Prep Books Are The Best!

(a sample of the <u>hundreds of letters</u> REA receives each year)

" A guaranteed "5" on the AP Biology. The book's strength is its six full-length exams with multiple-choice questions. "

AP Biology Student, Stanford University, Stanford, CA

" REA's AP Biology test prep is a good reference source with good tests. It has an excellent review section and the tests are complete. "

AP Biology Student, Detroit, MI

" Your book was such a better value and was so much more complete than anything your competition has produced — and I have them all! "

Teacher, Virginia Beach, VA

" Compared to the other books that my fellow students had, your book was the most useful in helping me get a great score. "

Student, North Hollywood, CA

" Your book was responsible for my success on the exam, which helped me get into the college of my choice... I will look for REA the next time I need help. "

Student, Chesterfield, MO

" Just a short note to say thanks for the great support your book gave me in helping me pass the test... I'm on my way to a B.S. degree because of you! "

Student, Orlando, FL

(more on next page)

(continued from front page)

" I just wanted to thank you for helping me get a great score
on the AP U.S. History exam... Thank you for making great test preps! "
Student, Los Angeles, CA

" Your *Fundamentals of Engineering Exam* book was the absolute best
preparation I could have had for the exam, and it is one of the major
reasons I did so well and passed the FE on my first try. "
Student, Sweetwater, TN

" I used your book to prepare for the test and found that the advice and the
sample tests were highly relevant... Without using any other material, I earned
very high scores and will be going to the graduate school of my choice. "
Student, New Orleans, LA

" What I found in your book was a wealth of information sufficient to shore up
my basic skills in math and verbal... The practice tests were challenging and
the answer explanations most helpful. It certainly is
the *Best Test Prep for the GRE*! "
Student, Pullman, WA

" I really appreciate the help from your excellent book. Please keep up
the great work. "
Student, Albuquerque, NM

" I am writing to thank you for your test preparation... Your book helped me
immeasurably and I have nothing but praise for your *GRE* preparation. "
Student, Benton Harbor, MI

THE BEST TEST PREPARATION FOR THE

ADVANCED PLACEMENT EXAMINATION

AP BIOLOGY

Seventh Edition

AP Biology Review by

Laurie Ann Callihan

Edited by Stephen Hart

AP Lab Reviews by

James M. Buckley, Jr.

Science Teacher
Edwards-Knox Central School
Russell, New York

Practice Tests by

Joyce A. Blinn

Reading Specialist – Biology
Bowling Green State University
Bowling Green, Ohio

Shira Rohde

Instructor of Physiology
Santa Rosa Junior College
Santa Rosa, California

Jay Templin, Ed.D.

Assistant Professor of Biology
Widener University
Wilmington, Delaware

Research & Education Association

61 Ethel Road West • Piscataway, New Jersey 08854

The Best Test Preparation for the
AP BIOLOGY EXAM

Copyright © 2005 by Research & Education Association, Inc.
Prior editions copyright © 2003, 2000, 1998, 1995, 1992, 1988 by
Research & Education Association, Inc.

Printed in the United States of America

Library of Congress Control Number 2004094939

International Standard Book Number 0-7386-0054-7

REA® is a registered trademark of Research & Education Association, Inc.,
Piscataway, NJ 08854.

REA supports the effort to conserve and
protect environmental resources by
printing on recycled papers.

CONTENTS

BIOLOGY SUBJECT REVIEWS

PRACTICE TESTS

AP BIOLOGY LAB REVIEWS

INDEX

ABOUT OUR BIOLOGY REVIEW AUTHOR

Laurie Ann Callihan received a B.S. in Biology from Christian Heritage College in El Cajon, California, and pursued post-graduate study at ICR Graduate School, in Santee, California, and at Albany State University, in Albany, New York. Ms. Callihan began her educational career over 20 years ago as Laboratory Manager at Santana Public High School in Santee, California. She has taught at Christian High School in El Cajon, California; NC3 Academy in Valley Forge, Pennsylvania; and Sauquoit Valley Central School District in Sauquoit, New York. Currently a home-school educator in Arcadia, Florida, Ms. Callihan also teaches CLEP preparation classes throughout the United States. Her publications include *The Guidance Manual for the Christian Home School,* published by Career Press, the forthcoming *Science by the Book,* and a weekly column found on Crosswalk.com. Her educational work makes her a frequent radio and television guest.

ABOUT OUR BIOLOGY REVIEW EDITOR

Stephen Hart is a writer and editor specializing in science, medicine, and technology. After majoring in zoology, Mr. Hart went on to earn his M.A.T. in Biology at the University of Washington. He has worked as an editorial consultant for Prentice Hall, Saunders, and the American Society of Plant Physiologists. His freelance writing has included assignments for Time-Life Books, ABCNews.com, and the NASA Astrobiology Web site.

ACKNOWLEDGMENTS

In addition to our authors, we would like to thank Larry B. Kling, Manager, Editorial Services; Pam Weston, Production Manager, for ensuring press readiness; Alicia Shapiro, Project Manager, along with Craig Yetsko, Amy Jamison, and Amy Laurent for their editorial contributions; Christine Saul, Senior Graphic Artist, for her graphic arts contributions; Jeff LoBalbo, Senior Graphic Artist, for post-production file mapping; and Network Typesetting for typesetting revisions for this new edition.

ABOUT RESEARCH & EDUCATION ASSOCIATION

Founded in 1959, Research & Education Association is dedicated to publishing the finest and most effective educational materials—including software, study guides, and test preps—for students in middle school, high school, college, graduate school, and beyond. Today, REA's wide-ranging catalog is a leading resource for teachers, students, and professionals. We invite you to visit us at REA.com to find out how "REA is making the world smarter."

AP BIOLOGY
Independent Study Schedule

The following study schedule allows for thorough preparation for the AP Biology Examination. Although it is designed for six weeks, it can be condensed into a three-week course by collapsing each two-week period into a single week. Be sure to set aside at least two hours each day to study. Bear in mind that the more time you spend studying, the more prepared and relaxed you will feel on the day of the exam.

Week	Activity
1	Read and study Chapter 1, which will introduce you to the AP Biology Examination. Carefully read and study the Biology Review included in Chapter 2 of this book.
2 & 3	Carefully read and study the Biology Review included in Chapters 3-8 of this book.
4	Take AP Biology Practice Tests I and II in this book. After scoring your exam, carefully review all incorrect answer explanations. If any particular subjects seem difficult, review them by referring back to the appropriate section of the Biology Review. If possible, read biology-related articles from science magazines (available at your local library or bookstore). This will help familiarize you with current events in science and technology related to biology, as well as terminology and style used by scientists (including those who write questions for the AP Biology Exam).
5	Take Practice Tests III and IV, and after scoring your exam, carefully review all incorrect answer explanations. If any particular subjects seem difficult, review them by referring back to the appropriate section of the Biology Review.
6	Take Practice Tests V and VI. After scoring them, review all incorrect answer explanations. Study any areas in which you consider yourself to be weak by using the Biology Review and any other reliable sources you have on hand. Review our practice tests again to be sure you understand the problems that you originally answered incorrectly.

CHAPTER 1
PASSING THE
AP BIOLOGY
EXAMINATION

Chapter 1

PASSING THE AP BIOLOGY EXAMINATION

ABOUT THIS BOOK

This book provides an accurate and complete representation of the Advanced Placement Examination in Biology. Our six practice tests are based on the format of the most recently administered Advanced Placement Biology Exam. Each model exam lasts three hours (including a 10-minute for reading period) and includes every type of question that you can expect to encounter on the real test. Following each of our practice tests is an answer key, complete with detailed explanations designed to clarify the material for you. Also included in this book is a targeted biology course review. We provide it as a quick and handy reference for the topics covered on the AP Biology Exam. By using the subject reviews, completing all six practice tests, and studying the explanations that follow, you will pinpoint your strengths and weaknesses and, above all, put yourself in the best possible position to do well on the actual test.

ABOUT THE EXAM

The Advanced Placement Biology Examination is offered each May at participating schools and multi-school centers throughout the world.

The Advanced Placement Program is designed to allow high school students to pursue college-level studies while attending high school. The participating colleges, in turn, grant credit and/or advanced placement to students who do well on the examinations.

The Advanced Placement Biology Course is designed to be the equivalent of a college introductory biology course, often taken by biology majors in their first year of college. The AP Biology Exam covers material in three major areas:

1. Molecules and Cells – 25%
2. Heredity and Evolution – 25%
3. Organisms and Populations – 50%

The exam is divided into two sections:

1. **Multiple-Choice:** Composed of 100 multiple-choice questions designed to test your ability to recall and understand various biological facts and concepts. This section of the exam is 80 minutes long, and is worth 60% of the final grade.

2. **Free-Response:** Consists of four mandatory questions designed to test your ability to think clearly and present ideas in a logical and coherent way. The answers must be in essay form. Outlines alone, or unlabeled and unexplained diagrams are not acceptable. Each of the four questions is weighted equally, and topics covered are as follows:

Molecules and Cells – one question
Heredity and Evolution – one question
Organisms and Populations – two questions

Any one of these four questions may require you to analyze or interpret data or information from their laboratory experience as well as classroom lectures. This section of the exam is 90 minutes long, and counts for 40% of the final grade.

A 10-minute reading period is included on the exam.

You may find the AP Biology Exam considerably more difficult than many classroom exams. In order to measure the full range of your ability in biology, the AP Exams are designed to produce average scores of approximately 50% of the maximum possible score for the multiple-choice and essay sections. Therefore, you should not expect to attain a perfect or even near-perfect score.

HOW TO USE THIS BOOK

What do I study first?

Read over the course review and the suggestions for test-taking. Next, take the first practice test to pinpoint your area(s) of weakness, and then go back and focus your study on those specific problems. Studying the reviews thoroughly will reinforce the basic skills you will need to do well on the exam. Make sure to take the six practice tests to become familiar with the format and procedures involved with taking the actual exam.

To best utilize your study time, follow our Independent Study Schedule, which you will find in the front of this book. The schedule is based on a six-week program, but if necessary can be condensed to three weeks by combining each two-week program into one week.

When should I start studying?

It is never too early to start studying for the AP Biology Examination. The earlier you begin, the more time you will have to sharpen your skills. Do not procrastinate! Cramming is *not* an effective way to study, since it does not allow you the time needed to learn the test material. The sooner you learn the format of the exam, the more time you will have to familiarize yourself with it.

CONTENT OF THE AP BIOLOGY EXAMINATION

The AP Biology course covers the material one would find in a college-level general biology class. The exam stresses basic facts and principles, as well as general theoretical approaches used by biologists.

The approximate breakdown of topics is as follows:

25% Molecular and Cellular Biology

- Chemistry of life
- Cells
- Cellular energy

25% Heredity and Evolution

- Heredity
- Molecular genetics
- Evolutionary biology

50% Organisms and Populations

- Diversity of organisms

- Structure and function of plants and animals

- Ecology

ABOUT OUR REVIEW SECTION

This book contains an AP Biology Course Review that can be used as both a primer and as a quick reference while taking the practice exams. Our 120-page review is meant to complement your AP Biology textbook and is by no means exhaustive. By studying our review along with your text, you will be well prepared for the exam.

SCORING THE AP BIOLOGY EXAMINATION

How do I score my practice tests?

The multiple-choice section of the exam is scored by crediting each correct answer with one point, and deducting only partial credit (one-fourth of a point) for each incorrect answer. Questions omitted do not receive a deduction or a credit. Use this formula to calculate a raw score:

$$\underset{\substack{\text{number} \\ \text{right}}}{\underline{\hspace{1.5cm}}} - (\underset{\substack{\text{number} \\ \text{wrong*}}}{\underline{\hspace{1.5cm}}} \times 0.25) = \underset{\text{raw score}}{\underline{\hspace{1.5cm}}}$$

* Do not include unanswered questions

Then,

$$\underset{\substack{\text{raw} \\ \text{score}}}{\underline{\hspace{1.5cm}}} \times 0.90 = \underset{\text{multiple-choice raw score}}{\underline{\hspace{2.5cm}}}$$

The four essays are given a maximum score of 15 points each. Higher scores are awarded to essays that demonstrate in-depth knowledge and understanding of the subject or topic. The score should be given by a person who is both knowledgeable in biology and is able to be impartial, such as a teacher. Add the four scores together to calculate a second raw score. Use this formula:

$$\underset{\text{essay \#1}}{\underline{\hspace{1cm}}} + \underset{\text{essay \#2}}{\underline{\hspace{1cm}}} + \underset{\text{essay \#3}}{\underline{\hspace{1cm}}} + \underset{\text{essay \#4}}{\underline{\hspace{1cm}}} = \underset{\text{essay raw score}}{\underline{\hspace{2.5cm}}}$$

Now you can determine your composite score. To do this, add the raw scores from both sections. Use this formula:

$$\underline{\hspace{4cm}} + \underline{\hspace{4cm}} = \underline{\hspace{4cm}}$$

   multiple-choice score   essay score   composite score
                   (round to nearest whole number)

You may then convert your composite score to an AP Biology Test grade by using the scale that follows. Please note that there is not a fixed composite score range that is consistent from year to year. The following scale should be used as an estimate only.

COMPOSITE SCORE	AP GRADE
101–150	5 (extremely well qualified)
82–100	4 (well qualified)
62–81	3 (qualified)
40-61	2 (possibly qualified)
0-39	1 (no recommendation)

When will I know my score?

In July, a grade report will be sent to you, your high school, and the college you chose to notify. The report will include scores for all the AP Exams you have taken up to that point.

Your grade will be used by your college of choice to determine placement in its biology program. This grade will vary in significance from college to college, and is used with other academic information to determine placement. Normally, colleges participating in the Advanced Placement Program will recognize grades of 3 or better. Contact your college admissions office for more information regarding its use of AP grades.

STUDYING FOR THE AP BIOLOGY EXAMINATION

It is very important for you to choose the time and place for studying that works best for you. Some students may set aside a certain number of hours every morning, while others may choose to study at night before going to sleep. Other students may study during the day, while waiting in line, or even while eating lunch. Only you can determine when and where your study time will be most effective. But be consistent and use your time wisely. Work out a study routine and stick to it.

When you take the practice tests, create an environment as much like the actual testing environment as possible. Turn your television and radio off, and sit down at a quiet table free from distraction. Make sure to time yourself, breaking the test down by section.

As you complete each practice test, score your test and thoroughly review the explanations to the questions you answered incorrectly; however, do not review too much at one time. Concentrate on one problem area at a time by reviewing the question and explanation, and by studying our review until you are confident that you completely understand the material.

Keep track of your scores and mark them on the Scoring Worksheet. By doing so, you will be able to gauge your progress and discover general weaknesses in particular sections. You should carefully study the reviews that cover areas with which you have difficulty, as this will build your skills in those areas.

TEST-TAKING TIPS

Although you may not be familiar with standardized tests such as the AP Biology Examination, there are many ways to acquaint yourself with this type of examination and help alleviate any test-taking anxieties. Listed below are ways to help you become accustomed to the AP exams, some of which may be applied to other standardized tests as well.

Become comfortable with the format of the exam. Stay calm and pace yourself. After simulating the test a couple of times, you will boost your chances of doing well, and you will be able to sit down for the actual exam with more confidence.

Read all of the possible answers. Just because you think you have found the correct response, do not automatically assume that it is the best answer. Read through each choice to be sure that you are not making a mistake by jumping to conclusions.

Use the process of elimination. Go through each answer to a question and eliminate as many of the answer choices as possible. By eliminating just two answer choices, you give yourself a better chance of getting the item correct, since there will only be three choices left from which to make your guess.

Work quickly and steadily. You will have only 80 minutes to work on 100 questions in the multiple-choice section, so work quickly and steadily to avoid focusing on any one question too long. Taking the practice tests in this book will help you learn to budget your time.

Beware of test vocabulary. Words such as *always, every, none, only*, and *never* indicate there should be no exceptions to the answer you choose. Words like *generally, usually, sometimes, seldom, rarely*, and *often* indicate there may be exceptions to your answer.

Learn the directions and format for each section of the test. Familiarizing yourself with the directions and format of the exam will save you valuable time on the day of the actual test.

Answer every question. There is no penalty for guessing, so answer every question before you run out of time, even if you are not sure of the answer.

THE DAY OF THE EXAM

Before the exam

On the day of the test, you should wake up early (preferably after a good night's rest) and have a good breakfast. Make sure to dress comfortably, so that you are not distracted by being too hot or too cold while taking the test. Also plan to arrive at the test center early. This will allow you to collect your thoughts and relax before the test, and will also spare you the anxiety that comes with being late.

Before you leave for the test center, make sure that you have your admission form, social security number, and another form of identification, which must contain a recent photograph, your name, and signature (i.e., driver's license, student identification card, or current alien registration card). You will not be allowed to take the test if you do not have proper identification. You will also need to bring your school code. Also, bring several sharpened No. 2 pencils with erasers for the multiple-choice questions and black or blue pens for the free-response questions.

You may wear a watch, but only one without a beep or alarm. No dictionaries, textbooks, notebooks, compasses, correction fluid, highlighters, rulers, computers, cell phones, beepers, PDAs, scratch paper, listening and recording devices, briefcases, or packages will be permitted and drinking, smoking, and eating are prohibited while taking the test.

During the exam

Once you enter the test center, follow all of the rules and instructions given by the test supervisor. If you do not, you risk being dismissed from the test and having your scores canceled.

After the exam

You may immediately register when taking the exam to have your score sent to the college of your choice; you may also wait and later request to have your AP score reported to the college of your choice.

CONTACTING THE AP PROGRAM

For registration bulletins or more information about the AP Biology exam, contact:

AP Services
P.O. Box 6671
Princeton, NJ 08541-6671
Phone: (609) 771-7300 or (888) 225-5427
Website: www.collegeboard.com

▼

CHAPTER 2
THE CHEMISTRY
OF BIOLOGY

Chapter 2

THE CHEMISTRY OF BIOLOGY

CHEMICAL COMPOSITION OF LIVING THINGS

Matter — Atoms, Elements, Molecules

The study of matter is known as chemistry. In order to understand why cells behave the way they do, you must first understand some basic chemistry. All matter is made up of **atoms.** The properties of matter are a result of the structure of atoms and their interaction with each other.

An **element** is a substance that cannot be broken down into any other substances. The simplest unit of an element that retains the element's characteristics is known as an atom. Each atom of a given element has a nucleus containing a unique number of **protons** and about the same number of **neutrons**. The nucleus is surrounded by **electrons**.

Elements are listed by atomic number on the **periodic table of the elements**. The atomic number is the number of protons found in the nucleus of an atom of that element. In an uncharged atom, the number of protons is equal to the number of electrons.

Electrons have much less mass than protons and neutrons. Electrons have a charge of -1, while protons have a charge of +1. Neutrons have no charge. The number of protons in the nucleus of an atom carries a positive charge equal to this number; that is, if an atom's nucleus contains 4 protons, the charge is +4. Since positive and negative charges attract, the positive charges of the nucleus attract an equal number of negatively charged electrons.

Electrons travel freely in a three-dimensional space that may be called an **electron cloud**, an **electron shell**, or an **orbital**. Current models of the atom follow the principles of quantum mechanics, which predict the

Periodic Table of the Elements

1	2	3	4	5	6	7	8	9	10	11	12	13	14	15	16	17	18
1 H 1.01																	2 He 4.00
3 Li 6.94	4 Be 9.01											5 B 10.81	6 C 12.01	7 N 14.01	8 O 16.00	9 F 19.00	10 Ne 20.18
11 Na 22.99	12 Mg 24.30											13 Al 26.98	14 Si 28.09	15 P 30.97	16 S 32.07	17 Cl 35.45	18 Ar 39.95
19 K 39.10	20 Ca 40.08	21 Sc 44.96	22 Ti 47.87	23 V 50.94	24 Cr 52.00	25 Mn 54.94	26 Fe 55.84	27 Co 58.93	28 Ni 58.69	29 Cu 63.55	30 Zn 65.39	31 Ga 69.72	32 Ge 72.61	33 As 74.92	34 Se 78.96	35 Br 79.90	36 Kr 83.80
37 Rb 85.47	38 Sr 87.62	39 Y 88.91	40 Zr 91.22	41 Nb 92.91	42 Mo 95.94	43 Tc (98)	44 Ru 101.07	45 Rh 102.91	46 Pd 106.42	47 Ag 107.87	48 Cd 112.41	49 In 114.82	50 Sn 118.71	51 Sb 121.76	52 Te 127.60	53 I 126.90	54 Xe 131.29
55 Cs 132.91	56 Ba 137.33		72 Hf 178.49	73 Ta 180.95	74 W 183.84	75 Re 186.21	76 Os 190.23	77 Ir 192.22	78 Pt 195.08	79 Au 196.97	80 Hg 200.59	81 Tl 204.38	82 Pb 207.20	83 Bi 208.98	84 Po (209)	85 At (210)	86 Rn (222)
87 Fr (223)	88 Ra (226)		104 Rf (261)	105 Db (262)	106 Sg (263)	107 Bh (264)	108 Hs (265)	109 Mt (268)	110 Uun (269)	111 Uuu (272)	112 Uub (277)						

57 La 138.91	58 Ce 140.12	59 Pr 140.91	60 Nd 144.24	61 Pm (145)	62 Sm 150.36	63 Eu 151.96	64 Gd 157.25	65 Tb 158.93	66 Dy 162.50	67 Ho 164.93	68 Er 167.26	69 Tm 168.93	70 Yb 173.04	71 Lu 174.97
89 Ac (227)	90 Th 232.04	91 Pa 231.04	92 U 238.03	93 Np (237)	94 Pu (244)	95 Am (243)	96 Cm (247)	97 Bk (247)	98 Cf (251)	99 Es (252)	100 Fm (257)	101 Md (258)	102 No (259)	103 Lr (262)

Fig. 2-1: The Periodic Table of the Elements. Elements are listed by atomic number.

Common Elements

Atomic Number	Symbol	Common Name
1	H	Hydrogen
2	He	Helium
6	C	Carbon
7	N	Nitrogen
8	O	Oxygen
11	Na	Sodium
12	Mg	Magnesium
14	Si	Silicon
15	P	Phosphorous
16	S	Sulphur
17	Cl	Chlorine
19	K	Potassium
20	Ca	Calcium
24	Cr	Chromium
26	Fe	Iron
29	Cu	Copper
30	Zn	Zinc
47	Ag	Silver
53	I	Iodine
79	Au	Gold
80	Hg	Mercury
82	Pb	Lead
86	Rn	Radon

probabilities of an electron being in a certain area at a certain time. Although the term "orbital" is used, electrons do not orbit the nucleus like a planet orbiting a sun. The orbital (or electron cloud, or electron shell) represents a probability of finding an electron at a particular location.

Each shell has a particular amount of energy related to it, and is therefore also referred to as an **energy level**. Energy levels are named utilizing a quantum number and a letter designation (i.e., 1s, 2s, 2p, etc.). The quantum number of the energy level closest to the nucleus is 1, and progresses as the levels get farther from the nucleus (2, 3, etc.). The letter designation indicates the shape of that particular energy level. The energy level closest to the nucleus has the least energy related to it; the furthest has the most. Each energy level has a limited capacity for holding electrons and each energy level requires a different number of electrons to fill it. Lower energy levels (closer to the nucleus) have less capacity for electrons than those farther from the nucleus.

Since electrons are attracted to the nucleus, electrons fill the electron shells closest to the nucleus (lowest energy levels) first. Once a given level is full, electrons start filling the next level out. The outermost occupied energy level of an element is called the **valence shell**. The number of electrons in the valence shell will determine the combinations that this atom will be likely to make with other atoms. Atoms are more stable when every electron is paired and are most stable when their valence shell is full. The tendency for an atom toward stability means that elements having unpaired or partially filled valence shells will easily gain or lose electrons in order to obtain the most efficient configuration.

Chemical Bonds

Valence properties of atoms provide opportunities for them to bond with other atoms. A **covalent bond** between atoms is formed when atoms share electrons. For instance, hydrogen has only one electron, which is unpaired, leaving the 1s valence shell one electron short of full. Oxygen has 6 electrons in the valence shell; it needs 2 more electrons in the valence shell for that shell to be full. It is easy for 2 hydrogen atoms to share their electrons with the oxygen, making the effective valence shells of each full. Covalent bonds are the strongest type of chemical bond.

A **molecule** is two or more atoms held together by shared electrons (covalent bonds). A **compound** is formed when two or more different atoms bond together chemically to form a unique substance (ex. H_2O, CH_4).

Charged atoms are called **ions**. An atom that loses one or more electrons becomes a positively charged particle, or a positive ion. An atom that gains one or more electrons becomes a negative ion. Positive and negative ions are attracted to each other in a bond called an **ionic bond**. An ionic bond is weaker than a covalent bond. Na^+Cl^-(sodium chloride or table salt) is an example of a substance held together by ionic bonds.

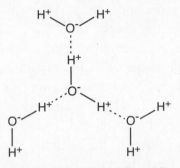

Fig. 2-2: Hydrogen Bonds. Dotted lines represent hydrogen bonds between water molecules.

Some molecules have a weak, partial negative charge at one region of the molecule and a partial positive charge in another region. Molecules that have regions of partial charge are called **polar molecules**. For instance, water molecules (which have a net charge of 0) have a partial negative charge near the oxygen atom and a partial positive charge near each of the hydrogen atoms. Thus, when water molecules are close together, their positive regions are attracted to the negatively charged regions of nearby molecules; the negative regions are attracted to the positively charged regions of nearby molecules. The force of attraction between water molecules, shown above as a dotted line, is called a **hydrogen bond**. A hydrogen bond is a weak chemical bond.

Chemical Reactions

Chemical reactions occur when molecules interact with each other to form one or more molecules of another type. Chemical reactions that occur within cells provide energy, nutrients, and other products that allow the organism to function.

There are several categories of chemical reactions. Chemical reactions are symbolized by an equation where the reacting molecules (**reactants**) are shown on one side and the newly formed molecules (**products**) on the other, with an arrow between indicating the direction of the reaction. Some chemical reactions are simple, such as the breakdown of a compound into its components, (a **decomposition** reaction):

$$AB \rightarrow A + B$$

A simple **combination** reaction is the reverse of decomposition:

$$A + B \rightarrow AB$$

When one compound breaks apart and forms a new compound with a free reactant it is called a **replacement** reaction:

$$AB + C \rightarrow AC + B$$

Chemical reactions may require an input of energy or they may release energy. Reactions that require energy are called **endothermic** reactions. Reactions that release energy are termed **exothermic**.

In a study of biology, it is crucial to understand endothermic and exothermic reactions. It is through endothermic reactions on the cellular level that living things are able to store energy in the form of chemical bonds.

All chemical reactions are subject to the **laws of thermodynamics**. The first law of thermodynamics (also known as the law of conservation of matter and energy) states that matter and energy can neither be created nor destroyed. In other words, the sum of matter and energy of the reactants must equal that of the products. The second law of thermodynamics, or the law of increasing disorder (or entropy), asserts that all reactions spread energy, which tends to diminish its availability. So, although we know from the first law that the energy must be equal on both sides of a reaction equation, reaction processes also tend to degrade the potential energy into a form that cannot perform any cellular work.

Properties of Water

Water exhibits unique characteristics that affect the processes of life. Water is able to dissolve many types of organic and inorganic substances. This property promotes several biological processes such as muscle contraction, nerve stimulation, and transport across membranes (permeability).

Because water molecules are polar, certain types of chemicals dissociate in water. Some chemicals yield protons and others accept protons when dissolved in water. An **acid** is a chemical that donates protons (H+ ions) when dissolved in water. Acidity then, is a measure of the concentration of H+ ions in a solution. A chemical that accepts protons (H+ ions) when dissolved in water is a **base**. The **pH** (standing for potential of hydrogen) scale is a measurement of H+ ions in solution. The pH of a substance can range from 0-14. A pH of 7 is neutral (as is pure water). A pH below 7 is acidic and a pH above 7 is basic (or alkaline). Acids and bases tend to neutralize each other when dissolved together in water. The neutralization of an acidic solution with a basic solution produces a **salt** (an ionic compound) and water. Acids, bases, and salts are important chemicals to many life processes.

The transparent quality of water keeps it from disturbing processes within cells that require light (such as in photosynthetic and light-sensing cells).

Water also exhibits unique responses to temperature change. Most substances contract upon becoming a solid; however, water expands as it solidifies (a process we call freezing), forming a loose lattice structure (crystal). This crystalline form also makes frozen water (ice) less dense than liquid water. This accounts for lakes and other bodies of water freezing on the top first (insulating the water and organisms below from harsh temperature changes).

Water has a high specific heat; it resists changes in temperature. The presence of water in an environment will tend to moderate the effect of harsh temperature changes.

Hydrogen bonds between water molecules also give water a high surface tension, allowing small particles, and even some organisms (such as the water strider) to rest on the surface. This surface tension also causes liquid water in air to form drops (rain).

Chemical Structure of Organic Compounds

Organic compounds are the building blocks of all living things. The special properties exhibited by the various types of organic molecules allow for the specialized functions within the cells and tissue of living things. **Organic compounds** are defined as those that contain carbon. Organic molecules may also include hydrogen, oxygen, nitrogen, sulfur, phosphorous, and some metal ions. It is important to have a basic understanding of the properties and chemical structure of carbohydrates, proteins, and other organic compounds. Organic substances include many types of molecules active in biological processes (or biomolecules), such as carbohydrates, lipids, proteins, and nucleic acids.

Carbohydrates

Carbohydrates are made of varying combinations of only carbon, hydrogen, and oxygen. The ratio of hydrogen to oxygen in carbohydrates is always 2:1, just as in water (H_2O)—thus the name carbo (carbon) hydrate (plus water).

Sugars and **starches** are both forms of carbohydrates. The basic sugar unit is a **monosaccharide**, which usually contains 3 to 7 carbon atoms plus attached oxygen and hydrogen atoms. The most common monosaccharides are called hexoses (six carbon sugars); they are usually in a ring-shaped (or cyclic) structure.

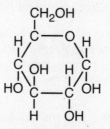

Fig. 2-3: Structural formula of Cyclic Glucose (a common hexose).

Two monosaccharide molecules may join together, producing a **disaccharide** and liberating a molecule of water. Table sugar is a disaccharide of glucose and fructose (the most common monosaccharides). When three monosaccharides join together, the chain is then called a **trisaccharide**. When more than three merge the resultant molecule is known as a **polysaccharide**.

Plants store energy by synthesizing polysaccharides known as **starches**. Starches are stored within the plant's cells until energy is needed. Plants also synthesize starches that provide structure to their cells; the most common is a plant fiber known as **cellulose** (a long chain of water-insoluble polysaccharides).

Glycogen is a polysaccharide composed of many joined glucose units. Many animals use glycogen as a short-term storage molecule for energy. In mammals, glycogen is found in muscle and liver tissue.

Lipids

Lipids are organic compounds composed of carbon, hydrogen, and oxygen. The ratio of hydrogen to oxygen in lipids is always greater than 2:1. Lipids are hydrophobic (water fearing) and will not dissolve in water. Lipids include waxes, steroids, phospholipids, and fats. These various types of substances perform many functions within cells. Some form structural components of cell membranes (phospholipids), some provide moisture barriers (waxes), and others are primarily used to store energy (fats). Other lipids serve as vitamins or hormones.

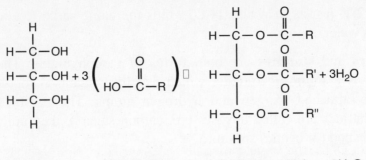

glycerol + 3 fatty acids = fat (triglyceride) + $3H_2O$

Fig. 2-4: Production of Fat. The bonding of three fatty acids to a molecule of glycerol produces a fat (triglyceride) molecule and releases 3 water molecules. The release of water allows for the compacting of the high-energy fatty acids into a more concentrated form—the fat molecule.

Fats are highly efficient lipid molecules used for long-term energy storage. When an organism takes in more carbohydrates than are necessary for its current energy use, the excess energy is stored in fat molecules. The energy is stored in chemical bonds between the atoms of lipid molecules. When these bonds are broken, energy is released. In addition to storing energy, fats also function in organisms to provide a protective layer that insulates internal organs and maintains heat within the body.

Proteins

Proteins are present in every living cell. Proteins are large unbranched chains of **amino acids**. Amino acids are single links (**monomers**) that join together to form linear chains with many links (**polymers**). Amino acids contain carbon, hydrogen, oxygen, nitrogen, and sometimes sulfur and phosphorous. There are twenty common amino acids that can combine in various sequences to form thousands of different proteins. Amino acids are connected into chains by a water-releasing (dehydration) reaction that forms peptide bonds. For this reason, proteins may also be called **polypeptides**.

Proteins found in living things may have dozens or hundreds of amino acids. The long linear strings of amino acids form unique shapes by folding up in various ways. The shape of different protein molecules is the characteristic that allows them to perform specific functions within cells.

Enzymes are special proteins that act as **catalysts** for reactions. A catalyst is a substance that changes the speed of a reaction without being affected itself. Enzyme names have the suffix -*ase* (such as polymerase, lactase).

Nucleic Acids

There are two groups of nucleic acids, deoxyribonucleic acid (**DNA**) and ribonucleic acid (**RNA**). Each type is composed of chains of **nucleotides**. Nucleotides are the monomers that form nucleic acids, which are polymers. Each nucleotide has a sugar (from the pentose group) attached to a phosphate group and a nitrogenous base. The sugar and phosphate groups alternate in long chains, forming the backbone of the DNA or RNA molecule. In DNA, the sugar molecule is deoxyribose; in RNA it is ribose. RNA chains are generally single strands, but DNA strands pair up to form a shape like a twisted ladder. This **double-helix** structure of DNA was discovered and modeled by two scientists, James Watson and Francis Crick, in the 1950s. DNA and RNA structure is therefore known as the **Watson-Crick** model.

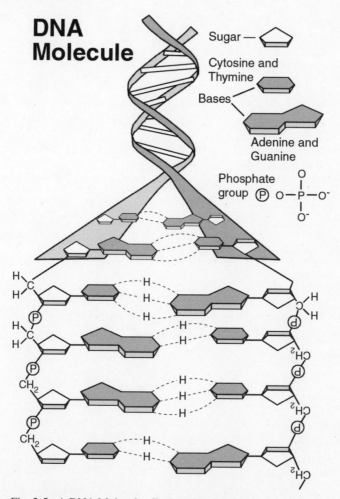

Fig. 2-5: A DNA Molecule. Each molecule of DNA consists of a chain of nucleotides (each containing a phosphate group, a sugar, and a nitrogenous base). Two chains bond together with hydrogen bonds, forming a double-helix structure.

The nitrogen bases in DNA include adenine, cytosine, guanine, and thymine (A, C, G, and T). In RNA, thymine is replaced by the base uracil (U). The nucleic acid bases form complementary pairs, that is, cytosine (C) and guanine (G) pair together forming hydrogen bonds, while thymine (T - or uracil in RNA - U) pairs with adenine (A). [A sequence of GATTACA would then pair with the sequence CTAATGT, or with the RNA sequence CUAAUGU.] This pairing allows DNA and RNA strands to accurately duplicate themselves and to encode the order of amino acids in proteins.

CHAPTER 3
CELLULAR AND
MOLECULAR
BIOLOGY

Chapter 3

CELLULAR AND MOLECULAR BIOLOGY

THE STRUCTURE AND FUNCTION OF CELLS

The **cell** is the smallest and most basic unit of most living things (**organisms**). Many species have only a single cell, others are multicellular. (Although viruses are sometimes considered to be living, they are noncellular and cannot fulfill the characteristics of life without invading the cell of another organism.) Cell structure varies according to the function of the cell and the type of living thing.

Scientists first began to describe cells after the invention of the **light microscope** in the mid 1600s. **Antonie van Leeuwenhoek** observed tiny organisms (he called them "animalcules") with the use of microscopes. We now know these tiny organisms were one-celled bacteria. **Robert Hooke** was the first to use the term "cells," when he observed cell walls of dead cork under a light microscope.

There are two main types of cells: prokaryotic and eukaryotic. **Prokaryotes** have no nucleus or any other membrane-bound **organelles** (cell components that perform particular functions). The DNA in prokaryotic cells usually forms a single chromosome, which floats within the cytoplasm. Prokaryotic organisms have only one cell and include all bacteria. Plant, fungi, and animal cells, as well as protozoa, are **eukaryotic**. Eukaryotic cells contain membrane-bound intracellular organelles, including a nucleus. The DNA within eukaryotes is organized into chromosomes.

In the mid-nineteenth century, two German scientists (Matthias Schleiden and Theodor Schwann) developed the **cell theory**. It contains the following tenets:

1.   All living things are made up of one or more cells.

2.   Cells are the basic units of life.

3. All cells come from pre-existing cells.

These tenets of the cell theory developed by scientists over 150 years ago are still accurate today.

A single organism can be unicellular (consisting of just one cell), or multicellular (consisting of many cells). A multicellular organism may have many different types of cells that differ in structure to serve different functions. Individual cells may contain organelles that assist them with specialized functions. For example, muscle cells tend to contain more mitochondria (organelles that make energy available to the cells) since muscle requires the use of extra energy.

Animal cells differ in structure and function from photosynthetic cells, which are found in plants, some bacteria, and some protists. Photosynthetic cells have the added job of producing food, so they are equipped with specialized photosynthetic organelles. Plant cells also have a central vacuole and cell walls, structures not found in animal cells.

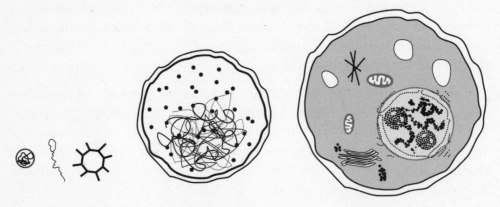

Viruses　　　　Prokaryotic Cell　　　　Eukaryotic Cell

Fig. 3-1: Viruses and Cells. Viruses are much smaller than cells, ranging from approximately 0.05 - 0.1 micrometers. The prokaryotic cell has no nucleus or other membrane-bound organelles and is approximately 1-10 micrometers in diameter. The eukaryotic cell has membrane-bound organelles, including a nucleus containing the chromosomes. Eukaryotic cells are approximately 10-100 micrometers in diameter.

Viruses

Viruses are much smaller than even the smallest cells. Scientists do not agree as to whether viruses are actually alive. Although they can reproduce, they do not have the ability to conduct metabolic functions on their own. Virus structure consists of only a protein capsule, DNA, or RNA, and sometimes enzymes. Viruses survive and replicate by invading a living cell. The virus then utilizes the cell's mechanisms to reproduce itself, sometimes destroying the cell in the process.

Cell Organelles of Plants and Animals

The light microscope is useful in examining most cells and some cell organelles (such as the nucleus). However, many cell organelles are very small and require the magnification and resolution power of an **electron microscope.**

All cells are enclosed within the **cell membrane** (or plasma membrane). Near the center of each eukaryotic cell is the **nucleus**, which contains the chromosomes. Between the nucleus and the cell membrane, the cell contains a region called the **cytoplasm**. Since all of the organelles outside the nucleus but within the cell membrane exist within the cytoplasm, they are all called **cytoplasmic organelles**.

The shape and size of cells can vary widely. The longest nerve cells (neurons) may extend over a meter in length with an approximate diameter of only 4-100 micrometers (1 millimeter = 1,000 micrometers, μm). A human egg cell may be 100 micrometers in diameter. The average size of a bacterium is 0.5 to 2.0 micrometers. However, most cells are between 0.5 and 100 micrometers in diameter. The size of a cell is limited by the ratio of its volume to its surface area. In the illustration below, note the variation of shape of cells within the human body:

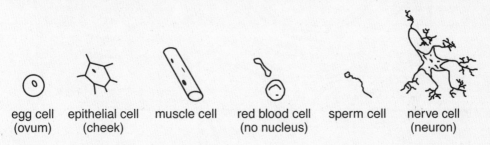

| egg cell (ovum) | epithelial cell (cheek) | muscle cell | red blood cell (no nucleus) | sperm cell | nerve cell (neuron) |

Fig. 3-2: Varying Cell Types. The six sketches of human cell types show some of the diversity in shape and size among cells with varying functions. The sketches are not sized to scale.

Animal Cells

1.   The **cell membrane (1a)** encloses the cell and separates it from the environment. It may also be called a plasma membrane. This membrane is composed of a double layer (bilayer) of phospholipids with globular proteins embedded within the layers. The membrane is extremely thin (about 80 angstroms; 10 million angstroms = 1 millimeter) and elastic. The combination of the lipid bilayer and the proteins embedded within it allow the cell to determine what molecules and ions can enter and leave the cell, and regulate the rate at which they enter and leave.

Endocytic vesicles (1b) form when the plasma membrane of a cell surrounds a molecule outside the membrane, then releases a membrane-

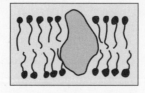

Fig. 3-3: Cell Membrane. A phospholipid bilayer with embedded globular proteins.

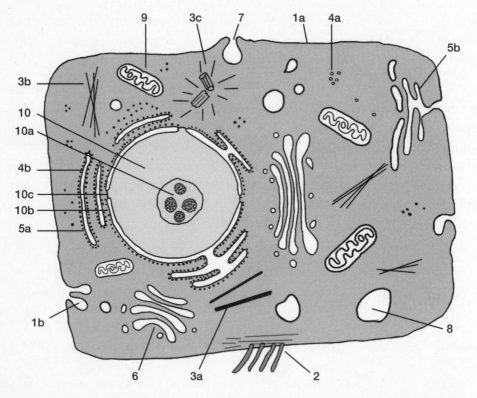

Fig. 3-4: A Generalized Animal Cell (cross-section). Since there are many types of animal cells, this diagram is generalized. In other words, some animal cells will have all of these organelles, others will not. However, this illustration will give you a composite picture of the organelles within the typical animal cell. It is also important to note the function of each organelle. Each labeled component above is explained by the corresponding text below.

bound sack containing the desired molecule or substance into the cytoplasm. This process allows the cell to absorb larger molecules than would be able to pass through the cell membrane, or that need to remain packaged within the cell.

2. Microvilli are projections of the cell extending from the cell membrane. Microvilli are found in certain types of cells, for example, those involved in absorption (such as the cells lining the intestine). These filaments increase the surface area of the cell membrane, increasing the area available to absorb nutrients. They also contain enzymes involved in digesting certain types of nutrients.

3.   The **cytoskeleton** provides structural support to a cell. **Microtubules (3a)** are long, hollow, cylindrical protein filaments, which give structure to the cell. These filaments are scattered around the edges of a cell and form a sort of loose skeleton or framework for the cytoplasm. Microtubules also are found at the base of cilia or flagella (organelles which allow some cells to move on their own) and give these organelles the ability to move. **Microfilaments (3b)** are double-stranded chains of proteins, which serve to give structure to the cell. Together with the larger microtubules, microfilaments form the cytoskeleton, providing stability and structure. **Centrioles (3c)** are structural components of many cells, and are particularly common in animal cells. Centrioles are tubes constructed of a geometrical arrangement of microtubules in a pinwheel shape. Their function includes the formation of new microtubules, but is primarily the formation of structural skeleton around which cells split during mitosis and meiosis. Basal bodies are structurally similar to centrioles, but their function is to anchor and aid in the movement of flagella or cilia.

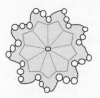

Fig. 3-5: Cross-section of a Centriole.
Centrioles are tubes constructed of a
geometrical arrangement of microtubules in a pinwheel shape.

4.   **Ribosomes** are the site of protein synthesis within cells. Ribosomes are composed of certain protein molecules and RNA molecules (ribosomal RNAs, or rRNAs). **Free ribosomes (4a)** float unattached within the cytoplasm. The proteins synthesized by free ribosomes are made for use in the cytoplasm, not within membrane-bound organelles. **Attached ribosomes (4b)** are attached to the ER (see No. 5). Proteins made at the site of attached ribosomes are destined for use within the membrane-bound organelles.

5.   The **endoplasmic reticulum,** a large organization of folded membranes, is responsible for the delivery of lipids and proteins to certain areas within the cytoplasm (a sort of cellular highway). **Rough endoplasmic reticulum** or **RER (5a)** has attached ribosomes. In addition to packaging and transport of materials within the cell, the RER is instrumental to protein synthesis. **Smooth endoplasmic reticulum** or **SER (5b)** is a net-

work of membranous channels. Smooth endoplasmic reticulum does not have attached ribosomes. The endoplasmic reticulum is responsible for processing lipids, fats, and steroids, which are then packaged and dispersed by the Golgi apparatus.

6.   The **Golgi apparatus** (also known as Golgi bodies, or the Golgi complex) is instrumental in the storing, packaging, and shipping of proteins. The Golgi apparatus looks much like stacks of hollow pancakes and is constructed of folded membranes. Within these membranes, cellular products are stored, or packaged by closing off a bubble of membrane with the proteins or lipids inside. These packages are shipped (via the endoplasmic reticulum) to the part of the cell where they will be used, or to the cell membrane for secretion from the cell.

7.   **Secretory vesicles** are packets of material packaged by either the Golgi apparatus or the endoplasmic reticulum. Secretory vesicles carry substances produced within the cell (a protein, for example) to the cell membrane. The vesicle membrane fuses with the cell membrane in a process called **exocytosis**, allowing the substance to escape the cell.

8.   **Lysosomes** are membrane-bound organelles containing digestive enzymes. Lysosomes digest unused material within the cell, damaged organelles, or materials absorbed by the cell for use.

9.   **Mitochondria** are centers of cellular respiration (the process of breaking up covalent bonds within sugar molecules with the intake of oxygen and release of ATP, adenosine tri-phosphate). ATP molecules store energy that is later used in cell processes. Mitochondria (plural of mitochondrion) are more numerous in cells requiring more energy (muscle, etc.). Mitochondria are self-replicating, containing their own DNA, RNA, and ribosomes. Mitochondria have a double membrane; the internal membrane is folded. Cellular respiration reactions occur along the folds of the internal membrane (called **cristae**). Mitochondria are thought to be an evolved form of primitive bacteria (prokaryotic cells) that lived in a symbiotic relationship with eukaryotic cells more than 2 billion years ago. This concept, known as the **endosymbiont hypothesis,** is a plausible explanation of how mitochondria, which have many of the necessary components for life on their own, became an integral part of eukaryotic cells.

10. The **nucleus** is an organelle surrounded by two lipid bilayer membranes. The nucleus contains chromosomes, nuclear pores, nucleoplasm, and nucleoli. The **nucleolus (10a)** is a rounded area within the nucleus of the cell where ribosomal RNA is synthesized. This rRNA is incorporated into ribosomes after exiting the nucleus. Several nucleoli (plural of nucleolus) can exist within a nucleus. The **nuclear membrane**

(10b) is the boundary between the nucleus and the cytoplasm. The nuclear membrane is actually a double membrane, which allows for the entrance and exit of certain molecules through the nuclear pores. **Nuclear pores (10c)** are points at which the double nuclear membrane fuses together, forming a passageway between the inside of the nucleus and the cytoplasm outside the nucleus. Nuclear pores allow the cell to selectively move molecules in and out of the nucleus. There are many pores scattered about the surface of the nuclear membrane.

Plant Cells

The structure of plant cells differs noticeably from animal cells with the addition of three organelles: the cell wall, the chloroplasts, and the central vacuole. In Figure 3-6, the organelles numbered 1 to 7 function the same way in plant cells as in animal cells (see above).

1. **Golgi apparatus**

2. **Mitochondria**

3. **Rough endoplasmic reticulum**

4. **Ribosome**

5. **Nucleus**

6. **Nucleolus**

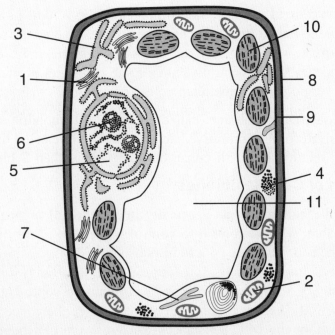

Fig. 3-6: A Typical Plant Cell.

7. Smooth endoplasmic reticulum

8. Cell walls surround plant cells. (Bacteria also have cell walls.) Cell walls are made of cellulose and lignin, making them strong and rigid (whereas the cell membrane is relatively weak and flexible). The cell wall encloses the cell membrane providing strength and protection for the cell. The cell wall allows plant cells to store water under relatively high concentration. The combined strength of a plant's cell walls provides support for the whole organism. Dry wood and cork are essentially the cell walls of dead plants. The structure of the cell wall allows substances to pass through it readily, so transport in and out of the cell is still regulated by the cell membrane.

9. The **cell membrane** (or plasma membrane) functions in plant and animal cells in the same way. However, in some plant tissues, channels connect the cytoplasm of adjacent cells.

10. Chloroplasts are found in plant cells (and also in some protists). Chloroplasts are the site of photosynthesis within plant cells. **Chlorophyll** pigment molecules give the chloroplast their green color, although the chloroplasts also contain yellow and red carotenoid pigments. In the fall, as chloroplasts lose chlorophyll, these pigments are revealed, giving leaves their red and yellow colors. The body (or **stroma**) of the chloroplast contains embedded stacked, disk-like plates (called **grana**), which are the site of photosynthetic reactions.

11. The **central vacuole** takes up much of the volume of plant cells. It is a membrane-bound (this particular membrane is called the **tonoplast**), fluid-filled space, which stores water and soluble nutrients for the plant's use. The tendency of the central vacuole to absorb water provides for the rigid shape (turgidity) of some plant cells. (Animal cells may also contain vacuoles for varying purposes, and these too are membrane-bound, fluid-filled spaces. For instance, contractile vacuoles perform the specific function of expelling waste and excess water from single-celled organisms.)

Properties of Cell Membranes

The cell membrane is an especially important cell organelle with a unique structure, which allows it to control movement of substances into and out of the cell. Made up of a fluid phospholipid bilayer, proteins, and carbohydrates, this extremely thin (approximately 80 angstroms) membrane can only be seen clearly with an electron microscope. The selective permeability of the cell membrane serves to manage the concentration of substances within the cell. Substances can cross the cell membrane by passive transport, facilitated diffusion, and active transport. During **passive transport,** substances freely pass across the membrane without the cell expending any energy. **Facilitated diffusion** does not require added energy, but it cannot occur without the help of specialized proteins. Transport requiring energy output from the cell is called **active transport**.

Simple diffusion is one type of passive transport. **Diffusion** is the process whereby molecules and ions flow through the cell membrane from an area of higher concentration to an area of lower concentration (thus tending to equalize concentrations). Where the substance exists in higher concentration, collisions occur, which tend to propel them away toward lower concentrations. Diffusion generally is the means of transport for ions and molecules that can slip between the lipid molecules of the membrane. Diffusion requires no added energy to propel substances through a membrane.

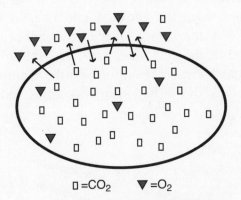

□ =CO_2 ▼ =O_2

Fig. 3-7: Diffusion. CO_2 diffuses out of the cell since its concentration is higher inside the cell. O_2 diffuses into the cell because its concentration is higher outside. Molecules diffuse from areas of high concentration to areas of lower concentration.

Another type of passive transport is **osmosis,** a special process of diffusion occurring only with water molecules. Osmosis does not require the addition of any energy, but occurs when the water concentration inside the cell differs from the concentration outside the cell. The water on the side of the membrane with the highest water concentration will move through the membrane until the concentration is equalized on both sides. When the water concentration is equal inside and outside the cell, it is called isomotic or isotonic. For instance, a cell placed in a salty solution will tend to lose water until the solution outside the cell has the same concentration of water molecules as the cytoplasm (the solution inside the cell).

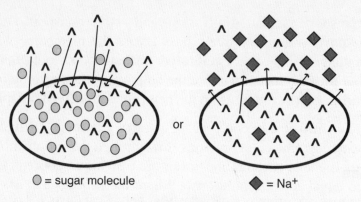

○ = sugar molecule   ◆ = Na⁺

∧ = water molecule

Fig. 3-8: Osmosis. Water crosses the membrane into a cell that has a higher concentration of sugar molecules than the surrounding solution. Water crosses the membrane to leave the cell when there is a higher concentration of Na⁺ ions outside the cell than inside the cell.

Facilitated diffusion is another method of transport across the cell membrane. Facilitated diffusion allows for transfer of substances across the cell membrane with the help of specialized proteins. These proteins, which are embedded in the cell membrane, are able to pick up specific molecules or ions and transport them through the membrane. The special protein molecules allow the diffusion of molecules and ions that cannot otherwise pass through the lipid bilayer.

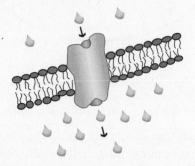

Fig. 3-9: Facilitated Diffusion. Specialized proteins embedded in the cell membrane permit passage of substances of a particular shape and size.

Active transport, like facilitated diffusion, requires membrane-bound proteins. Unlike facilitated diffusion, active transport uses energy to move molecules across a cell membrane against a concentration gradient (in the opposite direction than they would go under normal diffusion circumstances). With the addition of the energy obtained from ATP, a protein molecule embedded in the membrane changes shape and moves a molecule across the membrane against the concentration gradient.

Large molecules are not able to pass through the cell membrane, but may be engulfed by the cell membrane. **Endocytosis** is the process whereby large molecules (i.e. some sugars or proteins) are taken up into a pocket of membrane. The pocket pinches off, delivering the molecules, still inside a membrane sack, into the cytoplasm. This process, for instance, is used by white blood cells to engulf bacteria. **Exocytosis** is the reverse process, exporting substances from the cell.

Enzymes

Enzymes are protein molecules that act as catalysts for organic reactions. (A catalyst is a substance that lowers the activation energy of a reaction. A catalyst is not consumed in the reaction.) Enzymes do not make reactions possible that would not otherwise occur under the right energy conditions, but they lower the activation energy, which increases the rate of the reaction.

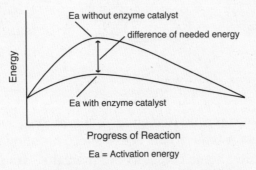

Fig. 3-10: Effect of Enzyme on a Reaction. Adding an enzyme lowers the activation energy for a reaction.

Enzymes are named ending with the letters -ase, and usually begin with a syllable describing the catalyzed reaction (i.e., hydrolase catalyzes hydrolysis reactions, lactase catalyzes the breakdown of the sugar lactose). Thousands of reactions occur within cells, each controlled by one or more enzymes. Enzymes are synthesized within the cell at the ribosomes, as all proteins are.

Enzymes are effective catalysts because of their unique shapes. Each enzyme has a uniquely shaped area, called its **active site**. For each enzyme, there is a particular substance known as its **substrate**, which fits within the active site (like a hand in a glove). When the substrate is seated in the active site, the combination of two molecules is called the **enzyme-substrate complex**. An enzyme can bind to two substrates and catalyze the formation of a new chemical bond, linking the two substrates. An enzyme may also bind to a single substrate and catalyze the breaking of a chemical bond, releasing two products. Once the reaction has taken place, the unchanged enzyme is released.

The operation of enzymes lowers the energy needed to initiate cellular reactions. However, the completion of the reaction may either require or release energy. Remember from Chapter 2 that reactions requiring energy are called endothermic reactions. Reactions that release energy are called exothermic reactions. Endothermic reactions can take place in a cell by being coupled to the breakdown of ATP or a similar molecule. Exothermic reactions are coupled to the production of ATP or another molecule with high-energy chemical bonds.

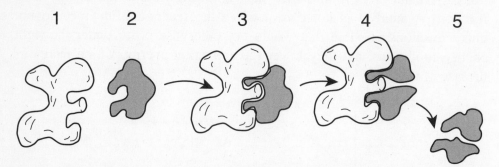

Fig. 3-11: Enzyme Reaction. 1 - enzyme; 2 - substrate; 3&4 - enzyme-substrate complex; 5 - products.

Some enzymatic reactions require a non-protein substance called a **cofactor**. The cofactor binds to the active site. This allows the substrate to fit into the active site. Some cofactors are inorganic. **Inorganic cofactors** include metal ions—for example, iron, copper, or zinc. Other cofactors are organic molecules. **Organic cofactors** are also called **coenzymes**. Some coenzymes are not made by cells but must be obtained in the diet. Most vitamins are coenzymes (or precursors of coenzymes). **Prosthetic groups** are similar to cofactors; they also facilitate the enzyme reaction. However, prosthetic groups are bound to the enzyme, rather than being separate atoms or molecules.

In some cases, other substances compete to attach to an enzyme's active site. If one of these substances, known as an **inhibitor**, attaches to the enzyme first, the cellular reaction will not take place. Environmental conditions within the cell, such as high temperature or acidity, may also inhibit an enzymatic reaction. These conditions may change the shape of the active site and render the enzyme ineffective.

Enzyme reactions may also be controlled by mechanisms within the cell. Enzyme control (or **regulation**) may occur when the product of the reaction is also an inhibitor to the reaction. This slows down the production rate as the concentration of the product increases. In other cases, a particular molecule serves as a regulator, by changing the structure of the active site making the enzyme more or less effective.

Energy Transformations

All living things require energy. Ultimately, the source of most energy for life on Earth is the sun. Photosynthetic organisms (plants, some protists, and some bacteria) are able to harvest solar energy and transform it into chemical energy eventually stored within covalent bonds of molecules (such as carbohydrates, fats, and proteins). These organisms are called primary producers. Consumers eat producers and utilize the chemical energy stored in them to carry on the functions of life. Other organisms then consume the consumers. In each of these steps along the food chain, some energy is lost as heat (see discussion of thermodynamic laws in Chapter 2).

Cellular metabolism is a general term, which includes all types of energy transformation processes, including photosynthesis, respiration, growth, movement, etc. Energy transformations occur as chemicals are broken apart or synthesized within the cell. The process whereby cells build molecules and store energy (in the form of chemical bonds) is called **anabolism**. **Catabolism** is the process of breaking down molecules and releasing stored energy.

ATP

Energy from the sun is transformed by photosynthetic organisms into chemical energy in the form of ATP. ATP (adenosine triphosphate) is known as the energy currency of cellular activity. While energy is stored in the form of carbohydrates, fats, and proteins, the amount of energy contained within the bonds of any of these substances would overwhelm (and thus kill) a cell if released at once. In order for the energy to be released in small packets usable to a cell, large molecules need to be broken down in steps. ATP is an efficient storage molecule for the energy needed for cellular processes. ATP consists of a nitrogenous base (adenine), a simple sugar (ribose), and three phosphate groups. When a cellular process requires energy, a molecule of ATP can be broken down into ADP (adenosine diphosphate) plus a phosphate group. Even more energy is released when ATP is decomposed into AMP (adenosine monophosphate) and two phosphate groups. These energy-releasing reactions are then coupled with energy-absorbing reactions.

Photosynthesis

The process of **photosynthesis** includes a crucial set of reactions. These reactions convert the light energy of the sun into chemical energy usable by living things. Photosynthetic organisms carry out photosynthesis. They use the converted energy for their own life processes, and also store energy that may be used by organisms that consume them.

Although the process of photosynthesis actually occurs through many small steps, the entire process can be summed up with the following equation:

$$6CO_2 + 6H_2O + \text{light energy} \rightarrow C_6H_{12}O_6 + 6O_2$$

(carbon dioxide + water $\rightarrow$ glucose + oxygen)

Chlorophyll is a green pigment (a pigment is a substance that absorbs light energy). Photosynthesis occurs in the presence of chlorophyll, as the chlorophyll is able to absorb a photon of light. Chlorophyll is contained in the grana of the chloroplast (see discussion of plant cells earlier in this chapter). Photosynthesis can only occur where chlorophyll is present. It is not used up in the photosynthetic process, but must be present for the reactions to occur.

There are two phases of the photosynthetic process, the light reaction, or **photolysis,** and the dark reaction, or **CO$_2$ fixation**. During photolysis, the chlorophyll pigment absorbs a photon of light, leaving the chlorophyll in an excited (higher energy) state. The light reaction is a decomposition reaction, which separates water molecules into hydrogen and oxygen atoms utilizing the energy from the excited chlorophyll pigment. Oxygen, which is not needed by the cell, combines to form O_2 (gas) and is released into the environment. The free hydrogen is grabbed and held by a particular molecule (called the hydrogen acceptor) until it is needed. The excited chlorophyll also supplies energy to a series of reactions that produce ATP from ADP and inorganic phosphate (Pi).

The dark reaction (CO_2 fixation) then occurs in the stroma of the chloroplast. This second phase of photosynthesis does not require light; however, it does require the use of the products (hydrogen and ATP) of photolysis. In this phase, six CO_2 molecules are linked with hydrogen (produced in photolysis) forming glucose (a six-carbon sugar). This is a multi-step process, which requires the ATP produced in the photolysis phase. Glucose molecules can link to form polysaccharides (starch or sugar), which are then stored in the cell.

Cellular Respiration

Unlike photosynthesis (which only occurs in photosynthetic cells), respiration occurs in all cells. Respiration is the process that releases energy for use by the cell. There are several steps involved in cellular respiration. Some require oxygen (that is, they are **aerobic**) and some do not (that is, they are **anaerobic** reactions).

Glycolysis is the breaking down of the six-carbon sugar (glucose) into smaller carbon-containing molecules yielding ATP (glyco = sugar, lysis = breakdown). It is the first step in all respiration pathways and occurs in the cytoplasm of all living cells. Each molecule of glucose (six carbons) is broken down into two molecules of pyruvic acid (or pyruvate with three carbons each), two ATP molecules, and two hydrogen atoms (attached to NADH, nicotinamide adenine dinucleotide). This is an **anaerobic reaction** (no oxygen is required). After glycolysis has occurred, respiration will continue on one of two pathways, depending upon whether oxygen is present or not. The process of glycolysis is summarized by the following chemical equation:

glucose (6 C) + 2ADP + 2 Pi + 2NAD$^+$ → 2 pyruvic acid (3 C each) + 2ATP + 2NADH + 2H$^+$

Aerobic Pathways

Aerobic respiration (in the presence of oxygen) begins with glycolysis and proceeds through two major steps, the **Krebs cycle** (also known as the citric acid cycle) and **electron transport**. The first step, the Krebs cycle, occurs in the matrix of a cell's mitochondria and breaks down pyruvic acid molecules (three carbons each) into CO_2 molecules, H$^+$ (protons), and 2 ATP molecules. The Krebs cycle also liberates electrons, which then enter the next step.

The second step occurs along the electron transport system, or ETS, which captures the energy (in the form of electrons) released by the Krebs cycle. The ETS is a series of **cytochromes**, which exist on the cristae of the mitochondria. Cytochromes are pigment molecules, which include a protein and a **heme** (iron containing) group. The iron in heme groups may be either oxidized (loses electron to form Fe^{+3}) or reduced (gains electron to form Fe^{+2}) as electrons are passed along the ETS. As electrons pass from one cytochrome to another, energy is given off. Some of this energy is lost as heat; the rest is stored in molecules of ATP. This process can produce the most ATP molecules per cycle, 32 ATPs per glucose molecule. The final step of the electron transport chain occurs when the last electron carrier transfers two electrons to an oxygen atom that simultaneously combines with two protons from the surrounding medium to produce water.

Anaerobic Pathways

If no oxygen is present within the cell, respiration will proceed anaerobically after glycolysis. Anaerobic respiration is also called **fermentation**. Anaerobic respiration breaks down the two pyruvic acid molecules (three carbons each) into end products (such as ethyl alcohol, C_2H_6O or lactic acid $C_3H_6O_3$), plus carbon dioxide (CO_2). The net gain from anaerobic respiration is two ATP molecules per glucose molecule. Fermentation is not as efficient as aerobic respiration; it uses only a small part of the energy available in a glucose molecule.

CHEMICAL NATURE OF THE GENE

In Chapter 2, the Watson-Crick model of DNA was explained and illustrated. Watson and Crick were responsible for explaining the structure of the DNA molecule, research that laid the foundation of our current understanding of the function of chromosomes and genes. Today, through the discoveries of these two scientists, and through the collaborative work of scientists worldwide, the study of chromosomes and genetic inheritance has proceeded to discover the intricacies of the **genomes** (sum total of genetic information) of many organisms, including humans.

A **gene** is a length of DNA that encodes a particular protein. Each protein the cell synthesizes performs a specific function in the cell. The function of one protein, or the function of a group of proteins, is called a trait.

DNA Replication

In order to replicate, a portion of a DNA molecule unwinds, separating the two halves of the double helix. (This separation is aided by the enzyme helicase.) Another enzyme (DNA polymerase) binds to each strand and moves along them as it collects nucleotides using the original DNA strands as templates. The new strand is complementary to the original template and forms a new double helix with one of the parent strands. If no errors occur during DNA synthesis, the result is two identical double helix molecules of DNA.

The process of DNA replication, however, is occasionally subject to a mistake known as a **mutation.** All the DNA of every cell of every organism is copied repeatedly to form new cells for growth, repair, and reproduction. A mutation can result from an error that randomly occurs during replication. Mutations can also result from damage to DNA caused by exposure to certain chemicals, such as some solvents or the chemicals in cigarette smoke, or by radiation, such as ultraviolet radiation in sunlight or x-rays. Cells have built-in mechanisms for finding and repairing most DNA errors, however, they do not fix them all. The result of a DNA error, a mutation, expresses itself in a change (small or large) in the cell structure and function.

DNA carries the information for making all the proteins a cell can make. The DNA information for making a particular protein can be called the gene for that protein. Genetic traits are expressed, and specialization of cells occurs, as a result of the combination of proteins encoded by the DNA of a cell. Protein synthesis occurs in two steps called transcription and translation.

Transcription refers to the formation of an RNA molecule, which corresponds to a gene. The DNA strand "unzips" and replicates; individual RNA nucleotides are strung together to match the DNA sequence by the enzyme RNA polymerase. The new RNA strand (known as messenger RNA or **mRNA**) migrates from the nucleus to the cytoplasm, where it is modified in a process known as **post-transcriptional processing**. This processing prepares the mRNA for protein synthesis by removing the non-coding sequences. In the processed RNA, each unit of three nucleotides or **codon** encodes a particular amino acid.

The next phase of protein synthesis is called **translation**. In order for the protein synthesis process to continue, a second type of RNA is required, transfer RNA or **tRNA**. Transfer RNA is the link between the "language" of nucleotides (codon and anticodon) and the "language" of amino acids (hence the word "translation"). Transfer RNA is a chain of about 80 nucleotides. At one point along the tRNA chain, there are three unattached bases, which are called the anticodon. This anticodon will line up with a corresponding codon during translation. Each tRNA molecule also has an attached, specific amino acid.

Translation occurs at the ribosomes. A ribosome is a structure composed of proteins and ribosomal RNA (rRNA). A ribosome attaches to the mRNA strand at a particular codon known as the start codon. This codon is only recognized by a particular initiator tRNA. The ribosome continues to add tRNA whose anticodons make complementary bonds with the next codon on the mRNA string, forming a peptide bond between amino acids as each amino acid is held in place by a tRNA. At the end of the translation process, a terminating codon stops the synthesis process and the protein is released.

Structural and Regulatory Genes

Genes encode proteins of two varieties. **Structural genes** code proteins that form organs and structural characteristics. **Regulatory genes** code proteins that determine functional or physiological events, such as growth. These proteins regulate when other genes start or stop encoding proteins, which in turn produce specific traits.

Transduction and Transformation

In most organisms, DNA replication preserves a continuity of traits throughout the organism's lifespan. However, the genetic makeup of bacteria can be changed through one of two processes, transduction or transformation. **Transduction** is the transfer of genetic material (portions of a bacterial chromosome) from one bacterial cell to another. The transfer is mediated by a bacteriophage (a virus that targets bacteria). Bacteria may also absorb and incorporate pieces of DNA from their environment (usually from dead bacterial cells), a process called **transformation**.

Cell Division

The process of cell reproduction is called **cell division**. The process of cell division centers on the replication and separation of strands of **DNA**.

Structure of Chromosomes

Chromosomes are long chains of subunits called **nucleosomes**. Each nucleosome is composed of a short length of DNA wrapped around a core of small proteins called **histones**. The combination of DNA with histones is called **chromatin**. Each nucleosome is about 11 nm in diameter (a nanometer is one billionth of a meter) and contains a central core of eight histones with the DNA double helix wrapped around them. Each gene spans dozens of nucleosomes. The DNA plus histone strings are then tightly packed and coiled, forming chromatin.

In a cell that is getting ready to divide, each strand of chromatin is duplicated. The two identical strands (called **chromatids**) remain attached to each other at a point called the **centromere**. During cell division, the chromatin strands become more tightly coiled and packed, forming a chromosome, which is visible in a light microscope. At this stage, a chromosome consists of two identical chromatids, held together at the centromere, giving each chromosome an **X** shape.

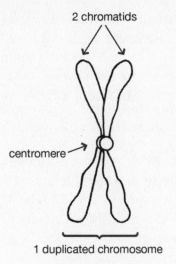

Fig. 3-12: A Chromosome.

Within the nucleus, each chromosome pairs with another of similar size and shape. These pairs are called **homologs**. Each set of homologous chromosomes has a similar genetic constitution, but the genes are not necessarily identical. Different forms of corresponding genes are called **alleles.**

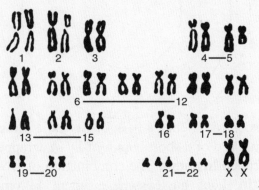

Fig. 3-13: Paired Homologous Chromosomes.

Restriction Enzymes

The study of DNA has been greatly aided by the discovery of restriction enzymes (restriction endonucleases). Restriction enzymes cut sections of DNA molecules by cleaving the sugar-phosphate backbone at a particular nucleotide sequence.

Scientists have isolated hundreds of different restriction endonucleases that act on a few hundred different DNA sequences. Restriction enzymes are made by bacteria and act to destroy foreign DNA (for example, viral DNA) that has entered the bacterial cell.

In the laboratory, restriction enzymes are used to cut DNA into small strands of DNA for study. Restriction enzymes are generally named after their host of origin, rather than the substrate upon which they act. For example, EcoRI is from the host *Escherichia coli*, Hind II and Hind III from *Haemophilus influenzae*, XhoI from *Xanthomonas holcicola*, etc.

The Cell Cycle

A cell that is going to divide progresses through a particular sequence of events ending in cell division, which produces two daughter cells. This is known as the **cell cycle** (see Fig. 3-14). The time taken to progress through the cell cycle differs with different types of cells, but the sequence is the same. Cells in many tissues never divide.

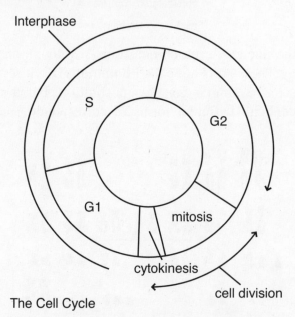

The Cell Cycle

Fig. 3-14: The Cell Cycle. Interphase includes the G1, S, and G2 phases. The cell division phase includes mitosis and cytokinesis.

There are two major periods within the cell cycle: interphase and mitosis (also called the M phase or cell division phase). **Interphase** is the period when the cell is active in carrying on its function. Interphase is divided into three phases. During the first phase, the G_1 **phase**, metabolism and protein synthesis are occurring at a high rate, and most of the growth of the cell occurs at this time. The cell organelles are produced (as necessary) and undergo growth during this phase. During the second phase, the **S phase**, the cell begins to prepare for cell division by replicating the DNA and proteins necessary to form a new set of chromosomes. In the final phase, the **G$_2$ phase**, more proteins are produced, which will be necessary for cell division, and the centrioles (which are integral to the division process) are replicated as well. Cell growth and function occur through all the stages of interphase.

Mitosis

Mitosis is the process by which a cell distributes its duplicated chromosomes so that each daughter cell has a full set of chromosomes. Mitosis progresses through four phases: prophase, metaphase, anaphase, and telophase (see Fig. 3-15).

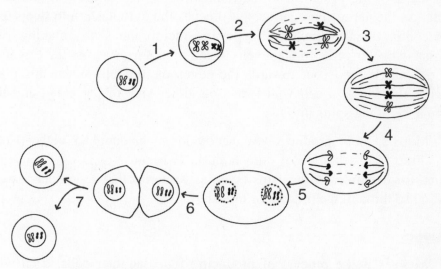

Fig. 3-15: Mitosis. See explanations of numbered steps below.

During **prophase (1, 2)**, the first stage of mitosis, the chromatin condenses into chromosomes within the nucleus and becomes visible through a light microscope. The centrioles move to opposite ends of the cell, and **spindle fibers** begin to extend from the centromeres of each chromosome toward the center of the cell. At this point, although the chromosomes become visible, the nucleolus no longer is. During the second part of prophase, the nuclear membrane dissolves and the spindle fibers attach to the centromeres forming a junction called a **kinetochore**. The chromosomes then begin moving in preparation for the next step, metaphase.

During **metaphase (3)**, the spindle fibers pull the chromosomes into alignment along the equatorial plane of the cell, creating the metaphase plate. This arrangement insures that one copy of each chromosome is distributed to each daughter cell.

During **anaphase** (**4**), the chromatids are separated from each other when the centromere divides. Each former chromatid is now called a chromosome. The two identical chromosomes move along the spindle fibers to opposite ends of the cell. **Telophase** (**5**) occurs as nuclear membranes form around the chromosomes. The chromosomes disperse through the new nucleoplasm, and are no longer visible as chromosomes under a standard microscope. The spindle fibers disappear. After telophase, the process of **cytokinesis** (**6**) produces two separate cells (**7**).

Cytokinesis differs somewhat in plants and animals. In animal cells, a ring made of the protein actin surrounds the center of the cell and contracts. As the actin ring contracts, it pinches the cytoplasm into two separate compartments. Each cell's plasma membrane seals, making two distinct daughter cells. In plant cells, a cell plate forms across the center of the cell and extends out towards the edges of the cell. When this plate reaches the edges, a cell wall forms on either side of the plate, and the original cell then splits into two.

Mitosis, then, produces two nearly identical daughter cells. (Cells may differ in distribution of mitochondria or because of DNA replication errors, for example.) Organisms (such as bacteria) that reproduce asexually, do so through the process of mitosis.

Meiosis

Meiosis is the process of producing four daughter cells, each with single unduplicated chromosomes (**haploid**). The parent cell is **diploid**, that is, it has a normal set of paired chromosomes. Meiosis goes through a two-stage process resulting in four new cells, rather than two (as in mitosis). Each cell has half the chromosomes of the parent. Meiosis occurs in reproductive organs, and the resultant four haploid cells are called **gametes** (egg and sperm). When two haploid gametes fuse during the process of fertilization, the resultant cell has one chromosome set from each parent, and is diploid. This process allows for the huge genetic diversity available among species.

Two distinct nuclear divisions occur during meiosis, reduction (or meiosis 1, steps **1 to 5** in Fig. 3-16), and division (or meiosis 2, steps **6 to 10**). **Reduction** affects the **ploidy** (referring to haploid or diploid) level, reducing it from 2n to n (i.e., diploid to haploid). **Division** then distributes the remaining set of chromosomes in a mitosis-like process.

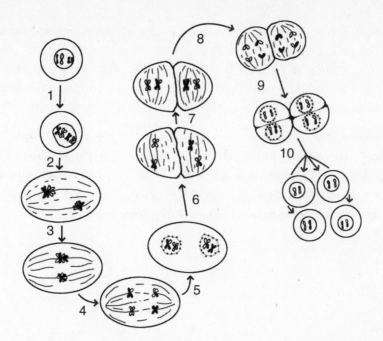

Fig. 3-16: Meiosis. See explanations of numbered steps, above and below.

The phases of meiosis 1 are similar to the phases of mitosis, with some notable differences. As in mitosis, chromosome replication (**1**) occurs before prophase; then during prophase 1 (**2**), homologous chromosomes pair up and join at a point called a **synapse** (this happens only in meiosis). The attached chromosomes are now termed a tetrad, a dense four-stranded structure composed of the four chromatids from the original chromosomes. At this point, some portions of the chromatid may break off and reattach to another chromatid in the tetrad. This process, known as **crossing over**, results in an even wider array of final genetic possibilities.

The nuclear membrane disappears during late prophase (or prometaphase). Each chromosome (rather than each chromatid) develops a kinetochore, and as the spindle fibers attach to each chromosome, they begin to move.

In metaphase 1 (**3**), the two chromosomes (a total of four chromatids per pair) align themselves along the equatorial plane of the cell. Each homologous pair of chromosomes contains one chromosome from the mother and one from the father from the original sexual production of that organism. When the homologous pairs orient at the cell's center in preparation for separating, the chromosomes randomly sort. The resulting cells from this meiotic division will have a mixture of chromosomes from each parent. This increases the possibilities for variety among descendent cells.

Anaphase 1 (**4**) occurs next as the chromosomes move to separate ends of the cell. This phase differs from the anaphase of mitosis where one of each chromosome pair (rather than one chromatid) separates. In telophase 1 (**5**), the nuclear envelope may or may not form, depending on the type of organism. In either case, the cell then proceeds to meiosis 2.

The nuclear envelopes dissolve (if they have formed) during prophase 2 (**6**) and spindle fibers form again. All else proceeds as in mitosis, through metaphase 2 (**7**), anaphase 2 (**8**), and telophase 2 (**9**). Again, as in mitosis, each chromosome splits into two chromatids. The process ends with cytokinesis (**10**), forming four distinct gamete cells.

CHAPTER 4
PLANTS
(BOTANY)

Chapter 4

PLANTS (BOTANY)

Most of us commonly recognize plants as organisms that produce their own food through the process of photosynthesis. (Some bacteria are also photosynthetic.) However, the plant kingdom is divided into several classifications according to physical characteristics.

Vascular plants (tracheophytes) have tissue organized in such a way as to conduct food and water throughout their structure. These plants include some that produce seeds (such as corn or roses) as well as those that do not produce any seeds (such as ferns). **Nonvascular** plants (bryophytes), such as mosses, lack special tissue for conducting water or food. They produce no seeds or flowers and are generally only a few centimeters in height.

Another method of classifying plants is according to their method of reproduction. **Angiosperms** are plants that produce flowers as reproductive organs. **Gymnosperms**, on the other hand, produce seeds without flowers. These include conifers (cone-bearers) and cycads.

Plants that survive only through a single growing season are known as **annuals**. Other plants are **biennial**; their life cycle spans two growing seasons. **Perennial** plants continue to grow year after year.

PLANT ANATOMY

Plants have structures with attributes that equip them to thrive in their environment. Angiosperms and Gymnosperms differ mostly in the structure of their stems and reproductive organs. Gymnosperms are mostly trees, with woody, instead of herbaceous stems. Gymnosperms do not produce flowers; instead they produce seeds in cones or cone-like structures.

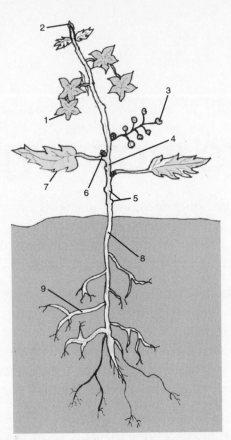

Fig. 4-1: A Typical Flowering Plant (angiosperm).
Note descriptions of numbered structures in text.

Angiosperms

The shoot system of angiosperms includes the stem, leaves, flowers, and fruit, as well as growth structures such as nodes and buds (see Fig. 4-1:1-7). The signature structure of an angiosperm is the **flower (1)**, the primary reproductive organ. Before the flower blooms, it is enclosed within the **sepals (1-a)**, small, green, leaf-like structures, which fold back to reveal the flower **petals (1-b)**. The petals usually are brightly colored; their main function is to attract insects and birds, which may be necessary to the process of pollination. The short branch of stem, which supports the flower, is called the **pedicel (1-c).**

Usually (but depending on the species), a single flower will have both male and female reproductive organs. The **pistil** is the female structure, and includes the stigma, style, ovary, and ovules. The **stigma (1-d)** is a sticky surface at the top of the pistil, which traps pollen grains. The stigma sits above a slender vase-like structure, the **style (1-e)**, which encloses the ovary. The **ovary (1-f)** is the hollow, bulb-shaped structure in the lower interior of the pistil. (After seeds have formed, the ovary will ripen and

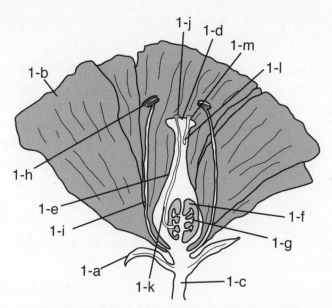

Fig. 4-2: Typical Flower. Note numbered explanations in text.

become fruit.) Within the ovary are the **ovules (1-g)**, small round cases each containing one or more egg cells. (If the egg is fertilized, the ovule will become a seed.) In the process of meiosis in the ovule, an egg cell is produced, along with smaller bodies known as polar nuclei. The polar nuclei will develop into the endosperm of the seed when fertilized by sperm cells.

The male structure is the stamen, consisting of the **anther (1-h)** atop the long, hollow **filament (1-i)**. The anther has four lobes and contains cells (microspore mother cells) that become pollen. Some mature **pollen grains (1-j)** are conveyed (usually by wind, birds, or insects) to a flower of a compatible species, where they stick to the stigma. The stigma produces chemicals, which stimulate the pollen to burrow into the style, forming a hollow **pollen tube (1-k)**. This tube is produced by the tube **nucleus (1-l)**, which has developed from a portion of the pollen grain. The pollen tube extends down toward the ovary. Behind the tube nucleus are two **sperm nuclei (1-m)**. When the sperm nuclei reach the ovule, one will join with an egg cell, fertilizing it to become a zygote (the beginning cell of the embryo). The other sperm nucleus merges with the polar bodies forming the endosperm, which will feed the growing embryo.

The **shoot apex (2)** is composed of **meristem** tissue (consisting of undifferentiated cells capable of quick growth and specialization), and is the region where elongation of the stem occurs. The **terminal bud** (the beginning of a new set of leaves) is also located at the shoot apex. Each year, as the plant continues to grow taller, a new terminal bud and shoot apex are produced. The spot where the previous year's terminal bud was located is then called a **terminal bud scar**.

Fruit (3) is a matured ovary, which contains the seeds (mature fertilized ovules). The fruit provides protection for the seeds, as well as a method to disburse them. For instance, when ripened fruit is eaten by animals the seeds are discarded or excreted in the animal's waste, transferring the seed to a new location for germination. Fruits that develop from a single ripened ovary are known as **simple fruits** (i.e., apple, corn, olive, acorn, cucumber). **Compound fruits** develop from many separate ovaries. They may be an **aggregate fruit,** in which many ovaries of a single flower fuse together (i.e., raspberry), or a **multiple fruit,** which forms from the fusing of several ovaries of separate flowers during ripening (i.e., strawberry or pineapple).

Each **seed** contains a tiny embryonic plant, stored food, and a seed coat for protection. When the seed is exposed to proper moisture, temperature, and oxygen, it germinates (begins to sprout and grow into a new plant). Stored food in a seed is found in the cotyledon. Angiosperms are also classified according to the structure of their cotyledons. Plants with two cotyledons in each seed are known as dicotyledons (**dicots**); those with only one are known as monocotyledons (**monocots**). The following chart outlines the major differences between monocots and dicots:

Dicots	Monocots
ex. oaks, flowers, vegetables	ex. grasses, lilies, palm trees
two cotyledons in seed	one cotyledon in seed
leaves have branched or networked veins	leaves have parallel veins
vascular bundles (collections of xylem and phloem tubes) are arranged in rings	stems have random arrangement of vascular bundles
taproot system with smaller secondary roots	fibrous roots
flowers with petals in multiples of four or five	flowers with petals in multiples of three

The **stem (4)** is the main support structure of the plant. The stem produces leaves and lateral (parallel with the ground) branches. **Nodes (5)** are the locations along the stem where new leaves sprout, and the space between nodes is the **internode**. New leaves begin as **lateral buds (6)**, which can be seen on growing plants.

The stem is also the main organ for transporting food and water to and from the leaves. In some cases the stem also stores food, for instance a potato is a tuber (stem) that stores starch. The stem also contains meristem tissue.

Most of the stem tissue is made of **vascular tissue**, including two varieties—**xylem** and **phloem**. Xylem tissue is composed of long tubular cells, which transport water up from the ground to the branches and leaves. Phloem tissue, made of stacked cells connected by sieve plates (which allow nutrients to pass from cell to cell), transports food made in the leaves (by photosynthesis) to the rest of the plant.

The **leaf (7)** is the primary site of photosynthesis in most plants. Most leaves are thin, flat, and joined to a branch or stem by a petiole (a small stem-like extension). The petiole houses vascular tissue, which connects the veins in the leaf with those in the stem.

The **cuticle**, which maintains the leaf's moisture balance, covers most leaf surfaces. Considering a cross-section of a leaf, the outermost layer is the **epidermis (7-a, e).** The epidermis is generally one cell thick. It secretes the waxy cuticle and protects the inner tissue of the leaf.

The mesophyll is composed of several layers of tissue between the upper and lower epidermis. The uppermost, the **palisade layer (7-b)**, contains vertically aligned cells with numerous chloroplasts. The arrangement of these cells maximizes the potential for exposure of the chloroplasts to needed sunlight. Most photosynthesis occurs in this layer.

The sugars produced by photosynthesis are transported throughout the plant via the **vascular bundles (7-c)** of xylem and phloem. The vascular bundles make up the veins in the leaf.

The next layer beneath the palisade cells is the **spongy layer (7-d)**, a layer of parenchyma cells separated by large air spaces. The air spaces allow for the exchange of gases (carbon dioxide and oxygen) for photosynthesis.

On the underside of the leaf there are openings ringed by **guard cells (7-f).** The openings are called **stomata (7-g)** (or stomates). The stomata serve to allow moisture and gases (carbon dioxide and oxygen) to pass in and out of the leaf, thus facilitating photosynthesis.

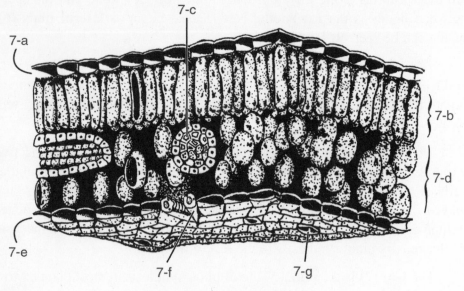

Fig. 4-3: Cross-section of a Leaf.

The root system of a typical angiosperm includes the **primary roots (8)**, which extend downward and the **lateral roots (9)**, which develop secondarily and extend horizontally, parallel with the ground surface. Roots function to provide water and needed nutrients to the plant. Roots are structured to provide a large surface area for absorption. The network of the root system also anchors the plant.

Roots have four major structural regions, which run vertically from bottom to top. The **root cap** is composed of dead, thick-walled cells, and covers the tip of the root, protecting it as the root pushes through soil. The **meristematic region** is just above the root cap. It consists of undifferentiated cells, which carry on mitosis, producing cells that grow to form the **elongation region**. In the elongation region, cells differentiate, large vacuoles are formed, and cells grow. As the cells differentiate into various root tissues, they become part of the **maturation region**.

A cross-section of root tissue above the maturation region would reveal several types of **primary root tissue.** In the maturation region, the epidermis produces **root hairs (9-a)**, extensions of the cells, which reach between soil particles and retrieve water and minerals. The primary tissues include the outermost layer, the **epidermis (9-b)**. The epidermis is one cell layer thick and serves to protect the internal root tissue and absorb nutrients and water.

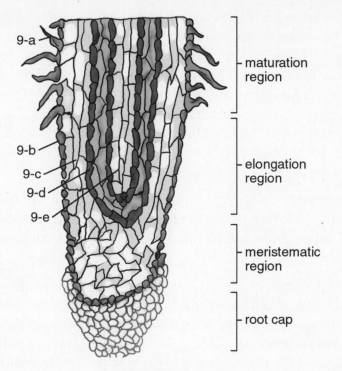

9-a

maturation
region

9-b

9-c

9-d

9-e

elongation
region

meristematic
region

root cap

Fig. 4-4: Root Cross-section.

Inside the epidermis is a ring known as the **cortex (9-c)**, made of large parenchyma cells. **Parenchyma** cells are present in many tissues of plants; they are thin-walled cells loosely packed to allow for flow of gases and uptake of minerals.

Inside the cortex is a ring of **endodermis (9-d)**, a single layer of cells, which are tightly connected so no substances can pass between cells. This feature allows the endodermis to act as a filter; all substances entering the vascular tissues from the root must pass through these cells. In the center of the root is the **vascular cylinder (9-e)**, including xylem and phloem tissue.

PLANT PHYSIOLOGY

Water and Mineral Absorption and Transport

Although plants produce their own sugars and starches for food, they must obtain water, carbon dioxide, and minerals from their environment. Vascular plants have well-developed systems for absorption and transport of water and minerals.

Water is essential to all cells of all plants, so plants must have the ability to obtain water and transport water molecules throughout their structure. Most water is absorbed through the plant's root system, then makes its way in one of two pathways toward the xylem cells, which will transport water up the stem and to the leaves and flowers. The first pathway is for water to seep between the epidermal cells of the roots and between the parenchyma cells of the cortex. When water reaches the endodermal tissue, it enters the cells and is pushed through the vascular tissue toward the xylem.

A second pathway is for the water to pass through the cell wall and plasma membrane. Water travels along this intracellular route through channels in the cell membranes (plasmodesmata), until it reaches the xylem.

Once water reaches the xylem, hydrogen bonding between water molecules (known as **cohesion**) causes tension that pulls water through the water column up through the stem and on to the leaves (known as the **cohesion-tension process**). Some water that has traveled up through the plant to the leaves is evaporated, a process known as **transpiration**. As water is evaporated, it causes a siphoning effect (like sucking on a straw), which continues to pull water up from the root xylem, through the length of the plant and to the leaves.

Food Translocation and Storage

Food is manufactured by photosynthesis mostly in the leaves. The rest of the plant must have this food (carbohydrates) imported from the leaves. The leaves have source cells, which store the manufactured sugars. The food molecules are transferred from the source cells to phloem tissue through active transport (energy is expended to move molecules across the plasma membrane against the concentration gradient—from low concentration to high concentration). Once in the phloem, the sugars begin to build up causing osmosis to occur (water enters the phloem lowering the sugar concentration). The entrance of water into the phloem causes pressure, which pushes the water-sugar solution through **sieve plates** that join the cells. This pressure thrusts the water-sugar solution to all areas of the plant, making food available to all cells in the plant.

PLANT REPRODUCTION AND DEVELOPMENT

The reproductive cycle of plants occurs through the alternation of haploid (n) and diploid (2n) phases. [Remember from Chapter 3 that the haploid cells have one complete set of chromosomes (n). Diploid cells have two sets of chromosomes (2n).] Diploid and haploid stages are both capable of undergoing mitosis in plants. The diploid generation is known as a **sporophyte**. The reproductive organs of the sporophyte produce **gametophytes** through the process of meiosis. Gametophytes may be male or female and are haploid. The male gametophyte produces **sperm** (**male gamete**); the female produces an **egg cell** (**female gamete**). When a sperm cell **fertilizes** an egg cell (haploid cells join to form a diploid cell) they produce a **zygote**. The zygote will grow into an **embryo**, which resides within the growing seed.

We are accustomed to identifying particular plants according to their adult phase, which is only one phase of the life cycle. Various phyla of plants have their own identifiable life cycles, which include an **alternation of generations**.

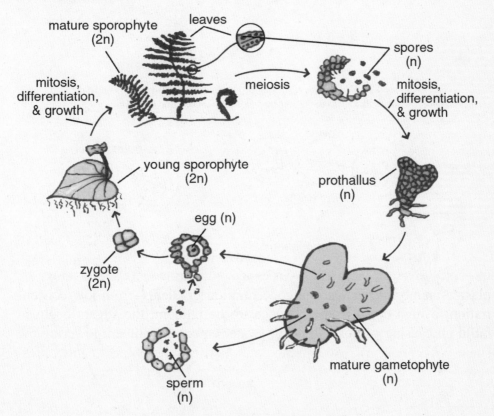

Fig. 4-5: Alternation of Generations in Ferns.

Mosses and ferns alternate haploid and diploid phases, developing two distinct generations of the plant, each with its own recognizable form. One generation is haploid, the other diploid. The haploid phase is most prominent in mosses, while in ferns; the diploid stage is most prominent.

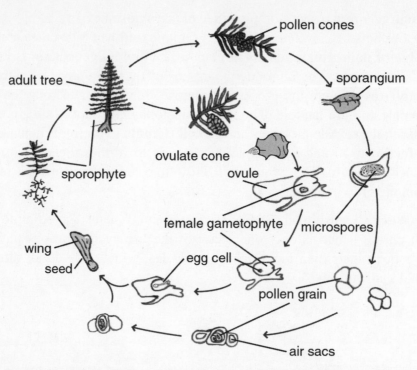

Fig. 4-6: Pine Life Cycle. The adult tree produces both male (pollen) and female (ovulate) cones that form the pollen and ovules that combine to produce a seed.

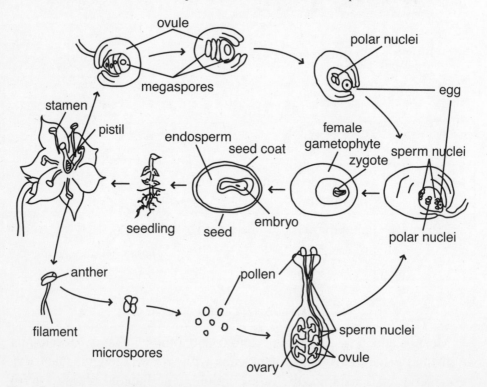

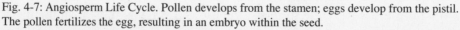

Fig. 4-7: Angiosperm Life Cycle. Pollen develops from the stamen; eggs develop from the pistil. The pollen fertilizes the egg, resulting in an embryo within the seed.

In conifers (such as pines), the sporophyte generation (diploid) is the familiar adult of the species. The process of meiosis produces the haploid gametophytes (male and female) from the male and female cone scales. The male gametophyte forms the male pollen grain and its attached air bladders, which assist it in being borne by the wind. The pollen contains sperm cells and tube cells, which will fertilize an egg cell of a female scale when they are brought into contact.

In angiosperms, the dominant adult generation is also the sporophyte—the flowering plant.

Asexual Plant Reproduction

Some plants may also reproduce through **vegetative propagation**—an asexual process. Asexual reproduction occurs through mitosis only (it does not involve gametes), and produces offspring genetically identical to the parent. While sexual reproduction leads to genetic variation and adaptation, asexual reproduction of a plant with a desirable set of genetic traits, preserves these intact in successive generations. Many plants reproduce through a combination of sexual and asexual reproduction, reaping the advantages of each.

There are several types of plants that produce structures specifically designed to carry on vegetative propagation. These are described in the chart below:

Reproductive Structure	Description of Structure	Plants with these Structures
tubers	underground storage stems, develop new shoots after dormant season	potatoes
rhizomes	underground runners that develop into new plant	irises
stolens	above-ground runners that grow roots of their own then develop into new plant	strawberries
bulbs	underground storage units that grow into many new plants via division	amaryllis
corms	resemble bulbs but with enlarged, solid stem for food storage	gladiolus, crocus

PLANT GROWTH AND DEVELOPMENT

Hormones are chemicals that regulate the growth, development, and function of an organism. Plant cells produce hormones that bring about physiological changes within plant tissues. Each type of hormone affects changes in particular cells known as target cells. The traits regulated by hormones are many and varied, but there are some particularly important ones in plants. Note the most common hormones and their functions in the following chart:

Hormone	Process Regulated or Influenced
giberellins (65 hormones)	cell division & cell elongation
cytokinins	cell division & fruit development
abscisic acid	opening and closing of stomata (controlling water lost through transpiration and formation of winter buds that put plant in dormant state)
ethylene	ripening of fruit (spoiling releases ethylene which stimulates ripening of surrounding fruit); metabolic activity (i.e., producing female flowers to increase fertilization)
auxins	growth factors (i.e., tropisms)

A **tropism** is an involuntary response of an organism to an external stimulus such as light, water, gravity, or nutrients. For instance, plant stems are usually positively **phototropic** (they grow towards light), while plant roots are negatively phototropic (they grow away from light). Plant roots are positively **geotropic**; they grow toward the center of the earth, while stems are negatively geotropic, growing against gravity. Tropisms are thought to be caused by plant hormones, which react to the external stimulus causing some cells to grow quickly and others to grow slowly. Variations of auxin levels also influence the strength of petioles and stems, regulating when leaves or fruit drop.

There are other factors (besides hormones), which influence plant growth and development. For instance, plants respond to relative periods of light and darkness, a characteristic known as **photoperiodicity**. Light-sensitive chemicals in the leaves trigger a response in the plant, which encourages growth, flowering, or other reactions. It is this trait that causes flowering and growth of varying plants at different times of year.

CHAPTER 5
ANIMALS
(ZOOLOGY)

Chapter 5

ANIMALS (ZOOLOGY)

The animal kingdom includes a wide variety of phyla that have a range of body plans. This range includes certain invertebrates with relatively simple body plans as well as highly complex vertebrates (including humans). There are specific characteristics that differentiate animals from other living things. Organisms in the animal kingdom share the following traits:

1. Animal cells do not have cell walls or plastids.

2. Adult animals are multicellular with specialized tissues and organs.

3. Animals are heterotrophic (they do not produce their own food).

4. Animal species are capable of sexual reproduction, although some are also capable of asexual reproduction (ex. hydra).

5. Animals develop from embryonic stages.

In addition to the above traits, most adult animals have a symmetrical anatomy. Adult animals can have either radial symmetry (constituent parts are arranged radiating symmetrically about a center point) or bilateral symmetry (the body can be divided along a center plane into equal, mirror-image halves). There are a few exceptions to this rule, including the adult sponge whose body is not necessarily symmetrical. While there is wide variation in the physical structure of animals, the animal kingdom is usually divided into two broad categories—invertebrates and vertebrates. There are many more species of invertebrates than vertebrates.

Invertebrates are those species having no internal backbone structure; **vertebrates** have internal backbones. Invertebrates include sponges and worms, which have no skeletal structure at all, and arthropods, mollusks, crustaceans, etc., which have exoskeletons. In fact, there are many more phyla of invertebrates than vertebrates (about 950,000 phyla of invertebrates and only about 40,000 phyla of vertebrates).

ANIMAL ANATOMY

Tissues

Like all multicellular organisms, animal bodies contain several kinds of tissues, made up of different cell types. Differentiated cells may organize into specialized tissues performing particular functions. There are eight major types of animal tissue:

1) **Epithelial tissue** consists of thin layers of cells. Epithelial tissue makes up the layers of skin, lines ducts and the intestine, and covers the inside of the body cavity. Epithelial tissue forms the barrier between the environment and the interior of the body.

2) **Connective tissue** covers internal organs and composes ligaments and tendons. This tissue holds tissues and organs together, stabilizing the body structure.

3) **Muscle tissue** is divided into three types—smooth, skeletal, and cardiac. **Smooth** muscle makes up the walls of internal organs and functions in involuntary movement (breathing, etc.). **Skeletal** muscle attaches bones of the skeleton to each other and surrounding tissues. Skeletal muscle's function is to enable voluntary movement. **Cardiac** muscle is the tissue forming the walls of the heart. Its strength and electrical properties are vital to the heart's ability to pump blood.

4) **Bone tissue** is found in the skeleton and provides support, protection for internal organs, and ability to move as muscles pull against bones.

5) **Cartilage tissue** reduces friction between bones, and supports and connects them. For example, it is found at the ends of bones and in the ears and nose.

6) **Adipose tissue** is found beneath the skin and around organs providing cushioning, insulation, and fat storage.

7) **Nerve tissue** is found in the brain, spinal cord, nerves, and ganglion. It carries electrical and chemical impulses to and from organs and limbs to the brain. Nerve tissue in the brain receives these impulses and sustains mental activity.

8) **Blood tissue** consists of several cell types in a fluid called plasma. It flows through the blood vessels and heart, and is essential for carrying oxygen to cells, fighting infection, and carrying nutrients and

wastes to and from cells. Blood also has clotting capabilities, which preserve the body's functions in case of injury.

Tissues are organized into organs, and organs function together to form systems, which support the life of an organism. Studying these systems allows us to understand how organisms thrive within their ecosystem.

Systems

Many different body plans exist amongst animals, and each type of body plan includes systems necessary for the organism to live. Our discussion of systems here focuses on those found in most vertebrates. Vertebrates are highly complex organisms with several systems working together to perform the functions necessary to life. These include the digestive, gas exchange, skeletal, nervous, circulatory, excretory, and immune systems.

Digestive System

The **digestive system** (see Fig. 5-1) serves as a processing plant for ingested food. The digestive system in animals generally encompasses the processes of **ingestion** (food intake), **digestion** (breaking down of ingested particles into molecules that can be absorbed by the body), and **egestion** (the elimination of indigestible materials). In most vertebrates, the digestive organs are divided into two categories, the **alimentary canal,** and the **accessory organs**. The alimentary canal is also known as the **gastrointestinal** (or GI) **tract** and includes the mouth, pharynx, esophagus, stomach, small intestine, large intestine, rectum, and anus. The accessory organs include the teeth, tongue, salivary glands, liver, gallbladder, and pancreas.

The **mouth** (oral cavity, **1**) is the organ of ingestion and the first organ of digestion in the GI tract. The first step in digestion in many vertebrates occurs as food is chewed. Chewing is the initial step in breaking down food into particles of manageable size. Chewing also increases the surface area of the food and mixes it with saliva, which contains the starch-digesting enzyme amylase. Saliva is secreted by the **salivary glands** (**2**). Chewed food is then swallowed and moved toward the **stomach** (**3**) by peristalsis (muscle contraction) of the **esophagus** (**4**). The stomach is a muscular organ that stores incompletely digested food. The stomach continues the mechanical and chemical breakdown of food particles begun by the chewing process. The lining of the stomach secretes mucous to protect it from the strong digestive chemicals necessary in the digestive process. The stomach also secretes digestive enzymes and hydrochloric acid, which continue the digestive process to the point of producing a watery soup of nutrients, which then proceeds through the pyloric sphincter into the small intestine (the duodenum). The **pancreas** (**5**) and **gall bladder** (**6**) release more enzymes into the small intestine, the site where the final steps of digestion and most absorption occurs. The cells lining the **small intestine** (**7**) have protrusions out into the lumen of the intestine called **villi**. Villi provide a large surface area for absorption of nutrients. Nutrients move into the capillaries through or between the cells making up the villi. The enriched blood travels to the **liver** (**8**), where some sugars are removed and stored. The indigestible food proceeds from the small intestine to the **large intestine** (**9**) where water is absorbed back into the body. The waste (**feces**) is then passed through the **rectum** (**10**) and excreted from the **anus** (**11**).

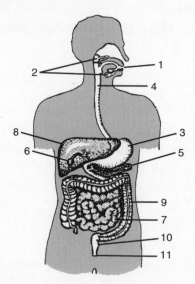

Fig. 5-1: Human Digestive System.

There are, of course, variations in the digestive system among animals of various classifications. Some vertebrates such as cows and deer are **ruminants**; they consume large amounts of vegetation. These animals have several chambers in their stomachs. Chewed vegetation is regurgitated from the first two stomach chambers as **cud**, and is chewed again, allowing much of their food to be broken down mechanically. Bacteria in the digestive track then break down cellulose, the main constituent of a ruminant's diet.

Many invertebrates, such as insects and earthworms, have digestive systems resembling those of vertebrates, including a mouth, esophagus, stomach, and intestines. Many of these species also have a **crop**, an organ that stores food until it is processed for absorption. Other animals have only a sac-like digestive cavity that performs the necessary functions of digestion.

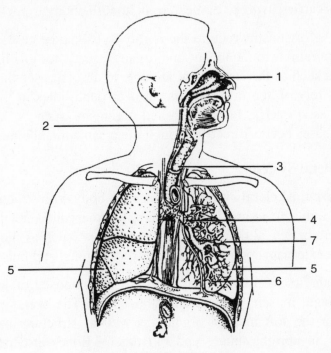

Fig. 5-2: Human Respiratory System.

Respiratory or Gas Exchange System

Also known as the **respiratory system** (see Fig. 5-2), the **gas exchange system** is responsible for the intake and processing of gases required by an organism, and for expelling gases produced as waste products. In humans, air is taken in primarily through the **nose** (although gases may be inhaled through the mouth, the nose is better at filtering out pollutants in the air). The **nasal passages (1)** have a mucous lining to capture foreign particles. This lining is surrounded by epithelial tissue with embedded capillaries, which serve to warm the entering air. Air then passes through the **pharynx (2)** and into the **trachea (3)**. The trachea includes the windpipe or **larynx** in its upper portion, and the **glottis**, an opening allowing gases to pass into the two branches known as the bronchi. The glottis is guarded by a flap of tissue, the **epiglottis**, which prevents food particles from entering the bronchial tubes. The **bronchi (4)** lead to the two **lungs (5)** where they branch out in all directions into smaller tubules known as **bronchioles (6)**. The bronchioles end in **alveoli (7)**, thin-walled air sacs, which are the site of gas exchange. The bronchioles are surrounded by capillaries, which bring blood with a high density of carbon dioxide and a low concentration of oxygen from the pulmonary arteries. At the alveoli, the carbon dioxide diffuses from the blood into the alveoli and oxygen diffuses from the alveoli into the blood. The oxygenated blood is carried away to tissues throughout the body.

All living organisms require the ability to exchange gases, and there are several variations to the means and organs utilized for this life process. Invertebrates such as the earthworm are able to absorb gases through their skin. Insects rely on the diffusion of gases through holes in the exoskeleton known as spiracles. In single-celled organisms such as the amoeba, diffusion of gases occurs directly through the plasma membrane.

Musculoskeletal System

The **musculoskeletal system** provides the body with structure, stability, and the ability to move. By definition, the musculoskeletal system is unique to vertebrates, although some invertebrates (such as mollusks and insects) have external support structures (exoskeletons) and muscle.

In humans, the musculoskeletal system is composed of joints, ligaments, cartilage, muscle groups, and 206 bones. The skeleton provides protection for the soft internal organs, as well as structure and stability allowing for an upright stature and movement. Bones also perform the important function of storing calcium and phosphates, and producing red blood cells within the bone marrow. The 206 bones forming the human skeleton are linked with movable joints, and joined by muscle systems controlling movement.

Skeletal muscles are voluntary—they are activated by command from the nervous system. **Smooth muscle** lines most internal organs, protecting their contents and function, and generally contracting without conscious intent. For instance, the involuntary (automatic) contraction of smooth muscle in the esophagus and lungs facilitates digestion and respiration. **Cardiac muscle** is unique to the heart. It is involuntary muscle (like smooth muscle), but cardiac muscle also has unique features, which cause it to "beat" rhythmically. Cardiac muscle cells have branched endings that interlock with each other, keeping the muscle fibers from ripping apart during their strong contractions. In addition, electrical impulses travel in waves from cell to cell in cardiac muscle, causing the muscle to contract in a coordinated way with a rhythmic pace.

Nervous System

The **nervous system** is a communication network that connects the entire body of an organism, and provides control over bodily functions and actions. Nerve tissue is composed of nerve cells known as **neurons**. Neurons carry impulses via electrochemical responses through their **cell body** and **axon** (long root-like appendage of the cell). Nerve cells exist in networks, with axons of neighbor neurons interacting across small spaces (**synapses**). Chemical neurotransmitters send messages along the nerve network causing responses specific to varying types of nerve tissue. The nervous system allows the body to sense stimuli and conditions in the environment and respond with necessary reactions. **Sensory organs**— skin, eyes, nose, ears, etc.—transmit signals in response to environmental stimuli to the **brain**, which then conveys messages via nerves to glands and muscles, which produce the necessary response.

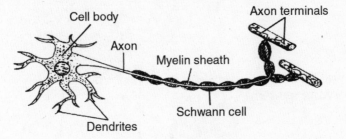

Fig. 5-3: A typical neuron.

The human nervous system (and that of many mammals) is anatomically divided into two systems, the central nervous system, and the peripheral nervous system. The following outline shows the components of each portion of the nervous system.

I. Central Nervous System (CNS) - two main components, the **brain** and the **spinal cord**. These organs control all other organs and systems of the body. The spinal cord is a continuation of the brain stem, and acts as a conduit of nerve messages.

II. Peripheral Nervous System (PNS) - a network of nerves throughout the body.

A) **Sensory Division**

    1. **visceral sensory nerves** - carry impulses from body organs to CNS

    2. **somatic sensory nerves** - carry impulses from body surface to CNS

B) **Motor Division**

    1. **somatic motor nerves** - carries impulses to skeletal muscle from CNS

2. **autonomic**

   a.) **sympathetic** nervous system - carries impulses that stimulate organs

   b.) **parasympathetic** nervous system - carries impulses back from organs

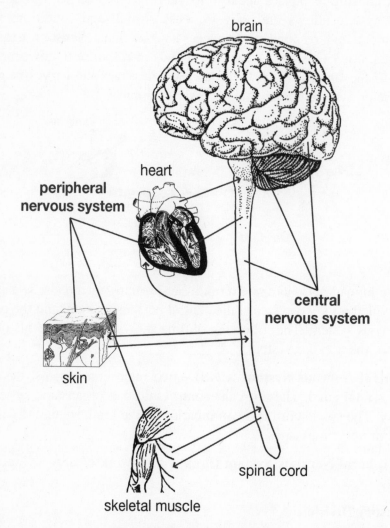

Fig. 5-4: Human Nervous System.

    The brain of vertebrates has three major divisions, the forebrain, midbrain, and hindbrain. The **forebrain** is located most anterior, and contains the **olfactory lobes** (sense smell), **cerebrum** (controls sensory and motor responses, memory, speech, and most factors of intelligence), as well as the **thalamus** (integrates senses), **hypothalamus** (is involved in hunger, thirst, blood pressure, body temperature, hostility, pain, pleasure, etc.), and **pituitary gland** (releases various hormones). The **midbrain** is between the forebrain and hindbrain and contains the **optic lobes** (visual center connected to the eyes by the optic nerves). The **hindbrain** consists of the **cerebellum** (controls balance, equilibrium, and muscle coordination) and the **medulla oblongata** (controls involuntary response such as breathing and heartbeat).

Within the brain, nerve tissue is grayish in color and is called **gray matter**. The nerve cells, which exist in the spinal cord and throughout the body, have insulation covering their axons. This insulation (called the **myelin sheath**) speeds electrochemical conduction within the axon of the nerve cell. Since the myelin sheath gives this tissue a white color, it is called **white matter**. The myelin sheath is made up of individual cells called Schwann cells.

The nervous systems of vertebrates and some invertebrates are highly sophisticated, providing conscious response and unconscious controls. However, the nervous systems of some species of invertebrates (such as jellyfish) are relatively simple networks of neurons that control only some aspects of their body functions.

Circulatory System

The **circulatory system** is the conduit for delivering nutrients and gases to all cells and for removing waste products from them.

In invertebrates, the circulatory system may consist entirely of diffusion in the gastrovascular cavity, or it may be an **open circulatory system** (where blood directly bathes the internal organs), or a **closed circulatory system** (where blood is confined to vessels).

Closed circulatory systems are also typical of vertebrates. In vertebrates, **blood** flows throughout the circulatory system within **vessels**. Vessels include **arteries**, **veins**, and **capillaries**. The pumping action of the **heart** (a hollow, muscular organ) forces blood in one direction throughout the system. In large animals, valves within the heart, and some of the vessels in limbs, keep blood from flowing backwards (being pulled downward by gravity).

Blood carries many products to cells throughout the body, including minerals, infection-fighting white blood cells, nutrients, proteins, hormones, and metabolites. Blood also carries dissolved gases (particularly oxygen) to cells and waste gases (mainly carbon dioxide) away from cells. The process of cellular metabolism is a fundamental process of life and cannot proceed without a continuous supply of oxygen to every living cell within the body.

Capillaries (tiny vessels) surround all tissues of the body and exchange carbon dioxide for oxygen. Oxygen is carried by **hemoglobin** (containing iron) in red blood cells. Oxygen enters the blood in the lungs and travels to the heart, then through **arteries** (larger vessels that carry blood away from the heart), **arterioles** (small arteries), to capillaries. The blood picks up carbon dioxide waste from the cells and carries it through capillaries, then **venules** (small veins), and **veins** (vessels that carry blood toward the heart), back to the heart and on to the lungs. Thus, blood is continually cycled.

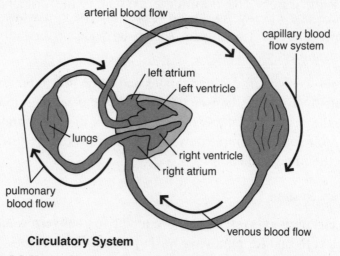

Circulatory System

Fig. 5-5: Human Circulatory System. Blood flows from the heart through arteries to the capillaries throughout the body and returns via the veins.

Excretory System

The **excretory system** is responsible for collecting waste materials and transporting them to organs that expel them from the body. There are many types of waste that must be expelled from the body, and there are many organs involved in this process.

The primary excretory organs of most vertebrates are the kidneys. The **kidneys** filter metabolic wastes from the blood and excrete them as **urine** into the urinary tract. The urinary tract carries the fluid that is eventually expelled from the body. Urine is typically 95% water, and may contain urea (formed from breakdown of proteins), uric acid (formed from breaking down nucleic acids), creatinine (a byproduct of muscle contraction), and various minerals and hormones.

The **liver** produces **bile** from broken down pigments and chemicals (often from pollutants and medications) and secretes it into the small intestine, where it proceeds to the large intestine and is expelled in the feces.

The liver also breaks down some nitrogenous molecules (including some proteins), excreting them as urea.

The **lungs** are the sites of excretion for carbon dioxide. The **skin** is an accessory excretory organ; salts, urea, and other wastes are secreted with water from sweat glands in the skin.

Immune System

The **immune system** functions to defend the body from infection by bacteria and viruses. The **lymphatic system** is the principal infection-fighting component of the immune system. The organs of the lymphatic system in humans and other higher invertebrates include the lymph, lymph nodes, spleen, thymus, and tonsils. **Lymph** is a collection of excess fluid that is absorbed from between cells into a special system of vessels, which circulates through the lymphatic system and finally dumps into the bloodstream. Lymph also collects plasma proteins that have leaked into interstitial fluids.

Lymph nodes are small masses of lymph tissue whose function is to filter lymph and produce lymphocytes. **Lymphocytes** and other cells are involved in the immune system. Lymphocytes begin in bone marrow as stem cells and are collected and distributed via the lymph nodes. There are two classes of lymphocytes, B cells, and T cells. **B cells** emerge from the bone marrow mature, and produce **antibodies**, which enter the bloodstream. These antibodies find and attach themselves to foreign **antigens** (toxins, bacteria, foreign cells, etc.). The attachment of an antibody to an antigen marks the pair for destruction.

The **spleen** contains some lymphatic tissue, and is located in the abdomen. It filters larger volumes of lymph than nodes can handle. The **tonsils** are a group of lymph cells connected together and located in the throat.

The **thymus** is another mass of lymph tissue, which is active only through the teen years, fighting infection and producing T cells. **T cells** mature in the thymus gland. Some T cells (like B cells) patrol the blood for antigens, but T cells are also equipped to destroy antigens themselves. T cells also regulate the body's immune responses.

Homeostatic Mechanisms

All living cells, tissues, organs, and organisms must maintain a tight range of physical and chemical conditions in order for them to live. Conditions such as temperature, pH, water balance, sugar levels, etc., must be monitored and controlled in order to keep them within the accepted ranges that will not inhibit life. When the conditions of an organism are within acceptable ranges, it is said to be in **homeostasis**. Organisms have a special set of mechanisms that serve to keep them in homeostasis. Homeostasis is a state of dynamic equilibrium, which balances forces tending toward change and forces acceptable for life functions.

Homeostasis is achieved mostly by actions of the sympathetic and parasympathetic nervous systems by a process known as **feedback control**. For instance, when the body undergoes physical activity, muscle action causes a rise in temperature. If not checked, rising temperature could destroy cells. In this instance, the nervous system detects rising temperature and reacts with a response that causes sweat glands to produce sweat. The evaporation of sweat cools the body.

There are many instances of feedback control. These take effect when any situation arises that may drive levels out of the normal acceptable range. In other words, the homeostatic mechanism is a reaction to a stimulus. This reaction, called a **feedback response**, is the production of some counter force that levels the system.

Hormonal Control in Homeostasis and Reproduction

Hormones are chemicals produced in the endocrine glands of an organism, which travel through the circulatory system and are taken up by specific targeted organs or tissues, where they modify metabolic activities.

Hormonal control occurs through one of two processes. The first is the **mobile receptor mechanism**. A hormone is manufactured in response to a particular **stimulus**. The hormone (for instance a **steroid**) enters the bloodstream from one of the ductless endocrine glands that manufacture hormones. The steroid passes through the cell membrane of the targeted cell and enters the cytoplasm. The hormone combines with a particular protein known as a receptor, creating the **hormone-receptor complex**. This complex enters the nucleus and binds to a DNA molecule causing a gene to be transcribed. The mRNA molecule leaves the nucleus for the endoplasmic reticulum, where it encodes a particular protein. The protein migrates to the site of the stimulus and counteracts the source of the stimulus. The result is homeostasis, a balance of the counterproductive forces.

The second process targets receptors on a cell's membrane. A particular **receptor** exists on the membrane when the cell is in a particular condition (for instance containing an excess of glucose). When the hormone binds with the receptor on the membrane, the receptor changes its form. This triggers a chain of events within the cytoplasm resulting in the production or destruction of proteins, thus moderating the conditions.

Hormones control many physiological functions, from digestion, to conscious responses and thinking, to reproduction. In humans, for instance, women of childbearing age have a continuous cycle of hormones. The hormone cycle causes the release of eggs at specific times. If the egg is fertilized, a different combination of hormones stimulates a chain of events that promotes the development of the embryo.

ANIMAL REPRODUCTION AND DEVELOPMENT

Reproduction in multicellular animals is a complex process that generally proceeds through the steps of **gametogenesis** (gamete formation) and then **fertilization**.

Gametes are the sex cells formed in the reproductive organs—sperm and eggs. When a sperm of one individual combines with the egg cell of another, the resulting cell is known as a **zygote. A zygote** then develops into a new individual. In the case of **spermatogenesis** (sperm formation), diploid **primary spermatocytes** are formed from special cells (**spermatogonia**) in the testes. The primary spermatocytes then undergo meiosis I, forming haploid **secondary spermatocytes** with a single chromosome set. (Please see the section on meiosis in Chapter 3.) The secondary spermatocytes go through meiosis II, forming **spermatids**, which are haploid. These spermatids then develop into the **sperm cells**.

In human female reproductive organs, egg cells are formed through a similar process known as **oogenesis. Primary oocytes** are typically present in great number in the female's ovaries at birth. Primary oocytes undergo meiosis I, forming one **secondary oocyte** and one smaller **polar body**. Both the secondary oocyte and the polar body undergo meiosis II; the polar body producing two polar bodies (not functional cells), and the oocyte producing one more polar body and one haploid **egg cell**. The egg cell is now ready for fertilization, and if there are sperm cells present, the egg may be fertilized, forming a diploid cell with a new combination of chromosomes, the zygote.

All multicellular organisms that reproduce sexually begin life as a zygote. The zygote then undergoes a series of cell divisions known as **cleavage**. After the first few divisions, the cluster of cells is called a morula. The **morula** then continues cell division, and the cluster begins to take shape as a thin layer of cells surrounding an internal cavity, the **blastula**. As cell division continues, the cells migrate and rearrange themselves, transforming the blastula into a two-layered cup shape, called the **gastrula** (a process known as **gastrulation**). As the gastrula develops, the cup shape reforms itself into a double-layered tube. The outer layer of the gastrula tube will become the **ectoderm**, which later will develop into the skin, some endocrine glands, and the nervous system. The inner layer of the tube will become the **endoderm**, the precursor of the gut lining and various accessory structures. With further development, a third layer, between the ectoderm and endoderm arises—the **mesoderm**. The mesoderm layer will eventually form muscles, and organs of the skeletal, circulatory, respiratory, reproductive, and excretory systems. The ectoderm, mesoderm, and endoderm form through the process of gastrulation and are collectively called the **germ layers**. As the germ layers develop, the embryo becomes recognizable, and differentiation continues until the organ systems are fully developed.

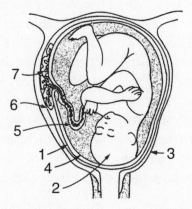

Fig. 5-6: Human Extraembryonic Membranes.

In addition to forming the tissues and organ systems of vertebrates, the germ layers also develop into **extraembryonic membranes** (i.e., membranes not part of the embryos themselves, see Fig. 5-6). The first of these membranes is the **chorion** (**1**). In egg-laying vertebrates, the chorion lies in contact with the innermost surface of the shell, while in other vertebrates it is the outermost membrane surrounding the **embryo** (**2**) and in contact with the **uterus** (**3**). In both cases, the chorion functions in regulating the passage of gases and water from the embryo to its surrounding environment. In embryos without shells, the chorion also controls passage of nutrients and wastes between the embryo and the mother.

Within the chorion is the **amnion** (**4**), a fluid-filled (**amniotic fluid**) sac enclosing the embryo. The amniotic fluid cushions the embryo and helps keep temperatures constant. The fluid also keeps the amnionic membrane from sticking to the developing embryo.

The third membrane is the **allantois** (**5**). It arises from the developing digestive tract. In humans and other vertebrates that bear live young, the allantois appears in the third week of development and becomes part of the **umbilical cord**. It contains blood vessels, which function to exchange gases and nutrients between the embryo and the mother. In egg-laying reptiles, the allantois is a reservoir for wastes. It fuses with the chorion, forming the **chorioallantoic membrane**, which regulates gas exchanges through the shell.

The **yolk sac membrane** (**6**), enclosing the **yolk sac** (**7**), also forms from the developing digestive tract and also becomes part of the umbilical cord. The yolk sac stores nutrients for use by the embryo. The yolk sac is larger and contains more material in egg-laying species, since there is no continuing contact with the mother. The yolk sac cells also give rise to gametes, which develop in reproductive organs of the embryo.

In mammals, the outer cells of the embryo and the inner cells of the uterus combine to form the **placenta**. The placenta is the connection between the mother and embryo; it is the site of transfer for nutrients, water, and wastes between them. The embryo synthesizes its own blood that is kept separate from the mother's blood. In the placenta, the vessels (that connect the circulatory system of the embryo through the umbilical cord to the placenta) pass right next to the mother's blood vessels. Nutrients, water, and oxygen diffuse from the mother's blood to the embryo's, while wastes and carbon dioxide diffuse into the mother's blood supply.

CHAPTER 6
PRINCIPLES OF HEREDITY
(GENETICS)

Chapter 6

PRINCIPLES OF HEREDITY (GENETICS)

The process by which characteristics pass from one generation to another is known as **inheritance**. The study of the principles of heredity (now called genetics) advanced greatly through the experimental work of **Gregor Mendel** (c. 1865). Mendel studied the relationships between traits expressed in parents and offspring, and the hereditary factors that caused expression of traits.

Mendel systematically bred pea plants to determine how certain hereditary traits passed from generation to generation. First, he established true-breeding plants, which produce offspring with the same traits as the parents. For example, the seeds of pea plants with yellow seeds would grow into plants that produced yellow seeds. Green seeds grow into plants that produce green seeds. Mendel named this first generation of true-breeding plants the parent or P_1 **generation**; he then bred the plant with yellow seeds and the plant with green seeds. Mendel called the first generation of offspring the F_1 **generation**. The F_1 generation of Mendel's yellow seed/green seed crosses contained only yellow seed offspring.

Mendel continued his experiment by crossing two individuals of the F_1 generation to produce an F_2 **generation**. In this generation, he found that some of the plants (one out of four) produced green seeds. Mendel performed hundreds of such crosses, studying some 10,000 pea plants, and was able to establish the rules of inheritance from them. The following are Mendel's main discoveries:

- Parents transmit hereditary factors (now called **genes**) to offspring. Genes then produce a characteristic, such as seed-coat color.

- Each individual carries two copies of a gene, and the copies may differ.

- The two genes an individual carries act independently, and the effect of one may mask the effect of the other. Mendel coined the terms geneticists still use: "dominant" and "recessive."

MODERN GENETICS

We now know that **chromosomes** carry all the genetic information in most organisms. Most organisms have corresponding pairs of chromosomes that carry genes for the same traits. These pairs are known as **homologous chromosomes**. Genes that produce a given trait exist at the same position (or **locus**) on homologous chromosomes. Each gene may have different forms, known as **alleles.** For instance, yellow seeds and green seeds arise from different alleles of the same gene. A gene can have two or more alleles, which differ in their nucleotide sequence. That difference can translate into proteins that function differently, resulting in variations of the trait.

Sexual reproduction (meiosis) produces gamete cells with $\frac{1}{2}$ the genetic information of the parents (paired chromosomes are separated and sorted independently). Therefore, each gamete may receive one of any number of combinations of each parent's chromosomes.

In addition, a trait may arise from one or more genes. (However, because one-gene traits are easiest to understand, we will use them for most of our examples.) If a trait is produced from a gene or genes with varying alleles, several possibilities for traits exist. The combination of alleles that make a particular trait is the **genotype**, while the trait expressed is the **phenotype**.

An allele is considered **dominant** if it masks the effect of its partner allele. The allele that does not produce its trait when present with a dominant allele is **recessive**. That is, when a dominant allele pairs with a recessive allele, the expressed trait is that of the dominant allele.

A **Punnett square** is a notation that allows us to easily predict the results of a genetic cross. In a Punnett square, a letter is assigned to each gene. Uppercase letters represent dominant traits, while lower case letters represent recessive traits (a convention begun by Mendel). The possible alleles from each parent are noted across the top and side of a box diagram; then the possible offspring are represented within the internal boxes. If we assign the allele that produces yellow seeds the letter **Y**, and the allele that produces green seeds **y**, we can represent Mendel's first cross between pea plants (**YY** × **yy**) by the following Punnett square:

	Y	Y
y	Yy	Yy
y	Yy	Yy

One parent pea plant had green seeds (green seeds is its phenotype), so it must not have had any of the dominant genes for yellow seeds (**Y**), therefore it must have the genotype **yy**. If the second parent had one allele for yellow and one for green then some of the offspring would have inherited two genes for green. Since Mendel started with true-breeding plants, we may deduce that one parent had two genes for green seeds (**yy**) and the other two genes for yellow seeds (**YY**).

When both alleles for a given gene are the same in an individual (such as **YY** or **yy**), that individual is **homozygous** for that trait. Furthermore, the individual's genotype can be called homozygous. Both of the above parents (P_1) were homozygous. The children in the F_1 generation all have one dominant gene (**Y**) and one recessive gene (**y**), their phenotype is yellow, and their genotype is **Yy**. When the two alleles for a given gene are different in an individual (**Yy**), that individual is said to be **heterozygous** for that trait; its genotype is heterozygous.

Breeding two F_1 offspring from the example above produces the following Punnett square of a double heterozygous (both parents **Yy**) cross:

	Y	y
Y	YY	Yy
y	Yy	yy

Through this Punnett square, we can determine that three-fourths of the offspring will produce yellow seeds. This is consistent with Mendel's findings. However, there are two different genotypes represented among the yellow seed offspring. One-half of the offspring were heterozygous yellow (**Yy**), while one-fourth is homozygous yellow (**YY**).

The example above shows a **monohybrid cross**—a cross between two individuals where only one trait is considered. Mendel also experimented with crossing two parents while considering two separate traits, a **dihybrid cross.**

The laws investigated by Mendel form the basis of modern genetics. However, Mendel's laws now incorporate modern terminology (i.e., "genes" rather than "hereditary factors," etc.).

The Law of Segregation

The first law of Mendelian genetics is the **law of segregation.** The law of segregation states that traits are expressed from a pair of genes in the individual (on homologous chromosomes). Each parent provides one chromosome of every pair of homologous chromosomes. Paired chromosomes (and thus corresponding genes) separate and randomly recombine during gamete formation.

The Law of Dominance

Mendel determined that one gene usually expressed itself over the other (was dominant). This is the **law of dominance**, Mendel's second law of inheritance. In Mendel's experiments, the first generation produced no plants with green seeds, leading him to recognize the existence of genetic dominance. The yellow-seed allele was clearly dominant.

The Law of Independent Assortment

Mendel also investigated whether genes for one trait always were linked to genes for another. In other words, Mendel experimented not only with pea seed-coat color, but also with pea-plant height (and a number of other traits in peas and other plants). He wanted to determine whether if the parent plant had green seeds and was tall, all plants with green seeds would be tall. These dihybrid cross experiments demonstrated that most traits were independent of one another. That is, a pea plant could be green and tall or green and short, yellow and tall or yellow and short. In most cases, genes for traits randomly sort into pairs (although some genes lie close to others on a chromosome and can therefore be inherited together). Since homologous chromosomes separate and independently sort in gamete formation, alleles are also separated and independently sorted, an assertion known as the **law of independent assortment**.

The following Punnett square demonstrates independent assortment. **Y** stands for the allele for yellow color, **y** for the allele for green, **T** for the allele tall, and **t** for short:

	TY	Ty	tY	ty
TY	TTYY	TTYy	TtYY	TtYy
Ty	TTYy	TTyy	TtYy	Ttyy
tY	TtYY	TtYy	ttYY	ttYy
ty	TtYy	Ttyy	ttYy	ttyy

Incomplete Dominance

Some traits have no genes that are dominant and instead produce offspring that are a mix of the two parents. For instance, in snapdragons a plant with red flowers crossed with a plant with white flowers produces offspring with pink flowers. This is known as **incomplete dominance** or **co-dominance**. Neither white nor red is dominant over the other. In incomplete dominance, the conventional way to symbolize the alleles is with a capital letter designating the trait (in this case **C** for color) and a superscript designating the allele choices (in this case ^{R} for red, ^{W} for white), making the possible alleles C^R and C^W. The following Punnett square represents the incomplete dominance of the allele for red flowers (C^R), the allele for white as (C^W), and the combination resulting in pink as (C^RC^W).

	C^R	C^R
C^W	C^RC^W	C^RC^W
C^W	C^RC^W	C^RC^W

In this case, two plants, one with white flowers, one with red, cross to form all pink flowers. If two of the heterozygous offspring of this cross are then bred, the outcome of this cross ($C^RC^W \times C^RC^W$) will be:

	C^R	C^W
C^R	C^RC^R	C^RC^W
C^W	C^RC^W	C^WC^W

One-fourth of the offspring will be red, one-half pink, and one-fourth white, a 1:2:1 ratio.

Multiple Alleles

In the instances above, two possible alleles exist in a species, so the genotype will be a combination of those two alleles. There are some instances where more than two choices of alleles are present. For instance, for human blood types there is a dominant allele for type A blood, another dominant allele for type B blood, as well as a recessive allele for neither A nor B, known as O blood. There are three different alleles and they may combine in any way. In multiple-allele crosses, it is conventional to denote the chromosome by a letter (in this case **I** for dominant, **i** for recessive), with a subscript letter representing the allele types (in this case **A**, **B**, or **O**). The alleles for A and B blood are co-dominant, while the allele for O blood is recessive. The possible genotypes and phenotypes then are as follows:

genotype	phenotype
$I^A I^A$	Type A blood
$I^B I^B$	Type B blood
$I^B i^O$	Type B blood
$I^A i^O$	Type A blood
$I^A I^B$	Type AB blood
$i^O i^O$	Type O blood

[Note: There is another gene responsible for the Rh factor that adds the + or - to the blood type.]

Linkage

While Mendel had established the law of independent assortment, later study of genetics by other scientists found that this law was not always true. In studying fruit flies, for instance, it was found that some traits are always inherited together; they were not independently sorted. Traits that are inherited together are said to be **linked**. Genes are portions of chromosomes, so most traits produced by genes on the same chromosome are inherited together. (The chromosomes are independently sorted, not the individual genes.)

However, an exception to this rule complicates the issue. During metaphase of meiosis I, when homologous chromosomes line up along the center of the dividing cell, some pieces of the chromosomes break off and move from one chromosome to another (change places). This random breaking and reforming of homologous chromosomes allows genes to change the chromosome they are linked to, thus changing the genome of that chromosome. This process, known as **crossing over**, adds even more possibility of variation of traits among species. It is more likely for crossing over to occur between genes that do not lie close together on a chromosome than between those that lie close together.

Gender is determined in an organism by a particular homologous pair of chromosomes. The symbols **X** and **Y** denote the sex chromosomes. In mammals and many insects, the male has an **X** and **Y** chromosome (**XY**), while the female has two **X**'s (**XX**). Genes that are located on the gender chromosome **Y** will only be seen in males. It would be considered a **sex-limited trait.** An example of a sex-limited trait is bar coloring in chickens that occurs only in males.

Some traits are **sex-linked**. In sex-linked traits, more males (**XY**) develop the trait because males have only one copy of the **X** chromosome. Females have a second **X** gene, which may carry a gene coding for a functional protein for the trait in question that may counteract a recessive trait. These traits (for example, hemophilia and colorblindness) occur much more often in males than females.

Still other traits may be **sex-influenced**. In this case, the trait is known as autosomal—it only requires one recessive gene to be expressed if there is no counteracting dominant gene. A male with one recessive allele will develop the trait, whereas a female would require two recessive genes to develop it. An example of a sex-influenced trait is male-pattern baldness.

Polygenic Inheritance

While the best-studied genetic traits arise from alleles of a single gene, most traits, such as height and skin color, are produced from the expression of more than one set of genes. Traits produced from interaction of multiple sets of genes are known as **polygenic traits.** Polygenic traits are difficult to map and difficult to predict because of the varied effects of the different genes for a specific trait.

CHAPTER 7
POPULATION
BIOLOGY

Chapter 7

POPULATION BIOLOGY

ECOLOGY

Ecology is the study of how organisms interact with other organisms, and how they influence or are influenced by their physical **environment**. The word "ecology" is derived from the Greek term *oikos* (meaning "home" or "place to live") and *ology* (meaning "the study of"), so ecology is a study of organisms in their home. This study has revealed a number of patterns and principles that help us understand how organisms relate to their environment. First, however, it is important to grasp some basic vocabulary used in ecology.

The study of ecology centers on the ecosystem. An **ecosystem** is a group of populations found within a given locality, plus the inanimate environment around those populations. A **population** is the total number of a single species of organism found in a given ecosystem. Typically, there are many populations of different species within a particular ecosystem. The term **organism** refers to an individual of a particular species. Each species is a distinct group of individuals that are able to interbreed (mate), producing viable offspring. Although species are defined by their ability to reproduce, they are usually described by their morphology (their anatomical features).

Populations that interact with each other in a particular ecosystem are collectively termed a **community**. For instance, a temperate forest community includes pine trees, oaks, shrubs, lichen, mosses, ferns, squirrels, deer, insects, owls, bacteria, fungi, etc.

The part of the Earth that includes all living things is called the **biosphere**. The biosphere also includes the **atmosphere** (air), the **lithosphere** (ground), and the **hydrosphere** (water).

A **habitat** refers to the physical place where a species lives. A species' habitat must include all the factors that will support its life and reproduction. These factors may be **biotic** (i.e., living - food source, predators, etc.) and **abiotic** (i.e., nonliving - weather, temperature, soil features, etc.).

A species' **niche** is the role it plays within the ecosystem. It includes its physical requirements (such as light and water) and its biological activities (how it reproduces, how it acquires food, etc.). One important aspect of a species' niche is its place in the food chain.

Ecological Cycles

Every species within an ecosystem requires resources and energy in varying forms. The interaction of organisms and the environment can be described as cycles of energy and resources that allow the community to flourish. Although each ecosystem has its own energy and nutrient cycles, these cycles also interact with each other to form bioregional and planetary biological cycles.

The **energy cycle** supports life throughout the environment. There are also several **biogeochemical cycles** (the water cycle, the carbon cycle, the nitrogen cycle, the phosphorous cycle, etc.), which are also important to the health of ecosystems. A biogeochemical cycle is the system whereby the substances needed for life are recycled and transported throughout the environment.

Carbon, hydrogen, oxygen, phosphorous, and nitrogen are called macronutrients; they are used in large quantities by living things. Micronutrients, those elements utilized in trace quantities in organisms, include iodine, iron, zinc, and copper.

Energy Cycle (Food Chain)

Since all life requires the input of energy, the **energy cycles** within the ecosystem are central to its well-being. On Earth, the Sun provides the energy that is the basis of life in most ecosystems. (An exception is the hydrothermal vent communities that derive their energy from the heat of the Earth's core.) Without the constant influx of solar energy into our planetary ecosystem, most life would cease to exist. Energy generally flows through the entire ecosystem in one direction—from producers to consumers and on to decomposers (consumers may also consume decomposers) through the **food chain.**

Photosynthetic organisms—such as plants, some protists, and some bacteria—are the first link in most food chains; they use the energy of Sunlight to combine carbon dioxide and water into sugars, releasing oxygen gas (O_2). Photosynthetic organisms are called producers, since they synthesize sugar and starch molecules using the Sun's energy to link the carbons in carbon dioxide. Primary consumers (also known as herbivores) are species that eat photosynthetic organisms. Consumers utilize sugars and starches stored in cells or tissues for energy. Secondary consumers feed on primary consumers, and on the chain goes, through tertiary, quarternary (etc.) consumers. Finally, decomposers (bacteria, fungi, some animals) are species that recycle the organic material found in dead plants and animals back into the food chain.

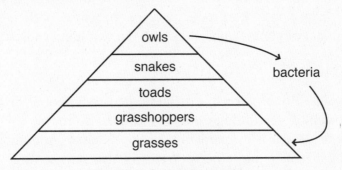

Fig. 7-1: A food chain pyramid.

Animals that feed only on other animals are called **carnivores** (meat-eaters), whereas those that consume both photosynthetic organisms and other animals are known as **omnivores**.

The energy cycle of the food chain is subject to the laws of thermodynamics. Energy can neither be created nor destroyed. However, every use of energy is less than 100% efficient, about 10% is lost as heat. When we call photosynthetic organisms producers, we mean that they produce food, using the Sun's energy to form chemical bonds in sugars and other biomolecules. Other organisms can use the energy stored in the bonds of these biomolecules.

The steps in the food chain are also known as **trophic levels**. Consider the pyramid diagram (Fig. 7-1) as one example of a food chain with many trophic levels. Grasses are on the bottom of the pyramid; they are the producers, the first trophic level. Producers are also known as **autotrophs**, as they produce their own food. Each trophic level is greater in **biomass** (total mass of organisms) than the level above it.

Grasshoppers represent the **second trophic level,** or primary consumers in this example of a food chain. Grasshoppers consume plants and are consumed (in this example) by toads, the secondary consumers, which represent the **third trophic level**. Snakes consume toads, and are in turn consumed by owls—making these the **fourth and fifth trophic levels**. In this example, bacteria are the decomposers that recycle some of the nutrients from dead owls (and other levels) to be reused by the first trophic level.

The pyramid illustrates a food chain; however, in nature it is never actually as simple as shown. Owls consume snakes, but they may also consume toads (a lower level in the pyramid) and fish (from an entirely different pyramid). Thus, within every ecosystem there may be numerous food chains interacting in varying ways to form a **food web**. Furthermore, all organisms produce waste products that feed decomposers. The food web represents the cycling and recycling of both energy and nutrients within the ecosystem. The productivity of the entire web is dependent upon the amount of photosynthesis carried out by photosynthesizers.

Water Cycle

The availability of water is crucial to the survival of all living things. Water vapor circulates through the biosphere in a process called the **hydrologic cycle**. Water is evaporated via solar radiation from the ocean and other bodies of water into clouds. Water is also released into the atmosphere from vegetation (leaves) by transpiration. Some water is also evaporated directly from soil, but most water in the ground flows into underground aquifers, which eventually empty into the oceans. Water above ground flows into waterways, which also eventually flow into the ocean (a process known as runoff). Water vapor is then redistributed over land (and back into oceans as well) via clouds, which release water as precipitation.

The water cycle also has a profound effect on Earth's climate. Clouds reflect the Sun's radiation away from the Earth, causing cool weather. Water vapor in the air also acts as a **greenhouse gas**, reflecting radiation from the Earth's surface back toward the Earth, and therefore trapping heat. The water cycle also intersects nearly all the other cycles of elements and nutrients.

Nitrogen Cycle

Nitrogen is another substance essential to life processes, since it is a key component of amino acids (components of proteins) and nucleic acids. The nitrogen cycle recycles nitrogen. Nitrogen is the most plentiful gas in the atmosphere, making up 78% of the air. However, neither photosynthetic organisms nor animals are able to use nitrogen gas (N_2), which does not readily react with other compounds, directly from the air. Instead, a process known as nitrogen fixing makes nitrogen available for absorption by the roots of plants. **Nitrogen fixing** is the process of combining nitrogen with either hydrogen or oxygen, mostly by **nitrogen-fixing bacteria**, or to a small degree by the action of **lightning**.

Nitrogen-fixing bacteria live in the soil and perform the task of combining gaseous nitrogen from the atmosphere with hydrogen, forming ammonium (NH_4^+ ions). (Some cyanobacteria, also called blue-green bacteria, are also active in this process.) Ammonium ions are then absorbed and used by plants. Other types of nitrogen-fixing bacteria live in symbiosis on the nodules of the roots of legumes (beans, peas, clover, etc.), supplying the roots with a direct source of ammonia.

Some plants are unable to use ammonia, instead, they use **nitrates**. Some bacteria perform **nitrification**, a process, which further breaks down ammonia into nitrites (NO_2^-), and yet again by another bacteria, which converts nitrites into nitrates (NO_3^-).

Nitrogen compounds (such as ammonia and nitrates) are also produced by natural, physical processes such as volcanic activity. Another source of usable nitrogen is lightning, which reacts with atmospheric nitrogen to form nitrates.

In addition, nitrogen passes along through the food chain, and is recycled through decomposition processes. When plants are consumed, the amino acids are recombined and used, a process that passes the nitrogen-containing molecules on through the food chain or web. Animal waste products, such as urine, release nitrogen compounds (primarily ammonia) back into the environment, yet another source of nitrogen. Finally, large amounts of nitrogen are returned to the Earth by bacteria and fungi, which decompose dead plant and animal matter into ammonia (and other substances), a process known as **ammonification.**

Various species of bacteria and fungi are also responsible for breaking down excess nitrates, a process known as **denitrification**, which releases nitrogen gas back into the air. The nitrogen cycle involves cycling nitrogen through both living and non-living entities.

Carbon Cycle

The carbon cycle is the route by which carbon is obtained, used, and recycled by living things. Carbon is an important element contained in the cells of all species. The study of organic chemistry is the study of carbon-based molecules.

Earth's atmosphere contains large amounts of carbon in the form of carbon dioxide (CO_2). Photosynthetic organsims require the intake of carbon dioxide for the process of photosynthesis, which is the foundation of the food chain. Most of the carbon within organisms is derived from the production of carbohydrates in photosynthetic organisms through photosynthesis. The process of photosynthesis also releases oxygen molecules (O_2), which are necessary to animal respiration. Animal respiration releases carbon dioxide back into the atmosphere in large quantities.

Since plant cells consist of molecules containing carbon, animals that consume photosynthetic organisms are consuming and using carbon from the photosynthetic organisms. Carbon is passed along the food chain as these animals are then consumed. When animals and photosynthetic organisms die, decomposers, including the detritus feeders, bacteria, and fungi, break down the organic matter. Detritus feeders include worms, mites, insects, and crustaceans, which feed on dead organic matter, returning carbon to the cycle through chemical breakdown and respiration.

Carbon dioxide (CO_2) is also dissolved directly into the oceans, where it is combined with calcium to form calcium carbonate, which is used by mollusks to form their shells. When mollusks die, the shells break down and often form limestone. Limestone is then dissolved by water over time and some carbon may be released back into the atmosphere as CO_2, or used by new ocean species.

Finally, organic matter that is left to decay, may, under conditions of heat and pressure be transformed into coal, oil, or natural gas (the **fossil fuels**). When fossil fuels are burned for energy, the combustion process releases carbon dioxide back into the atmosphere, where it is available to plants for photosynthesis.

Phosphorous Cycle

Phosphorous is another mineral required by living things. Unlike carbon and nitrogen, which cycle through the atmosphere in gaseous form, phosphorous is only found in solid form, within rocks and soil. Phosphorous is a key component in ATP, NADP (a molecule that, like ATP, stores energy in its chemical bonds), and many other molecular compounds essential to life.

Phosphorous is found within rocks and is released by the process of erosion. Water dissolves phosphorous from rocks, and carries it into rivers and streams. Here phosphorous and oxygen react to form phosphates that end up in bodies of water. Phosphates are absorbed by photosynthetic organisms in and near the water and are used in the synthesis of organic molecules. As in the carbon and nitrogen cycles, phosphorous is then passed up the food chain and returned through animal wastes and organic decay.

New phosphorous enters the cycle as undersea sedimentary rocks are thrust up during the shifting of the Earth's tectonic plates. New rock containing phosphorous is then exposed to erosion and enters the cycling process.

POPULATION GROWTH AND REGULATION

The population growth of a species is regulated by limiting factors that exist within the species' environment. Population growth maintains equilibrium in all species under normal conditions because of these limiting factors. A population's overall growth rate is affected by the birth rate (**natality**) and death rate (**mortality**) of the population. The rate of increase within a population is represented by the birth rate minus the death rate. When the birth rate within a population equals the death rate, the population remains at a constant level.

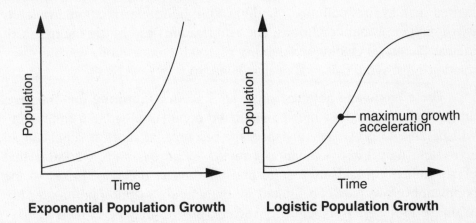

Exponential Population Growth **Logistic Population Growth**

There are two models of population growth, the exponential curve (or J-curve) and the logistic curve (or the S-curve). The exponential curve represents populations in which there is no environmental or social limit on population size, so the rate of growth accelerates over time. Exponential population growth exists only during the initial population growth in a particular ecosystem, since as the population increases the limiting factors become more influential. In other words, a fish population introduced into a pond would experience exponential population growth until food and space supplies began to limit the population.

The logistic curve reflects the effects of limiting factors on population size, where growth accelerates to a point, then slows down. The logistic curve shows population growth over a longer period of time, and represents population growth under normal conditions.

Population growth is directly related to the life characteristics of the population such as the age at which an individual begins to reproduce, the age of death, the rate of growth, etc. For instance, species that grow quickly, mature sexually at an early age, and live a long life would have a population growth rate that exceeds that of species with a short life span and short reproductive span.

In general, most populations have an incredible ability to increase in numbers. A population without limiting factors could overpopulate the world in several generations. It is the limits existing within each ecosystem that keep this from happening.

Limiting Factors

Many factors affect the life of an ecosystem, which may be permanent or temporary. Populations within an ecosystem will be affected by changes in the environment from **abiotic factors** (physical, non-living factors such as fire, pollution, Sunlight, soil, light, precipitation, availability of oxygen, water conditions, and temperature) and **biotic factors** (biological factors, including availability of food, competition, predator-prey relationships, symbiosis, and overpopulation).

These biotic and abiotic factors are known as **limiting factors** since they will determine how much a particular population within a community will be able to grow. For instance, the resource in shortest supply in an ecosystem may limit population growth. As an example, we know that photosynthetic organisms require phosphorous in order to thrive, so the population growth will be limited by the amount of phosphorous readily available in the environment. Conversely, growth may be limited by having more of an element (such as heat or water) than it can tolerate. For example, plants need carbon dioxide to grow; however, a large concentration of carbon dioxide in the atmosphere is toxic.

Ecologists now commonly combine these two ideas to provide a more comprehensive understanding of how conditions limit growth of populations. It may be stated that the establishment and survival of a particular organism in an area is dependent upon both 1) the availability of necessary elements in at least the minimum quantity, and 2) the controlled supply of those elements to keep it within the limits of tolerance.

Limiting factors interact with each other and generally produce a situation within the ecosystem that supports homeostasis (a steady-state condition). **Homeostasis** is a dynamic balance achieved within an ecosystem functioning at its optimum level. Homeostasis is the tendency of the ecological community to stay the same. However, the balance of the ecosystem can be disturbed by the removal, or decrease, of a single factor or by the addition, or increase, of a factor.

Populations are rarely governed by the effect of a single limiting factor; instead, many factors interact to control population size. Changes in limiting factors have a domino effect in an ecosystem, as the change in population size of one species will change the dynamics of the entire community. The number of individuals of a particular species living in a particular area is called the population **density** (number of organisms per area).

Both abiotic and biotic limiting factors exist in a single community, however one may be dominant over the other. Abiotic limiting factors are also known as **density-independent factors**. That is, they are independent of population density. For instance, the populations around Mount St. Helens were greatly affected by its eruption in 1980, and this effect had nothing to do with the population levels of the area before the eruption. In this situation, the density-independent physical factors dominated the population changes that took place.

Pollution is a major density-independent factor in the health of ecosystems. Pollution is usually a byproduct of human endeavors and affects the air or water quality of an ecosystem with secondary effects. In addition to producing pollution, humans may deliberately utilize chemicals such as pesticides or herbicides to limit growth of particular species. Such chemicals can damage the homeostatic mechanisms within a community, causing a long term upset in the balance of an ecosystem.

In other situations, biotic factors, called **density-dependent factors** may be the dominant influence on population in a given area. Density-dependent factors include population growth issues and interactions between species within a community.

Within a given area, there is a maximum level the population may reach at which it will continue to thrive. This is known as the **carrying capacity** of the environment. When an organism has reached the carrying capacity of the ecosystem, the population growth rate will level off and show no net growth. Populations also occupy a particular geographic area with suitable conditions. This total area occupied by a species is known as the **range**. Typically, populations will have the greatest density in the center of their range, and lower density at the edges. The area outside the range is known as the area of intolerance for that species, since it is not able to survive there. Environmental changes will affect the size and location of the range, making it a dynamic characteristic.

Over time, species may move in or out of a particular area, a process known as **dispersion**. Dispersion occurs in one of three ways—through **emigration** (permanent one way movement out of the original range), **immigration** (permanent one way movement into a new range), and **migration** (temporary movement out of one range into another, and back). Migration is an important process to many species and communities, since it allows animals that might not survive year round in a particular ecosystem to temporarily relocate for a portion of the year. Therefore, migration gives the opportunity for greater diversity of species in an ecosystem.

Two or more species living within the same area and that overlap niches (their function in the food chain) are said to be in **competition** if the resource they both require is in limited supply. If the niche overlap is minimal (other sources of food are available) then both species may survive. In some cases, one of the species may be wiped out in an area due to competition, a situation called **competitive exclusion**. This is a rare but plausible occurrence.

A **predator** is simply an organism that eats another. The organism that is eaten is known as the **prey**. The **predator/prey** relationship is one of the most important features of an ecosystem. As seen in our study of the energy cycle, energy is passed from lower trophic levels to higher trophic levels, as one animal is consumed by another. This relationship not only provides transfer of energy up the food chain, it also is a population control factor for the prey species. In situations where natural predators are removed from a region, the overpopulation occurring amongst the prey species can cause problems in the population and community. For instance, the hunting and trapping of wolves in the United States has led to an overpopulation of deer (the prey of wolves), which in turn has caused a shortage of food for deer in some areas, causing these deer populations to starve.

When two species interact with each other within the same range it is known as **symbiosis**. **Amensalism** is one type of symbiosis where one species is neither helped nor harmed while it inhibits the growth of another species. **Mutualism** is another form of symbiosis where both species benefit. **Parasitism** is symbiosis in which one species benefits, but the other is harmed. (Parasites are not predators, since the parasitic action takes a long period of time and may not actually kill the host.)

When the entire population of a particular species is eliminated, it is known as **extinction**. Extinction may be a local phenomenon, the elimination of a population of one species from one area. However, species extinction is a worldwide phenomenon, where all members of all populations of a species die.

The extinction of a single species may also cause a chain reaction of secondary extinctions if other species depend on the extinct species. Conversely, the introduction of a new species into an area can also have a profound effect on other populations within that area. This new species may compete for the niche of native population or upset a predator/prey balance. For example, the brown tree snake (native to Australia) was introduced into islands in the Pacific years ago. (They probably migrated on ships.) The brown snake has caused the extinction of several species of birds on those Pacific islands. The bird populations could not withstand the introduction of this new predator.

Ultimately, the survival of a particular population is dependent on maintaining a **minimal viable population** size. When a population is significantly diminished in size, it becomes highly susceptible to breeding problems and environmental changes that may result in extinction.

Community Structure

Community structure refers to the characteristics of a specified community, including the types of species that dominate, major climatic trends of the region and, whether the community is open or closed. A **closed community** is one whose populations occupy essentially the same range with very similar distributions of density. These types of communities have sharp boundaries called **ecotones** (such as a pond aquatic ecosystem that ends at the shore). An **open community** has indefinite boundaries, and its populations have varying ranges and densities (such as a forest). In an open community, the species are more widely distributed and animals may actually travel in and out of the area.

An open community is often more able to respond to calamity and may be therefore more resilient. Since the boundaries are subtler, the populations of a forest, for instance, may be able to move as necessary to avoid a fire. If, however, a closed community is affected by a traumatic event (for example, a pond being polluted over a short period of time) it may be completely wiped out.

Communities do grow and change over time. Some communities are able to maintain their basic structure with only minor variations for very long periods of time. Others are much more dynamic, changing significantly over time from one type of ecosystem to another. When one community completely replaces another over time in a given area, it is called **succession**. Succession occurs both in terrestrial and aquatic biomes.

Succession may occur because of small changes over time in climate or conditions, the immigration of a new species, disease, or other slow-acting factors. It may also occur in direct response to cataclysmic events such as fire, flood, or human intervention (for example, clearing a forest for farmland). The first populations that move back into a disturbed ecosystem tend to be hardy species that can survive in bleak conditions. These are known as **pioneer communities.**

An example of terrestrial succession occurs when a fire wipes out a forest community. The first new colonization will come from quick growing species such as grasses, which will produce over time a grassland ecosystem. The decay of grasses will enrich the soil, providing fertile ground for germination of seeds for shrubs brought in by wind or animals. The shrubs will further prepare the soil for germination of larger species of trees, which over time will take over the shrub-land and produce a forest community once again.

When succession ends in a stable community, the community is known as the **climax community**. The climax community is the one best suited to the climate and soil conditions, and one that achieves a homeostasis. Generally, the climax community will remain in an area until a catastrophic event (fire, flood, etc.) destroys it.

BIOMES

A **biome** is an ecosystem that is generally defined by its climate characteristics. Each biome includes many types of community interacting within the climatic region. There are several major biomes that have been identified by ecologists. There are two basic types of biomes—terrestrial and aquatic. **Terrestrial biomes** are those that exist on land, **aquatic biomes** are within large bodies of water. The following table gives the name of the major biomes with their major characteristics:

Biome	Temperature	Precipitation Level	Features
Tropical Rain Forest	warm	high	dense forest, heavy rainfall, abundant vegetation, relatively poor soil
Savanna	warm	moderate	grassland, light seasonal rains
Chaparral	hot summer, temperate winter	low in summer, high in winter	trees, shrubs, small animals, prolonged summer
Temperate Grassland	moderate and seasonal	low for most of year	large land tracts of grassland, shrubs and annuals, rodents, and some larger carnivores
Desert	extreme hot or cold	very low	sandy or rocky terrain, sparse vegetation, mainly succulents, small animals, rodents, reptiles
Tundra	extreme cold	low	modified grassland, permafrost, short growing season w/ some plants and animals
Taiga	cold	moderate	snow most of year, thick coniferous forests, wide variety of animal life
Temperate Deciduous Forest	moderate, seasonal	moderate	many trees (that lose leaves in cold season), mosses, grasses, shrubs, abundant animal life
Marine Aquatic	varied	not applicable	large amounts of dissolved minerals (particularly salts) in the water, huge array of aquatic animal and plant life
Freshwater Aquatic	varied	not applicable	still or running water with little dissolved minerals, large array of aquatic plant and animal life

Island Biogeography

Biogeography is the study of how photosynthetic organisms and animals are distributed in a particular location, plus the history of their distribution in the past. Island biogeography is a subdiscipline that investigates the distribution of species in an island habitat. The study of island biogeography is of particular interest to ecologists, since islands are closer to being a closed system (that is they have less interaction with other ecosystems) than other environments.

Since islands are by nature separated from other land ecosystems, species of both photosynthetic organisms and animals found on a particular island usually have arrived there by natural **dispersal** processes (by air or sea). For instance, there are many plant species with adapted seeds, which will float in water or be carried long distances by air and remain viable. Birds are adapted for dispersion, as are many species of insect, and many sea animals (tortoises, snails, etc.). Dispersal to an island is dependent on geographic as well as historical factors. Distance from other land masses is an important geographic factor. Obviously, the closer the island is to other land, the easier dispersal of species to that island will be. Conversely, islands separated by long stretches of water will have less dispersion. Prevailing winds and ocean currents are also geographic factors that will affect species introduction. Historical factors such as climate shifts (for instance, the shift to an ice age), drought, volcanic action, plate shifting (where the continental plates of the Earth's crust move slowly), etc., will also affect which species are able to travel to a given island. In recent history, dispersion has also occurred through human intervention. Species that inhabit a given ecosystem because humans transported them there are known as **introduced** species.

In some cases, new species develop from parents that were dispersed to the island. These new species are **native** to that island. Arrival of a species on an island, however, does not insure that it will survive and thrive there. In order to become an established part of the island ecosystem, a species must find a suitable habitat and niche. Ultimately, the species must be able to reproduce for many generations in its new setting, or it will not remain a part of the ecosystem. If the island contains a habitat suitable for the newly arrived species, then that species has a chance of survival in its new environment. Islands may contain several habitats; consequently, islands that support numerous habitats will be more likely to have a wider diversity of species.

Islands may also develop new habitats over time as the climate and geology change, and depending on the size and age of the island. In general, the larger the island and the older the island, the more species it will support. The one exception to this is an old island whose soil has eroded and lost its nutrients. In this case, its habitats may not be able to support life. Also, the harsher the climate (high or low temperature or water conditions) of the island, the fewer species it will have. The geology of the island (whether it is volcanic in origin, for instance) determines the characteristics of the soil, and thus has a direct effect on habitability as well.

PRINCIPLES OF BEHAVIOR

The study of **ethology** involves studying how animals act and react within their environments. Behavior simply is what an organism does and how it does it. Some behavioral characteristics are learned; others are instinctive (inherited).

Behavioral characteristics of animals may include how they acquire food, how they seek out and relate to a mate, how they respond to danger, or how they care for young. Behavior may be as simple as a reflex or may involve responses and interactions between the endocrine, nervous, and musculoskeletal systems.

Some behaviors are extremely simple in nature, they are a response to an environmental stimulus. These basic behaviors are innate; they exist from birth and are genetic in origin (they are inherited). **Innate behaviors** are the actions in animals we call **instincts**. Innate behaviors are highly stereotyped; all individuals of a species perform these behaviors in the same way. **Stereotyped behaviors** are of four basic varieties:

- **taxes** (plural of taxis) are directional responses either toward or away from a stimulus,

- **kineses** are changes in speed of movement in response to stimuli,

- **reflexes** are an automatic movement of a body part in response to a stimulus, and

- **fixed action patterns** (FAP) are complex but stereotyped behavior in response to a stimulus.

The fixed action pattern is the most complex of stereotyped behaviors. It is a pre-programmed response to a particular stimulus known as a **releaser** or a **sign stimulus**. FAPs include courtship behaviors, circadian rhythms, and feeding of young. Organisms automatically perform FAPs without any prior experience (FAPs are not learned).

Some animal behaviors are learned. **Learned behaviors** may have some basis in genetics, but they also require learning. Generally, there are three types of learned behavior in animals: conditioning, habituation, and imprinting.

Conditioning involves learning to apply an old response to a new stimulus. The classic example of conditioning is that of Pavlov's dogs. Ivan Pavlov was a scientist who studied animal behavior. Dogs have an innate behavior to begin salivating when they see food. Pavlov was able to train dogs to salivate when they heard a bell ring. He trained, or conditioned, them by ringing the bell every time he fed the dogs. The dogs were conditioned to produce an instinctive behavior (salivating) in response to a new stimulus (bell).

B.F. Skinner was another scientist who studied conditioning. Skinner started with the thesis that learning happens through changes in overt behavior. Skinner believed that when a particular behavior is rewarded, the individual is being conditioned to repeat that behavior. Reinforcement of good behaviors results in repeating that behavior.

Habituation is a learned behavior where the organism produces less and less response as a stimulus is repeated, without a subsequent negative or positive action. For instance, a cat might innately respond to a dog's approach by hissing and raising its hair. However, if the dog regularly approaches, but never attacks, the cat eventually learns that the dog is not a threat and ceases to exhibit the fear behavior. Habituation safeguards species from wasting energy on irrelevant stimuli.

Imprinting is a learned behavior that develops in a critical or sensitive period of the animal's lifespan. Konrad Lorenz (a behavioral scientist) was able to show that baby geese responded to their mother's physical appearance shortly after birth. During the critical period after birth, the gosling learns to recognize his mother. However, if another object is exposed to the gosling during that critical period (immediately following hatching) the gosling would interpret the substituted object to be its mother. Imprinting generally involves learning a new releaser for an established FAP.

Social Behavior

Some animal species demonstrate **social behavior**—behavior patterns that take into account other individuals. One aspect of animal behavior regards the physical land area that an individual lives in. Animals will develop a **home range** (an area in which they spend most of their time). Animals may also develop an area of land as their **territory**, which lies within the home range, but is the area the individual will defend as his own. The establishment of a territory implies the recognition by one individual that other individuals exist, thus it is a simple social behavior.

Sexual and mating behaviors often rely on complex interactions of the endocrine, nervous, and musculoskeletal systems. In many cases, an individual will compete with another for a particular mate. There are often complex rituals, which are performed before the actual mating experience, involving many instinctive responses to stimuli and learned behaviors. The sexual and parenting behaviors of animals are social traits that are extremely diverse between species.

In some species, social interactions are highly complex, for instance an entire population may function as a hierarchy (or society), where individuals have specified roles and status. Insects such as ants and bees, some species of birds, and many primates are among the groups that form societies.

A **society** is an organization of individuals in a population in which tasks are divided, in order for the group to work together. For instance, bees are social insects with a hierarchy (including a queen bee and worker bees). Some individuals are responsible for caring for the queen, others work within the nest, and others gather nectar from outside sources to be brought to the nest. Most of the population is female; the males are called drones and their only responsibility is mating. This division of labor allows the society to perform a higher function than if each individual acted on it own. Within a society, the individuals may be constantly growing, changing, and adapting, while the functions of the community remain the same over time.

While the social behavior of insects is more a question of division of labor, societies of primates are built around the idea of **dominance**. Older, more established individuals, compete for status within the community. A hierarchy is formed through actual competitions among individuals. The community member(s) at the top of the hierarchy enjoy privileges related to their selection of food and mates. This hierarchy is challenged as individuals mature, causing a succession of leaders.

Social behavior is highly dependent on communication within the population, and the ability of individuals to adapt behavior according to the needs of the society as a whole. Social animals exhibit a characteristic known as **altruism**, that is, having traits that tend to serve the needs of the society as a whole in addition to its own individual needs.

SOCIAL BIOLOGY

Human Population Growth

As with the study of population growth among other species, human population growth is a direct function of human birth and death rates (natality and mortality). People are able to reason around many of the limiting factors (for example, problems of food shortage or disease), making human population growth a much more complex situation. Furthermore, reproductive behaviors of humans are also subject to the reasoning process, unlike the instinctual mating behaviors of most animals.

The development of vaccines and antibiotics has greatly increased the life-span of people in recent history, decreasing the mortality rate. Infant mortality rates have steeply declined in the last 150 years, as safer birthing processes and infant care have been developed. On the other hand, the development of contraceptives has reduced the natality rate in many countries.

Thomas Malthus is one of the most famous human population scientists. In the 1780s Malthus recognized the exponential properties of population growth and calculated that the Earth's food supply would eventually be exhausted by human overpopulation. However, Malthus's calculations did not take into account new technologies allowing for higher yield of food production. So, while the Earth's population has indeed increased exponentially (passing the six billion mark in 2000), and the doubling time (the amount of time it takes for a population to double in size) is decreasing significantly, the Earth has so far been able to support its population for the most part. (The Earth has an adequate food supply at present, yet people may currently starve because they are unable to produce food in their region and/or may be politically unable to import food.)

A theory known as **demographic transition** proposes that there are progressive demographic time periods of human population growth. In the first period, birth and death rates are approximately equal, allowing the population to be in equilibrium with the environment. Social evolution (ability to fight disease, mass produce food, etc.) causes the birth rate to overtake the death rate, in turn causing rapid population growth throughout another period. Agrarian lifestyles (where families have numerous children to "work the farm") become less common and children become a liability in urban society. However, **biomedical progress** of urban society causes a lowering of the infant mortality rate. Society then faces a period of dramatic population growth, most of it within cities. The final stage occurs as developed industrialized nations work to lower birth rates through contraceptive practices.

As the human population proceeds through demographic transition, the **age composition** (the relative numbers of individuals of specific ages within the population) changes. As birth rates increase, the population tends to shift toward youth, whereas medical advancements may increase the average age of the population. For instance, in 1900 approximately 40% of Americans were under 18, in 1960, 36% and in 1996, only 26% of Americans were under 18. Demographic transition also has an effect on the population growth rate.

Meanwhile, the introduction of **genetic engineering** in recent history has produced a complex array of implications. Genetic engineering is the intentional alteration of genetic material of a living organism. Genetic engineering of plant species has produced species able to resist drought, disease, or other threats—providing for more abundant food production. Genetic engineering is also responsible for disease-fighting breakthroughs such as the production of human insulin to fight diabetes. (Insulin is produced industrially using genetically engineered bacteria that produce human insulin.) The future of genetic engineering, however, is uncertain as we confront the ethical questions regarding the possibility of choosing characteristics of children, or cloning humans.

The growth of human population has also had a profound effect on the biosphere. **Environmental pollution** (the addition of contaminants to the air and water by human intervention and industry) has profoundly affected the ecosystems of the Earth. Most pollution has occurred in recent decades as industrialization has increased.

Progress has been made in the **management of resources** in the recent past. In our discussion of energy and biochemical cycles (early in this chapter), we noted that our biosphere has natural mechanisms that allow for the recycling of energy and nutrients. Careful resource management, including the active human intervention of recycling energy, water, nutrients, and chemicals, will encourage the natural cyclic processes within the biosphere to maintain a viable balance.

CHAPTER 8
EVOLUTION

Chapter 8

EVOLUTION

HISTORY OF EVOLUTIONARY CONCEPTS

Evolutionary concepts are the foundation of much of the current study in biology. The term **evolution** refers to the gradual change of characteristics within a population, producing a change in species over time. Evolution is driven by the process of **natural selection**, a feature of population genetics first articulated by Charles Darwin in his book *The Origin of Species by Means of Natural Selection, or The Preservation of Favoured Races in the Struggle for Life* (published in 1859). Darwin was the first to explain natural selection as a driving force, and the first to lay out the full range of evidence for evolution. However, scientists before Darwin had already promoted some of the ideas inherent in evolutionary biology.

Carolus Linnaeus, the well-known botanist (who is credited with developing the classification system for organisms still used widely today) speculated on the origin of and relationships between groups of species

ORIGIN OF SPECIES.

INTRODUCTION.

WHEN on board H.M.S. 'Beagle,' as naturalist, I was much struck with certain facts in the distribution of the organic beings inhabiting South America, and in the geological relations of the present to the past inhabitants of that continent. These facts, as will be seen in the latter chapters of this volume, seemed to throw some light on the origin of species—that mystery of mysteries, as it has been called by one of our greatest philosophers. On my return home, it occurred to me, in 1837, that something might perhaps be made out on this question by patiently accumulating and reflecting on all sorts of facts which could possibly have any bearing on it. After five years' work I allowed myself to speculate on the subject, and drew up some short notes; these I enlarged in 1844 into a sketch of the conclusions, which then seemed to me probable: from that period to the present day I have steadily pursued the same object. I hope that I may be excused for entering on these personal details, as I give them to show that I have not been hasty in coming to a decision.

My work is now (1859) nearly finished; but as it will take me many more years to complete it, and as my health is far from strong, I have been urged to publish this Abstract. I have more especially been induced to do this, as Mr. Wallace, who is now studying the natural history of the Malay archipelago, has arrived at almost exactly the same general conclusions that I have on the origin of species. In 1858 he sent me a memoir on this subject, with a request that I would forward it to Sir Charles Lyell, who sent it to the Linnean Society, and it is published in the third volume of the Journal of that Society. Sir C. Lyell and Dr. Hooker, who both knew of my work—the latter having read my sketch of 1844—honoured me by thinking it advisable to publish, with Mr. Wallace's excellent memoir, some brief extracts from my manuscripts.

This Abstract, which I now publish, must necessarily be imperfect. I cannot here give references and authorities for my

Introduction to the 1859 edition of
Charles Darwin's *Origin of Species*.

in the mid-1700s. The French scientist Lamarck proposed that organisms acquire traits over their life span that equip them to survive within their environment and pass those traits on to their offspring. He presented the idea that, for example, giraffes developed longer necks during their life-time from their efforts to reach food high on tree branches. The children, born with longer necks would then further lengthen their necks reaching for high branches, passing these even longer necks on to their children. This Lamarckian theory of acquired characteristics has since been discredited.

Darwinian Concept of Natural Selection

Current theories of evolution have their basis in the work of Charles Darwin and one of his contemporaries, Alfred Russell Wallace. Darwin's book, however, served to catalyze the study of evolution across scientific disciplines. A synopsis of Darwin's ideas follows.

From our study of populations in Chapter 7, we know that population growth and maintenance of a species is dependent on limiting factors. Individuals within the species that are unable to acquire the minimum requirement of resources, are unable to reproduce. The ecosystem can support only a limited number of organisms—known as the carrying capacity (usually designated by the letter K).

Once the carrying capacity (K) is reached, a competition for resources ensues. Darwin considered this competition to be the basic *struggle for existence*. Some of the competitors will fail to survive. Within every population, there is variation among traits. Darwin proposed that those individuals who win the competition for resources pass those successful traits on to their children. Only the surviving competitors reproduce successfully generation after generation. Therefore, traits providing the competitive edge will be represented most often in succeeding generations.

Modern Concept of Natural Selection

Although the concepts of natural selection put forth by Darwin still form the basis of evolutionary theory today, Darwin had no real knowledge of genetics when he put forth his ideas.

Several years after Darwin's writings, Mendel's work (on experimental genetics) was rediscovered independently by three scientists. The laws of genetics served to support the suppositions Darwin had made. Over the next 40 years, the study of genetics included not only individual organisms but also population genetics (how traits are preserved, changed, or introduced within a population of organisms). Progress in the studies of bioge-ography and paleontology of the early 1900s also served to reinforce Darwin's basic observations.

The modern concept of natural selection emerged from Darwin's original ideas, with additions and confirmations of genetics, population studies, and paleontology. This **modern synthesis** focused on the concept that evolution was a process of gradual (over thousands or hundreds of thousands of generations) adaptive change in traits among populations.

Mechanisms of Evolution

Modern understanding of the process of natural selection recognizes that there are some basic mechanisms that support evolutionary change. Mutations happen only in individuals, and natural selection happens to individuals. However, modern theories focus on the change that occurs among populations, not in individuals.

All evolution is dependent upon genetic change. The entire collection of genes within a given population is known as its **gene pool.** Individuals in the population will have only one pair of alleles for a particular single-gene trait. Yet, the gene pool may contain dozens or hundreds of alleles for this trait. Evolution does not occur through changes from individual to individual, but rather as the gene pool changes through one of a number of possible mechanisms.

One mechanism that drives the changing of traits over time in a population is **differential reproduction.** Natural selection assumes some individuals within a population are more suited for survival, given environmental conditions. Differential reproduction takes this supposition one step further by proposing that those individuals within a population that are most adapted to the environment are also the most likely individu-als to reproduce successfully. Therefore, the reproductive processes tend to strengthen the frequency of expression of desirable traits across the population. Differential reproduction increases the number of alleles for desirable traits in the gene pool. This trend will be established and strengthen gradually over time, eventually producing a population where the desirable trait is dominant, if environmental conditions remain the same.

Another mechanism of genetic change is mutation. As discussed in Chapter 6, a **mutation** is a change of the DNA sequence of a gene, result-ing in a change of the trait. Although a mutation can cause a very swift change in the genotype (genetic code) and possibly phenotype (expressed trait) of the offspring, mutations do not necessarily produce a trait desirable for a particular environment. Mutation is a much more random occurrence than differential reproduction.

Although mutations occur quickly, the change in the gene pool is minimal, so change in the population occurs very slowly (over multiple generations). Mutation does provide a vehicle of introducing new genetic possibilities; genetic traits, which did not exist in the original gene pool, can be introduced through mutation.

A third mechanism recognized to influence the evolution of new traits is known as **genetic drift.** Over time, a gene pool (particularly in a small population) may experience a change in frequency of particular genes simply due to chance fluctuations. In a finite population, the gene pool may not reflect the entire number of genetic possibilities of the larger genetic pool of the species population. Over time, the genetic pool within this finite population changes, and evolution has occurred. Genetic drift has no particular tie to environmental conditions, and thus the random change in gene frequency is unpredictable. The change of gene frequency may produce a small or a large change, depending on what traits are affected. The process of genetic drift, as opposed to mutation, actually causes a reduction in genetic variety.

Genetic drift occurs within finite separated populations, allowing that population to develop its own distinct gene pool. However, occasionally an individual from an adjacent population of the same species may immigrate and breed with a member of the previously locally isolated group. The introduction of new genes from the immigrant results in a change of the gene pool, known as **gene migration.** Gene migration is also occasionally successful between members of different, but related, species. The resultant hybrids succeed in adding increased variability to the gene pool.

The study of genetics shows that in a situation where random mating is occurring within a population (which is in equilibrium with its environment), gene frequencies and genotype ratios will remain constant from generation to generation. This law is known as the **Hardy-Weinberg Law of Equilibrium,** named after the two men (G.H. Hardy and Wilhelm Weinberg, c. 1909) who first studied this principle in mathematical studies of genetics. The Hardy-Weinberg Law is a mathematical formula that shows why recessive genes do not disappear over time from a population.

According to the Hardy-Weinberg Law, the sum of the frequencies of all possible alleles for a particular trait is 1. That is,

$$p + q = 1$$

where the frequency of one allele is represented by **p** and the frequency of another is **q**. It then follows mathematically that the frequency of genotypes within a population can be represented by the equation:

$$p^2 + 2pq + q^2 = 1$$

where the frequency of homozygous dominant genotypes is represented by p^2, the homozygous recessive by q^2, and the heterozygous genotype by $2pq$.

For instance, in humans the ability to taste the chemical phenylthiocarbamide (PTC) is a dominant inherited trait. If **T** represents the allele for tasting PTC and **t** represents the recessive trait (inability to taste PTC) then the possible genotypes in a population would by **TT**, **Tt**, and **tt**. If the frequency of non-tasters in a particular population is 4% or 0.04 (that is, $q^2 = 0.04$), then the frequency of the allele **t** equals the square root of 0.04 or 0.2. It is then possible to calculate the frequency of the dominant allele, **T**, in the population using the equation:

$$p + 0.2 = 1$$
$$so, p = 0.8$$

The frequency of the allele for tasting PTC is 0.8. The frequency of the various possible genotypes (**TT**, **Tt**, and **tt**) in the population can also be calculated since the frequency of the homozygous dominant is p^2 or 0.64 or 64%. The frequency of the heterozygous genotype is $2pq$.

$$2pq = 2(0.8)(0.2) = 0.32 = 32\%.$$

Frequency of TT = 64%, Tt = 32%, tt is 4% . . . totaling 100%
or 0.64 + 0.32 + 0.04 = 1

In order for Hardy-Weinberg equilibrium to occur, the population in question must meet several conditions, viz., random mating (no differential reproduction) must be taking place and no migration, mutation, selection, or genetic drift can be occurring. When these conditions are met, Hardy-Weinberg equilibrium can occur, and there will be no changes in the gene pool over time. Hardy-Weinberg is important to the evolutionary process because it shows that alleles that have no current selective value will be retained in a population over time.

Speciation

A species is an interbreeding population that shares a common gene pool and produces viable offspring. Up to this point we have been considering mechanisms that produce variation within species. It is apparent that to explain evolution on a broad scale we must understand how genetic change produces new species. There are two mechanisms that produce separate species, allopatric speciation and sympatric speciation.

In order for a new species to develop, substantial genetic changes must occur between populations, which prohibit them from interbreeding. These genetic changes may result from genetic drift or from mutation that take place separately in the two populations. **Allopatric speciation** occurs when two populations are geographically isolated from each other. For instance, a population of squirrels may be geographically separated by a catastrophic event such as a volcanic eruption. Two populations (separated by the volcanic flow) continue to reproduce and experience genetic drift and/or mutation over time. This limits each population's gene pool and produces changes in expressed traits. Later, the geographical separation may be eliminated as the volcanic flow subsides; even so, the two populations have now experienced too much change to allow them to successfully interbreed again. The result is the production of two separate species.

Speciation may also occur without a geographic separation when a population develops members with a genetic difference, which prevents successful reproduction with the original species. The genetically different members reproduce with each other, producing a population, which is separate from the original species. This process is called **sympatric speciation**.

As populations of an organism in a given area grow, some will move into new geographic areas looking for new resources or to escape predators. (In this case, a natural event does not separate the population; instead, part of the population moves.) Some of these adventurers will discover new niches and advantageous conditions. Traits possessed by this traveling population will grow more common over several generations through the process of natural selection. Over time the species will specially adapt to live more effectively in the new environment. Through this process, known as **adaptive radiation,** a single species can develop into several diverse species over time. If the separated populations merge again and are able to successfully interbreed, then by definition new species have not been developed. Adaptive radiation is proven to have occurred when the species remerge and do not interbreed successfully.

All of the above evolutionary mechanisms are dependent upon reproduction of organisms over a long period of time, a very gradual process. **Punctuated equilibrium** is an entirely different method of explaining speciation. Punctuated equilibrium is a scientific model that proposes that adaptations of species arise suddenly and rapidly. Punctuated equilibrium states that species undergo a long period of equilibrium, which at some point is upset by environmental forces causing a short period of quick mutation and change.

Punctuated equilibrium was first proposed as paleontologists studied the fossil record. Gradualism would produce slowly changing and adapting species over many generations. However, the fossil record seems to show that organisms in general survive many generations in many areas with very little change over long periods of geologic time. New species appear in the fossils suddenly, without transitional forms, though "sudden" in this context needs to be understood on a geologic time scale.

Scientists still do not agree on the degree to which gradualism, punctuated equilibrium, or a combination of these processes is responsible for speciation.

There are also beliefs about origins (e.g., intelligent design, scientific creationism, and theistic evolution) involving neither of these ideas that depend instead on faith in an intelligent creator. These beliefs have survived in spite of scientific investigators having concluded that, as the National Academy of Sciences has put it, "the same forces responsible for the evolution of all other life forms on Earth can account for the evolution of human beings."

PLANT AND ANIMAL EVOLUTION

Evolution of the First Cells

The modern theory of the evolution of life on Earth assumes the earliest forms of life began approximately four billion years ago. It is presumed that conditions on Earth were very different from conditions today. The pre-life Earth environment would have been rich in water, ammonia, and methane, all compounds rich in hydrogen. In order for life to arise on Earth, organic molecules such as amino acids (the building blocks of proteins), sugars, acids, and bases would need to have formed from the available chemicals.

Over the last century there has been much research into plausible mechanisms for the origin of life. The **Oparin Hypothesis** is one theory regarding origin of life, developed by a Russian scientist (A.I. Oparin) in 1924. Oparin proposed that the Earth was approximately 4.6 billion years old and that the early Earth had a reducing atmosphere, meaning there was very little free oxygen present. Instead, there was an abundance of ammonia, hydrogen, methane, and steam (H_2O), all escaping from volcanoes. The Earth was in the process of cooling down, so there was a great deal of heat energy available, as well as a pattern of recurring violent lightening storms providing another source of energy. During this cooling of the Earth, much of the steam surrounding the Earth would condense, forming hot seas. In the presence of abundant energy, the synthesis of simple organic molecules from the available chemicals became possible. These organic substances then collected in the hot, turbulent seas (sometimes referred to as the "primordial soup").

As the concentration of organic molecules became very high, they began forming into larger, charged, complex molecules. Oparin called these highly absorptive molecules "coacervates." Coacervates were also able to divide.

Oparin's research involved finding experimental evidence to support his ideas that amino acids could combine to form proteins in early Earth conditions. Oparin knew proteins were catalysts so they could encourage further change and development of early cells.

Stanley Miller provided support for Oparin's hypotheses in experiments where he exposed simple inorganic molecules to electrical charges similar to lightning. Miller recreated conditions as they were supposed to exist in early Earth history, and was successful in his attempt to produce complex organic molecules including amino acids under these conditions. Miller's experiments served to support Oparin's hypotheses.

Sidney Fox, a major evolution researcher of the 1960s, conducted experiments that proved ultraviolet light may induce the formation of dipeptides from amino acids. Under conditions of moderate dry heat, Fox showed formation of proteinoids, polypeptides of up to 18 amino acids. He also showed that polyphosphoric acid could increase the yield of these polymers, a process that simulates the modern role of ATP in protein synthesis. These proteins formed small spheres known as microspheres; these showed similarities to living cells.

Further strides were made by researcher Cyril Ponnamperuma who demonstrated that small amounts of guanine formed from the thermal polymerization of amino acids. He also proved the synthesis of adenine and ribose from long-term treatment of reducing atmospheric gases with electrical current.

Once organic compounds had been synthesized, primitive cells most likely developed that contained genetic material in the form of RNA, and that used energy derived from ATP. These primitive cells were prokaryotic and similar to some bacteria now found on Earth.

The endosymbiont theory suggests that original prokaryotic cells took in other cells that performed various tasks. For instance, an original cell could absorb several symbiotic bacteria that then evolve into mitochondria. Several cells that lived in symbiosis would have combined and evolved to form a single eukaryotic cell.

Plant Evolution

The evolution of plant species is considered to have begun with heterotrophic prokaryotic cells. Since it is presumed that the early Earth's atmosphere was lacking in oxygen, early cells were anaerobic. Over time, some bacteria evolved the ability to carry on photosynthesis (cyanobacteria), thus becoming autotrophic, which in turn introduced significant amounts of oxygen into the atmosphere. As oxygen is poisonous to most anaerobic cells, a new niche opened up: cells able not only to survive in the presence of oxygen, but also to use it in metabolism.

Cyanobacteria were incorporated into larger aerobic cells, which then evolved into photosynthetic eukaryotic cells. Cellular organization increased, nuclei and membranes formed, and cell specialization occurred, leading to multicellular photosynthetic organisms, that is, plants.

The earliest plants were aquatic, but as niches filled in marine and freshwater environments, plants began to move onto land. Anatomical changes occurred over time allowing plants to survive in a nonaqueous environment. Cell walls thickened, and tissues to carry water and nutrients developed. As plants continued to adapt to land conditions, differentiation of tissues continued, resulting in the evolution of stems, leaves, roots, and seeds. The development of the seed was a key factor in the survival of land plants. Asexual reproduction dominated in early species, but sexual reproduction developed over time, increasing the possibilities of diversity.

Processes of adaptive radiation, genetic drift, and natural selection continued over long periods of time to produce the incredible diversity seen in the plant world today.

Animal Evolution

The evolution of animals is thought to have begun with marine protists. Although there is no fossil record, going back to the protist level, animal cells bear the most similarity to marine protist cells. Fossilized burrows from multicellular organisms begin to appear in the geological record approximately 700 million years ago, during the Precambrian period. These multicellular animals had only soft parts—no hard parts, which could be fossilized.

During the Cambrian period (the first period of the Paleozoic Era), beginning about 570 million years ago, the fossil record begins to show multicellular organisms with hard parts, namely exoskeletons. The fossil record at this time includes fossil representations from all modern day (and some extinct) phyla. This sudden appearance of multitudes of differentiated animal forms is known as the **Cambrian explosion**.

At the end of the Paleozoic Era, the fossil record attests to several mass extinction events. These combined events resulted in the extinction of about 95% of animal species developed to this point. Fossils indicate that many organisms, such as Trilobites, that were numerous in the Cambrian era, did not survive the end of the Paleozoic Era.

Approximately 505 million years ago was the beginning of the Ordovician period, which lasted until about 440 million years ago. The Ordovician period was marked by diversification among species that survived past the Cambrian extinctions. The Ordovician is also known for the development of land plants. Early forms of fish arose in the Cambrian, but developed during the Ordovician, these being the first vertebrates to be seen in the fossil record. Again, the end of the Ordovician is marked by vast extinctions, but these extinctions allowed the opening of ecological situations, which in turn encouraged adaptive radiation.

Adaptive radiation is the mechanism credited with the development of new species in the next period, the Silurian, from 440 to 410 million years ago. The Silurian period is marked by widespread colonization of landmasses by plants and animals. Large numbers of insect fossils are recognizable in Silurian geologic sediments, as well as fish and early amphibians. The mass movement onto land by formerly marine animals required adaptation in numerous areas including gas exchange, support (skeletal), water conservation, circulatory systems, and reproduction.

In the study of animal evolution, attention is paid to two concepts, homology, and analogy. Structures that exist in two different species because they share a common ancestry are called **homologous**. For instance, the forelimbs of a salamander and an opossum are similar in structure because of common ancestry. **Analogous** structures are similar because of their common function, although they do not share a common ancestry. Analogous structures are the product of **convergent evolution**. For instance, birds and insects both have wings, although they are not relatives. Rather the wings evolved as a result of convergence. Convergence occurs when a particular characteristic evolves in two unrelated populations. Wings of insects and birds are analogous structures (they are similar in function regardless of the lack of common ancestors).

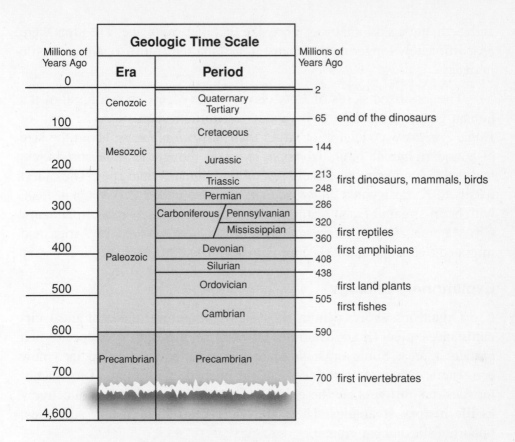

Geologic Time Scale		
Era	**Period**	

(Millions of Years Ago, left scale: 0, 100, 200, 300, 400, 500, 600, 700, 4,600)

Era	Period	Millions of Years Ago / events
Cenozoic	Quaternary / Tertiary	2
	Cretaceous	65 — end of the dinosaurs
Mesozoic	Jurassic	144
	Triassic	213 — first dinosaurs, mammals, birds / 248
	Permian	286
	Carboniferous / Pennsylvanian	320
	Mississippian	360 — first reptiles
Paleozoic	Devonian	408 — first amphibians
	Silurian	438
	Ordovician	505 — first land plants
	Cambrian	590 — first fishes
Precambrian	Precambrian	700 — first invertebrates

The process of **extinction** has played a large part in the direction evolution has taken. Extinctions occur at a generally low rate at all times. It is presumed that species that face extinction have not been able to adapt appropriately to environmental changes. However, there have also been several "extinction events" that have wiped out up to 95% of the species of their time. These events served to open up massive ecological niches, encouraging evolution of multitudes of new species.

Approximately 400 million years ago, the first amphibians gave rise to early reptiles that then diversified into birds, then mammals. One branch of mammals developed into the tree dwelling primates, considered the ancestors of humans.

Human Evolution

Humans are thought to have evolved from primates who over time developed larger brains. A branch of bipedal primates gave rise to the first true hominids about 4.5 million years ago. The earliest known hominid fossils were found in Africa in the 1970s. The well-known "Lucy" skeleton was named *Australopithecus afarensis*. It was determined from the skeleton of *Australopithecus* that it was a biped. It had a human-like jaw and teeth, but a skull that was more like that of a small ape. The arms were proportionately longer than humans, indicating the ability to still be motile in trees.

The fossilized skulls of *Homo erectus*, the oldest known fossil of the human genus, is thought to be about 1.8 million years old. The skull of *Homo erectus* was quite a lot larger than *Australopithecus*, about the size of a modern human brain. *Homo erectus* was thought to walk upright and had facial features more closely resembling humans than apes. The oldest fossils to be designated *Homo sapiens* are also called Cro-Magnon man, with brain size and facial features essentially the same as modern humans. Cro-Magnon *Homo sapiens* are thought to have evolved in Africa and migrated to Europe and Asia approximately 100,000 years ago.

Evolutionary Ecology

Organisms evolve within ecosystems; therefore, the ecological circumstances affect (if not determine) the course of evolution of species in a particular area. Some organisms are better suited to develop in a new ecosystem. Others only thrive in an established equilibrium. The characteristics that differentiate these types of organisms are known collectively as **life history strategies**. There are two types of life history strategies: opportunistic and equilibreal.

Organisms with **opportunistic** life history strategies (also known as r-selected) tend to be pioneer species in a new or recently devastated community. In addition to traits that allow them to succeed in the long term, they also have traits that help make them succeed in a changing or new ecosystem. They tend to have short maturation times and short overall life spans. They tend to have high mortality rates. Often reproduction is asexual, with high numbers of offspring. They find it easy to disperse over large areas. They do not parent their young. These are rapidly reproducing species that are also easily wiped out by more sophisticated populations that follow. For example, dandelions are an opportunistic species.

Species with **equilibreal** life strategies (also known as K-selected) are those organisms that overtake the opportunistic pioneer species. These tend to have long life spans with a long maturation time and corresponding low mortality rate. They reproduce sexually and produce fewer (longer-living) offspring that they tend to parent. They tend to stay within their established borders rather than dispersing. These characteristics form the basis for particular species to dominate in varying ecosystems. For example, an oak tree is an equilibreal species.

One of the most interesting ecological behaviors to explain through evolution is **altruism** (social behavior where organisms seem to place the needs of the community over their own need). An altruistic trait may actually decrease the fitness of the individual with the trait (known as the cost of altruism), while it increases the fitness of the community (the benefit of altruism). When you look at altruism in terms of the individual it would not have been an evolved trait since it decreases the individual's fitness. However, when looked at in terms of the community, an altruistic trait has value. In order for the traits of altruism to evolve it would be necessary for some other factor to influence the preservation and proliferation of those traits. This is thought to occur in nature through a process known as **kin selection**.

Kin selection is the tendency of an individual to be altruistic toward a close relative, resulting in the preservation of its genetic traits. Close relatives have a greater likelihood of passing on identical traits to their offspring. For instance, kin selection for a gene that causes an animal to share food with its close relatives, would result in this altruistic trait being spread throughout the gene pool and passed on to future generations. Thus, those relatives are more likely to survive, and their genes are passed on to the offspring, thus preserving the altruistic trait in future generations.

Since the communities that have altruistic individuals are more likely to persevere, natural selection will work to maintain those communities, while the weaker communities die out. It is widely accepted that those communities containing altruistic individuals are made up of close relatives that have been able to preserve the altruism through kin selection.

Classification of Living Organisms

The study of **taxonomy** seeks to organize living things into groups based on morphology, or more recently, genetics. Scientists have sought to categorize the great diversity of life on Earth for hundreds of years.

Carolus Linnaeus, who published his book *Systema Naturae* in 1735, first developed our current methods of taxonomy. Linnaeus based his taxonomic keys on the morphological (outward anatomical) differences seen among species. Linnaeus designed a system of classification for all known and unknown organisms according to their anatomical similarities and differences. Although Linnaeus was a Biblical creationist who sought to show the great diversity of creation, and although he devised his system over 100 years before Darwin's *Origin of Species*, his system remains as the basis of our classification system today.

Linnaeus used two Latin-based categories—*genus* and *species*—to name each organism. Every genus name could include one or more types of species. We refer to this two-word naming of species as **binomial nomenclature** (literally meaning "two names" in Latin). For example, Linnaeus named humans *Homo sapiens* (literally "man who is wise"). *Homo* is the genus name and *sapiens* the species name. *Homo sapiens* is the only extant species left from the genus *Homo*.

Beyond genus and species, Linnaeus further categorized organisms in a total of seven levels. Every **species** also belongs to a **genus**, **family**, **order**, **class**, **phylum**, and **kingdom**. *Kingdom* is the most general category, *species* the most limited. Taxonomists now also add "sub" and "super" categories to give even more opportunity for grouping similar organisms, and have added categories even more general than kingdom (that is, **domains**).

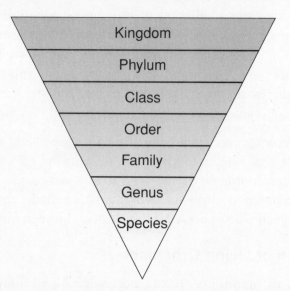

Although Linnaeus's system was designed before evolution was understood, the system he designed remains in use because it is based on similarities of species. An evolutionary classification system would use these same criteria. However, today, the classification system also serves to show relationships between organisms. When one constructs a **phylogenetic tree** (an evolutionary family tree of species) the result will generally show the same relationships represented with Linnaeus's taxonomy.

The most modern classification system contains three domains: the **Archaea,** the **Eubacteria**, and the **Eukaryota**. The organisms of the domain Archaea are prokaryotic, have unique RNA, and are able to live in the extreme ecosystems on Earth. The domain Archaea includes methane-producing organisms, and organisms able to withstand extreme temperatures and high salinity. The domain Eubacteria contains the prokaryotic organisms we call bacteria.

[Note: Some taxonomists still use a system including five kingdoms and no domains. In this case, the kingdom Monera would include organisms that are considered by other taxonomists to be included within the domains Archaea and Eubacteria.]

The domain Eukaryota includes all organisms that possess eukaryotic cells. The domain Eukaryota includes the four kingdoms: **Kingdom Protista, Kingdom Fungi, Kingdom Animalia,** and **Kingdom Plantae.** The following chart gives the major features of the four kingdoms of the Eukaryota:

Kingdom	# Known Phyla/Species	Nutrition	Structure	Included Organisms
Protista	27/250,000 +	photosynthesis, some ingestion and absorption	large eukaryotic cells	algae & protozoa
Fungi	5/100,000 +	absorption	multicellular (eukaryotic) filaments	mold, mushrooms, yeast, smuts, mildew
Animalia	33/1,000,000 +	ingestion	multicellular, specialized eukaryotic motile cells	various worms, sponges, fish, insects, reptiles, amphibians, birds, and mammals
Plantae	10/250,000 +	photosynthesis	multicellular, specialized eukaryotic nonmotile cells	ferns, mosses, woody and non-woody flowering plants

There are nine major phyla within the **Kingdom Animalia.** The Phyla are as follows:

1. **Porifera** - the sponges

2. **Cnidaria** - jellyfish, sea anemones, hydra, etc.

3. **Platyhelminthes** - flat worms

4. **Nematoda** - round worms

5. **Mollusca** - snails, clams, squid, etc.

6. **Annelida** - segmented worms (earthworms, leeches, etc.)

7. **Arthropoda** - crabs, spiders, lobster, millipedes, insects

8. **Echinodermata** - sea stars, sand dollars, etc.

9. **Chordata** - fish, amphibians, reptiles, birds, mammals, lampreys

Vertebrates are within the phylum Chordata, which is split into three subphyla, the **Urochordata** (animals with a tail cord such as tunicates), the **Cephalochordata** (animals with a head cord, such as lampreys), and **Vertebrata** (animals with a backbone).

The subphylum Vertebrata is divided into two **super-classes**, the **Aganatha** (animals with no jaws), and the **Gnathostomata** (animals with jaws). The Gnathostomata includes six classes with the following major characteristics:

a. **Chondrichthyes** - fish with a cartilaginous endoskeleton, two-chambered heart, 5-7 gill pairs, no swim bladder or lung, and internal fertilization (sharks, rays, etc.).

b. **Osteichthyes** - fish with a bony skeleton, numerous vertebrae, swim bladder (usually), two-chambered heart, gills with bony gill arches, and external fertilization (herring, carp, tuna).

c. **Amphibia** - animals with a bony skeleton, usually with four limbs having webbed feet with four toes, cold-blooded (ectothermic), large mouth with small teeth, three-chambered heart, separate sexes, internal or external fertilization, amniotic egg (salamanders, frogs, etc.).

d. **Reptilia** - horny epidermal scales, usually have paired limbs with five toes (except limbless snakes), bony skeleton, lungs, no gills, most have three-chambered heart, cold-blooded (ecothermic), internal fertilization, separate sexes, mostly egg-laying (oviparous), eggs contain extraembryonic membranes (snakes, lizards, alligators).

e. **Aves** - spindle shaped body (with head, neck, trunk, and tail), long neck, paired limbs, most have wings for flying, four-toed foot, feathers, leg scales, bony skeleton, bones with air cavities, beak, no teeth, four-chambered heart, warm blooded (endothermic), lungs with thin air sacs, separate sexes, egg-laying, eggs have hard calcified shell (birds - ducks, sparrows, etc.).

f. **Mammalia** - body covered with hair, glands (sweat, scent, sebaceous, mammary), teeth, fleshy external ears, usually four limbs, four-chambered heart, lungs, larynx, highly developed brain, warm-blooded, internal fertilization, live birth (except for the egg-laying monotremes), milk producing (cows, humans, platypus, apes, etc.).

THE ADVANCED PLACEMENT EXAMINATION IN

BIOLOGY

TEST I

ADVANCED PLACEMENT
BIOLOGY EXAM I

SECTION I

100 Questions
80 Minutes

DIRECTIONS: For each question, there are five possible choices. Select the best choice for each question. Blacken the correct space on the answer sheet.

1. Hydrolysis of lipid molecules yields:

    (A) amino acids and water

    (B) amino acids and glucose

    (C) fatty acids and glycerol

    (D) glucose and glycerol

    (E) glycerol and water

2. Simple squamous tissue is a type of which of the following kinds of tissue?

    (A) connective   (D) nerve

    (B) epithelial   (E) vascular

    (C) muscle

3. The majority of ATP molecules derived from nutrient metabolism are generated by (the):

    (A) anaerobic fermentation and glycolysis

    (B) fermentation and electron transport chain

    (C) glycolysis and substrate phosphorylation

    (D) Krebs cycle and electron transport chain

    (E) substrate phosphorylation

4. An organism with genotype AaBb can produce a variety of different sex cell genotypes equaling:

   (A) 1   (D) 8

   (B) 2   (E) 16

   (C) 4

5. Fill in the missing blanks for the photosynthetic reaction:

   Water + _____(1)_____   Carbohydrate + ___(2)____

   (A) (1) carbon dioxide, (2) oxygen

   (B) (1) chlorophyll, (2) oxygen

   (C) (1) light, (2) carbon dioxide

   (D) (1) oxygen, (2) water

   (E) (1) sugar, (2) light

6. Two pink flowers (Rr), of the species Japanese four-o'clock plant, mate. Assuming incomplete dominance, the chance of obtaining a red-colored offspring is:

   (A) 0%   (D) 75%

   (B) 25%   (E) 100%

   (C) 50%

7. The human condition of colorblindness is:

   (A) caused by a recessive allele

   (B) equally common in both sexes

   (C) expressed by a heterozygous genotype in females

   (D) inherited by males from their fathers

   (E) produced by a homozygous genotype in males

8. A DNA strand in a double helix has a base sequence of ATACGT. The base sequence of its DNA complement is:

   (A) ACGUAU   (D) TGCATA

   (B) ATACGT   (E) UAUGCA

   (C) TATGCA

9. RNA is made by the process of:

   (A) duplication   (D) transcription

   (B) fermentation   (E) translation

   (C) replication

10. Select the light with the shortest wavelength absorbed during photosynthesis:

    (A) blue   (D) red

    (B) green   (E) yellow

    (C) orange

11. Genes control body chemistry by ultimately specifying the structure of:

    (A) carbohydrates   (D) proteins

    (B) lipids   (E) water

    (C) phospholipids

12. The gene that turns structural genes off and on in an operon is the:

    (A) cistron   (D) regulator

    (B) operator   (E) repressor

    (C) promotor

13. The variable portion of a DNA nucleotide is at its:

    (A) base   (D) ribose

    (B) deoxyribose   (E) sugar

    (C) phosphate group

14. Select the cell type containing the highest concentration of mitochondria.

    (A) erythrocyte   (D) neuron

    (B) leukocyte   (E) skin

    (C) muscle

15. Viral replication, in which the host cell bursts following each cycle, is termed:

    (A) conjugation   (D) transduction

    (B) lysogenic   (E) transformation

    (C) lytic

16. The largest, most general category of classification is the:

    (A) class   (D) phylum

    (B) genus   (E) species

    (C) kingdom

17. The function of phloem is to:
   (A) cover and protect
   (B) convert nutrients from the soil
   (C) strengthen and support
   (D) store reserve materials
   (E) transport organic solutes

18. In the binomial *Quercus alba*, the first term represents the organism's:
   (A) class
   (B) genus
   (C) order
   (D) phylum
   (E) species

19. The largest number of known species is represented by the phylum:
   (A) Arthropoda
   (B) Annelida
   (C) Echinodermata
   (D) Platyhelminthes
   (E) Porifera

20. A human birth defect produced by a dominant allele of a gene is:
   (A) albinism
   (B) diabetes mellitus
   (C) hemophilia
   (D) high cholesterol
   (E) low melanin levels

21. What type of leaf structures and environmental conditions promote gas exchange in plants?
   (A) Cortex, heat
   (B) Cortex, cold
   (C) Mesophyll, high humidity
   (D) Stomata, heat
   (E) Stomata, normal temperatures

22. Phloem conducts:
   (A) ions
   (B) glucose
   (C) glycogen
   (D) minerals
   (E) sucrose

23. The skin performs all of the following human body functions except:
   (A) identification of an individual
   (B) protection
   (C) sensation
   (D) storage
   (E) temperature regulation

24. The biceps brachii produce movements by pulling on:
    (A) bones   (D) nerves
    (B) joints   (E) skin
    (C) muscles

25. Which of the following can be said to be a semiconservative process?
    (A) conjugation   (D) translation
    (B) DNA replication   (E) translocation
    (C) RNA transcription

26. Neurons that conduct signals away from the central nervous system are classified as:
    (A) afferent   (D) motor
    (B) associative   (E) sensory
    (C) internuncial

27. The innermost layer of the eye is the:
    (A) choroid coat   (D) retina
    (B) cornea   (E) sclera
    (C) pupil

28. Which of the following is not a polymer?
    (A) DNA   (D) RNA
    (B) glycogen   (E) starch
    (C) glucose

29. Select the nonpathogenic bacterium:
    (A) *Clostridium*   (D) *Staphylococcus*
    (B) *Escherichia*   (E) *Treponema*
    (C) *Salmonella*

30. The largest number of chambers is found in the heart of a(n):
    (A) amphibian   (D) reptile
    (B) bird   (E) shark
    (C) fish

31. Which law explains the inhalation and exhalation of air in terms of pressure changes?

(A) Archimedes' law   (D) Dalton's law

(B) Aristotle's law   (E) Mendel's law

(C) Boyle's law

32. *Paramecium caudatum* is best classified into the kingdom:

(A) Animalia   (D) Plantae

(B) Fungi   (E) Protista

(C) Monera

33. Which of the following is a single bacterial cell?

(A) *Diplobacillus*   (D) *Streptococcus*

(B) *Gonococcus*   (E) *Streptomyces*

(C) *Staphylococcus*

34. Bacteria that can effectively carry out metabolism in the presence or absence of oxygen are described as:

(A) aerobic   (D) fermentative microbes

(B) anaerobic   (E) glycolytic

(C) facultative anaerobes

35. Each is an important assumption for maintenance of a Hardy-Weinberg equilibrium in a population except:

(A) asexual reproduction

(B) random mating among members

(C) large population size

(D) lack of emigration or immigration

(E) absence of new mutations

36. The free-swimming coelenterate larva is the:

(A) coral   (D) planula

(B) hydra   (E) polyp

(C) medusa

37. Plant-eaters can digest plant cell walls due to their utilization of which enzyme?

    (A) amylase

    (B) cellulase

    (C) chymotrypsin

    (D) pepsin

    (E) trypsin

38. A coelom is a(n):

    (A) body cavity bounded by mesoderm, in which the viscera are suspended.

    (B) digestive tract, which is endodermal in origin.

    (C) outer skin that is ectodermal in origin.

    (D) specialized region of the higher forebrain.

    (E) one of the four mammalian heart chambers.

39. Which of the following types of organisms occupies the trophic level of least biomass?

    (A) herbivores

    (B) plants

    (C) primary consumers

    (D) secondary consumers

    (E) tertiary consumers

40. The invertebrate phylum phylogenetically closest to the chordates is:

    (A) Annelida

    (B) Arthropoda

    (C) Cnidaria

    (D) Echinodermata

    (E) Mollusca

41. An insect metamorphic life cycle occurs in which of the following sequences?

    (A) adult-pupa-larva-egg

    (B) egg-larva-pupa-adult

    (C) larva-adult-egg-pupa

    (D) pupa-egg-larva-adult

    (E) pupa-adult-larva-egg

42. Highest pressure of circulating blood is found in a(n):

    (A) arteriole

    (B) artery

    (C) capillary

    (D) vein

    (E) venule

43.   Which of the following is part of a human's axial skeleton?

(A) clavicle   (D) rib

(B) fibula   (E) scapula

(C) humerus

44.   Glial cells:

(A) conduct signals   (D) support neurons

(B) contribute to movement   (E) transport oxygen

(C) cover the skin

45.   Select the disease caused by a protozoa:

(A) chicken pox   (D) measles

(B) common cold   (E) smallpox

(C) malaria

46.   Which of the following has a vitamin as a building block?

(A) apoenzyme   (D) mineral

(B) coenzyme   (E) protein

(C) holoenzyme

47.   The filtering of inhaled debris that travels through the upper respiratory tract occurs through the action of:

(A) cilia   (D) phagocytes

(B) goblet cells   (E) villi

(C) Leidig cells

48.   Substances in the blood are transported across the nephron tubules by mechanisms in the process of:

(A) bulk flow   (D) reabsorption

(B) filtration   (E) secretion

(C) osmosis

49.   A person receives the results of a hematocrit during a series of blood tests. A hematocrit is the:

(A) abundance of white blood cells in blood

(B) concentration of sugar in the blood

(C) level of circulating antibodies

(D) percentage of blood cellular material by volume

(E) typing of the blood by the ABO scheme

50. An insect is captured and studied in a laboratory. This insect has a pair of short, rigid wings, and a pair of thin veined wings. It also has chewing mouthparts. The insect will most likely be classified as a member of which of the following orders?

(A) Diptera

(B) Hemiptera

(C) Homoptera

(D) Lepidoptera

(E) Orthoptera

DIRECTIONS: The following groups of questions have five lettered choices followed by a list of diagrams, numbered phrases, sentences, or words. For each numbered diagram, phrase, sentence, or word choose the heading which most directly applies. Blacken the correct space on the answer sheet. Each heading may be used once, more than once, or not at all.

Questions 51 - 54 refer to the biomolecule diagrams below.

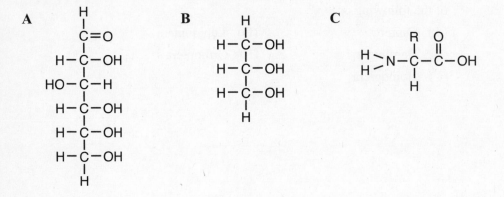

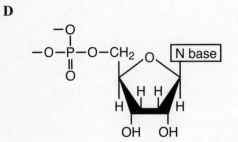

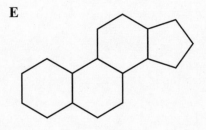

51.   carbohydrates

52.   lipids

53.   nucleic acid

54.   proteins

Questions 55 - 58 refer to the diagram below.

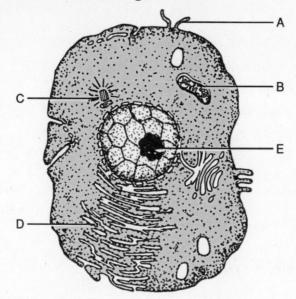

55.   organize cell division

56.   movement of the cell

57.   internal transport

58.   extraction of energy from nutrients

Questions 59-62 refer to stages of meiosis I.

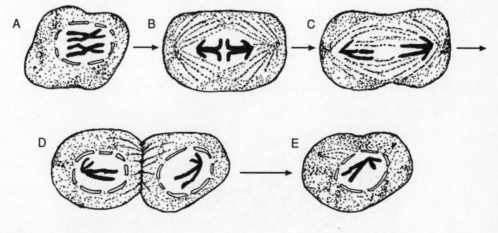

59.   anaphase

60.   metaphase

61.   prophase

62.   telophase

Questions 63 - 66 refer to the listed descriptions of skeletal muscle contraction types.

    (A) a short, individual contraction and relaxation

    (B) a sustained maximal response

    (C) an accumulation of an abundance of lactic acid

    (D) the merging of separate responses into a powerful output

    (E) tonic activity, as occurring in muscle tone

63.   fatigue

64.   simple twitch

65.   summation

66.   tetanus

Questions 67 - 70 refer to various descriptions of:

    (A) members have jointed appendages

    (B) flatworms; members lack segmentation

    (C) each member possesses a muscular foot

    (D) members possess a high degree of segmentation

    (E) closest phylogenetic relatives of the chordates

67.   Annelida

68.   Arthropoda

69.   Echinodermata

70.   Mollusca

Questions 71-73 refer to the drawing below.

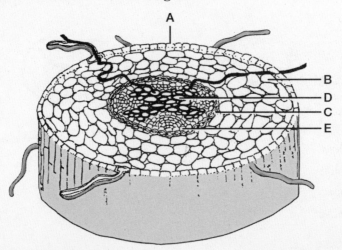

71.   The root cortex

72.   The root epidermis

73.   Root xylem

Questions 74-77 refer to the drawing below.

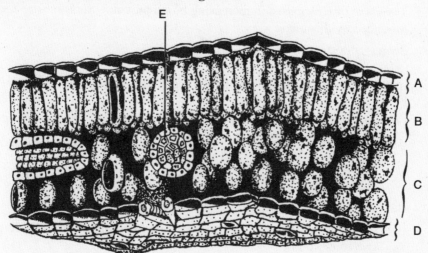

74.   Gas exchange occurs here.

75.   A waxy cuticle is thicker here.

76.   A higher chloroplast density occurs here.

77.   The highest humidity would be here.

Questions 78-81 refer to the diagram below.

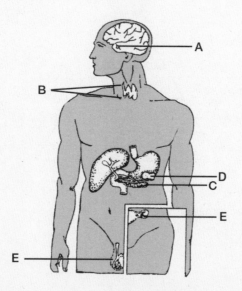

78. A sudden change in an organism's amount of extracellular fluid will be corrected by this organ.

79. A person eats three candy bars. Within minutes, this endocrine gland effects blood glucose homeostasis.

80. Substances that cause vasoconstriction change the diameters of blood vessels in order to assist in increasing blood pressure. Such substances are produced by this gland.

81. Secrete aldosterone

Questions 82 - 85 refer to the organelles of a cell and their function(s).

(A) site of mRNA translation

(B) contains a circular arrangement of 18 microtubules that surround 2 microtubules

(C) contains a circular arrangement of 27 microtubules

(D) site of rRNA synthesis

(E) contains a circular arrangement of nine microtubules surrounding two microtubules

82. centriole

83. cilium

84. nucleolus

85. ribosome

Questions 86 - 87 refer to the drawing below.

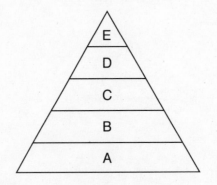

86. Producer biomass

87. Secondary consumer

DIRECTIONS: The following questions refer to experimental or laboratory situations or data. Read the description of each situation. Then choose the best answer to each question. Blacken the correct space on the answer sheet.

Question 88 - 90 refer to the diagram below.

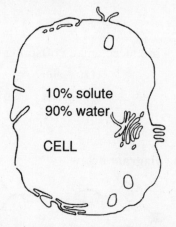

88.   The intracellular environment is best described as:

(A) hypertonic   (D) osmotic

(B) hypotonic   (E) permeable

(C) isotonic

89.   The extracellular environment will:

(A) gain water   (D) lose solute

(B) gain solute   (E) remain unchanged

(C) lose water

90.   Over time the cell will:

(A) become more hypertonic intracellularly

(B) enlarge and experience lysis

(C) experience crenation

(D) lose motility

(E) lose solute

Questions 91 - 92 refer to the genetic grid below.

	AB	Ab	aB	ab
Ab	1	2	3	4
ab	5	6	7	8

91. In the genetic cross, what is the percentage of genetic recombinations that are heterozygous for both loci?

    (A) 0   (D) 75
    (B) 25   (E) 100
    (C) 50

92. A genotype that is not produced among offspring from this cross:

    (A) AABb   (D) Aabb
    (B) AAbb   (E) aaBB
    (C) AaBb

Questions 93-95 refer to the diagram below.

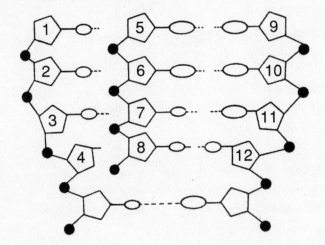

93. DNA nucleotide base #2 is cytosine. The RNA base of #6 is:

    (A) Adenine   (D) Thymine
    (B) Cytosine   (E) Uracil
    (C) Guanine

94. RNA base #7 is uracil. The DNA base at #3 is:

    (A) Adenine   (D) Thymine
    (B) Cytosine   (E) Uracil
    (C) Guanine

95. The DNA-base sequence from 1 to 4 is CGCT. The RNA base sequence from 5 to 8 is:

(A) ACGG   (D) GCGA

(B) CGCT   (E) TCGC

(C) CGCU

Questions 96 - 98 refer to the drawing below:

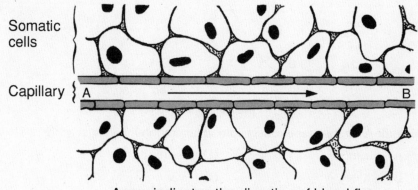

Arrow indicates the direction of blood flow.

96.　Region A:

(A) accepts carbon dioxide from cells

(B) receives blood from an arteriole

(C) receives nutrients from cells

(D) has a lower blood pressure than the blood pressure at B

(E) transports blood to an artery

97.　Region B:

(A) accepts oxygen from cells

(B) gives carbon dioxide to cells

(C) has a higher blood pressure than the blood pressure at A

(D) transports blood to a venule

(E) unloads nutrients to cells

98.　The best word to describe this blood vessel's function is:

(A) circulation   (D) pressurization

(B) exchange   (E) transport

(C) flow

Questions 99 - 100 refer to the graph below.

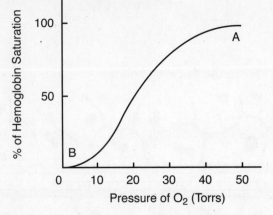

99.   Point A on the graph reflects blood hemoglobin behavior at the:

(A) heart   (D) tissue cell

(B) kidney   (E) vein

(C) lung

100.   Point B on the graph reflects blood hemoglobin behavior at the:

(A) artery   (D) lung

(B) kidney   (E) tissue cell

(C) liver

SECTION II

DIRECTIONS: Answer each of the following four questions in essay format. Each answer should be clear, organized, and well-balanced. Diagrams may be used in addition to the discussion, but a diagram alone will not suffice. Suggested writing time per essay is 22 minutes.

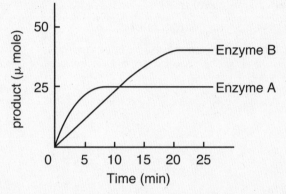

Graph I = condition of enzyme A, catalysis = 37°C, pH = 3, excess substrate A. Condition of enzyme B, catalysis = 37°C, pH = 8, excess substrate B.

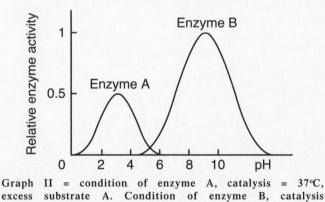

Graph II = condition of enzyme A, catalysis = 37°C, excess substrate A. Condition of enzyme B, catalysis = 37°C, excess substrate B.

1. Enzymes are important reaction catalyzers.

    (A) From the data given in Graph I, discuss the effectiveness of each enzyme.

    (B) Give an example of an enzyme in the human body that corresponds with enzyme A and another that corresponds with enzyme B.

    (C) Describe the effects an excess of carbon dioxide in the body would have on enzyme effectiveness.

2.   Describe the different types of mutations and the process of translation. Include a discussion of how point mutations affect proper protein synthesis at the level of translation.

3.   Defend the accuracy of this ecologically-based statement: "Energy flows through an ecosystem but materials cycle." Offer examples of food chains and biogeochemical cycles to support its accuracy.

4.   Describe how each of the following animal and plant cells perform its unique function by specialized structural traits.

        Animal = erythrocyte, neuron, muscle fiber.

        Plant = epidermal cell, tracheids, parenchyma cells.

ADVANCED PLACEMENT BIOLOGY EXAM I

ANSWER KEY

1.	(C)	26.	(D)	51.	(A)	76.	(B)
2.	(B)	27.	(D)	52.	(B)	77.	(E)
3.	(D)	28.	(C)	53.	(D)	78.	(A)
4.	(C)	29.	(B)	54.	(C)	79.	(C)
5.	(A)	30.	(B)	55.	(C)	80.	(D)
6.	(B)	31.	(C)	56.	(A)	81.	(D)
7.	(A)	32.	(E)	57.	(D)	82.	(C)
8.	(C)	33.	(B)	58.	(B)	83.	(B)
9.	(D)	34.	(C)	59.	(C)	84.	(D)
10.	(A)	35.	(A)	60.	(B)	85.	(A)
11.	(D)	36.	(D)	61.	(A)	86.	(A)
12.	(B)	37.	(B)	62.	(D)	87.	(C)
13.	(A)	38.	(A)	63.	(C)	88.	(A)
14.	(C)	39.	(E)	64.	(A)	89.	(C)
15.	(C)	40.	(D)	65.	(D)	90.	(B)
16.	(C)	41.	(B)	66.	(B)	91.	(B)
17.	(E)	42.	(B)	67.	(D)	92.	(E)
18.	(B)	43.	(D)	68.	(A)	93.	(B)
19.	(A)	44.	(D)	69.	(E)	94.	(D)
20.	(C)	45.	(C)	70.	(C)	95.	(C)
21.	(E)	46.	(B)	71.	(B)	96.	(B)
22.	(E)	47.	(A)	72.	(A)	97.	(D)
23.	(D)	48.	(E)	73.	(D)	98.	(B)
24.	(A)	49.	(D)	74.	(D)	99.	(C)
25.	(B)	50.	(E)	75.	(A)	100.	(E)

ADVANCED PLACEMENT BIOLOGY EXAM I

DETAILED EXPLANATIONS OF ANSWERS

SECTION I

1.   **(C)**

Hydrolysis is a type of chemical digestion. Amino acids are the digested building blocks of proteins. Glucose is a subunit of carbohydrates. Water molecules are required to split chemical bonds in hydrolysis but are not produced in the process.

2.   **(B)**

Epithelial tissue covers the free surfaces of the body. For example, simple (one cell layer) squamous (flat, platelike) epithelial tissue can be found on the surface of the skin, and acts as a protective barrier. Muscle tissue consists of muscle fibers, and contains no simple squamous tissue. Nerve tissue is made almost entirely of neurons and neuroglial cells. Connective tissue, such as bone, blood, and tendons, contain cells that are separated by and suspended in some sort of matrix. Vascular tissue is not a valid tissue category.

3.   **(D)**

Only a small fraction of ATP molecules is produced from anaerobic process of fermentation or glycolysis. Once pyruvic acid is formed, its entry into the aerobic Krebs cycle unleashes most of the original glucose molecule's energy. Krebs cycle reactions yield high energy electrons (oxidation) that are then shuttled down a series of transport acceptors located in the inner mitochondrial membrane until they finally combine with oxygen and H^+ to form water. During electron transport, a proton gradient is generated across the inner mitochondrial membrane. The collapse of this proton gradient provides energy for the production of ATP molecules from ADP molecules and inorganic phosphates.

4.   **(C)**

Mendel's law of Independent Assortment leads to AB, Ab, aB, and ab combinations in produced sex cells. The answer has a mathematical base, accounting for all possible combinations when one gene is selected from each of the two pairs.

5.   **(A)**

During photosynthesis, the gas carbon dioxide reacts with the hydrogen from water. Photolysis, or the chemical splitting of water by light, releases oxygen as one of the products. CO_2 reacts with the available hydrogen in coupled dark reactions to make the other product, a sugar such as glucose - $C_6H_{12}O_6$.

6.   **(B)**

The outcome of the mating of two pink flowers of genotype Rr, assuming incomplete dominance, is best displayed by a Punnett square:

	R	r
R	RR	Rr
r	Rr	rr

All offspring of genotype RR will be red; all offspring of genotype Rr will be pink; all those of genotype rr will be white. Therefore, there is a 25% chance that any offspring will be red.

7.   **(A)**

Many of the better-known sex-linked human conditions, such as hemophilia and colorblindness, are caused by recessive alleles. Sex-linked (X-linked) genes are located on the X-chromosome. Thus males, whose sex chromosomes are X and Y, have only one such gene. Assuming that there are only two alleles for this X-linked gene, males are genotypically either C—(normal) or c—(i.e. - colorblind). The Y-chromosome does not offer a second gene in this case. Males can thus not be homozygous. For females, whose sex chromosomes are X and X, three genotypes are possible: CC, Cc and cc. A woman of genotype Cc is a carrier of the disease but does not express the recessive effect of colorblindness. She can, however, pass on her recessive allele to her offspring. In order to produce a colorblind female (cc), a female carrier would have to mate with a colorblind male (c—). Each parent offers a C allele on the X chromosome for a c genotype in the offspring. This is unlikely and an infrequent event.

An example of a common cross is:

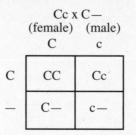

Cc x C—
(female) (male)
C   c

	C	c
C	CC	Cc
—	C—	c—

One-half of the males produced are color blind. One-half of the females produced are carriers.

8.   **(C)**

Two base-pairing rules must be memorized for DNA strand complementarity: A-T and G-C. Thus, the given DNA strand of six bases dictates only one possible complement.

9.   **(D)**

This is a rote-memory question. Duplication or replication refer to DNA copying. Translation is the RNA direction of protein synthesis.

10.   **(A)**

The choices are ranked in order of increasing wavelength: blue-green-yellow-orange-red. Green is reflected; red light has a wavelength range of 650 nm - 700 nm in the visible spectrum. Since light of 680 nm and 700 nm wavelength is utilized by photosystem II and photosystem I respectively, the light with the shortest wavelength absorbed during photosynthesis is blue light.

11.   **(D)**

DNA serves as a template for RNA synthesis and RNA serves as a template for protein synthesis. Proteins participate in a wide variety of body chemistry. For instance, as enzymes they catalyze nearly all chemical reactions in biological systems. They serve as transport molecules such as oxygen-carrying molecules, hemoglobins and myoglobins. They protect our bodies against foreign pathogens in the form of antibodies.

12.   **(B)**

In an operon, the operator gene is adjacent to the first of several consecutive structural genes that code for enzymes that are needed for a particular metabolic pathway. These structural genes are often arranged in the same order that the enzymes which they code for are used in the pathway. The promotor is located next to the operator gene, opposite the side of the linked structural genes and is the location at which the RNA polymerase, which generated the mRNA that is necessary for enzyme synthesis, binds. The regulator gene is at another location on the chromosome. This location can be near or far from the operon that it regulates.

13.   **(A)**

The base: adenine (A), cytosine (C), guanine (G) or thymine (T) varies from nucleotide to nucleotide building block in a DNA strand. Any DNA nucleotide is occupied by only one of these bases for four possible nucleotide structures. The other choices are constant in the nucleotide. Ribose is a component of an RNA nucleotide.

14.   **(C)**

Muscle cells are the engines of an animal, developing contractile pulling forces to produce work. Mitochondria, cell powerhouses to extract energy from nutrients, are most in demand here.

15.   **(C)**

Viruses are obligate, intracellular parasites. This means that they must enter host cells and use materials that are found within the cell to reproduce. Viruses lack ribosomes and ATP-generating systems. Thus, viruses enter the host cell and use the host cell's ribosomes and other organelles for their reproductive needs. Eventually, enough viral protein and viral DNA are produced, the new viruses are assembled, and the cell ruptures, releasing the new viruses. This frees new viral particles at the conclusion of this lytic life cycle. In an alternative lysogenic life cycle, viruses instead incorporate their DNA into the host's chromosome and remain latent. The virus may later start a lytic cycle. Transduction refers to the process of a virus taking along some of a host cell's DNA and injecting this DNA, along with its own viral DNA, into a new host cell. The other choices do not refer to viral life cycles.

16.   **(C)**

The hierarchy of classification levels is, from the most general down to most restrictive:

Kingdom
    Phylum
        Class
            Order
                Family
                    Genus
                        Species

17. **(E)**

Phloem is one of two types of plant vascular tissue. It transports organic solutes, especially sugars, both upward and downward throughout the plant body. Xylem, the other plant vascular tissue type, transports water and dissolved minerals upward through the plant from their absorption site in the roots. Epidermal tissue covers the plant. Large parenchymal cells in roots and leaves store certain substances as a reserve. Supportive cells include collenchyma and sclerenchyma, which have thick cell walls.

18. **(B)**

In the binomial system of organism nomenclature, the first taxonomic name is the genus name and is capitalized. It is followed by the species name, which begins with a lowercase letter. This is the scientific name of the white oak tree.

19. **(A)**

There are more arthropod species than species of any other phylum. Arthropods include such well-known groups as arachnids, crustaceans, and insects.

Annelids are segmented worms; echinoderms include sea urchins and sea anemones; poriferans are sponges; phylum Platyhelminthes represents the flatworms.

20. **(C)**

Two well-known examples of recessive sex-linked traits in human beings are red-green color blindness and hemophilia. These recessive sex-linked traits occur in a higher frequency in men than in women.

Albinism is an autosomal recessive disease. An individual heterozygous for albinism appears normal because one normal gene can be sufficient for making enough of the functional enzyme that make melanin pigments. Albinism is associated with low melanin levels.

Diabetes mellitus is characterized by an elevated level of glucose in blood and urine and arises from a deficiency of insulin. The causes for the disease are not clear but there is evidence that this defect has molecular basis such as abnormally formed insulin.

High cholesterol level is a genetic disease resulting from a mutation at a single autosomal locus coded for the receptor for LDL (low-density lipoprotein). Whether a trait is dominant or recessive does not apply to this disease because the heterozygotes suffer from a milder problem than the homozygotes. The heterozygotes possess functional LDL receptors though they are present at a deficient level.

21. **(E)**

Stomata control gas exchange by either opening or closing, thereby regulating the amount of air that enters the leaf. At normal temperatures, stomata are open. At high temperatures, the guard cells that surround each stoma will expand, thereby sealing each stoma.

22.　　**(E)**

Sucrose is the major carbohydrate molecule transported in plants and most of the movement of carbohydrates is through the phloem. Xylem transports ions (minerals). The other carbohydrates listed are not common in plants and glucose is not a transported molecule.

23.　　**(D)**

A study of skin structure reveals skin's ability to perform all but one of the listed capabilities, i.e., fingerprints for identification, blood vessels to vent body heat, receptors to sense stimuli, and layers to protect.

24.　　**(A)**

The biceps brachii are the muscles on the ventral portion of the upper arm that pull and bend the forearm. Bones are the rigid bars that yield to skeletal muscles' pulling force. Movable joints allow a source of mobility between articulating bones. Skeletal muscles are stimulated by nerves. Lacking this stimulation they will not respond.

25.　　**(B)**

DNA replication is referred to as a semiconservative process because, after replication is completed, each of the two daughter molecules of DNA contains one strand from the parent DNA molecule. The other strand of each daughter molecule is assembled from nucleotides present in the nucleus.

26.　　**(D)**

Sensory or afferent neurons send signals toward the central nervous system (CNS). Associative, or internuncial, neurons are within the CNS. Motor or efferent neurons, with axons outside and directed away from the CNS, send signals out to peripheral points.

27.　　**(D)**

The retina contains the receptor cells that receive and register incoming light rays. The choroid is a middle layer of darkly pigmented and highly vascularized tissue. This structure provides blood to the eye and absorbs light to prevent internal reflection that may blur the image. The outer sclera (white of the eye) includes the transparent cornea. The pupil is an opening in the donut-shaped, colored iris interior to the cornea. The size of the pupil is regulated by the contraction and relaxation of the iris, which controls the amount of light admitted into the eye.

28.   **(C)**

A polymer is a long complex molecule formed by the bonding of simpler, repetitive subunits. DNA and RNA are polymers of nucleotides. Glycogen and starch are polysaccharides. Polysaccharides are polymers of simple sugars, including glucose. Glucose is a subunit, not a polymer.

29.   **(B)**

Clostridium can cause botulism and tetanus. *Staphylococcus* can infect a wound and cause blood poisoning. *Salmonella* can cause food poisoning. *E. coli* lives normally in the human large intestine, or colon. *Treponema* can cause syphilis.

30.   **(B)**

A four-chambered heart with a complete separation of sides is a characteristic of mammals and birds, the warm-blooded vertebrates. Most of the cold-blooded vertebrates do not have a completely separated four-chambered heart. For instance, fish (e.g. shark) has a two-chambered heart composed of an atrium and a ventricle. No mixing of oxygenated and deoxygenated blood occurs in fish because of a single pathway of blood circulation: gills Æ systemic circulation Æ heart Æ gills. Amphibians and reptiles, with the exception of crocodilians, have a 3-chambered heart composed of a left and a right atrium and an incompletely divided ventricle. Blood in amphibians and reptiles circulates through a pulmonary and a systemic pathway in each cycle with very little mixing of oxygenated and deoxygenated blood.

31.   **(C)**

Boyle's law states that air pressure is inversely proportional to volume. As the chest cavity increases due to the flattening of the diaphragm and rib elevation, internal pressure drops below that of the atmosphere, causing an inrush of air.

32.   **(E)**

Paramecium caudatum, according to the currently recognized five-kingdom system, is a protist. Animalia includes all multicellular animals. Fungi consists of unicellular and multicellular organisms that do not possess chlorophyll and that require the presence of organic matter in order to survive. Monera is made up of bacteria and blue-green algae. Plantae consists of unicellular and multicellular plants.

33.   **(B)**

"Di" means two, "strepto" means chain, and "staphylo" means bunch. *Gonococcus* is a single, spherically shaped bacterial cell that causes gonorrhea.

34.   **(C)**

Facultatively anaerobic organisms, under normal aerobic conditions, will use oxygen in their metabolism, as humans do; in the absence of sufficient oxygen, however, such organisms can metabolize molecules other than oxygen. Aerobic is a term applied to situations involving oxygen, while anaerobic is a term applied to those involving no oxygen. Fermentation is the synthesis of alcohol via the glycolytic pathway. Glycolysis is the series of anaerobic metabolic reactions that converts glucose to pyruvic acid.

35.   **(A)**

All other choices represent important conditions necessary to maintain a consistency of a population's gene frequencies. Sexual reproduction with random mating is an important requirement for this equilibrium.

36.   **(D)**

Coral and hydra are types of adult coelenterates. Medusa and polyp are alternating adult body forms of many coelenterate species.

37.   **(B)**

Use of cellulases allows herbivores to digest cellulose, the major component of cell walls. Amylase (ptyalin) breaks starch down into monosaccharides and disaccharides. Chymotrypsin, trypsin, and pepsin all are proteases.

38.   **(A)**

This is an exact definition of the coelom.

39.   **(E)**

Energy flows from plants (producers) to herbivores (primary consumers) to additional levels of consumers in the food chain. Each succeeding link has less remaining available energy. Generally, only about 10% of the energy from one trophic level is passed to the next level. Loss of energy can be attributed to the respiration of organisms and the consequent dissipation of heat, due to the inability of most animals to digest the cellulose of plants.

40.   **(D)**

Based on embryonic development, two evolutionary lines have been distinguished. One evolutionary line, containing the phyla Annelida, Arthropoda, and Mollusca, is called Protostomia; the blastopores of protostomes develop into mouths. The other evolutionary line, containing the phyla Chordata and Echinodermata, is called Deuterostomia; the blastopores of members of these phyla become anuses. Coelenterates are more primitive than either the Protostomia or the Deuterostomia.

41.   **(B)**

The metamorphic life cycle of insects can be exemplified by the life cycle of a butterfly. From a butterfly's egg will hatch a caterpillar (the larval form). The caterpillar, after a period of growth, will spin itself a cocoon and become a pupa. Eventually, the adult butterfly will emerge from the cocoon.

42.   **(B)**

Blood flows through the circulatory system due to a pressure gradient. The blood will flow from a region of higher pressure to one of lower pressure. Therefore, blood pressure must be greatest at the beginning of blood's circuit, namely, the aorta, or artery.

43.   **(D)**

The rib is one of the twelve pairs of bones which form a rib cage to protect the lungs and heart. Along with the skull and vertebral column, the rib cage forms the axial skeleton. The bones of the paired appendages, the pectoral and pelvic girdles belong to the appendicular skeleton.

44.   **(D)**

Glial cells bind neurons together. They offer nerve cells support, protection, and nutritional supply.

45.   **(C)**

Malaria is caused by protozoans of the genus *Plasmodium*, of the class Sporozoa. The other choices represent diseases caused by viruses.

46.   **(B)**

All enzymes are composed primarily of protein. The more complex enzymes have non-protein portions called cofactors; the protein portion of the enzyme is called an apoenzyme. If the cofactor is an easily separated organic molecule, it is called a coenzyme. Many coenzymes are related to vitamins. An enzyme deprived of its vitamin is thus incomplete, leading to the nonexecution of a key step in metabolism. Holoenzyme refers to the RNA polymerase, with its core enzyme and sigma subunit associated together.

47.   **(A)**

Cilia line the upper respiratory tract, waving against air inflow to filter out unneeded debris. Villi are fingerlike extensions of the membranes of cells lining the small intestine. They increase surface area to facilitate absorption of digested nutrients. Goblet cells line the same region and secrete mucus. Leidig cells are in the male testis.

48.   **(E)**

Filtration first moves blood plasma substances from the glomerulus (capillary) into the cuplike Bowman's capsule at the nephron's origin. After monitoring these solute concentrations (e.g. - glucose, sodium, etc.), reabsorption returns them to the blood <u>from</u> the nephron tubule at high percentage rates. Secretion is a third step, moving materials from the blood (peritubular capillaries) to the *distal convoluted tubule* for exit and elimination.

49.   **(D)**

Hematocrit is the percentage of blood cells in blood by volume. For males this value is normally 47 ± 5; for females, it is 42 ± 5. Thirty-two percent is abnormally low, indicating anemia - a diminished capacity of the blood carry oxygen.

50.   **(E)**

The traits that are mentioned in question 50 are those of Orthopterans. Members of this order include grasshoppers and cockroaches. Dipterans, such as houseflies, have one pair of wings and sucking mouthparts. Hemipterans, the true bugs, have one pair of wings that are thicker proximally and membranous distally, and a pair of wings that are totally membranous. Homopterans have either no wings, or two pairs of arched wings. Lepidopterans, such as butterflies, have two pairs of scale-covered wings and sucking mouthparts.

51. **(A)**   52. **(B)**   53 **(D)**   54. **(C)**

Formula A shows a hexose sugar molecule. By adding the number of different types of atoms from the structural formula, the molecular formula is $C_6H_{12}O_6$ with <u>six</u> carbon atoms in a chain. This particular hexose sugar is glucose, a monosaccharide. Formula B shows but three carbon atoms in a chain. The base ratio is also not 1-2-1 for carbon-hydrogen-oxygen as it is in simple carbohydrates. B is the alcohol, glycerol, that bonds to fatty acids in a lipid or fat molecule. Formula C is an amino acid, the repetitive building block for protein macromolecules. The amino group, NH_2, and carboxylic acid group, COOH, are identifying functional groups of an amino acid. D is the structural formula for a nucleotide, the building block subunit for nucleic acids such as DNA and RNA. Its identifying components are a 5-carbon sugar, a varying nitrogen base, and a phosphate group. Formula E is a carbon skeleton for a steroid molecule.

55. (C)   56. (A)   57. (D)   58. (B)

Centrioles are paired, cylinder- shaped organelles at right angles to one another. Located near the cell nucleus, they coordinate cell division. Cilia are numerous, hairlike projections of the cell membrane that beat in synchrony to propel the cell in movement. The endoplasmic reticulum is a winding, tubular system that establishes a channel for internal transport. The mitochondrion is an oblong, football-shaped organelle with a double membrane. Its inner one forms pockets, or cristae and has enzymes to run cell respiration. The darkstaining spherical nucleolus in the nucleus does not appear as an answer.

59. (C)   60. (B)   61. (A)   62. (D)

Note, from the illustration, the synapsis (pairing and attraction) of homologous chromosomes. This phenomenon, along with their crossing over denotes <u>prophase</u> of meiosis one. The chromosomes align along the central plane of the spindle in <u>metaphase</u>. The homologs separate in <u>anaphase</u> with cell cytokinesis and complete separation into two daughter cells occurring in <u>telophase</u>. Illustration E is a meiosis II stage.

63. (C)   64. (A)   65. (D)   66. (B)

As a skeletal muscle receives separate, well-spaced stimuli of sufficient intensity, it will twitch to each stimulus. Each twitch is marked by contraction and relaxation of a muscle. As the rate of stimulation increases, the muscle does not have sufficient time to totally relax between contractions. The muscle then contracts from an already partially contracted position, producing greater force than that produced by a normal twitch. Rapid signals from the nervous system causes this to occur quite often; each time, the muscle is more contracted prior to the next signal and subsequent contraction. In this way, the contractions summate to produce a greater muscular force than the force of a single simple twitch. At some point, the neural impulses arrive at so rapid a rate, that the muscle has absolutely no time to relax between impulses. It is at this point that the muscle has reached a state of tetanus. Overwhelming a muscle with demands beyond its ability to receive new nutrients and oxygen yields accumulation of lactic acid, the source of muscle fatigue. Muscles, when not producing movement, still remain somewhat taut or maintain muscle tone (tonus).

67. (D)   68. (A)   69. (E)   70. (C)

Annelids, or segmented worms, display a high degree of somatic segmentation. Arthropods ("arthro" = joint + "pods" = foot), such as insects, have many jointed appendages. There is a great deal of evidence to support the statement that echinoderms are more closely related to chordates than any other group (both undergo cleavage that is indeterminate and radial during their ontogenies; both are deuterostomes). All mollusks possess a muscular foot.

71.   **(B)**

The cortex is the deep layer of primarily parenchymal cells beneath the outer epidermis. The cells store starch.

72.   **(A)**

Epidermis is the single-layered outer covering tissue. Root epidermis has no waxy cuticle, since its function is water absorption.

73.   **(D)**

Tubular cells of xylem are in the stele, or vascular conducting core. The starlike points formed by thick-walled xylem cells alternate with patches of phloem. Xylem plays a role in water and mineral transportation.

74.   **(D)**

The lower epidermal layer has stomata for gas exchange.

75.   **(A)**

Cuticle is the waxy layer that covers both the upper and the lower epidermis of a leaf and it is generally thicker on the upper epidermis. This protects the internal tissue of a leaf from excessive water loss, from fungal infection, and from mechanical injury.

76.   **(B)**

Internal parenchyma cells contain chloroplasts for photosynthesis. Parenchyma cells lie in the entire region between the upper and the lower epidermis, forming a soft tissue called mesophyll. The upper palisade mesophyll is composed of vertically arranged cylindrical parenchyma cells. The lower spongy mesophyll consists of irregularly shaped parenchyma cells. Intercellular spaces in these two mesophyll layers are important in communication with the stomata for gas exchange. A high chloroplast density occurs within the upper palisade mesophyll. This gives the plant an advantage, in that the upper surface of a leaf facing the sun's rays receives most sunlight and photosynthesis can then be carried out at its optimal rate.

77.   **(E)**

The intercellular space in the spongy mesophyll usually has a 100% humidity. A thin film of water is formed on the surface of mesophyll cells. Gases dissolve in this water film before they enter into the cells.

78.   **(A)**

The pituitary gland is composed of an anterior and a posterior lobe. The stalk of the posterior lobe is connected to the hypothalamus. Antidiuretic hormone (ADH) is produced in the hypothalamus and stored in the posterior pituitary. Upon nervous stimulation from the hypothalamus, the posterior pituitary releases ADH which acts on kidney tubule to reabsorb water.

79.   **(C)**

The pancreas secretes insulin to lower blood sugar and maintain equilibrium.

80.   **(D)**

The adrenal glands produce adrenaline. This hormone is a well-known constrictor of blood vessels. The principle demonstrated here is that of negative feedback: a stimulus met by a response that reverses the trend of the stimulus. A dropping blood pressure must be opposed and corrected. Constricting blood vessels forces the same amount of blood to travel through a region of decreased volume; this causes a rise in blood pressure.

81.   **(D)**

The hormone aldosterone is secreted by the adrenal cortex to promote sodium reabsorption in the kidney.

82. **(C)**   83. **(B)**   84. **(D)**   85. **(A)**

The answers to questions 82 - 85 are self-explanatory.

86.   **(A)**

Producers are the first organisms in a food chain. Through photosynthesis, producers obtain a great amount of energy to build the highest biomass among the different trophic levels in an ecosystem.

87.   **(C)**

After the producer tier at A, the primary consumers (herbivores) are next, at B. Secondary consumers, carnivores, compose the next food chain link and biomass tier.

88.   **(A)**

Since the extracellular environment has a 95% concentration of water, the extracellular environment has a greater concentration of water than the intracellular environment does. Therefore, water will flow <u>into</u> the cell due to osmosis. Terms of "tonicity" refer to the solute concentration in water. The inside cell setting has a higher, <u>hyper</u>, solute concentration. Its solute concentration is not less, <u>hypo</u>, or equal, <u>iso</u>, to the extracellular environment.

89.　　**(C)**

As explained in solution 88, water will flow into the cell. Therefore, the extracellular environment will lose water.

90.　　**(B)**

Osmosis is the movement of water from an area of a higher level of concentration to one of lower concentration through a semipermeable membrane. Water concentration is higher outside, 95%, and lower inside. The semipermeable membrane allows it to flow in.

The cell will eventually rupture, or lyse.

91. **(B)**　92. **(E)**

The complete Punnett square for the cross AaBb x Aabb appears as follows:

	AB	Ab	aB	ab
Ab	AABb 1	AAbb 2	AaBb 3	Aabb 4
ab	AaBb 5	Aabb 6	aaBb 7	aabb 8

Only cells 3 and 5 (1/4 of total) show genetic recombinations heterozygous for both gene pairs. Of all the genotypes listed in problem 92, only aaBB does not appear in the Punnett square, and therefore is not a possible genotype for the offspring.

93.　　**(B)**

If base #2 is cytosine, then base #10 must be guanine, which is the complement of cytosine. Base #6, therefore, must be complement of base #10 (guanine), or cytosine.

94.　　**(D)**

If RNA base #7 is uracil, than DNA base #11 must be adenine. (Uracil, not thymine, is the RNA complement of adenine). DNA base #3 must therefore be thymine.

95.   **(C)**

A left-hand DNA sequence CGCT is complementary to a right-hand base sequence of GCGA. This is transcribed as CGCU.

96.   **(B)**

Blood pressure is greatest in blood vessels closest to the heart and decreases as blood flow away from the heart. Aorta, arteries, anterioles, capillaries, venules, veins, and vena cava are the blood vessels arranged in order of decreasing blood pressure. Such a gradient of blood pressure is essential for a one-direction flow and is a result of friction between the flowing blood and the wall of blood vessels.

97.   **(D)**

This is the capillary end that connects with a venule, is lower in pressure, and receives carbon dioxide and waste products from cells for transport to venules and veins.

98.   **(B)**

This term best indicates the two-way traffic of molecules between the blood and the cells around the capillary.

99.   **(C)**

Blood, and its hemoglobin, flows to the lung to load up oxygen. Hence, hemoglobin is highly saturated with oxygen.

100.   **(E)**

Blood hemoglobin is relatively unsaturated at tissue cells, as it liberates the oxygen to these cells.

SECTION II

ESSAY I

Enzymes are globular proteins with distinct surface geometries that result from the folding of the amino acid sequence of a polypeptide chain. They accelerate the rate of a reaction toward equilibrium without changing the position of equilibrium. This catalyzation makes reactions occur within a reasonable time frame as well as within physiological constraints such as temperature. Enzymes lower the activation energy of a reaction, which allows the reaction to proceed.

Contained within the conformation of the enzyme is an active site, which is specific to a certain substrate, or substance, upon which the enzyme acts. The substrate binds to the active site through weak non-covalent bonds such as hydrogen bonds, van der Waals forces, and hydrophobic interactions that arise between the active groups of the amino acid and the substrate. This binding of the substrate to the active site distorts the geometry of the enzyme and changes the concentrations of the reactants, which make the reaction progress.

Graph I shows the rate of two enzyme-catalyzed reactions. The steeper slope for enzyme A indicates a faster rate of catalyzation than B. Enzyme A has a lower level of production than enzyme B and therefore gives less product. Since the effectiveness of a catalyst is determined by how quickly a reaction reaches its equilibrium, and the maximum production corresponds to a property of the reaction that is unaffected by enzymes, enzyme A is more efficient than B.

Enzyme A exhibits its maximum activity at a pH of 3; enzyme B's greatest activity was at 8, according to Graph II. An enzyme sharing the same characteristics given of enzyme A is pepsin, which is found in the stomach. It breaks down proteins by cleaving the peptide bond between amino acids. Gastric juice containing hydrochloric acid is secreted during digestion, making the environment of the stomach acidic, and activating pepsinogen to become pepsin.

Enzyme B is characteristic of trypsin, an enzyme found in the small intestine. It is secreted by the pancreas and is also a proteolytic enzyme. Its inactive form is trypsinogen. When bile is secreted, full of bicarbonate ions, in the small intestine, it makes the chyme from the stomach alkaline. This pH change stimulates enterokinases to cleave trypsinogen to become trypsin.

As carbon dioxide levels increase in the bloodstream, the pH of the blood lowers from its approximately neutral pH. This acidic change affects the structure and activity of enzymes. As evidenced in Graph II, different enzymes have varying activities and efficiencies at similar pH. Therefore, making the blood more acidic could result in a denaturation of enzymes, and thus, a loss of specific 3-D conformation. The consequence is a loss of function, since it can no longer bind the specific substrate. Acidic pHs could also activate enzymes that function more efficiently at lower pHs. Cumulative effects can be felt on the level of metabolism, whose function hinges on the positive and negative activity of enzymes to alter the availability of substrates.

ESSAY II

A mutation is a change in the base sequence of a gene which leads to the formation of a new allele. Mutations can be classified into point mutations, chromosomal mutations, and genomic mutations.

Point mutations affect small regions of a chromosome. Substitution is a point mutation in which nucleotides are replaced by different ones. Substitution can occur spontaneously through the mispairing of bases during DNA replication. Deletion causes a gene to have several bases less than normal while addition gives the opposite result.

Chromosomal mutations affect larger regions of a chromosome and are usually initiated by a breakage in the DNA backbone. Translocation is the interchange of chromosome segments between two nonhomologous chromosomes. It is different from crossing-over, a normal genetic process that gives rise to variation. Crossing-over involves two homologous chromosomes. Deletion results in a karyotype that has lost a segment or segments of chromosome. A segment of chromosome without a centromere does not attach to any chromosome, it does not move with the spindle fiber during cell division, and is not incorporated into either daughter cell. A karyotype has a chromosome longer than normal because of a duplicate segment at its end. When a broken segment reattaches to its original position in a reversed order, a change in genetic order results without loss or gain of total gene count. This is called inversion. Translocation and inversion cause new groupings of genes. The favorable groupings are conserved by natural selection while the unfavorable ones are selected out.

Genomic mutations involve changes in the number of chromosomes present in the karyotype. This abnormality results from nondisjunction, a process in which homologous chromosomes fail to separate and move to opposite poles during cell division. This results in one daughter cell receiving an extra chromosome while the other daughter cell receives one less. Trisomy is a condition where three chromosomes of one type are present in the nucleus. For example, Down's Syndrome is also called Trisomy 21 because of the presence of three chromosome #21 in the nucleus of the affected individual.

Messenger RNA (mRNA) is synthesized in the nucleus by the process of transcription from a DNA template. mRNA is transported to the cytoplasm for translation. Ribosomes convert the nucleotide sequence of mRNA into the amino acid sequence of the polypeptide chain. Ribosomes consist of two subunits. The smaller subunit is responsible for binding the mRNA, and the larger subunit contains the enzymes that catalyze the formation of peptide bonds. An mRNA molecule associated with several ribosomes is called a polysome, which allows protein to be synthesized before mRNA becomes degraded. Protein synthesis is invariably started at AUG, the start codon. mRNA is translated from the 5' end to the 3' end and polypeptides are synthesized from the left amino end to the right carboxyl end. Specific amino acids are brought to the mRNA ribosome complex by tRNA which has an anticodon complementary to the triplet codon of the mRNA. Three nucleotides of the mRNA sequence are read at a time. The translocation of a ribosome along the mRNA, three nucleotides to the right, is an energy requiring process. During protein synthesis, adjacent amino acids are linked together by peptide bonds formed through dehydration. Once a stop codon is encountered, protein synthesis stops and the complex of mRNA, ribosome, and nascent polypeptide chain dissociates. There are three stop codons among the 64 triplet codes and these stop codons have no tRNA anticodon complementary to them. Some nascent polypeptides have to be modified before they become useful.

A single base substitution changes a codon to another of the 64 possible genetic codes. Substitution at the third base of a codon may not cause any effect because some amino acids are coded by multiple codons which differ from each other at the third base position, e.g., both UUA and UUG code for leucine. However, the results of an amino acid substitution can be serious. The degree of seriousness increases when the exchanged amino acid belongs to a different charge group, such as a nonpolar amino acid being substituted by a polar one, etc. Also, amino acid substitution at the functional site of a protein, such as the active site of an enzyme, has a more serious effect than at other locations. Sometimes, base substitution changes a coding codon to a stop codon, and this leads to premature termination of protein synthesis. The effect is deleterious if this extra stop codon is close to the start codon.

Deletion or addition of a three base multiple results in the deletion or insertion of amino acids. The significance depends on the location of the deletion or insertion. If it happens on a region such that the functional site of a protein is malformed, this mutation can be deleterious. Deletion or addition of bases not at a multiple of three causes a reading-frame shift, where the order in which the mRNA is read is shifted according to the number of amino acids. Starting from the site of mutation, the mRNA is translated into a different polypeptide chain. Proteins formed this way cannot carry out their normal functions. This type of mutation is usually deleterious as well.

ESSAY III

The original source of energy to any ecosystem of the planet earth is the sun. Its radiant energy is trapped by chlorophyll-containing organisms. Through photosynthesis, such organisms convert the energy of light into the stored energy of chemical bonds of sugars, the product of photosynthesis. From this initial process, different populations of organisms in a community are integrated by nutrition, their feeding levels in a food chain.

Photosynthetic organisms serve in the role of producers and as initiators of the food chain. Subsequent links in the chain denote different levels of consumers; primary consumer, secondary consumer, etc. and decomposers. Primary consumers in a given food chain are herbivores, plant eaters. Subsequent links are carnivores, eating animal flesh, and decomposers correspond to the end of a food chain and consist of bacteria and fungi, the organisms of decay. As a concrete example: oak tree (producer) - insect (primary consumer, herbivore) - snake (secondary consumer, carnivore) - owl (tertiary consumer, carnivore, etc.) An example from a pond could be: alga - minnow - sunfish - bass - grizzly bear.

Each chemical energy transfer, link by link in the food chain, is accompanied by a major conversion to heat. Useful chemical energy remains stored in chemical bonds. It becomes a component of organism protoplasm, available by feeding through predation at the next food chain link. Because of the large heat conversion at each step, up to 90% of the number of links in a food chain is limited usually to four or five. Heat is dissipated and cannot be changed back to a usable chemical form. Therefore, constant useful energy input is required from sunlight and photosynthesis converting light energy into chemical energy for utilization by other organisms. Turn off the sunlight to the earth and food chains will eventually run down.

Materials, on the other hand, are reusable. A copper atom can remain a copper atom if it is not changed chemically. It can continually be reshuttled between the biotic and abiotic sectors of the environment. Current shortage of materials, as with certain metals, stems from a lack in efficiency of recycling to keep such materials available. Without such recycling, a metal is kept tied up in one sector. It is thus unavailable while taken out of circulation.

One simple example of such a biogeochemical cycle is the phosphorous cycle. Phosphorous is an essential element to protoplasm (bio), but has its abiotic reservoir in the earth's geological structure (geo). Acceleration of mining and erosion practices has released large amounts of rock phosphorous into waterways as phosphate ions. The dissolved phosphate is used by plants and reaches animals through the food chain. Phosphatizing bacteria work on plant and animal carcasses and wastes, returning the phosphorous to the waterways. This return and subsequent reuse is characteristic of circulation or a cycle.

ESSAY IV

Erythrocytes synthesize, store, and transport hemoglobins. Hemoglobin binds O_2 and CO_2. Its affinities for these gases depend on the pH of the medium modulated by CO_2 concentration. Mature erythrocytes are enucleated in higher vertebrates and are biconcave disk-shaped. These special structures give the erythrocyte a larger surface area to accommodate hemoglobin and the diffusion of gases across its membrane. Hemoglobin embedded in the stroma of an erythrocyte is advantageous in that no free floating hemoglobin is present to disturb the osmotic relationship between blood and tissue fluid.

Neurons are capable of conducting and transmitting electric impulses rapidly. They consist of a cell body containing the nucleus and other organelles, extensively branched dendrites, and a long, single axon which may branch at its terminal end.

Dendrites receive and direct impulses to the cell body. Axons transmit impulses away from the cell body. The capability of forming synapsis with other neurons and target organs allows neurons to form long conducting pathways to various parts of the body. Axons in the central nervous system are wrapped in glial cells while those outside the central nervous system are enveloped in Schwann cells. These two kinds of cells form myelin sheaths that speed up the conduction of impulses in the axon.

Muscles in our body can be differentiated into skeletal muscles, smooth muscles, and cardiac muscles. Skeletal muscle fiber is cylindrical, coenocytic (with many nuclei) with a striated appearance. Bundles of skeletal muscle fibers attach to bone and are responsible for rapid action under the control of the voluntary nervous system. Smooth muscle fibers are nonstriated, thin, and elongated cells, and they form a sheet of muscle tissue which serves as the walls of the viscera and blood vessels. Cardiac muscle fibers are striated, their activity similar to smooth muscle. Muscle fiber is composed of a sheath enclosing numerous myofibrils. The contractile materials of the myofibril are thin actin and thick myosin filaments. A special structure called a crossbridge is formed when the globular heads of myosin filament are in contact with the actin molecule of the thin filament. This crossbridge is responsible for the sliding together of the thick and thin filaments which produce muscle contraction.

Epidermal cells are relatively flat with a thicker outer cell wall. These irregularly shaped cells interlock to form the surface tissue of stem, roots, and leaf with no intercellular spaces for the prevention of water loss. Some epidermal cells are specialized to perform different functions. For example, guard cells are sausage-shaped epidermal cells that regulate the size of stomata. Epidermal cells of root tissue are devoid of cuticle and have hairlike processes to facilitate water absorption.

Tracheids and vessel cells are the two main elements of the xylem of plant's vascular tissue. Tracheids are elongated, tapering cells with pits on their cell walls. These pits are particularly numerous at the tapering ends and the vertically linked pattern of the tracheids form an upward transport system for water and dissolved substances. Tracheids have liquefied secondary cell walls which serve as a supportive structure for the plant.

Parenchyma cells are relatively unspecialized vegetative cells found in roots, stems, and leaves. They have a thin primary cell wall and usually lack a secondary cell wall. They are capable of cell division. Parenchyma cells in leaves contain a high density of chloroplasts and are photosynthetic. Those located in stem and root serve to store nutrients and water. Turgid parenchyma cells help to give shape and support to the plant. Their large vacuoles take in water and push against the cell wall to maintain turgidity.

THE ADVANCED PLACEMENT EXAMINATION IN

BIOLOGY

TEST II

ADVANCED PLACEMENT BIOLOGY EXAM II

SECTION I

100 Questions
80 Minutes

DIRECTIONS: For each of the following questions or incomplete sentences, there are five choices. choose the answer which is most correct. Darken the corresponding space on your answer sheet.

1. Semiconservative replication of DNA refers to the fact that

   (A) the daughter DNA is an entirely new duplex and thus the original DNA is intact

   (B) pieces of the old and new DNA duplexes are jumbled together in the daughter generation

   (C) each strand of the parent DNA serves as a template for the synthesis of its new partner strand. Thus one strand is conserved in each new double helix

   (D) DNA replication is modest in its ATP requirements

   (E) DNA replication occurs by base pairing between adenine and thymine and between guanine and cytosine

2. The following statements about the codon are true EXCEPT

   (A) The codon is a triplet of nucleotides on messenger RNA (mRNA)

   (B) The codon is a triplet of bases on transfer RNA (tRNA)

   (C) The codon base pairs with the anticodon

   (D) The codon is degenerate, i.e. most amino acids are represented by more than one codon

(E) A codon represents an amino acid, or a signal to initiate or terminate protein synthesis

3. Wobble of the anticodon

(A) refers to the freedom in the pairing of the third base of the codon

(B) refers to the inaccuracy of base pairing, i.e. if adenine were to pair with guanine, or uracil with cytosine

(C) is represented, for example, by the codons UUG and CUG, both of which code for leucine

(D) refers to imprecision in the pairing of the first base of the codon

(E) occurs only in initiating and terminating codons

4. The dark reactions of photosynthesis, in which carbon dioxide fixation occurs, are called

(A) Krebs cycle   (D) Cyclic AMP

(B) Calvin cycle   (E) Carbon cycle

(C) Cori cycle

5. All of the following processes occur in the nitrogen cycle, EXCEPT

(A) Ammonification   (D) Denitrification

(B) Nitrification   (E) Nitrogen fixation

(C) Deamination

6. All the statements about circadian rhythms are true, EXCEPT

(A) They cycle over a 24-hour period

(B) They are exemplified in plants by leaf orientations, which change from day to night

(C) They are exemplified in humans by the sleep-wake cycle

(D) They are exemplified in humans by changes in body temperature throughout the day and night

(E) They are entirely controlled by exogenous factors (such as the light-dark cycle)

7. In comparing photosynthesis to respiration, which of the following statements is true?

(A) Carbohydrate is produced in respiration, but not in photosynthesis

(B) Oxygen is produced in respiration, but not in photosynthesis

(C) Carbon dioxide is produced in photosynthesis, but not in respiration

(D) Water is produced in photosynthesis, but not in respiration

(E) Oxygen is produced in photosynthesis, but not in respiration

8. All of the following fates for sugar produced during photosynthesis are possible in a plant cell, EXCEPT

(A) its polymerization into starch for storage purposes

(B) its decomposition for energy production

(C) its polymerization into glycogen for storage purposes

(D) its use in the synthesis of other organic molecules

(E) its use in the synthesis of sucrose

9. An enzyme functions to increase the rate of a reaction by

(A) increasing the concentration of the substrate

(B) decreasing the E_a (energy of activation)

(C) competing with the substrate

(D) breaking down ATP

(E) hydrolyzing the substrate

10. PKU (phenylketonuria) is an example of an inborn error of metabolism. These "errors" refer to

(A) congenital birth defects

(B) hormonal overproduction

(C) inherited lack of an enzyme

(D) nondisjunction

(E) atrophy of endocrine glands

11. All living organisms are classified as eukaryotes (true nucleus) or prokaryotes (before the nucleus). The only example of a prokaryote listed below is

(A) AIDS virus   (D) an oak tree

(B) *E. coli*   (E) amoeba

(C) *Homo sapiens*

12. With respect to the electron transport chain and chemiosmosis, all of the following statements are true EXCEPT

(A) each NADH yields three ATPs

(B) each $FADH_2$ yields two ATPs

(C) the cytochrome enzymes utilize NAD^+ and FAD as their coenzyme

(D) hydrogen ions are pumped from the mitochondrial matrix into the intermembranal space

(E) the cytochrome enzymes utilize iron as their cofactors

13. All of the following statements concerning ATP are true EXCEPT

(A) it can be formed in anaerobic glycolysis

(B) it can be formed in aerobic respiration

(C) it can be formed in muscle from phosphocreatine

(D) it can be formed from cAMP (cyclic AMP)

(E) it can be formed from ADP

Questions 14 - 15 refer to the diagram below.

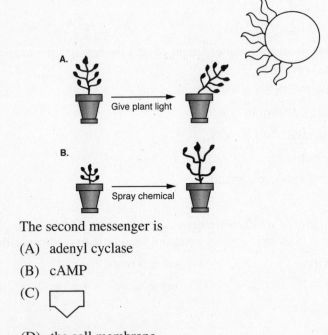

14. The second messenger is

(A) adenyl cyclase

(B) cAMP

(C)

(D) the cell membrane

(E) ATP

15. The symbol ⬔ represents

    (A) a steroid hormone (D) glucose
    (B) an operator   (E) an antibody
    (C) a protein hormone

16. Lichen, in which an alga and a fungus live in harmony, is an example of

    (A) mutualism   (D) predation
    (B) commensalism   (E) competition
    (C) parasitism

17. Konrad Lorenz researched the phenomenon of imprinting. To test his ideas, he had newly hatched ducks see him first. Subsequently, the ducks were allowed to see their mother. These ducks would tend to follow

    (A) their true mother   (D) no one in particular
    (B) other ducks   (E) Konrad Lorenz
    (C) other chickens

18. The binomial nomenclature for man is *Homo sapiens*. Classify man, in proper order starting with its Kingdom and working through its order.

    (A) Chordata, Animalia, Primates, Mammalia, Vertebrata
    (B) Animalia, Chordata, Vertebrata, Mammalia, Primates
    (C) Animalia, Vertebrata, Chordata, Mammalia, Primates
    (D) Primates, Mammalia, Vertabrata, Chordata, Animalia
    (E) Animalia, Chordata, Vertabrata, Primates, Mammalia

19. All of the following structures in a leaf may function in photosynthesis, EXCEPT:

    (A) cuticle   (D) chloroplasts
    (B) mesophyll   (E) spongy layer
    (C) guard cells

20. Which of the following statements does not apply to members of Class Aves?

    (A) They have feathers
    (B) They have compact hollow bones
    (C) They are homeothermic
    (D) They excrete urea
    (E) They use song in mating behavior

21. Darwin's theory of natural selection includes all of the following stipulations EXCEPT

   (A) every organism produces more organisms than can survive

   (B) due to competition, not all organisms survive

   (C) some organisms are more fit, i.e., they are able to survive better in the environment

   (D) the difference in survivability is due to variations between organisms

   (E) variation is due, at least in part, to mutations

22. Hemophilia is a disease caused by a sex-linked recessive gene on the X chromosome; therefore,

   (A) females have twice the likelihood of having the disease, since they have two X chromosomes

   (B) mothers can pass the gene with equal probability to either a son or daughter

   (C) females can never have the disease, they can only be carriers

   (D) inbreeding has no effect on the incidence of the disease, since it is purely sex-linked

   (E) a hemophiliac son is always produced if his father has the gene and, hence, the disease

23. All of the following statements about vitamin D are correct EXCEPT

   (A) a deficiency causes rickets.

   (B) it can be produced in the skin in the presence of ultraviolet light.

   (C) dairy products are a good source.

   (D) night blindness may result from a deficiency.

   (E) it helps absorb calcium from the digestive tract and helps incorporate the calcium into bone.

24. In certain flowers, color is inherited by incomplete dominance. A cross between a homozygous red flower (RR) and a homozygous white flower (rr) will always yield pink flowers. When these pink flowers are subsequently crossed, the expected probabilities may include:

   (A) 25% pink

   (B) 50% red

   (C) 0% white

   (D) 50% pink

   (E) 100% pink

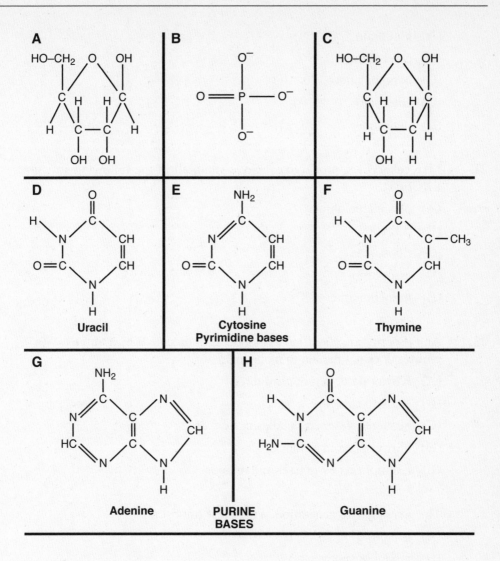

A HO–CH₂ O OH

B O⁻

C HO–CH₂ O OH

D Uracil

E Cytosine
Pyrimidine bases

F Thymine

G Adenine

H PURINE BASES Guanine

25.   The structures of the components of a nucleotide are illustrated above. The pentose sugars, the phosphate group and the five nitrogenous bases are depicted. The two molecules that would be found only in DNA, but not RNA are represented by the letters

(A) A and D

(B) B and E

(C) C and F

(D) C and D

(E) A and F

26.   The relatively large size of the mammalian brain, allowing for greater learning, association, and memory, is due to the enlargement of the

(A) hindbrain

(B) cerebellum

(C) hypothalamus

(D) cerebrum

(E) midbrain

27. Like eukaryotes, prokaryotes may contain all of the following structures EXCEPT

(A) plasma membrane

(B) cell wall

(C) ribosomes

(D) cytoplasm

(E) mitochondria

28. Angiosperms are classified as monocots or dicots. Which of the following phrases does not pertain to monocots?

(A) Flower parts in groups of three

(B) Netted leaf veins

(C) Scattered vascular bundles in stem

(D) Flower parts in groups of six

(E) Exemplified by grasses and orchids

29. The gametophyte generation in the plant life cycle

(A) is diploid

(B) produces spores

(C) is haploid

(D) has become more dominant in the evolution of plants

(E) is a zygote

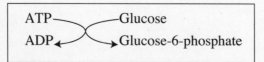

30. The enzyme-catalyzed sequence depicted above represents

(A) the dephosphorylation of glucose

(B) the phosphorylation of ADP

(C) the first step of glycolysis

(D) phosphofructokinase activity

(E) a reaction occurring within the mitochondrial matrix

31. In humans, there are many anatomical adaptations that function to increase surface area for chemical reactions and transport mechanisms. All of the following are examples EXCEPT

(A) the alveoli of the lungs

(B) the microvilli of the small intestine

(C) the cristae of the inner mitochondrial membrane

(D) the villi of the small intestine

(E) the sensory hairs (cilia) in the cochlea of the inner ear

32. Concerning the development of the vertebrate brain,

(A) the prosencephalon consists of the pons and cerebellum.

(B) the mesencephalon develops into the myelencephalon and meten-cephalon.

(C) the rhombencephalon consists of the pons, medulla oblongata, and cerebellum.

(D) the telencephalon develops into the prosencephalon and diencephalon.

(E) the cerebellum is part of the diencephalon.

33. Adaptations of desert plants to hot, dry environments, may include all of the following, EXCEPT

(A) wide spacing between plants

(B) deep penetrating roots

(C) deciduous leaves

(D) thick, waxy cuticles

(E) superficial stomata

34. There are various types of plant stems that have different functions. Which of the following is not a type of stem?

(A) tendrils

(B) nodes

(C) tubers

(D) rhizomes

(E) corms

35.   Acquired characteristics

   (A) refer to traits inherited as genes

   (B) are not transmitted to the next generation

   (C) are the basis of Darwin's theory of natural selection

   (D) are exemplified by the lengthening of the giraffe's neck over evolution-ary time, due to stretching toward trees

   (E) can, for instance, explain the lack of pigment in an albino

36.   All of the following statements about embryonic induction are true, EX-CEPT

   (A) it is exemplified by the development of the vertebrate lens

   (B) neurulation is an example

   (C) it refers to the interaction whereby certain cells can stimulate the development of nearby cells

   (D) it refers to cleavage

   (E) it most likely occurs due to chemical factors

37.   Which of the following statements concerning alternation of generations in plants is true?

   (A) The diploid generation consists of gametophytes

   (B) The haploid generation consists of sporophytes

   (C) Gametes result from mitosis

   (D) Gametophytes result from the fusion of gametes

   (E) Meiosis produces sporophytes

38.   Deviation from a Hardy-Weinberg equilibrium may be the result of

   (A) absence of mutation

   (B) large population size

   (C) migration

   (D) no natural selection

   (E) lack of differential reproduction

39.   The period of human gestation is divided into three trimesters. The event that is correctly matched to its trimester of occurrence is the following:

   (A) the third trimester is characterized by development and differentiation.

   (B) the greatest growth in size occurs in the first trimester.

   (C) the limb buds develop in the first trimester.

(D) kicking is felt by the mother in the first trimester.

(E) organ development begins in the second trimester.

40. Which of the following statements about the gymnosperms is not true?

(A) They are seed plants

(B) They include ginkgo and cycads

(C) They are cone-bearers

(D) They are the flowering plants

(E) They are referred to as the "naked seed" plants

DIRECTIONS: The following groups of questions have five lettered choices followed by a list of diagrams, numbered phrases, sentences, or words. For each numbered diagram, phrase, sentence, or word choose the heading which most directly applies. Blacken the correct space on the answer sheet. Each heading may be used once, more than once, or not at all.

Questions 41 - 43 refer to the diagram below showing DNA replication.

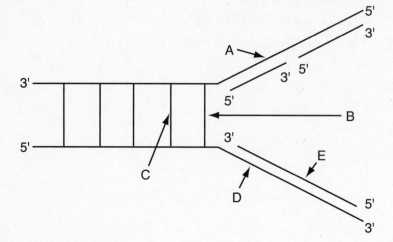

41.   The lagging strand

42.   A base pair

43.   The replication fork

Questions 44 - 47 refer to various transport processes encountered in biology

    (A) Transfusion

    (B) Translocation

    (C) Transcription

    (D) Translation

    (E) Transpiration

44.   This nuclear process refers to the transfer of information from DNA to RNA

45.   The transfer of sucrose in sieve tubes.

46.   Protein synthesis as directed by messenger RNA.

47.   The introduction of blood directly into the bloodstream.

Questions 48 - 50 refer to the stages of the cell cycle.

    (A) Anaphase

    (B) Prophase

    (C) Interphase

    (D) Metaphase

    (E) Telophase

48.   Cytokinesis accompanies this stage of mitosis.

49.   This phase, in which DNA is replicated, is not part of mitosis

50.   This stage of mitosis is characterized by the condensation of the chromo-somes.

Questions 51 - 54 deal with anatomical and physiological aspects of the first meiotic prophase (Prophase I).

    (A) Synapsis

    (B) Crossing over

    (C) Sister chromatids

    (D) Chiasma

    (E) Centromeres

51.   The site of crossover between attached homologous chromosomes.

52.   The constricted point on the chromosome at which sister chromatids are attached.

53.   Close pairing of homologous chromosomes to form tetrads.

54.   Non-sister chromatids of homologous chromosomes exchange segments.

Questions 55 - 56 distinguish between different biomes.

    (A) Tundra

    (B) Taiga

    (C) Desert

    (D) Tropical rainforest

    (E) Deciduous forest

55.   The Arctic exemplifies this biome.

56.   Hot humid weather and no seasonal changes are characteristic of this biome.

Questions 57 - 59 deal with different mechanisms that cause reproductive isolation.

    (A) Mechanical isolation

    (B) Gamete isolation

    (C) Hybrid inviability

    (D) Behavioral isolation

    (E) Temporal isolation

57.   Size, shape, and length of reproductive organs influence mating.

58.   Pollination/mating is a seasonal event.

59.   Courtship rituals are required for mating.

Questions 60 - 62 distinguish five animal phyla.

    (A) Porifera

    (B) Arthropoda

    (C) Echinodermata

    (D) Mollusca

    (E) Platyhelminthes

60.   These freshwater and marine filter feeders are sessile and contain spongin or spicules as supportive structures.

61.   This phylum includes the parasitic flukes and the tapeworms.

62.   As is phylum Chordata, this phylum is classified as Deuterostome.

Questions 63 - 66 show examples of organic nutrients.

    (A) monosaccharide

    (B) disaccharide

    (C) oligosaccharide

    (D) saccharin

    (E) polysaccharide

63.   Fructose

64.   Lactose

65.   Sucrose

66.   Starch

Questions 67 - 70 describe different human cells that are to be matched with the organelle that is most associated with the cell's function.

(A) Mitochondria

(B) Cilium

(C) Rough endoplasmic reticulum

(D) Lysosome

(E) Flagella

67. Especially numerous in skeletal muscle cells

68. Found only in sperm cells

69. Leukocyte

70. Pancreatic acinar cell

Questions 71 - 72 refer to the following blood-typing experiment. Two students type their blood in biology lab using antiserum A and antiserum B. The results of their tests are below:

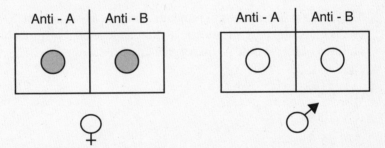

71. When they marry and have children, the possible phenotypes will be:

(A) AB only

(B) Type O only

(C) Type A and Type B

(D) Type AB and Type O

(E) Type B only

72. The male ( ) depicted above is called a universal donor because

(A) he has no antigens on his red blood cells

(B) he has both antibodies in his plasma

 (C) he has no antibodies in his plasma

 (D) he has no antibodies on his red blood cells

 (E) he has no antigens in his plasma

Questions 73 - 74 refer to the pedigree below. A square indicates a male; a circle indicates a female. A hollow shape indicates the lack of trait; a darkened shape indicates the presence of trait.

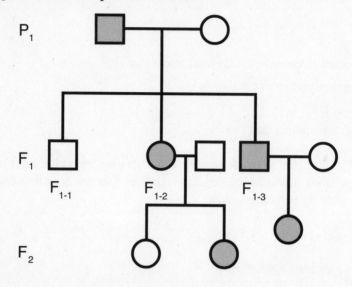

73. The trait, a preauricular gill remnant, which is a tiny hole in the front of the ear, is transmitted by an autosomal dominant gene. The probability that the children of F_{1-1}, should he marry an unafflicted woman, will have the trait is

 (A) 50%

 (B) 0%

 (C) 100%

 (D) 25%

 (E) Cannot be determined with the information given.

74. F_{1-3} and his wife just had a baby girl afflicted with this trait. The probability that their next son will have the trait is

 (A) 0% - half the kids should have the trait, and one just received it so the next one should not.

 (B) 50%

 (C) 100% - all the sons will show the trait

 (D) 25%

 (E) Cannot be determined with the information given.

Questions 75 - 76 refer to the drawings of the two plants. You have two plants in which you wish to stimulate growth. Plant A receives light and responds as indicated below. Plant B receives a chemical and responds as below.

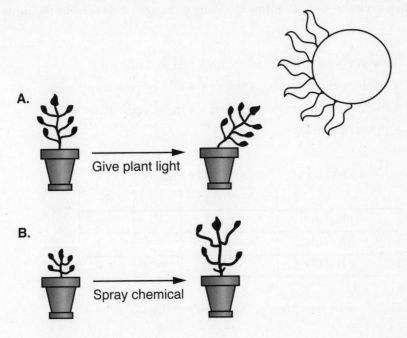

A.   Give plant light

B.   Spray chemical

75.   The hormone responsible for the growth movements seen in plant A is

    (A)   auxin

    (B)   florigen

    (C)   cytokinin

    (D)   abscisic acid

    (E)   ethylene

76.   The chemical given to plant B, a genetic dwarf, must be

    (A)   ethylene

    (B)   gibberellins

    (C)   cytokinins

    (D)   growth hormone

    (E)   florigen

Questions 77 - 80 refer to an experiment in digestion. Digestions of fat yields glycerol and fatty acids. You wish to determine if and how bile salts and pancreatic juice affect fat digestion. You prepare three tubes as indicated below. While incubating them in a 37°C bath, you measure the pH in the test tubes over the next 45 minutes. Your data are presented in the table below.

Tube A contains 4 mls. of cream + pinch of bile salts

Tube B contains 4 mls. of cream + 4 mls. of pancreatic juice

Tube C contains 4 mls. of cream + 4 mls. of pancreatic juice + pinch of bile salts

Data on pH		Time (mins.)		
	0	15	30	45
pH-Tube A	7	7	7	7
pH-Tube B	7	6.9	6.7	6.3
pH-Tube C	7	6.3	6.0	5.4

77.   Digestion of the cream occurs most rapidly in

(A) Tube A

(B) Tube B

(C) Tube C

(D) No digestion occurred

(E) Cannot be determined from the data

78.   If you only have two test tubes with which to do your experiment and you wish to figure out the role of bile salts, it is necessary to prepare

(A) Tubes A and B

(B) Tubes B and C

(C) Tubes A and C

(D) Just Tube C

(E) Just Tube A

79.   It is clear that the ingredient necessary for digestion of fats is

(A) cream

(B) water

(C) bile salts

(D) pancreatic juice

(E) not in any of the tubes

80. The function of bile salts is to

    (A) digest the fat

    (B) chemically degrade the fat

    (C) emulsify the fat into smaller globules

    (D) activate the enzymes in pancreatic juice

    (E) acidify the solution which it is in

Questions 81 - 84 refer to a urinalysis report. A lab technician forgets to label three patients' recent urine samples and a sample of distilled water. He performs various tests on these samples to try to determine which urine belongs to which patient. One patient was on a high-salt diet; one was on a high-protein diet; and one had uncontrolled diabetes mellitus. The results of the tests on the three urine samples and the distilled water tube are shown below:

	A	B	C	D
Specify gravity	1.030	1.029	1.010	1.000
Glucose	negative	299 mg/dl	negative	negative
pH	6.3	5.2	5.0	7
Odor	aromatic	sweet	aromatic	none
Volume	130 mls	160 mls	96 mls	100 mls

81. The urine sample from the diabetic patient is in which test tube?

    (A) Tube A

    (B) Tube B

    (C) Tube C

    (D) Tube D

    (E) Cannot be determined from data available

82. Tube D must contain the distilled water because

    (A) by definition, the specific gravity of distilled water = 1.000

    (B) by definition, the pH of distilled water is 7

    (C) process of elimination leaves only Tube D for water

    (D) specific gravity is the weight of a volume of water divided by the weight of an equal volume of substance

    (E) there is no glucose in it

83.   The effect of a diuretic drug would most directly affect which of the following parameters?

(A) specific gravity

(B) glucose

(C) pH

(D) odor

(E) volume

84.   The tube with the highest concentration of hydrogen ions is

(A) Tube A

(B) Tube B

(C) Tube C

(D) Tube D

(E) Cannot be determined by the data available

The graph below indicates the interaction between a predator (solid) and prey (dotted) population over the years 1976 to 1980. Their population sizes are indicated on either side of the graph.

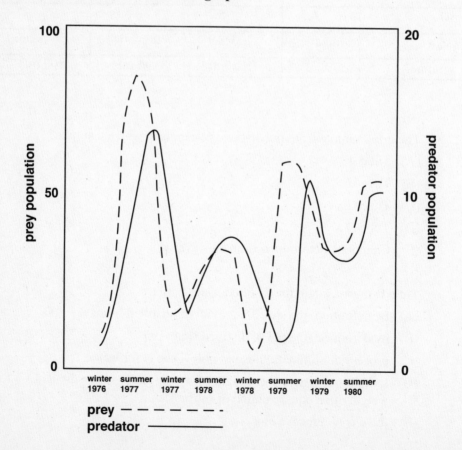

85.   The oscillations in the predator/prey population

(A) occur because an increase in prey population will increase predator population indefinitely.

(B) occur because an increase in prey population will allow an increase in predator population until the predators eat too many prey.

(C) occur because an increase in predator population causes a direct and immediate increase in prey population.

(D) occur because of seasonal changes

(E) are unique in this case and not seen in most predator/prey interactions.

86.   The drop in predator population during the winter months is probably due to

(A) cold

(B) snow

(C) drop in prey population

(D) hibernation

(E) coincidence

87.   The most mild winter probably occurred in the year

(A) 1976   (D) 1979

(B) 1977   (E) 1980

(C) 1978

88.   The peak prey population was achieved

(A) in the summer of 1977 with a population of 100

(B) in the summer of 1977 with a population of 75

(C) in the summer of 1977 with a population of 20

(D) in the summer of 1977 with a population of 15

(E) in the summer of 1977, population unknown

89.   In the winter of 1980, a chemical, toxic and fatal to the prey but not to the predator, is introduced into the environment; the subsequent effect to the predator will be

(A) no effect, since it is non-toxic to him

(B) a drop in population due to decreased food resources

(C) a rise in population

(D) independent of any changes in prey population

(E) a drop in population due to the yearly winter drop

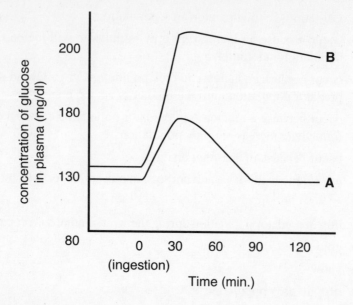

Questions **90 - 94 refer to the chart above, which illustrates this scenario: In a glucose tolerance test, two fasting subjects drink glucose solutions (in amounts that are proportional to their body weight). Plasma glucose levels are measured just before ingestion, and at 30-minute intervals for the next two hours.**

90.   The plasma glucose levels of the subjects, while still fasting, are

   (A) 0 minutes

   (B) 80 mg/dl

   (C) 130 mg/dl

   (D) 180 mg/dl

   (E) not depicted in the graph above

91.   Peak plasma glucose levels are reached

   (A) at the time of ingestion

   (B) at 30 minutes

   (C) at 60 minutes

   (D) at different times for the two subjects

   (E) at 30 mg/dl

92.   Graph A indicates

   (A) a normal response to glucose ingestion

   (B) a diabetic response to glucose ingestion

(C) a maximum plasma glucose level of 180 mg/dl

(D) a return to fasting glucose levels within a half hour

(E) a fasting glucose level of 130 mg/dl

93. Graph B indicates

(A) excess insulin has been secreted

(B) high tolerance to glucose

(C) a diabetic condition

(D) a maximum glucose level of 180 mg/dl

(E) rapid return to fasting glucose levels

94. Urinary excretion of glucose may occur

(A) in subject A

(B) in subject B

(C) in both subjects

(D) in neither subject

(E) but it is unrelated to plasma glucose levels

Questions 95 - 97 refer to transport processes through the cell membrane.

The following table indicates the effects of two cell poisons on the transport processes of the cell membrane. One group of cells was given ouabain, and another group was given cyanide. A "✓" indicates that the process is still functional, while an "**X**" indicates that the process cannot occur in the presence of the poison.

	Diffusion	Na$^+$-K$^+$ Pump	Endocytes
Ouabain	✓	X	✓
Cyanide	✓	X	X

95. Which of the following statements is true?

(A) Ouabain did not affect any active processes

(B) Cyanide did not affect any active processes

(C) Cyanide prevented ouabain from acting on endocytosis

(D) Passive processes were unaffected by either poison

(E) Only processes that do not require ATP were affected by cyanide

96.   The probable mechanisms of action are that

(A) cyanide inhibits the Na^+-K^+ pump directly

(B) ouabain inhibits the production of ATP

(C) cyanide inhibits the production of ATP and, hence, the activity of the Na^+-K^+ pump

(D) cyanide inhibits the activity of the Na^+-K^+ pump and, hence, the production of ATP

(E) ouabain inhibits the production of ATP directly and, hence, the activity of the Na^+-K^+ pump

97.   In the presence of ouabain,

(A) Na^+ will accumulate outside the cell

(B) K^+ will accumulate inside the cell

(C) K^+ will accumulate outside the cell due to diffusion

(D) K^+ will accumulate outside the cell due to active transport

(E) Na^+ will accumulate inside the cell due to endocytosis

Questions 98 - 100 refer to observations on simple plant tissues.

In a lab examination in your botany class, you are to identify the following three cell types A, B, and C. Your determinations are based on the following key observations.

	A	B	C
Capacity to divide (Mitosis)	Yes	No	No
High concentrations in mesophyll of leaves	Yes	No	No
High numbers in young stems	Yes	Yes	No

98.   To identify a parenchyma cell, the key observation that you would look at would be

(A) its presence in leaves, since leaves are alive at maturity

(B) its ability to divide, since it is the only live cell

(C) its presence in stems, since only stems function in food storage

(D) its presence in leaves, since leaves contain a lot of chloroplasts

(E) air spaces in the cells when viewed with a microscope

99.   According to the chart, the inability of cell C to divide

(A)   indicates that it must be a parenchyma cell, which is the least special-ized and thus cannot undergo mitosis, a specialized function

(B)   indicates that it must be a parenchyma cell, since the air spaces preclude the capacity to divide

(C)   indicates that it must be sclerenchyma cell, since dead cells cannot divide

(D)   indicates that it must be a parenchyma cell, since photosynthesizing cells cannot divide

(E)   is not a clue to the identification of any cell type

100.   Which of the following is true?

(A)   A is a sclerenchyma cell

(B)   B is a collenchyma cell

(C)   C is a parenchyma cell

(D)   A is a collenchyma cell

(E)   C is a collenchyma cell

SECTION II

DIRECTIONS: Answer each of the following four questions in essay format. Each answer should be clear, organized, and well-balanced. Diagrams may be used in addition to the discussion, but a diagram alone will not suffice. Suggested writing time per essay is 22 minutes.

1.   Discuss the complete oxidation of glucose by the processes of glycolysis, the Krebs cycle, and the electron transport chain. Be sure to include in which part of the cell each process occurs. Do not dwell on details and numerical balance of the reactions, but focus on the major reactants, products, and destinations of these products.

2.   Different patterns of genetic inheritance cause variation and sometimes speciation. Discuss how dominant/recessive alleles, incomplete dominance, codominance, and sex-linked inheritance can affect two populations of the same organism separated by geographic barriers, giving an example.

3.   Negative feedback plays an important role in the counteraction of stress.

   (A) Explain the mechanism's role in a stressful environment. Include how at least two bodily systems are affected.

   (B) Design a controlled experiment to test the postulate that adrenaline prepares the body for "Flight or Fight."

4.   Explain the role of plant hormones, including their effects.

   (A) Growth hormones

   (B) Postulated flowering hormone

   (C) Aging and ripening hormone

ADVANCED PLACEMENT BIOLOGY EXAM II

ANSWER KEY

1.	(C)	26.	(D)	51.	(D)	76.	(B)
2.	(B)	27.	(E)	52.	(E)	77.	(C)
3.	(A)	28.	(B)	53.	(A)	78.	(B)
4.	(B)	29.	(C)	54.	(B)	79.	(D)
5.	(C)	30.	(C)	55.	(A)	80.	(C)
6.	(E)	31.	(E)	56.	(D)	81.	(B)
7.	(E)	32.	(C)	57.	(A)	82.	(A)
8.	(C)	33.	(E)	58.	(E)	83.	(E)
9.	(B)	34.	(B)	59.	(D)	84.	(C)
10.	(C)	35.	(B)	60.	(A)	85.	(B)
11.	(B)	36.	(D)	61.	(E)	86.	(C)
12.	(C)	37.	(C)	62.	(C)	87.	(D)
13.	(D)	38.	(C)	63.	(A)	88.	(A)
14.	(B)	39.	(C)	64.	(B)	89.	(B)
15.	(C)	40.	(D)	65.	(B)	90.	(B)
16.	(A)	41.	(A)	66.	(E)	91.	(B)
17.	(E)	42.	(C)	67.	(A)	92.	(A)
18.	(B)	43.	(B)	68.	(E)	93.	(C)
19.	(A)	44.	(C)	69.	(D)	94.	(B)
20.	(D)	45.	(B)	70.	(C)	95.	(D)
21.	(E)	46.	(D)	71.	(C)	96.	(C)
22.	(B)	47.	(A)	72.	(A)	97.	(C)
23.	(D)	48.	(E)	73.	(B)	98.	(D)
24.	(D)	49.	(C)	74.	(B)	99.	(C)
25.	(C)	50.	(B)	75.	(A)	100.	(B)

ADVANCED PLACEMENT
BIOLOGY EXAM II

DETAILED EXPLANATIONS
OF ANSWERS

SECTION I

1.   **(C)**

DNA replicates by forming two daughter molecules from the original parent. There are three possible ways in which DNA can replicate by base pairing. In semiconservative replication, each strand of the double helix serves as a template for the synthesis of its new partner. Thus there are two identical molecules formed from the original one; the daughter molecules are also identical to the parent molecule. It is named semiconservative replication since only one original strand is conserved in each daughter molecule. This is the way in which DNA replicates.

The other proposed mechanisms by which DNA might replicate, are conservative and dispersive replication, neither of which occur. In conservative replication, the parent duplex is left intact and an entirely new double-stranded molecule is formed. In dispersive replication, pieces of parent and daughter DNA are mixed together in the new generation.

The three models are shown below. A solid line indicates a parent strand, while a dotted line indicates a newly synthesized strand.

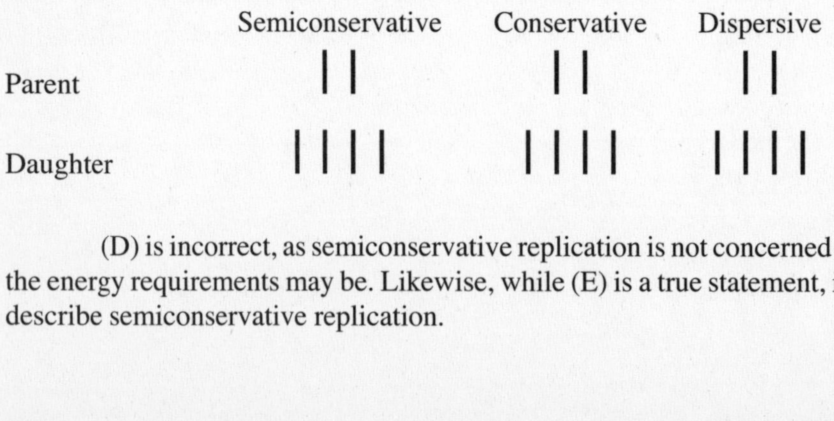

	Semiconservative	Conservative	Dispersive
Parent	‖	‖	‖
Daughter	‖‖	‖‖	‖‖

(D) is incorrect, as semiconservative replication is not concerned with what the energy requirements may be. Likewise, while (E) is a true statement, it does not describe semiconservative replication.

2.   **(B)**

The codon is a triplet of nucleotides on messenger RNA (mRNA). Since there are four nucleotides in RNA, a triplet sequence would yield 64 possible codons (4^3), 61 of which code for an amino acid. There are only twenty amino acids; therefore most of the amino acids are coded for by more than one codon. This is referred to as the degeneracy of the genetic code. Three of the triplet codons are a signal to stop, while the one that codes for the amino acid methionine, is also a signal to initiate protein synthesis.

The anticodon is a triplet of nucleotides on a loop of transfer RNA (tRNA). Since the tRNA is specific for an amino acid, when the mRNA codon base pairs with the tRNA anticodon, the tRNA will bring the appropriate amino acid to the elongating protein chain on mRNA.

3.   **(A)**

The codon is degenerate, meaning that most amino acids are represented by more than one codon. The difference in two or more different codons representing the same amino acid is usually the base of the third nucleotide in the sequence. This relative freedom in base-pairing at the third position is referred to as wobble. Thus UUC and UUU both code for the amino acid phenylalanine. While UUG and CUG do both code for leucine, this is not an example of wobble since the mismatch occurs at the first position.

Base pairing occurs between one purine and one pyrimidine base. In RNAs, adenine pairs with uracil while guanine pairs with cytosine.

While the stop codons show some degeneracy (UAA and UAG), most of the amino acids are represented by degenerate codons, and thus tRNA molecules bond to mRNA molecules allowing wobble at the third base.

4.   **(B)**

In 1961, Melvin Calvin elucidated the series of reactions in which six carbon dioxide molecules are converted to one glucose molecule (a six-carbon sugar) using NADPH and ATP during the dark reactions of photosynthesis. The Calvin cycle occurs in the stroma (the semifluid matrix) of the chloroplast and in many ways is analogous to the Krebs cycle occurring in the mitrochondrial matrix.

In the Calvin cycle, a five-carbon sugar, ribulose bisphosphate is regenerated in each turn of the cycle, whereas in the Krebs cycle, oxaloacetic acid, a four-carbon molecule, is regenerated every turn. Sir Hans Krebs described the sequence in 1937. Synonyms for the Krebs cycle are Citric Acid cycle and Tricarboxylic acid cycle, both names referring to the intermediates of the cycle.

The Cori cycle refers to the biochemical sequence whereby glucose is converted into lactate in skeletal muscle. The lactate then moves into the liver, in which it can be reconverted to glucose, which then becomes available to the muscle.

Cyclic AMP (adenosine monophosphate) is a ubiquitous substance synthesized from the catalysis of ATP by the enzyme adenyl cyclase. It functions as the "second messenger" in the action of many hormones, such as glucagon and epinephrine.

The carbon cycle refers to all the interrelationships whereby carbon is cycled between different inorganic and organic molecules. Photosynthesis and cellular respiration are the two major aspects of this cycle: in photosynthesis, carbohydrate is produced from carbon dioxide, whereas the reverse occurs in cellular respiration, maintaining a steady equilibrium. Photosynthesis occurs in plant cells, but both plant and animal cells undergo cellular respiration. Other aspects to be considered in the carbon cycle are the burning of fossil fuels, and environmental conditions. Note that the carbon cycle does not merely refer to the fixation of carbon dioxide.

5.   **(C)**

The nitrogen cycle involves several distinct types of bacteria that metabolize the various forms of nitrogen. Nitrification refers to the conversion of ammonia to nitrate in two oxidation steps: the nitrite bacteria convert ammonia (NH_3) to nitrite (NO_2) and then nitrate bacteria convert the nitrite to nitrate (NO_3).

In the absence of oxygen, denitrifying bacteria reduce nitrate or nitrite to atmospheric nitrogen (N_2). Nitrogen-fixing bacteria live in the soil and convert atmospheric nitrogen to organic nitrogen molecules. Ammonification refers to the process whereby nitrogenous organic remains are decomposed by soil bacteria and fungi, which utilize the proteins and amino acids for themselves and release the excess nitrogen as ammonia.

Deamination is the initial step in the degradation of amino acids. The amino group (NH_2) is removed and converted to ammonia, which will be eliminated in the form of urea ($H_2N-C-NH_2$).

O

6.   **(E)**

Circadian literally means "about a day," hence a circadian rhythm is a rhythm that cycles over a twenty-four hour period. Examples of these rhythms in humans can be as obvious as the sleep-wake cycle, or as obscure as the urinary excretion of ions. Other rhythms include fluctuations in body temperature and secretion of certain hormones. Metabolism of drugs may even follow a circadian rhythm.

Examples of circadian rhythms in the plant kingdom include the secretion of nectar from flowers. In certain leguminous plants, the orientation of the leaves, which lie horizontally in the daytime and yet more vertically at night, exemplifies a circadian rhythm.

Although circadian rhythms seem to follow the 24-hour light-dark cycle, if one were to experimentally alter the light-dark cycle, i.e. change it to a 28-hour day, the rhythms would gradually adapt to this new time schedule. This mechanism is called entrainment. Thus while the light-dark cycle is important in modifying the rhythm, it does not determine it. These rhythms can, in fact, persist in total darkness (although the exact timekeeping is lost). Hence the rhythms are generated by endogenous factors.

7.   **(E)**

The complete oxidation of glucose is basically the opposite process of photosynthesis. The reactions can be written as below:

energy

$$6CO_2 + 6\,H_2O \iff 6\,O_2 + C_6H_{12}O_6$$
$$\text{(glucose)}$$

in which photosynthesis is represented by the forward reaction and respiration by the reverse reaction.

Photosynthesis occurs in plants. In the presence of sunlight (energy), atmospheric CO_2, and water, plants can evolve oxygen and form glucose, which is stored as the polysaccharide carbohydrate starch.

Animals eat plant foods (starch) and respire: in the presence of oxygen, animals oxidize glucose completely to CO_2, and H_2O and form ATP (energy).

Thus, animals depend on plants for oxygen and plants depend on animals for carbon dioxide. Note that while animals do not photosynthesize, plants must respire.

8.   **(C)**

In photosynthesis, plant chloroplasts produce glucose and oxygen from carbon dioxide and water, in the presence of sunlight.

Glucose is a monosaccharide (simple sugar) that has many possible fates, depending upon the needs of the plant cell. Within the chloroplast, glucose can be polymerized into the polysaccharide starch. Alternatively, plant cells can respire: glucose can enter the cytoplasm and be oxidized/degraded to generate ATP. Cytoplasmic glucose can also participate in other chemical reactions, including the formation of the disaccharide sucrose (glucose + fructose) or other organic molecules.

Glycogen is the storage form of glucose in animal cells (liver and muscle cells). It is the analogue of plant starch, but is not found in plant cells.

9.   **(B)**

Enzymes are proteins that interact with specific substrates, and increase the rate of the chemical reaction which the substrate undergoes. While heat and increased concentration of substrate can increase the reaction rate by increasing the collision between molecules, the mechanism of action of enzymes is different.

All chemical reactions have an energy barrier that they must overcome in order for the reaction to occur. This is true of endothermic (energy-requiring) and exothermic (energy-releasing) reactions. This energy barrier is called the activation energy (E_a). It is analogous to lighting a fire: once lit, the fire will produce a lot of heat (energy), but you must first put energy in, i.e. light the match. An enzyme functions by lowering the energy of activation, and thus making it more likely that the colliding molecules will react, overcome the barrier, and form products. The mechanism of action of an enzyme is indicated below for both endothermic and exothermic reactions. Note that whether the reaction consumes or produces energy (ATP) will not affect the way an enzyme works. The decrease in the energy barrier in the presence of the enzyme is indicated by the dotted line.

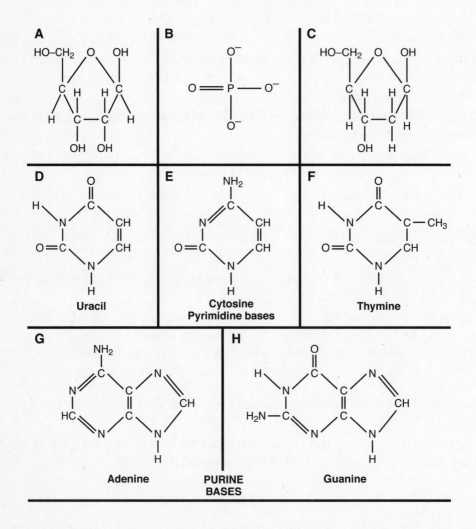

10.   **(C)**

Phenylketonuria is an inherited disease in which the enzyme phenylalanine hydroxylase, which converts the amino acid phenylalanine to the amino acid tyrosine, is missing. Phenylalanine therefore is diverted to other usually insignificant metabolic pathways. These alternate metabolites develop to high levels in body fluids. Mental retardation and early death by age 20 are characteristic of the disease.

Like other inborn errors of metabolism, this disease is caused by an inherited lack of an enzyme (or synthesis of a deficient form of the enzyme), which leads to the accumulation of abnormal, or excessive levels of normal metabolites (metabolic intermediates). Symptoms may appear shortly after birth. There is no obvious "defect" at birth, since the disease is only manifest upon ingestion of the amino acid. Furthermore, birth defects may be environmentally or medically induced, rather than genetically induced.

Disorders of endocrine glands often include overproduction or lowered production of a hormone. For instance, a tumor of a gland may cause excess secretion. Underproduction may be a result of atrophy of the gland.

Nondisjunction refers to the event whereby the chromosomes do not separate during meiosis: the resultant gamete therefore carries an extra chromosome, or lacks a chromosome.

11.   **(B)**

Cells are classified as eukaryotic or prokaryotic. The former are characterized by a membrane-bound nucleus, while the latter do not have an organized nucleus. All living things are grouped into one of five kingdoms. Only kingdom Monera consists of prokaryotic organisms. Monera include the cyanobacteria (blue-green algae) and the bacteria. *E. coli (Escherichia coli)* is a bacterium.

The other four kingdoms include only eukaryotic organisms. Kingdom Animalia, the animals, include the human being, or *Homo sapiens*. An oak tree falls into kingdom Plantae. *Amoeba* is a member of the kingdom Protista.

The AIDS (Acquired Immune Deficiency Syndrome) virus is not classified here because viruses are not truly living organisms; they depend on a living host (plant, animal, bacterium) for their metabolic and reproductive mechanisms.

12.   **(C)**

(See diagram). There are three sites along the electron transfer chain at which pairs of hydrogen ions are extruded (pumped) from the mitochondrial matrix into the intermembranal space. The hydrogen ions flow back into the matrix via special channel proteins that penetrate the inner mitochondrial membrane. ATP synthetases are on the ends of the channels facing the matrix; they sit like heads on the channel stalk. For each pair of hydrogen ions flowing through a protein channel due to the H^+ concentration gradient from the intermembrane space into the matrix, one ATP is produced.

Since NADH releases its electrons (and hydrogen ions) at the beginning of the electron transport chain, it causes three pairs of hydrogen ions to be extruded - one at each aforementioned site. Therefore, three pairs of hydrogen ions will re-enter the matrix and cause the formation of three ATP's. $FADH_2$ releases its electrons (and hydrogen ions) at a later site, bypassing the first site. Therefore only two pairs of electrons will re-enter the matrix and thus two ATPs will be formed.

Many of the enzymes that participate in electron transfer are cytochromes. Their active portions are iron-sulfur groups in which inorganic iron (Fe) is either in the ferrous, reduced (Fe^{+2}), or ferric, oxidized (Fe^{+3}), state.

NAD+ and FAD are coenzymes in the dehydrogenase enzymes, which predominate in the Krebs cycle. These coenzymes are reduced and pass their electrons to the electron transfer chain.

The term cofactor as opposed to coenzyme is merely a function of its chemical nature. A cofactor is inorganic, e.g. Fe, while a coenzyme is organic, e.g. NAD^+.

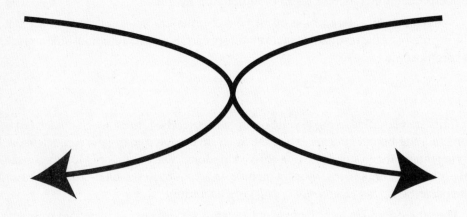

13.   **(D)**

ATP (adenosine triphosphate) is a nucleotide consisting of the purine nitrogenous base adenine, the pentose sugar ribose, and three phosphate groups. It is a high-energy compound by virtue of the bonds of the last two phosphate groups.

ATP can be synthesized under aerobic or anaerobic conditions although aerobic production is much more efficient. In anaerobic glycolysis, only a net yield of two ATPs are produced from one glucose molecule. However, in aerobic respiration, glucose is oxidized completely and 38 ATPs are formed. Oxidative phosphorylation refers to the coupling of electron transfer to the phosphorylation of ADP to form

$$ATP \ (ADP + P_i \rightarrow ATP, \text{ in which } P_i \text{ is inorganic phosphate}).$$

However, ATP can be synthesized directly from phosphocreatine, a high-energy compound in skeletal muscle. The reaction is as follows:

$$Phosphocreatine + ADP \leftrightarrow ATP + creatine.$$

Note that in this reaction, catalyzed by creatine kinase, a phosphate group is transferred from phosphocreatine to ADP. This reaction allows rapid, albeit short-lived, ATP production before the metabolic processes discussed above kick in.

cAMP (cyclic AMP) is not a precursor of ATP. Rather, ATP is converted to cAMP in certain cells.

14.   **(B)**

Protein hormones utilize the same mechanism of action as the amino-acid-derivative hormone epinephrine. The mechanism is described by the second messenger theory of hormone action. The hormone, illustrated by $\vee$, binds to a membrane receptor, illustrated by . This hormone-receptor complex activates an enzyme located on the inner surface of the plasma membrane. This enzyme, adenyl cyclase, represented by ●, catalyzes the conversion of ATP into cyclic adenosine-3'-5'-monophosphate abbreviated cAMP. cAMP is the second messenger (the hormone was the first messenger) that will activate a cascade of intracellular reactions, which vary with the hormone.

15.   **(C)**

Chemically, hormones are divided into three groups: proteins, steroids, and derivatives of the amino acid tyrosine. The steroid hormones include those of the adrenal cortex (i.e. aldosterone, corticosterone) and the sex steroids produced primarily in the gonads (i.e. testosterone, progesterone). The amino acid derivatives include epinephrine and the thyroid hormones. All other hormones are proteins. This includes all the hormones of the pituitary gland (i.e. growth hormone, prolactin, oxytocin, etc.), pancreas (glucagon and insulin), and many more.

Steroid hormones are lipid-soluble and diffuse into the cell. They bind to a cytoplasmic receptor. The hormone-receptor complex moves into the nucleus, where it can activate particular genes. Steroid hormones have no need for a second-messenger system.

Protein hormones cannot diffuse through the lipid membrane and thus must activate a membrane receptor facing the extracellular fluid. This receptor ultimately stimulates the cAMP system represented in the diagram.

While glucose and antibodies each have membrane receptors, they do not activate adenyl cyclase and ultimately the cAMP system. Receptors are quite specific, as are their mechanisms of activation.

An operator is a gene that regulates the transcription of particular genes.

16.   **(A)**

Symbiosis, which literally means "living together," refers to an association between organisms of distinct species. When both organisms benefit from the association, the symbiosis is called mutualism. An extreme example of this is a lichen, which, through evolutionary time, is now a single organism. A lichen is a combination of a fungus and an alga. The alga supplies the photosynthetically produced food for the fungus while the fungus provides water and minerals, and a mechanical support for the alga.

In a commensalistic symbiosis, one species benefits, while the other is neither benefitted nor harmed. Epiphytes grow in the branches of trees to maximize light exposure, with no ill effect on the tree.

In parasitism, one species benefits at the expense of the other species, designated the host. Parasites may live on or within the host's body. A hookworm (phylum Nematoda) bores through human skin and eventually comes to live in the intestine, causing diarrhea and anemia in the host.

Members of a predatory species kill and consume other organisms in order to survive.

Competition occurs between organisms that share a limited resource in the environment. It can be intraspecific as well as interspecific.

17.   **(E)**

Konrad Lorenz is a noted ethologist (one who studied behavior). He described the phenomenon of imprinting, a type of learning behavior pattern in which birds (e.g.: ducks, geese, chickens) form a strong attachment with whomever they are first exposed to in a critical time period shortly after hatching.

Under normal conditions, the bird first sees its mother and thus follows her around; the bird also thus learns to associate and mate with its own species. However, in his experiment, Lorenz had newly hatched ducks exposed to himself. The ducklings followed him as if he were their mother.

18.   **(B)**

Taxonomy is the classification of organisms and is based on categorizing similar organisms. The highest or broadest classification scheme is the kingdom. All living organisms are placed within one of the five kingdoms - Monera, Protista, Fungi, Plantae, or Animalia. The subsequent subdivisions are phylum, class, order, family, genus, and species. There may also be subdivisions (e.g. subphyla) and super-divisions (e.g. superclasses).

The last two names of the classification form the binomial nomenclature (a two-worded Latin name) that is unique for each species. The binomial nomenclature is underlined or italicized; the genus name is capitalized, while the species name is not.

The complete classification for man is as follows:

Kingdom	Animalia
Phylum	Chordata
Subphylum	Vertebrata
Class	Mammalia
Order	Primate
Family	Hominidae
Genus	Homo
Species	*Homo sapiens*

Thus *Homo sapiens* is the binomial nomenclature for the human being.

19.   **(A)**

Since chloroplasts are the photosynthetic organelles, it is important to identify those cells/structures in the leaf that contain chloroplasts. The middle section of the leaf, the mesophyll, contains the photosynthetic cells. These parenchymal cells are divided into two layers - the upper palisade layer and the lower spongy layer. The former is responsible for most of the photosynthesis although the latter contribute. The upper and lower layers of the leaf consists of epidermal cells. Stomata, or openings, penetrate the epidermis, in particular the lower epidermis. The pore sizes are regulated by two guard cells, which are specialized epidermal cells. The guard cells contain chloroplasts.

The epidermal cells secrete a waxy substance called cutin, which forms the cuticle. The cuticle forms the outer coating of the leaf. While it allows light to penetrate to the photosynthetic cells within the leaf, it does not participate in photosynthesis, since it contains no chloroplasts.

20.   **(D)**

Class Aves, within the phylum Chordata, refers to birds. Birds' unique feature is that they have feathers. They are homeotherms, or warm-blooded animals; i.e. like mammals, they maintain a constant and high body temperature. This is in contrast to reptiles, which are poikilothermic: these cold blooded animals have a body temperature that varies with the ambient temperature. As an adaption for flying, birds have air sacs and hollow bones, and thus do not weigh very much. Birds use song as a behavioral mechanism to identify their own species and territory, and for courtship practices.

Like terrestrial reptiles and insects, birds excrete uric acid crystals as the final waste product of nitrogen metabolism. In contrast, mammals excrete their nitrogen wastes as urea. Uric acid is less soluble than urea and thus little water is lost by its excretion.

21.   **(E)**

Charles Darwin is credited with formulating the most widely supported theory of evolution. The postulates of his theory came together in his book *On the Origin of Species by Means of Natural Selection* in 1859, and are recapitulated below.

All organisms overproduce gametes. Not all gametes form offspring, and of the offspring formed, not all survive. Those organisms that are most competitive (in various different aspects) will have greater likelihoods of survival. These survival traits vary from individual to individual but are passed on to the next generation, and thus over time, the best adaptions for survival are maintained. The environment determines which traits will be selected for or against; and these traits will change in time. A selected trait may later be disadvantageous.

The key drawback to Darwin's theory is that he did not suggest the key to variation in traits. It is now known that variation may be due to genetic mutations, gene flow due to migration, genetic drift, especially in small populations, and natural selection of genotypes, i.e. a differential ability to survive and/or reproduce.

22.   **(B)**

Hemophilia is a sex-linked recessive disease. Like color-blindness, the gene for hemophilia, h, is carried on the X-chromosome. If a male inherits the gene, he will have the genotype X^hY and will be a hemophiliac (a normal male is X^HY) since the recessive gene will be expressed. If a female inherits the gene, she will have the genotype X^HX^h and will carry the trait since her other X chromosome has the normal dominant gene, H.

The common pattern of transmittal is from carrier mothers to their sons. Note that a carrier mother X^HX^h has an equal (50%) chance of passing the gene on to either a son (X^hY) or a daughter (X^HX^h); however, the daughter will not express the disease. It is unlikely for a female to be a hemophiliac, X^hX^h, since she must have acquired the recessive gene from both her carrier mother and her hemophiliac father. However, this is possible, and as expected, the incidence increases when there is marriage between relatives.

If the gene were Y-linked, then a diseased father would always produce a hemophiliac son. However, a son inherits the gene only from his mother, since the mother contributes his sole X-chromosome.

23.   **(D)**

Vitamin D is a fat-soluble vitamin that is chemically similar to steroid compounds. Cholesterol is the precursor to the steroid hormones and vitamin D. Vitamin D is produced in the skin in the presence of ultraviolet (UV) light. Its synthesis requires enzymes in the kidneys and the lungs. Good sources of vitamin D include dairy products, such as milk, and fish liver oils. Among the functions attributed to vitamin D are an increase in calcium absorption from the gastrointestinal tract and the incorporation of calcium and phosphate into bones. Thus, a vitamin D deficiency manifests itself in bone problems. Children show rickets, malformed bones; adults show osteomalacia, a softening of the bones.

Night blindness is due to vitamin A deficiency, since vitamin A is a constituent of rhodopsin, a visual pigment.

24. **(D)**

In incomplete dominance, the "dominant" allele cannot completely mask the expression of the recessive allele. While the result of a cross between a dominant allele and a recessive allele may appear to be a blended trait, in future generations the dominant and recessive allele can each be independently expressed (i.e., the original traits will re-emerge); hence, no blending has occurred.

In certain flowers, color is inherited by incomplete dominance. The Punnett square for the cross between the red and white flower is shown below:

RED   x   WHITE
RR   x   rr

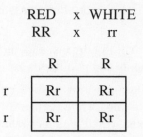

One hundred percent pink flowers (Rr) are produced. The Punnett square for a cross between two pink flowers is shown as follows:

PINK   x   PINK
Rr   x   Rr

	R	r
R	RR	Rr
r	Rr	rr

The expected probabilities of phenotypic expression are 25% red (RR), 50% pink (Rr), and 25% white (rr).

25. **(C)**

Nucleic acids are composed of polymers of nucleotides, each nucleotide consisting of a pentose sugar (five-carbon sugar), a phosphate group, and a nitrogenous base. DNA and RNA both contain the phosphate group (Figure B in the diagram). The only difference between DNA and RNA is the pentose sugar and the types of nitrogenous bases. The pentose sugars are deoxyribose (Figure C) in DNA, and ribose (Figure A) in RNA. DNA and RNA utilize both of the purine bases (double-ringed heterocyclic bases), adenine and guanine. They both also use the pyrimidine base (single-ringed heterocyclic base) cytosine. However, thymine (Figure F) is specific to DNA, while uracil (Figure D) is specific to RNA.

26.   **(D)**

The brains of all vertebrates are divided into the hindbrain, midbrain, and forebrain. In lower vertebrates, such as fish, the hindbrain is the dominant portion of the brain. It consists of the medulla oblongata and pons. The former deals with vital reflexes, such as cardiac activity, and it links the spinal cord to the rest of the brain. The latter contains the respiratory center, and like the former, it is the origin of many cranial nerves. The cerebellum is also part of the hindbrain: it functions in equilibrium and proprioception (awareness of body/limb position and movement).

The midbrains of fish process visual information and their forebrains function in olfactory (smell) sensation. These sensory functions are attributed to the cerebrum in higher vertebrates.

The midbrain is relatively small in humans, and, as the origin of several cranial nerves, it controls eye movements and pupillary size.

In all vertebrates, the forebrain consists of the diencephalon and the cerebrum. The diencephalon consists of the thalamus, a relay center for sensory input en route to the cerebrum, and the hypothalamus, which regulates many activities, including circadian rhythms, body temperature, emotions, food intake, and some hormone secretion. The cerebrum is highly developed in mammals: it constitutes 7/8 of the human brain. The cerebrum functions in learning, association, and memory. Birds also show great development of the cerebrum.

27.   **(E)**

Cells are broadly classified as prokaryotic ("before the nucleus") or eukaryotic ("true nucleus"). Kingdom Monera consists of organisms with prokaryotic cells, while the other four kingdoms (plant, animal, protista, and fungi) are characterized by eukaryotic organisms. The primary distinction between the two cell types is that prokaryotic cells do not have a membrane-bound nucleus, hence their name. Their DNA is contained within a nuclear region called a nucleoid.

Like eukaryotes, prokaryotes have a plasma membrane, which separates the cell from its external environment. All prokaryotic cells are further surrounded by a cell wall, while this is true of only certain eukaryotic cells (plant and fungal). They also have cytoplasmic ribosomes, which function in protein synthesis.

However, the eukaryotic cell has many other organelles, forming subcompartments in the cytoplasm. These organelles carry out specific functions. Two examples are the mitrocondrion, which functions in oxygen utilization and energy production, and the lysosome containing hydrolytic enzymes, which function in degradation and disposal of wastes.

28.   **(B)**

Angiosperms are flowering plants. There are two large subdivisions of them: The monocots (class Monocotyledoneae) and the dicots (class Dicotyledonae). Characteristics of the monocots (versus those of the dicots) follow: They have (1) one cotyledon (seed leaf) per seed (versus two); (2) flower parts occur in groups of three or multiples thereof (versus groups of four and five and multiples thereof); (3) parallel leaf veins (versus a netted pattern); and (4) "scattered" vascular bundles in the stem (versus forming a ring around the central pith). Examples of monocots are grasses, lilies, irises, and orchids. Herbs and many shrubs are dicots.

29.   **(C)**

In plants and some green algae, the organism's life cycle is characterized by an alternation of generations in which a diploid, spore-producing generation alternates with a haploid gamete-producing generation. The former is called the sporophyte generation while the latter is the gametophyte generation. Thus a gametophyte plant is composed of haploid cells. It undergoes mitosis to produce haploid gametes. Two gametes fuse to form the zygote, the first diploid cell of the new generation. The zygote develops into the sporophyte plant. The sporophyte consists of diploid cells. It undergoes meiosis to produce haploid spores, which may disperse. A spore need not fuse with another to develop into a new organism.

Depending upon the species, the two generations may appear similar or quite dissimilar, yet one generation is often the conspicuous one. In the evolution of plants, the sporophyte generation has become more dominant.

30.   **(C)**

The two reactions depicted occur simultaneously. ATP is converted (dephosphorylated) to ADP, while glucose is phosphorylated to glucose-6-phosphate. The phosphate group of ATP is transferred to glucose. This is the first step of glycolysis, which occurs in the cytoplasm. Since the phosphorylation of glucose requires energy, it is coupled to the breakdown of ATP. It is catalyzed by a hexokinase.

Glucose-6-phosphate is then isomerized to fructose-6-phosphate. Then phosphofructokinase (PFK) catalyzes the next energy requiring reaction of glycolysis in which the fructose-6-phosphate is phosphorylated to fructose-1,6-diphosphate. Phosphofructokinase is an important enzyme, as it is a chief site of regulation of glycolytic activity.

31.   **(E)**

Alveoli are tiny thin-walled air sacs within the lungs. There are widespread sheets of capillaries that cover the alveoli. The millions of alveoli in each lung increase the surface area through which gases can diffuse between air and blood.

The small intestine has many adaptions that increase its surface area for both digestion and absorption (transport of nutrients from the lumen into the blood or lymph). Firstly, the small intestine is very long (about 12 feet); secondly, the inner layer, or mucosa, is folded into villi that project into the lumen. Microvilli, which are folds of the epithelial cells composing the villi, further increase the surface area. Microvilli are also referred to as the brushborder. There are brushborder enzymes that complete chemical hydrolysis of nutrient molecules. Then the small monomers formed are absorbed.

The inner mitochondrial membrane has enzymes that function in the electron transport chain or as ATP synthetases. This inner membrane is folded into projections called cristae, which increase the surface area for these chemical reactions that sustain life.

Cilia are often considered to be cell projections that push substances past the cell. The hair cells in the cochlea of the inner ear are actually cilia. However, they are mechanoreceptors which, when distorted, will signal an auditory sensation. They thus have a neural function and do not function in chemical or transport reactions.

32.   (C)

All vertebrate brains have three primary divisions: the prosencephalon is the forebrain; the mesencephalon is the midbrain; and the rhombencephalon is the hindbrain.

The rhombencephalon develops into the myelencephalon (medulla oblongata) and the metencephalon (pons and cerebellum). The medulla oblongata and pons cooperate in the regulation of breathing. They are also the origin of many of the cranial nerves. The cerebellum deals with reflexes and equilibrium.

The mesencephalon is simply the midbrain; while it is a major association site in lower vertebrates such as fish, it is reduced in size and function in higher vertebrates. However, it maintains communication with the eyeball.

The prosencephalon develops into the diencephalon (thalamus and hypothalamus) and telencephalon (cerebrum). The thalamus functions as a relay center for sensory stimuli. The hypothalamus controls the pituitary gland; it also controls visceral activity via the autonomic nervous system. The cerebrum is highly developed in higher vertebrates such as birds and mammals; it functions in learning and other associative functions.

33.   (E)

Desert plants show many adaptations to their hot and arid environment. Plant life is relatively sparse, minimizing competition for water for widely spaced plants. The plants often have roots that penetrate deep and reach the groundwater. The leaves may be deciduous (able to fall off) during particularly stressful periods. The coating, or cuticle, of the plant leaf is often thick and waxy, thus functioning in water retention. Finally, water loss through the stomata (the openings between guard cells) is minimized by keeping the stomata hidden deep within the leaves.

34.   **(B)**

There are many types of stems that have specialized functions. The functions of stems generally may include transport of water and food between root and leaves, leaf support, and food storage.

Tendrils are modified stems that assist climbing plants such as the grapevine. Underground stems include tubers, rhizomes and corms. Tubers, found in the potato, function to store starch. Rhizomes, in ferns, function in vegetative propagation. Corms are found in gladiolus and are actually fleshy leaves that store food.

Nodes are not stems, but rather are the site on the stem at which the leaves attach. Internodes are thus the region between nodes.

35.   **(B)**

In the 1800's, two major theories of evolution were proposed. In 1800, Jean Baptiste Lamarck proposed a theory based on the inheritance of acquired characteristics. In other words, organs, and therefore animals, evolve through use. His classic example was his explanation for why the giraffe had such a long neck: He said that giraffes stretch their necks to reach the leaves high in trees. He assumed that an animal that stretched its neck could pass "a stretched and hence lengthened neck" on to its offspring.

Lamarck's theory was incorrect, since characteristics acquired in life cannot be passed on to the next generation, since the information is not in the genes. For instance, if a man develops his muscles by lifting weights, his offspring would not therefore be muscular as well.

In the 1830's, Charles Darwin started collecting information that would lead him to propose his theory of evolution based on natural selection. The basic premise of his theory is that individuals have differing capacities to cope with their environment. Some individuals have characteristics which are advantageous in the environment and hence, those individuals will tend to survive and reproduce.

According to Darwin's theory, a giraffe has a long neck because those giraffes that by chance had the selective advantage (long necks) would eat food in the trees, and hence survive and reproduce. Their offspring would be like the parents and hence have long necks. Giraffes with short necks would be selected against and not be able to survive and reproduce other short-necked giraffes.

Despite all of Darwin's insight, he never could explain the mechanism whereby traits were passed on. At about the same time, although unknown to Darwin, Gregor Mendel was experimenting with garden peas and was the first to introduce the concept of genes (the heritable factors), although he did not use that term.

Albinism is a genetic disease in which there is no production of melanin. Note that while many genetic diseases may be obvious at birth, others become manifest later in life. This does not mean that the disease is an acquired characteristic, for the genetic predisposition to develop the disease is present at birth, regardless of the age of manifestation of an inherited disease.

36.   **(D)**

Embryonic induction refers to the interaction between adjacent cells whereby one group of cells can determine the morphological development of a neighboring group. It is believed that this induction is due to the production and release of chemicals.

The classic example of induction is the formation of the vertebrate lens. When the optic vesicle contacts the overlying epidermis, it induces the formation of a lens from the epidermal tissue. The formation of the neural tube (neurulation) is yet another example of embryonic induction. The interaction occurs between the dorsal ectoderm and dorsal mesoderm.

Cleavage is the series of cell divisions whereby a zygote (fertilized egg) divides mitotically into two cells: the cells continue to divide into two cells until a hollow ball of cells called a blastula is formed.

37.   **(C)**

All plant life cycles exhibit an alternation of generations. The diploid generation is the sporophyte generation. It is characterized by a diploid (2n) number of chromosomes. The sporophyte plant divides by meiosis to produce spores that are haploid and hence the first cells of the new haploid generation. The spore divides mitotically to form the haploid gametophyte plant, which only has one of each pair of chromosomes. The gametophyte divides mitotically to produce gametes (egg and sperm cells). Haploid gametes of opposite sex fuse to produce a diploid zygote. This marks the beginning of the new diploid generation. This zygote grows into a sporophyte plant and the cycle begins anew.

38.   **(C)**

The Hardy-Weinberg equilibrium refers to a condition in which the proportion of alleles at a given locus remain constant. Four factors are required to maintain the equilibrium: large population size, no mutation, no migration, and no natural selection.

The best way to see why these factors are required is to study how evolution (and hence deviation from the equilibrium) may occur when the criteria are not met.

In a small population, chance alone may cause a shift in allele frequency. This random fluctuation is called genetic drift.

A mutation is a change in the DNA and as such is passed on to future generations.

Migration can be immigration (entrance) or emigration (exit) of individuals (and their genes!) to or from a population. This change in allele frequency due to migration is called gene flow.

Natural selection and differential reproduction are basically synonymous. This is the key factor of evolutionary change. Each individual of the population has a unique genotype (except identical twins, which have a common genotype) responsible for determining its phenotype. The environmental circumstances at the time determine whether that phenotype is at a survival advantage. Those individuals with the phenotypes that can cope best in the environment will differentially reproduce. Their genes will increase in frequency in the next generations.

39.   (C)

Human embryonic development takes nine months; these months are divided into three trimesters of three months each.

In the first trimester, cleavage and implantation occur within the first week. The embryonic membranes begin to develop, followed by gastrulation (the differentiation of the three primary cell layers: ectoderm, mesoderm, and endoderm) and neurulation (formation of the neural tube). By the end of the first month, organ development has begun - these organs include the eyes, heart, limb buds, and most other organs. In the second month, morphogenesis occurs. Morphogenesis refers to the development of form or structure. In short, the first trimester is a critical period of differentiation and development, but growth is not pronounced.

The second trimester is a period of rapid growth in size and weight. The mother may become aware of kicking in the baby. Growth continues and is most prominent in the final trimester.

40.   (D)

Seed-producing plants are evolutionarily advanced because their reproductive mechanisms do not depend on an aqueous medium in which their gametes must travel. The seed-producing plants include the gymnosperms (cone-bearers) and the angiosperms (the flowering plants). Seeds of gymnosperms are exposed, although embedded in cones. Thus the gymnosperms are referred to as "naked seed" plants, due to lack of protection afforded the seed. However, angiosperms have seeds that are well-protected within fruits.

All gymnosperms bear cones, as the cones are the reproductive structure - the site of seed production. Cones can be either male or female, and may or may not be found on the same plant.

41. (A)   42. (C)   43. (B)

The diagram illustrates semiconservative replication of DNA. The 3' and 5' illustrate the location of the phosphate group. The hydrogen bonds between the bases (labeled C in diagram) are broken, and the double-stranded DNA molecule begins to unwind. The replication fork (labeled B in the diagram) marks the area from which the single strands emerge. Each strand then serves as a template for DNA synthesis. The DNA polymerase enzyme reads the template in the 3' to 5' direction and hence synthesizes the new chain only in the 5' to 3' direction, since the two strands of the double helix are antiparallel (i.e. they run in opposite directions). Therefore, only one strand, designated the leading strand (labeled D in the diagram) will show continuous synthesis as the replication fork moves towards the DNA molecule's 5' end. The lagging strand (labeled A in the diagram) shows discontinuous synthesis. Nucleotides are added in short bursts in the appropriate 5' to 3' direction. Later these short polymers of nucleotides will be connected to form one strand.

44. (C)   45. (B)   46. (D)   47. (A)

Transcription is the nuclear process in which one strand of DNA dictates a complementary sequence of nucleotides in RNA. DNA unwinds in a particular region to expose particular genes and transcribe the necessary RNA. The DNA strand that is at this site is the template strand, while the other DNA strand is the anti-template strand. Note that the RNA transcript formed will contain the same sequence of bases as the anti-template strand, since it, too, had complementary base-pairing.

In plants, the term translocation refers to the movement of the organic products (such as sucrose) of photosynthesis from a leaf to other parts of the plant. This food is conducted through the phloem, the vascular tissue that consists of sieve tubes and companion cells.

Translation is the cytosolic process whereby a strand of messenger RNA dictates the amino acids that will be incorporated into protein. The messenger RNA has codons (triplets of nucleotides), which form base pairs with the anticodons on transfer RNA. Transfer RNAs carry the amino acids to the messenger RNA strand. Protein synthesis occurs on ribosomes, which are cytoplasmic organelles consisting of ribosomal RNA and protein. Hence all three types of RNA (messenger, transfer, and ribosomal) are involved in translation.

Transpiration is the loss of water vapor from plant stems and leaves. It occurs primarily through the stomata. This evaporated water loss may create a tension that will pull water upward from the root through the stem.

Transfusion is the direct infusion of blood into the bloodstream.

48. (E)   49. (C)   50. (B)

The cell cycle consists of, in continuous sequence: mitosis, in which the nucleus divides, cytokinesis, in which the cytoplasm divides, and interphase. Interphase is the longest period of the three and it is in this period that DNA is replicated. It consists of three distinct stages: G_1, a gap before DNA replicates, S, the stage of actual synthesis of DNA, and G_2, the gap after replication and prior to mitosis. It is the variable time spent in G_1 that is responsible for the widely variable times for the cell cycles of different cells.

Mitosis only occupies a small time segment of the total cell cycle. It consists of four stages. In prophase, the chromosomes condense into distinct rodlike structures. By metaphase, the nuclear membrane and nucleolus have disappeared completely. The chromosomes move to and align themselves along the spindle equator. In anaphase, sister chromatids of each replicated chromosome separate to each form a complete chromosome. Their migration to opposite poles of the cell seems to be based on the action of microtubules. Telophase is basically the opposite of prophase - the chromosomes decondense into a threadlike form. A new nuclear membrane is formed.

' In the strict sense, mitosis only refers to division of the nucleus. Cytokinesis, or cytoplasmic division, usually accompanies mitosis. It begins in late anaphase or in telophase and is marked by the formation of a depression called a cleavage furrow. At this site, the plasma membrane is pulled inward by a ring of microfilaments. The continual contraction of the microfilaments cuts the cytoplasm into usually equal halves. In plants, cytokinesis occurs via the formation of a cell plate. Now interphase will start anew.

51. (D)   52. (E)   53. (A)   54. (B)

While mitosis maintains the chromosome number, meiosis functions to halve the chromosome number. In meiosis, there are two sequential nuclear divisions (Meiosis I and Meiosis II). DNA duplication only precedes the first meiotic division; the interphase between the two divisions is short or absent; no duplication occurs.

Due to replication, there are two sister chromatids/chromosome. These chromatids are linked at the centromere, a constricted portion of the chromosome. In the first meiotic division (Anaphase I), the homologous chromosomes separate. These are the paired chromosomes that code for the same type of genetic trait. In the second meiotic division (Anaphase II), the sister chromatids of each chromosome separate.

Prophase I includes several important events that ultimately contribute to the uniqueness of each individual. Homologous chromosomes pair closely in a process called synapsis. The resultant four linked chromatids are called a tetrad. Non-sister chromatids in the tetrad can undergo a process called crossing over: they exchange segments of the homologous chromosomes at a site called the chiasma. Thus an original paternal and original maternal gene will end up in the same chromosome and hence in the same gamete. Recombination refers to this new combination of alleles. Note that there is no reason for sister chromatids to undergo crossing over, since they carry the same genetic material.

55. (A)   56. (D)

A biome is a broad yet distinct vegetational formation. Each biome is associated with particular fauna as well. A classification of biomes usually includes the following:

The tundra is a treeless region with long cold winters such as those that occur in the Arctic. A taiga is a coniferous forest, characterized by a preponderance of evergreens such as spruce and fir trees. The winters are long and harsh. A desert is a region of little rainfall, hot days, and cool nights. Plants, such as cacti, have adaptations to obtain and retain water. A tropical rainforest has much rainfall, high humidity, and high temperatures. There is little variation in this pattern throughout the year. The trees are tall and the vegetation is thick. A deciduous forest has alternating warm and cold seasons. The leaves fall (hence the term deciduous) in the winter. Examples of deciduous trees are oak, maple, and beech trees. The final biome, the grasslands, shows irregular rainfall. Grazing animals are numerous.

57. **(A)**   58. **(E)**   59. **(D)**

A mechanism that causes reproductive isolation is one that prevents interbreeding (breeding between different species). There are many types of these mechanisms, whose effects may manifest themselves before or after mating. That is, they may prevent the formation of the zygote or they may prevent the development of the zygote or the fertility of the organism.

Mechanical isolation refers to differences in the anatomy (i.e., size and length) or physiology of the reproductive organs such that mating is impossible.

Gamete isolation refers to an incompatibility (perhaps biochemically based) between the gametes of two different species.

Hybrid inviability is displayed if a hybrid embryo fails to develop, or, in the best of circumstances, develops normally, except for the fact that its reproductive system is nonfunctional. This is exemplified best by the sterile mule — a cross between a female horse and a male donkey.

Temporal isolation refers to a mechanism concerned with time. The mating seasons of two different species may not correspond.

Behavioral isolation involves courtship rituals, such as song and dance, which may be specific to each species.

60. **(A)**   61. **(E)**   62. **(C)**

Phylum Porifera, the sponges, consists of freshwater and marine animals. They are sessile filter feeders, and acquire food through their many pores. Needlelike spicules of calcium or fibers of spongin protein serve as supportive structures.

Members of phylum Arthropoda are characterized by jointed appendages and chitinous exoskeletons. Arthropods undergo molting to reform their exoskeletons. Examples include spiders, lobsters, and all insects.

Echinoderms are marine animals such as sea stars and sea cucumbers. They have radially symmetrical bodies. Echinoderms, as well as chordates, are classified as deuterostomes; this term refers to the fact that in the ontogeny of echinoderms and of chordates, the blastopore becomes the anus of the adult.

Mollusks have muscular or membranous mantles that protect the inner soft organs, called the visceral mass. In many cases, the mantle secretes a shell. Mollusks also have a muscular foot, which may function in locomotion or burrowing. Examples of mollusks include snails, clams, squid, scallops and oysters.

Phylum Platyhelminthes, the flatworms, include planarians, and parasitic flukes and tapeworms. The two parasitic types show reduced or absent nervous, digestive, respiratory and circulatory systems when compared to the planarians.

63. **(A)**   64. **(B)**   65. **(B)**   66. **(E)**

The organic nutrients that contribute calories to the diet are carbohydrates, lipids, and proteins. Carbohydrates have the empirical formula $C_nH_{2n}O_n$. Saccharum is

Latin for sugar; hence the simple sugars are called monosaccharides. These include glucose, fructose and galactose, all six-carbon sugars. Disaccharides are the chemical bonding of two monosaccharides. Glucose and fructose yield sucrose (table sugar); glucose and galactose yield lactose (milk sugar); and two glucoses combine to form maltose. An oligosaccharide is a molecule composed of a few monosaccharides - it typically contains around three to seven sugars in its structure, although the number is rather arbitrary. Polysaccharides are molecules composed of many monosaccharides; they are long polymers. The three major polysaccharides are all polymers of glucose. Plants store glucose in the form of starch which is edible. Animals store glucose as glycogen in the liver and muscle. Another polysaccharide in plants is cellulose - it is a component of plant cell walls and thus serves a structural role. However, unlike starch, cellulose found in wood and vegetable fibers, is not digestible by man due to lack of the enzyme that hydrolyzes it.

Saccharin is an artificial sweetener that was banned by the FDA (Food and Drug Administration) due to its possible carcinogenic (cancer-causing) properties.

67. (A)   68. (E)   69. (D)   70. (C)

Eukaryotic cells have many organelles that subserve specific functions. While most cells contain most of these organelles, some cells may have an abundance or a complete lack of certain organelles, depending on the function of the cell. Skeletal muscle cells are multinucleated and have an abundance of mitochondria. Skeletal muscle cells use a lot of energy for muscular contraction and hence need many mitochondria to supply the energy.

Sperm cells must swim to the egg and hence also have many mitochondria. However, a sperm cell is the only cell in the human body that has a flagellum. Flagella and cilia are cellular projections both based on a microtubular core and function in movement. The main differences are that a flagellum is a single, long projection which can propel the entire sperm cell, while cilia are short, numerous projections which move substances past the cell. The epithelial cells of the respiratory tract contain cilia to move mucus containing entrapped dust and debris up and out of the tract.

All secretory cells, such as the pancreatic acinar cell, which secretes pancreatic juice, have a preponderance of rough endoplasmic reticula. Ribosomes on the rough endoplasmic reticulum synthesize proteins that are destined for secretion by the cell (whereas free ribosomes synthesize proteins that will not be exported). The synthesized protein enters the rough endoplasmic reticulum as it is being synthesized on the ribosome; then the rough endoplasmic reticulum transports the protein, often to the Golgi apparatus for modifications before release.

Lysosomes contain hydrolytic enzymes that digest phagocytosed material such as bacteria and cell debris. Leukocytes (white blood cells) specialize in phagocytosis. In the process of endocytosis, a vesicle is formed around the bacterium, and this phagocytic vesicle fuses with the lysosomes, whose enzymes proceed to destroy the bacterium.

71. **(C)**   72. **(A)**

Red blood cells may contain antigens (markers) on their surfaces. Blood plasma contains the antibodies. A person only has antibodies against those antigens that he does not have. If he had antibodies against his own antigens, the antibodies and antigens would bind and agglutination (clumping) of the red blood cells would occur. In contrast to most antibodies that develop in response to exposure to an antigen, these plasma antibodies exist despite lack of exposure to the antigen.

Blood Type	A	B	AB	O
Antigens	A	B	A,B	---
Antibodies	anti-B	anti-A	---	anti-A anti-B

The female in the question showed agglutination with both antisera. The anti-A antiserum agglutinated with her A antigens, while the anti-B antiserum agglutinated with her B antigens. She has Type AB blood.

The male in the question showed no agglutination and therefore has no antigens on his red blood cells. He has Type O blood.

Type AB and Type O are the phenotypes of the students. Their genotypes are $I^A I^B$ and ii, respectively. Alleles I^A and I^B are codominant with each other, but each is dominant to the recessive allele i. A Punnett square shows the results of a cross between these two students:

Type AB x Type O

	I^A	I^B
i	$I^A i$	$I^B i$
i	$I^A i$	$I^B i$

The probabilities of their children's blood types are: Type A ($I^A i$), 50%; Type B ($I^B i$), 50%. Note that the phenotypes of the children are completely different from those of the parents.

The concern with blood transfusions is that a donor's red blood cells (by virtue of the antigens on them) will be agglutinated by the recipient's antibodies. There is not the opposite fear that a donor's plasma will agglutinate the recipient's red blood cells because the donor's plasma is diluted by the recipient's plasma, and thus the effects of the antibodies are minimized.

A subject with Type O blood, such as the male in the question, is said to be a universal donor. This is because he has no antigens on his red blood cells that could be agglutinated by the recipient's antibodies. Although he does have both plasma antibodies, his antibodies will be diluted by the recipient's plasma and thus will not cause harm. He can thus donate blood to anybody.

73. (B) 74. (B)

Since the trait is due to an autosomal dominant gene, if a family member does not express the trait, he does not carry it either. Suppose P stands for the preauricular gene and p represents the recessive normal gene. Thus, F_{1-1} (pp) does not contain the gene in his chromosomes and hence if he marries an unafflicted woman (pp), none of their children will have the trait.

For F_{1-2} (Pp) and F_{1-3} (Pp) both of whom show the trait, half the children should inherit the gene P while half should inherit the normal allele, p. This is evident in the children of F_{1-2}. For F_{1-3}, his next son (or daughter) has a 50% chance of inheriting the trait. The trait is not sex-linked. Each baby is independent of any other and thus, even though F_{1-3} already has an afflicted daughter, this will not affect the next outcome. Probability simply means that in the long run a 50-50 ratio is expected.

75. (A) 76. (B)

Auxin was the first of the plant hormones to be discovered. Auxins are responsible for the phototropic effect. They stimulate stem elongation. The auxin, probably indoleacetic acid (IAA) migrates and concentrates in the cells on the side of the plant away from the light and causes those cells to elongate. This causes the stem to bend in the opposite direction, towards the light, as depicted in experiment A.

Gibberellins also promote stem elongation. One particular gibberellin, gibberellic acid₃, (GA₃) is widely used in growth experiments. Dwarf plants treated with gibberellic acid will approach normal size, as depicted in experiment B.

Florigen is a postulated hormone that may play a role in the flowering process.

Cytokinins function in cytoplasmic division (cytokinesis), enhance leaf size, and slow the yellowing of leaves.

Abscisic acid was named according to its presumed, but now questioned role in abscission - the dropping of flowers, leaves, and fruits. However, its more important function is inhibitory in nature: it induces stomatal closure and seed dormancy.

Ethylene is an alkene with the structure $H_2C=CH_2$. It stimulates fruit ripening and promotes abscission.

Growth hormone is an animal hormone. In man, it increases bone and muscle growth, but also stimulates mitosis and protein synthesis in most other cells.

77. (C) 78. (B) 79. (D) 80. (C)

A triglyceride (neutral fat molecule) is one glycerol bound by ester bonds to three fatty acids. Digestion of fat thus yields free glycerol and fatty acids. The free fatty acids will decrease the pH of a solution. The pH drops the most and the most rapidly in tube C, which contains the fat source (cream), pancreatic juice, and bile salts.

To determine the function of bile salts, you must compare two tubes with exactly the same contents, except one will have bile salts as well, tube C has the same contents as tube B, but it also has bile salts. You would compare tubes A and C if you wished to elucidate the function of pancreatic juice. No real comparison can be made between tubes A and B since they only have cream in common. Of course, the most information would be obtained by looking at the data for tubes A, B, and C.

Each tube has the same fat source, cream. From tube A, it is apparent that bile salts have no enzymatic activity. It is clear that tube B contains the necessary ingredient for fat digestion, since fatty acids must have been produced in order for the pH to have dropped. That ingredient is pancreatic juice, which contains the enzyme lipase. Tube C contains bile salts in addition. Apparently bile salts are able to aid the pancreatic enzymes in their work. But bile salts alone have no enzymatic activity and therefore do not function in digestion. Digestion can be mechanical (e.g. churning) or chemical (e.g. enzymes).

The liver synthesizes bile, a fluid composed primarily of bile salts. The bile is then stored in the gallbladder until released as needed, such as after a fatty meal. The function of bile is to emulsify fats; it breaks fats up into smaller globules. This increases the surface area on which pancreatic enzymes can work. Thus tube C shows greatest digestion because the pancreatic enzymes have many smaller globules to digest. Note that the bile has no direct role in activating pancreatic enzymes. It simply increase the available surface area.

81. (B)   82. (A)   83. (E)   84. (C)

Tube A contained the urine of the subject on a high-salt diet. Tube B contained the diabetic's urine. Tube C contained the urine of the subject on a high-protein diet. Tube D contained the distilled water.

There are several clues that tube B contains the urine of the diabetic. The most obvious is that there is excess glucose in the urine (200 mg/dl). Excess glucose in the urine often draws water with it and a diabetic shows an osmotic diuresis. There is then a high volume of urine. Volume is a function of many factors, but compared to the other tubes, tube B contains the highest volume. Since a diabetic cannot utilize the blood sugar (the sugar will not be transported into the cells), he has excessive fatty acid oxidation for energy. This leads to the build-up of ketone bodies in the blood and urine. The ketone bodies are acetoacetic acid, B-hydroxybutyric acid and acetone. Acetone is the substituent in urine that casts off a sweet odor. The formation of these acids will lower the pH of the urine. Urinary pH is normally between 5 and 8. Diet influences urinary pH. A high protein diet often results in acidic urine, while a vegetarian diet results in more alkaline urine. The high concentration of solutes in a diabetic's urine increases the specific gravity. Specific gravity is defined as the weight of a volume of substance divided by the weight of an equal volume of distilled water. Therefore, by definition, the specific gravity of water is 1.000. Since urine is primarily water with solutes dissolved in it, it will always weigh more than an equal volume of pure water. Therefore, the specific gravity of urine is always greater than one. The higher the solute concentration, the higher the specific gravity, since the numerator is a higher number than the denominator. Urinary specific gravity varies between approximately 1.010 and 1.030. The man on the high-salt diet, as well as the diabetic, will also show relatively high specific gravities. The concentration of salt in the urine is due in part to diet. Although excess salt may be excreted with water, the specific gravity is still usually high. A high protein diet will not have much effect on specific gravity or volume.

Diuresis refers to an increased output of water. A diuretic drug is one that primarily affects urinary volume. Some diuretics also affect the output of specific urinary constituents. Thus the effect of diuretics on specific gravity is variable. pH is a measure of the concentration of hydrogen ions ($[H^+]$), or acidity of a solution. Mathematically, pH is defined as follows:

$$pH = \log [H^+]$$

However, it is an inverse relationship, in which an increase in $[H^+]$ causes a drop in pH. The pH scale varies from O to 14 in which pH 7 is neutral. At neutrality, there is a balance of H^+ and OH^- ions. Water is an example of a neutral compound. When the pH is less than 7, there is an excess of H^+ (over OH^- ions).

Tube C has the lowest pH (5.0) or highest $[H^+]$. It is 100 times more acidic that tube D with a pH of 7. Urinary pH normally varies between pH 5 - 8 depending on diet, drugs, and other factors.

85. **(B)**   86. **(C)**   87. **(D)**   88. **(A)**   89. **(B)**

Sizes of predator and prey populations fluctuate regularly and are interdependent. If the prey population is allowed to increase, this provides more food for the predator population, which then flourishes. However, more predators will eat more prey and the prey population will then decrease. Now the predator population will of necessity decrease as well, due to fewer food sources. The decrease in predator population allows the prey population to flourish and the cycle begins anew.

Note that while these oscillations occur independently of other factors, in the graph depicted, the oscillations coincide with seasonal changes. It appears that the prey succumb to the winter environment and hence the predator population will shrink as well. Note that the size of the predator population lags behind that of the prey population. There is no evidence that the winter poses any direct danger to the predator population, only that the population drop is due to the drop in prey population. The mildest winter was that of 1979 - although the normal oscillation occurred, the drop in prey population was not as severe as in other years.

The peak prey population was achieved in the summer of 1977, with a population of 100. At this time, the predator population was 15. Note the axes for population - the prey population size is read on the left; that of the predator is on the right.

The data for the graph ends in the summer of 1980. If in the following winter, a chemical were introduced into the environment which proved fatal to the prey, the predator population would decrease severely due to decreased food resources. Of course, if the predators had other sources of food, this drop need not occur; however, there is no evidence that this is the case, as their population size always lags behind that of the prey.

90. **(B)**   91. **(B)**   92. **(A)**   93. **(C)**   94. **(B)**

A glucose tolerance test is often administered to patients suspected of having diabetes. In this test, the patient fasts overnight to bring his plasma glucose to a stable basal level, often around 80 mg/dl. Both subjects A and B show the same fasting glucose level: 80 mg/dl. The subjects then ingest a sweet syrupy concoction. The volume ingested is proportional to body weight usually 1 gm of glucose per kg. of body weight. Normally, after a glucose load, the body responds by releasing insulin, a pancreatic hormone that stimulates glucose uptake by cells and hence lowers plasma glucose levels back to normal.

In the graphs, the rate of rise (slope) of plasma glucose level is the same for both subjects, although subject B shows a much higher glucose level for the given stress. In either case, the maximum plasma glucose levels are reached at 30 minutes, the time of the first of many blood tests used to measure the current glucose status. Thus, there is little latency between glucose ingestion and peak glucose levels.

Subject A exhibits a normal response to glucose ingestion: the plasma glucose reaches its maximum at about 130 mg/dl and returns to baseline within two hours. This is due to the release of insulin, which lowers plasma glucose.

Graph B indicates an abnormal response to glucose ingestion: the response given is indicative of diabetes. The peak plasma glucose level is close to 200 mg/dl and stays high. In two hours, the plasma glucose level is still excessively high. This indicates diminished tolerance to the glucose stress. The probable cause is diabetes, a disease in which the pancreas does not release insulin, and hence the body cannot counteract the glucose stress.

Not only do diabetics have high plasma glucose concentrations, but glucose is often excreted in the urine. When the plasma glucose level rises above 180 mg/dl (as it does in subject B), the kidneys cannot reabsorb all the glucose, and it begins to "spill over" into the urine.

95. **(D)**   96. **(C)**   97. **(C)**

It is evident that the two poisons have no effect on passive transport processes such as diffusion. They both affect active processes (processes that require the expenditure of ATP), either active transport and/or endocytosis. To determine the differences in their action, it would be most informative to first look at endocytosis, since it is blocked by only one of the poisons, cyanide. Endocytosis requires the presence of ATP, thus it is suggested that cyanide may inhibit ATP production. Furthermore, cyanide also blocks active transport, which also requires ATP. Since ouabain does not inhibit endocytosis, it presumably cannot affect the production of ATP. In comparing the effects of ouabain on active transport and on endocytosis, it is clear that the inhibition by ouabain on active transport is independent of the production of ATP. It is probable that ouabain directly inhibits the activity of the sodium-potassium pump, which would thus inhibit active transport, but not endocytosis, since the latter is independent of the pump. Cyanide and ouabain were not placed into the same cell, so one cannot determine cyanide's effect on ouabain.

Cyanide binds to the last enzyme of the electron transport chain and inhibits utilization of oxygen. Since oxidation is coupled to the phosphorylation of ADP to form ATP, cyanide inhibits ATP production.

Cyanide inhibits the ultimate production of ATP. There is a secondary inhibition of the activity of the pump (active transport) which requires the hydrolysis of ATP. In contrast, ouabain has a direct inhibitory effect on the pump with no effect on other active cell processes that do not utilize the pump, but do require ATP.

In the presence of ouabain, sodium cannot be pumped out of the cell into the extracellular fluid and potassium cannot be pumped in the opposite direction. However, these ions can still diffuse passively down their concentration gradients. Thus sodium, which is normally in higher concentration extracellularly (due to the pump), will diffuse into the cell, while potassium will diffuse out of the cell. Without active transport to maintain the gradient, the concentration gradient will dissipate by passive diffusion, and sodium will accumulate intracellularly and potassium will accumulate extracellularly relative to the standard conditions of the cell.

98. **(D)**   99. **(C)**   100. **(B)**

The three observations made were chosen because they can identify each of the cell types. A parenchyma cell contains chloroplasts, which are present in leaves. There are "air spaces" between the parenchyma cells composing the tissue; this does not mean that there are air spaces within any one cell. The upper and lower epidermis sandwich the palisade and spongy mesophyll layers. The latter layer, in particular, is laden with air spaces, which aid in nutrient and gas exchange. The chloroplasts are located in cells throughout the mesophyll layer. As the site of food production, leaves also store food. Food storage also occurs in stems and roots. While leaves are alive at maturity, so are the stems, roots, etc.

Both parenchyma and collenchyma cells are alive. While it can not be stated that every live cell will undergo mitosis, it is certainly true that a dead cell, such as a sclerenchyma cell, cannot divide. Note that the more specialized a cell is, the more likely that it will lose its capacity for division. Hence, parenchyma cells are the least specialized and are able to divide.

Since they serve a supportive role, one might correctly presume that collenchyma is present particularly in the stems. It is also present in leaf stalks and along the veins of leaves. Thus cell B is a collenchyma cell, cell A is a parenchyma cell, and cell C is a sclerenchyma cell.

SECTION II

ESSAY I

The complete oxidation of glucose is represented by the following equation:

$$\text{glucose} + 6\ O_2 \rightarrow 6\ CO_2 + 6\ H_2O = 38\ ATP$$

Glucose, in the presence of oxygen forms carbon dioxide, water, and ATP. ATP, or adenosine triphosphate, is the energy currency of the cell. Three major series of reactions are involved in the above reaction, with a total of about 30 individual steps. These reaction series are called glycolysis, Krebs cycle, and the electron transport chain. Each series occurs in a certain part of the cell, where the necessary enzymes are compartmentalized. A cell, with only the plasma membrane and one mitochondrion is depicted schematically below. The mitochondrion is the sole organelle required for energy synthesis. Of course, there are many mitochondria in cells, particularly in active cells such as skeletal muscle cells.

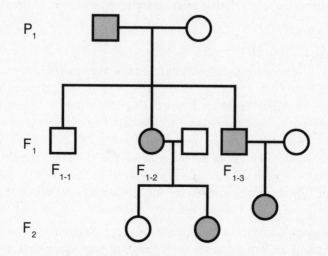

Note that the mitochondrion (plural, mitochondria) has two membranes. The inner membrane is folded and these folds are called cristae. The folding increases the surface area available for enzymatic reactions.

Glycolysis occurs in the cytoplasm. The Krebs cycle occurs in the mitochondrial matrix. The electron transport chain occurs on the inner mitochondrial membrane, including the cristae.

The process begins when glucose enters the cell as stimulated by the action of insulin. The first glycolytic enzyme is hexokinase. It transfers a phosphate group from ATP to form glucose-6-phosphate:

$$\text{Glucose} + \text{ATP} \quad \text{fi} \quad \text{Glucose-6-phosphate} + \text{ADP}$$

Note that although ultimately many ATPs will be formed, one ATP is required initially. In the next step, glucose-6-phosphate is isomerized to fructose-6-phosphate. The third step also requires an ATP molecule, since a phosphate group is added to fructose-6-phosphate to form fructose-1,6-diphosphate. In the next step, the six-carbon molecule is split into two three-carbon molecules. Several more steps are required to produce the final product of glycolysis, two molecules of pyruvic acid (or pyruvate, the salt form), a three-carbon molecule. Four molecules of ATP are produced and two molecules of NAD$^+$ (nicotinamide adenine dinucleotide) are reduced in those same steps.

Pyruvic acid has several fates in the cell. In yeast and other microorganisms, pyruvic acid is converted into ethanol in a process called alcoholic fermentation. This occurs in the absence of oxygen.

In the absence of oxygen, higher organisms such as ourselves produce lactic acid from pyruvic acid. Of interest here is the fate of pyruvic acid in the presence of oxygen. Pyruvic acid will enter the mitochondrial matrix, where it is converted to a two-carbon molecule called acetyl coenzyme A (acetyl CoA, for short). The third carbon is released as CO_2. The reaction catalyzed by this enzyme is summarized below:

$$\text{pyruvic acid} + \text{NAD}^+ + \text{CoA} \quad \text{fi} \quad \text{acetyl CoA} + CO_2 + \text{NADH}$$

Acetyl CoA is the starting point of the Krebs cycle. It is an important metabolic intermediate, as both fatty acids (via B-oxidation) and amino acids (via deamination) enter the Krebs cycle with acetyl CoA. Acetyl CoA enters the Krebs cycle by combining with a four-carbon molecule, oxaloacetate, to form the six-carbon citrate, or citric acid. The citrate undergoes several oxidation and decarboxylation steps to eventually become, once again, the four-carbon oxaloacetate. Each molecule of pyruvic acid that enters the Krebs cycle produces one molecule of GTP (guanosine triphosphate), and causes the reduction of three molecules of NAD$^+$ and one molecule of FAD, forming NADH and FADH$_2$, respectively.

The NADHs and FADH$_2$s formed in glycolysis and the Krebs cycle pass to the inner mitochondrial membrane to enter a series of oxidation/reduction reactions there. The oxidation of NADH yields 3 ATPs, whereas the oxidation of FADH$_2$ yields only 2 ATPs. The oxidation steps are coupled to the phosphorylation of ADP to form ATP, hence oxidative phosphorylation refers to the sequence of reactions of the electron transport, or respiratory, chain.

In the respiratory chain, the major group of electron carriers are cytochrome enzymes. The cytochromes can exist in an oxidized or a reduced form. Yet the cytochromes are pure electron carriers and do not pick up hydrogens. Like hemoglobin, cytochromes contain a heme group. Heme is an iron-containing pigment. Iron (Fe) can exist in the oxidized form Fe^{3+} or the reduced form Fe^{2+}. The electrons of the reducing equivalents are transferred to the cytochromes in a series of steps. The final step is catalyzed by cytochrome oxidase: oxygen is reduced to water as it oxidizes the cytochrome.

In 1961, Peter Mitchell proposed the chemiosmotic hypothesis to explain how oxidation is coupled to phosphorylation. The basic premise is that during electron transport, a proton (H^+) gradient develops across the inner mitochondrial membrane, with protons accumulating in the intermembranal space. This is due to the pumping of a pair of protons into this space at three sites along each respiratory chain. A "lollipop"-like enzyme traverses the inner mitochondrial membrane. The stalk penetrates the membrane, while the head faces the matrix. Protons flow back into the matrix through the stalk. The ATP synthetase portion is the head of the stalk. As protons flow back to the matrix down their gradient enough energy is generated to phosphorylate ADP to form ATP. Thus most of the ATP produced in the cell is due to oxidative phosphorylation. By comparison, glycolysis provides only a little ATP.

A diagram is shown below. Note that the original reaction is proven, where the reactants are glucose and oxygen and the products are water, carbon dioxide and ATP. These reactants and products are circled.

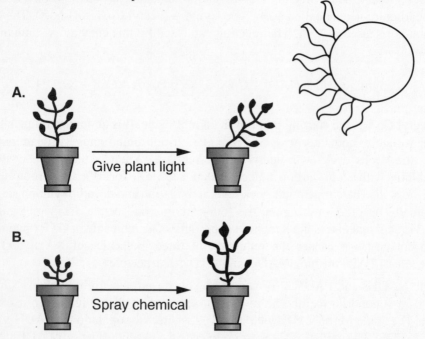

The energy that is required for the reaction that is catalyzed by the ATP synthetase, namely ADP + Pi → ATP is provided by the movement of protons (H^+) along their concentration gradient.

ESSAY II

Genes are the units of heredity, located on chromosomes. Genes occur in various forms, or alleles, the combinations of which code for the specific expression of traits. Each individual inherits one allele of each gene from his mother and one from his father. If an individual inherits two identical alleles of a gene, he is said to be homozygous for that trait; he is a homozygote. If the alleles are different, the individual is heterozygous for the trait; he is a heterozygote. The genotype is the individual's genetic constitution, whereas the phenotype refers to the expression of the genotype.

There are many different types of genetic inheritance patterns. The simplest is that of dominant and recessive inheritance. This is best exemplified by the inheritance of eye color in man. Let B represent the dominant allele for brown eyes and b represent the recessive allele for blue eyes. If an individual has the genotype BB, he is homozygous dominant and hence has the phenotype of brown eyes. An individual with the genotype bb is homozygous recessive and has the phenotype of blue eyes. A heterozygote, Bb, has brown eyes because B is dominant to b. Note that there are two genotypes (BB and Bb) that represent the phenotype brown eyes.

A Punnett square below shows a cross between two heterozygotes.

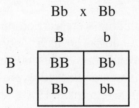

The parents are brown-eyed. Phenotypically, 75% of their offspring will have brown eyes and 25% will have blue eyes. The genotypes are 25% BB (homozygous dominant), 50% Bb (heterozygous) and 25% bb (homozygous recessive).

Some traits show incomplete dominance, whereby a dominant allele cannot fully mask the recessive allele. This is best exemplified in flower color. Let R be the dominant allele for red flower color and r be the recessive allele for white flower color. When a red flower (RR) is crossed with a white one (rr), the first generation plants are all pink (Rr). The Punnett square shows this cross:

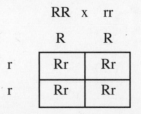

If the allele for red were fully dominant, the heterozygote plants would all be red.

In codominance, a heterozygote with two dominant alleles expresses them both equally. This is best exemplified by the inheritance of blood antigens. There are multiple alleles, I^A, I^B, and i, possible at the locus that codes for blood type. Of course, any one individual inherits only two alleles. I^A and I^B are dominant to i, yet are codominant with each other.

Type A blood is expressed by the genotypes $I^A I^A$ and $I^A i$. Recall that I^A is dominant to i. This person has only A-antigens on his red blood cells.

A phenotypically type B person has the genotype $I^B I^B$ or $I^B i$. This person has only B antigens on his red blood cells.

The AB phenotype is expressed by the genotype $I^A I^B$. These alleles are codominant and the person has both A and B antigens on his red blood cells.

The homozygous recessive genotype ii is expressed phenotypically by Type O blood. Type O blood only occurs when there is no dominant allele. This person has no antigens on his red blood cells.

Sex-linked inheritance is a little more complex. There are two sex chromosomes: X and Y. A female has XX, while a male has XY. Unlike other pairs of chromosomes, these chromosomes do not look alike. The X-chromosome is much larger than the Y. While the Y codes only for male sex, the X-chromosome contains other genes on it. The genes for color-blindness and hemophilia are carried on the X-chromosome. These two disorders are coded by recessive genes. Some types of baldness may be inherited in the same manner.

Since hemophilia and color-blindness are carried on the X-chromosome, these disorders are seen primarily in males, who have only one X-chromosome. The reason is that because males have only one X chromosome, when a male inherits an X-chromosome with the recessive gene, he will express the disease, since his Y-chromosome has no dominant allele to mask it. However, if a female inherits an X-chromosome with the recessive gene, she most likely will have the normal dominant allele on her other X-chromosome; thus she will carry the trait, but will not express it. For a female to express it, her father must have the disease while her mother must at least be a carrier. The likelihood of that combination is low, unless there is marriage between relatives.

The example provided deals with color blindness, although hemophilia is transmitted in an analogous manner. Suppose C is the dominant allele for normal color vision, and c is the allele for color blindness. A male is either normal ($X^C Y$) or color blind ($X^c Y$); a female is either normal ($X^C X^C$), a carrier ($X^C X^c$), or color blind ($X^c X^c$). A cross between "a carrier" mother and a normal father is shown below:

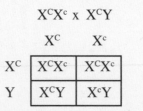

$$X^C X^c \times X^C Y$$

	X^C	X^c
X^C	$X^C X^C$	$X^C X^c$
Y	$X^C Y$	$X^c Y$

Note that the offspring are 25% of each of the following: normal female (X^CX^C), carrier female (X^CX^c), normal male (X^CY), and color blind male (X^cY). The normal mode of transmission is in this manner, i.e., from a carrier mother to her son. The disorder is not passed from fathers to their sons, because sons inherit the Y chromosome from their father and the Y chromosome does not contain these genes.

It is important to note that the <u>gene</u> for color blindness or hemophilia is passed equally to male and female offspring; however, it is <u>expressed</u> more often in the male due to lack of a dominant allele to mask it.

Also, when two populations of one organism are separated geographically, natural selection becomes a factor in the resulting phenotypical differences. As variance occurs through genetic inheritance, different environmental circumstances affect selection of characteristics. For example, if you separated a species of birds raised in the one environment, so that no interbreeding could occur, one could observe the differences. For example, if one group was kept in the same environment in which it was raised, and the other was placed in an environment where the bugs lived deep in the woods, one would expect that over generations, the second group would exhibit longer beaks. The different phenotype is expressed because it became favorable to survive in a different niche. Speciation is caused when the differences become incompatible with reproductive success.

ESSAY III

Homeostasis refers to the stability of the internal environment, which is composed of the extracellular fluid compartment (plasma and interstitial fluids). The concept was first introduced by Claude Bernard, who, around 1870, discussed the importance of the "milieu interieur." In the 1930s, Walter Cannon coined the term *homeostasis*. In short, all organ systems, but primarily the nervous and endocrine systems, strive to keep parameters of the internal environment constant, for this is the fluid in which our cells live. Some of the parameters monitored include the composition, temperature, osmotic pressure, and pH of the blood.

Stress causes an imbalance in the internal environment, be it external stress such as heat, noise, or surgery, or internal stress, such as infection or poison. The body compensates and counteracts the stress by homeostatic mechanisms. Thus, for instance, body temperature is normally regulated at 98.6 degrees F. (37^0 C), despite changes in the ambient temperature. If homeostasis were not functional, disease, and ultimately death, would ensue. Fever occurs when homeostasis of body temperature is non-functional; hypertension is a result of unregulated blood pressure; dehydration is due to a loss of blood and fluid volume; acidosis is evident when the pH of the blood drops.

The major mechanism that functions to maintain homeostasis is negative feedback. In feedback, the information about the status of a parameter (such as blood pressure, blood glucose) is monitored and reported to a central control region, which has a setpoint. The input (the status) is compared to the setpoint for the parameter. The control region then initiates a response if the status of the monitored parameter is not what it should be (the setpoint). In negative feedback, response of the body counteracts the effects of stress. Thus, a drop in blood glucose concentration elicits the release of glucagon to bring the concentration back up; the opposite input, a rise in the blood glucose level would elicit the release of insulin, which lowers the blood glucose level by transporting glucose into the cells.

While all the organ systems function in homeostasis (the respiratory system exchanges gases that are dissolved in the blood with gases that are present in alveoli; the kidneys regulate the volume and composition of the plasma), the major systems that control homeostasis are the nervous and endocrine systems. The nervous system has receptors that may detect an imbalance and send messages to counteract the imbalance or elicit hormonal secretion from endocrine glands. The nervous system sends action potentials that induce action immediately, albeit the signals are of short duration. In contrast, the endocrine system sends chemical signals, whose effects are longer-lasting, though there may be a latency to the effect.

A simplistic view of the homeostatic control of blood pressure and volume follows. Suppose the stress of hemorrhage occurs. The nervous system receives input concerning decreased blood pressure and blood volume. The nervous system responds by decreasing arterial baroreceptor activity. This causes vasoconstriction and an increase in heart rate. The vasoconstriction is an important way to increase blood pressure back to normal, while the increase in heart rate will increase cardiac output. The drop in blood volume is a signal to the hypothalamus to stimulate the posterior pituitary gland to release ADH (antidiuretic hormone). This hormone acts on the kidneys to reabsorb water into the blood and thus raise blood volume and ultimately blood pressure. Thus the interplay of nervous and endocrine activity functions in homeostasis.

To test if adrenaline and noradrenaline are important in preparing the body for "flight or fight," take four sets of mice, two test groups — one with their adrenal medulla destroyed, one group with normal adrenal medullas — and one control group for each. Artificially stimulate the adrenal glands for one group in each set. Monitor their heart rate, blood glucose level and respiration rate. Under a stressful condition, one would expect in a normal animal for all of the rates to be increased, as epinephrine and norepinephrine are known to exert those effects. The gas exchange will be increased because the hormone relaxes smooth muscle in the air passages. Compare the rates of the stimulated groups to each other and to the control groups. One would expect to find the normal mice with higher rates, above all of the other groups. To test the hypothesis further, inject the normal and mutant rats with epinephrine, and follow the same experiment. In this scenario, one would expect to find the test groups to have significantly different levels than the control group.

ESSAY IV

Just as an animal hormone is secreted by endocrine glands and released into the blood, a plant hormone is produced in one tissue and transported to another, exerting a specific effect. Only small amounts are needed to have the desired effect. Like animal hormones, plant hormones function in growth, development and metabolism. The major groups of plant hormones are the auxins, cytokinins, gibberellins, ethylene, abscisic acid, and perhaps florigen. Unlike animal hormones, a plant hormone may exert an effect on the tissue or cells in which it was produced.

Auxin was the first of the plant hormones to be discovered. The primary auxin is called IAA (indoleacetic acid). Auxin causes cell elongation and is responsible for the phototropic effect, whereby a plant bends toward a light source. This is due to cell elongation on the side of the plant that is away from the light, to which the auxin has migrated in response to the light. Auxin also plays a role in abscission, apical dominance, and the growth of fruit. Diminished concentrations of auxin promote fruit and leaf dropping.

Cytokinins function in cytoplasmic division, hence their name. They are especially important in tissues that are growing, such as germinating seeds. Yet they have other effects as well. They prevent the aging and abscission of leaves. It is of interest that cytokinins resemble the purine adenine, one of the nitrogenous bases in nucleic acids. Gibberellins were named after a fungus, *Gibberella fujikuroi*, which infected rice plants and caused hyperelongation of the stems, causing these rice plants to fall over. Gibberellins are thus useful in the treatment of genetically dwarfed plants, which can grow to normal size after being treated with gibberellins. Gibberellins also have secondary functions. They can induce cellular differentiation and seed germination by causing enzymes to convert food from the edospore into a usable form for seedlings.

Ethylene is a hydrocarbon gas ($H_2C = CH_2$) released from the burning of kerosene. It was discovered that ripening occurred more rapidly in the presence of kerosene combustion, although it was erroneously believed that it was the heat produced that caused the ripening. In fact, plants themselves produce ethylene just prior to fruit ripening. It also causes the aging and subsequent abscission, or dropping, of leaves. Other effects include a role in seed germination, and may determine sex in some flowers.

Abscisic acid is the primary inhibitory hormone, albeit named incorrectly for its postulated role in abscission. Abscisic acid in general does not cause abscission, but rather causes dormancy. It protects against unfavorable environmental conditions. For example it causes the stomata to close to prevent water loss. It encourages downward growth of roots if seedlings are in an unfavorable position.

Florigen is a postulated hormone that induces flowering. However, no specific hormone has been identified, and perhaps flowering is due to a combination of hormones. For instance, both auxin and gibberellin may induce flowering. There are probably also hormones that inhibit flowering. Florigen, the postulated flowering hormone, has not been isolated. Florigen is not a specific hormone, but probably a combination of plant hormones already identified. Auxin and gibberellin are two hormones which are likely to be identified as "florigen." It is possible that those hormones may inhibit flowering as well. The amount or level of each hormone present is likely to be a major determining factor.

THE ADVANCED PLACEMENT EXAMINATION IN

EXAMINATION IN

BIOLOGY

TEST III

ADVANCED PLACEMENT BIOLOGY EXAM III

SECTION I

100 Questions
80 Minutes

DIRECTIONS: For each question, there are five possible choices. Select the best choice for each question. Blacken the correct space on the answer sheet.

1. Water's ability to regulate environmental temperatures within a small range conducive to life is partially due to its
   (A) function as a universal solvent.
   (B) high heat capacity.
   (C) nonpolarity.
   (D) viscosity.
   (E) maximum density at zero degrees Celsius.

2. A factor that contributed greatly to the prolonged existences of simple organic molecules in Earth's prebiotic oceans was
   (A) the presence of simple amino acids.
   (B) the lack of high concentrations of atmospheric ammonia.
   (C) the presence of rudimentary enzymes.
   (D) the extremely low concentrations of atmospheric methane.
   (E) the virtual absence of atmospheric oxygen.

3. Name the bone that does not articulate with the humerus.
   (A) clavicle   (D) shoulder blade

(B) radius   (E) ulna

(C) scapula

4. A cell's nucleolus is found in its:
   - (A) cytoplasm
   - (B) E.R.
   - (C) mitochondrion
   - (D) nucleus
   - (E) plasma membrane

5. Removal of a cell's ribosomes would result in a cell's inability to utilize which of the following molecules?
   - (A) carbon dioxide
   - (B) carbon monoxide
   - (C) lysine
   - (D) oxygen
   - (E) phosphorus

6. Select the protease:
   - (A) amylase
   - (B) maltose
   - (C) pepsin
   - (D) ptyalin
   - (E) sucrase

7. Tetraploidy that occurs in an organism whose species normally has 80 chromosomes per cell will cause the organism's somatic cells to contain how many chromosomes?
   - (A) 20
   - (B) 40
   - (C) 60
   - (D) 80
   - (E) 160

8. A primary sex cell experiences one nondisjunction during meiosis. If the normal diploid number of chromosomes in the cell is 42, how many chromosomes are present in one of the defective gametes?
   - (A) 20
   - (B) 21
   - (C) 24
   - (D) 41
   - (E) 43

9. The term metastasis refers to the fact that cancer cells tend to:
   - (A) destroy
   - (B) divide
   - (C) reproduce
   - (D) shrink
   - (E) wander

10. Muscles pull on bones from their:

   (A) antagonists to prime movers

   (B) insertions to origins

   (C) origins to insertions

   (D) prime movers to synergists

   (E) synergists to antagonists

11. A cell is inhibited during the S phase of its cycle. It will not reproduce due to lack of:

   (A) ATP availability

   (B) centriole migration

   (C) centromere formation

   (D) DNA synthesis

   (E) plasma membrane structure

12. One of hemoglobin's subunits, about 150 amino acids long, requires a coded DNA sequence that contains how many nucleotides?

   (A) 3   (D) 150

   (B) 50   (E) 450

   (C) 100

13. Eye receptors and their function can best be summarized as:

   (A) cones - color discrimination, rods - twilight vision

   (B) cones - twilight vision, rods - color discrimination

   (C) ganglia - color discrimination, rods - twilight vision

   (D) lens - light refraction, cornea - light refraction

   (E) neurons - twilight vision, ganglia - color discrimination

14. Certain oncogenic viruses violate the central dogma of biochemical genetics by transferring genetic information in which of the following sequences?

   (A) DNA, protein, RNA

   (B) DNA, RNA, protein

   (C) RNA, DNA, protein

   (D) protein, DNA, RNA

   (E) RNA, protein, DNA

15.   Which stimulus will activate the lactose operon in a bacterial cell?

   (A) Absence of lactose

   (B) Availability of an inducer

   (C) Cistron repression

   (D) Regulator gene dominance.

   (E) Repressor molecule binding to the operator gene.

Question 16 refers to the diagram below.

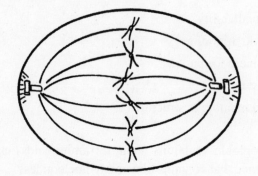

16.   This illustration shows a cell in the mitotic stage of:

   (A) anaphase   (D) prophase

   (B) interphase   (E) telophase

   (C) metaphase

17.   Four different DNA bases, transcribed in groups of three with possible base repetition, yield a number of codons, or three-letter combinations equaling:

   (A) 1   (D) 64

   (B) 4   (E) 128

   (C) 16

18.   During transcription, an RNA polymerase adds a uracil-containing nucleotide to the RNA molecule. The base on the strand of DNA that is not being transcribed is:

   (A) Adenine   (D) Thymine

   (B) Cytosine   (E) Uracil

   (C) Guanine

19. After chromosomal mapping, it is found that genes A and B are ten units apart, genes B and C are five units apart, and genes A and C are fifteen units apart. Their sequence on the chromosome is:

   (A) A C B   (D) C A B
   (B) B A C   (E) C B A
   (C) B C A

20. The sequence of stem layers from the inside out is:

   (A) cambium-xylem-phloem-pith-cortex
   (B) cortex-phloem-cambium-xylem-pith
   (C) phloem-xylem-pith-cambium-cortex
   (D) pith-xylem-cambium-phloem-cortex
   (E) xylem-phloem-cortex-pith-cambium

21. The pattern of xylem growth is:

   (A) cambium lays it down to the inside year by year
   (B) cambium lays it down to the outside year by year
   (C) it alternates with phloem bands year by year
   (D) it is internal to the pith as a thin layer
   (E) the oldest layers are closest to the cambium

22. The monosaccharide products of lactase-controlled hydrolysis are:

   (A) fructose and maltose
   (B) galactose and glucose
   (C) glucose and fructose
   (D) glucose and glucose
   (E) sucrose and fructose

23. A mother of blood type B-negative gives birth to an infant of blood type O-positive. Which of the following blood types could be that of the father?

   (A) AB-negative   (D) A-positive
   (B) AB-positive   (E) B-negative
   (C) O-negative

24. Which of the following organisms has the largest surface area-to-volume ratio and is listed with its proper relative metabolic rate?

   (A) dog - varying metabolism
   (B) elephant - rapid metabolism

(C) horse - slow metabolism

(D) human - varying metabolism

(E) shrew - rapid metabolism

25. Assuming a 1/2 probability of reproducing a male offspring, the chance for five successive male births in a family is:

(A) 1/4   (D) 1/32

(B) 1/8   (E) 1/64

(C) 1/16

26. Which of the following is a key component of Darwin's principles?

(A) Abundance of resources is available for organisms.

(B) More population members are produced than can survive.

(C) Organisms in a population are uniform.

(D) Population members contribute equally to a gene pool.

(E) Survival rates do not vary among a population's members.

27. Two parents of genotype AaBb mate. Assuming independent assortment and random recombination, the chance for an offspring to phenotypically express the dominant allele of the first gene and the recessive allele of the second gene is:

(A) 9/16   (D) 2/16

(B) 6/16   (E) 1/16

(C) 3/16

28. Among humans, a universal recipient is a person that has which blood type?

(A) A+   (D) O+

(B) AB+   (E) O-

(C) AB-

29. An organism with three independently sorting gene pairs, AaBbCc, can produce a number of genetically different sex cells equaling:

(A) 2   (D) 8

(B) 4   (E) 16

(C) 6

30. All of the following are terms that describe viruses except:
    (A) free-living
    (B) host-dependent
    (C) noncellular
    (D) protein and nucleic acid makeup
    (E) ultramicroscopic

31. Humans, great apes, and monkeys are all members of which of the following taxonomic categories?
    (A) genus
    (B) family
    (C) subfamily
    (D) order
    (E) species

32. A zygote will produce a 32-cell blastula after dividing mitotically by a number of divisions equaling:
    (A) 2
    (B) 4
    (C) 5
    (D) 7
    (E) 8

Question 33 refers to the drawing of the two pairs of chromatids below.

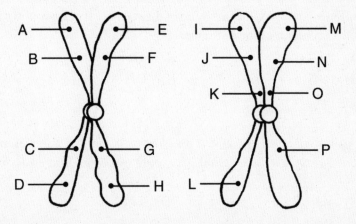

33. The two pairs of chromosomes are in a diploid cell that is in Prophase I of meiosis. If crossing-over of the medial chromosomes were to occur, one of the new chromosomes could have which of the following gene sequences?
    (A) ABGH
    (B) EFCD
    (C) EFKL
    (D) IJEF
    (E) IJKO

34. Greatest humidity is found in which region of a leaf ?
    (A) cuticle   (D) parenchyma
    (B) lower epidermis   (E) upper epidermis
    (C) mesophyll

35. Select the proper pair of phrases stating the condition and resulting plant growth of the chrysanthemum:
    (A) lateral leaf buds removed, terminal bud grows
    (B) lateral leaf buds remain, terminal bud inhibited
    (C) terminal bud remains, lateral buds grow
    (D) terminal bud removed, lateral buds unaffected
    (E) terminal bud removed, lateral buds grow

36. One thousand offspring are counted in a genetic cross. Five hundred and two appear dominant in phenotype while four hundred and ninety-eight appear recessive. The genotypes of the parents are most likely:
    (A) AA, AA   (D) Aa, aa
    (B) AA, Aa   (E) aa, aa
    (C) Aa, Aa

37. Following menses, the initiation of the menstrual cycle follows an increase in the secretion of the hormone:
    (A) ACTH   (D) GnRH
    (B) FSH   (E) GH
    (C) LH

38. A pair of mammalian kidneys reabsorbs 188 liters of water, eliminating 1.5 liters during that same period. The volume of water filtered during that time was:
    (A) 189.5 l (D) 141 l
    (B) 188 l (E) 1.5 l
    (C) 186.5 l

39. The two criteria used most often in taxonomic classifications are:
    (A) color and height
    (B) evolution and lifespan
    (C) lifespan and morphology

(D) morphology and phylogeny

(E) phylogeny and evolution

40. A heterozygous blood-type A person who is also Rh negative mates with a heterozygous blood-type B person who is Rh positive (heterozygous). The probability of producing an offspring of blood-type O-negative is:

(A) 0

(B) 1/8

(C) 3/8

(D) 1/2

(E) 5/8

41. Oak seeds are allowed to germinate in a Petri dish whose medium is fortified with high concentrations of auxin. As the seeds germinate into seedlings, the observed growth pattern is:

(A) lengthening of shoots and roots

(B) lengthening of shoots, inhibition of root growth

(C) inhibition of shoot and root growth

(D) inhibition of shoot growth, lengthening of the root

(E) no major effect on the roots or shoots

42. Tracheophytes:

(A) cannot conduct photosynthesis

(B) conduct and transport materials

(C) function as heterotrophs

(D) include fungi and mosses

(E) lack sexual reproduction

43. A protein currently synthesized by bacterial cells that have been altered by gene splicing is:

(A) actin

(B) AMP

(C) hemoglobin

(D) insulin

(E) myosin

44. The role of RNA polymerase is to:

(A) bind DNA nucleotides together during translation

(B) bind ribonucleotides together during transcription

(C) break down RNA during digestion

(D) destroy ribosomes during translation

(E) digest RNA nucleotides in an organism's diet

45. A person's blood pressure is taken, revealing a diastolic pressure of 90 mm Hg. The pulse pressure is 30 mm Hg. Systolic pressure is:

    (A) 30 mm Hg   (D) 120 mm Hg

    (B) 60 mm Hg   (E) 270 mm Hg

    (C) 90 mm Hg

46. An invertebrate is collected from a freshwater pond. Dissection of it shows three developmental body layers. It has a cuticle as its outer body covering. It belongs to the phylum:

    (A) Arthropoda   (D) Echinodermata

    (B) Annelida   (E) Porifera

    (C) Coelenterata

47. Rejection of a tissue graft in an organism is associated with heightened activity of:

    (A) B lymphocytes   (D) T monocytes

    (B) B monocytes   (E) neutrophils

    (C) T lymphocytes

48. A drug induces paralysis by blocking the function of acetylcholine. This drug specifically inhibits activity at which of the following structures?

    (A) cell body   (D) neurolemma

    (B) dendrite   (E) synapse

    (C) myelin sheath

49. Cells that sense sound are found in the ear's:

    (A) cochlea   (D) semicircular canals

    (B) eardrum   (E) vestibule

    (C) pinna

50. Blood normally circulates through vessels in which sequence?

    (A) artery - arteriole - capillary - venule - vein

    (B) arteriole - artery - capillary - vein - venule

    (C) capillary - arteriole - artery - vein - venule

    (D) vein - capillary - venule - artery - arteriole

    (E) vein - venule - arteriole - artery - capillary

51.   Primates are characterized by each of the following traits except:

(A) relatively large brains

(B) opposable thumbs

(C) rotating shoulder joints

(D) stereoscopic vision

(E) three-chambered hearts

52.   A randomly-mating population has an established frequency of 36% for organisms homozygous recessive for a given trait. The frequency of this recessive allele in the gene pool is:

(A) .24   (D) .6

(B) .36   (E) .64

(C) .5

53.   The abiotic source of nitrogen in the nitrogen cycle is in the:

(A) atmosphere   (D) minerals

(B) biomass   (E) water

(C) ground

54.   Primary consumers in a food chain are:

(A) animals   (D) decomposers

(B) bacteria   (E) herbivores

(C) carnivores

55.   A gas that causes asphyxiation by binding to hemoglobin thus preventing oxygen from doing so, is:

(A) carbon dioxide

(B) carbon monoxide

(C) nitrous oxide

(D) sulfur dioxide

(E) water vapor

56.   The chromosomal mutation by which a chromosome fragment attaches to a nonhomologous chromosome is termed a:

(A) deletion   (D) inversion

(B) diversion   (E) translocation

(C) duplication

57.   The order in which glands add seminal fluid to migrating semen is:

(A) Cowper's-seminal vesicle

(B) prostate-seminal vesicle-Cowper's

(C) prostate-Cowper's-seminal vesicle

(D) seminal vesicle-prostate-Cowper's

(E) seminal vesicle-Cowper's-prostate

58.   Most energy in a food chain will flow to:

(A) decomposers   (D) secondary consumers

(B) producers   (E) tertiary consumers

(C) primary consumers

DIRECTIONS: The following groups of questions have five lettered choices followed by a list of diagrams, numbered phrases, sentences, or words. For each numbered diagram, phrase, sentence, or word choose the heading which most directly applies. Blacken the correct space on the answer sheet. Each heading may be used once, more than once, or not at all.

Questions 59 - 62 refer to the drawings of functional groups below.

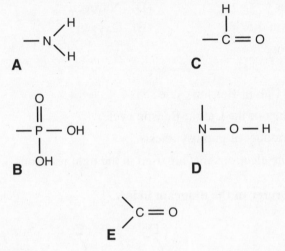

59.   amino acid
60.   fructose
61.   glucose
62.   nucleotide

Questions 63 - 65 refer to the diagram of the organelle below.

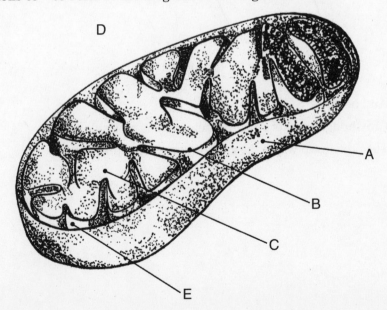

63.   The Krebs Cycle (citric acid cycle) occurs here.

64.   The majority of this organelle's energy harvest occurs here.

65.   Anaerobic metabolism of glucose occurs here.

Questions 66 - 69.

    (A) Water   (D) Nitrogen

    (B) Carbon dioxide   (E) Oxygen

    (C) Glucose

66.   Enters the Calvin-Benson cycle.

67.   Final product of the Calvin-Benson cycle.

68.   Gaseous product of photosynthesis.

69.   Provides the electrons that are used in the light reactions.

Questions 70 - 72 refer to the diagram below.

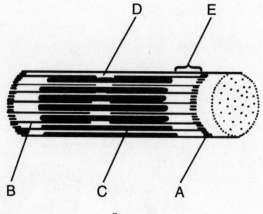

Sarcomere

70.   An I band.

71.   Crossbridges are specifically found on this molecule.

72.   The proteins to which the crossbridges temporarily bind.

Questions 73 - 74 refer to the diagram below.

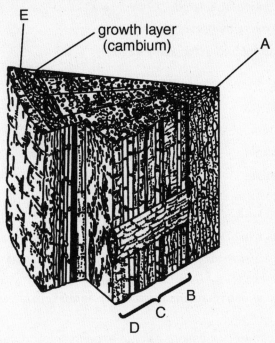

Three-Year Old Stem

73. A non-vascular layer is designated by this label.

74. The third-year growth layer is designated as this region.

Questions 75 - 77.

    (A) Ctenophora   (D) Annelida

    (B) Aschelminthes   (E) Mollusca

    (C) Arthropoda

75. Small, wormlike, and have flame cells, but lack circulatory and respiratory systems.

76. Radially symmetrical organisms with saclike bodies and mesogleal layers.

77. Organisms with a visceral mass and muscular foot.

Questions 78 - 81.

    (A) Sarcodina   (D) Sporozoa

    (B) Bacteriophage   (E) Ciliata

    (C) Mastigophora

78.   *Paramecium* is a member.

79.   Members move by flagella.

80.   Members move by pseudopodia.

81.   Parasites immobile in the adult stage.

Questions 82 - 85.

    (A) Porifera   (D) Platyhelminthes

    (B) Annelida   (E) Coelenterata

    (C) Chordata

82.   Organisms with some form of a dorsal supportive structure.

83.   Organisms which are radially symmetrical and possess nematocysts.

84.   These organisms are dorsoventrally flattened and have gastrovascular cavities.

85.   Organisms which retain many primitive animal characteristics.

Directions: The following questions refer to experimental or laboratory situations or data. Read the description of each situation. Then choose the best answer to each question. Blacken the correct space on the answer sheet.

Questions 86 - 88 refer to the diagram below.

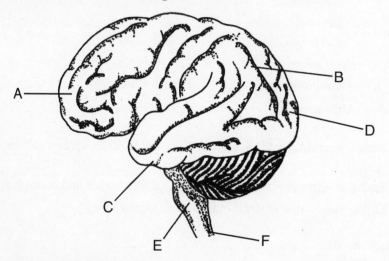

86.   A function of region F is:

    (A) abstract reasoning

    (B) control of blood pressure

    (C) hearing and vision processes

(D) memory

(E) vision

87.   Select the function not performed by region C.

(A) gustation   (D) taste

(B) hearing   (E) vision

(C) smell

88.   Region E is the:

(A) cerebellum   (D) medulla

(B) cerebrum   (E) pons

(C) hypothalamus

Questions 89 - 90 refer to the diagram below.

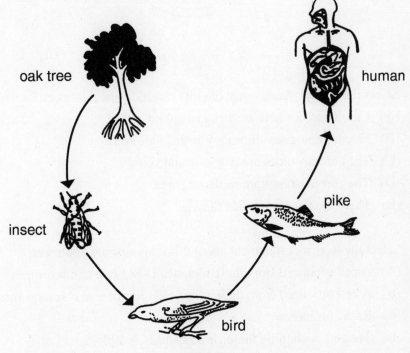

Food Chain

89.   In this food chain, which heterotroph receives the largest
       amount of useful energy?

(A) bird   (D) oak tree

(B) human   (E) pike

(C) insect

90.   Which of the following members of the food chain is an omnivore?

(A) bird   (D) oak tree

(B) human   (E) pike

(C) insect

Questions 91 - 93 refer to the drawing below.

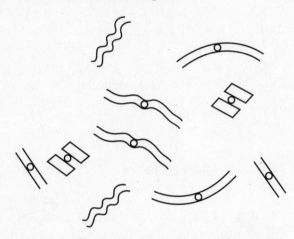

Chromosome extracted from a cell

91.   Select the correct statement about this chromosome allotment.

(A) Chromosomes here are from a haploid cell.

(B) Five homologous chromosome pairs are shown.

(C) The chromosomes are single-stranded.

(D) The chromosomes are triple-stranded.

(E) There are ten chromatids shown.

92.   Select the incorrect statement about this chromosome allotment.

(A) A cell produced from these meiotically has five chromosomes.

(B) A cell produced from these mitotically has twelve chromosomes.

(C) Each chromosome has a homologue.

(D) The cell containing these chromosomes is diploid.

(E) The chromosomes contain chromatids.

93.   An organized chromosome alignment made from this group is a:

(A) autosome   (D) karyotype

(B) complement   (E) sex linkage

(C) homologue

Questions 94 - 96 refer to the drawing below.

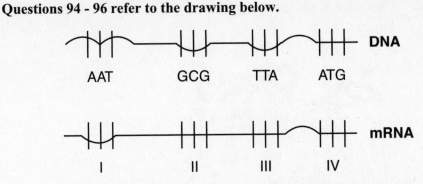

94.   RNA codons III and IV contain which of the following sequences?

(A) CCG and GCA   (D) AAT and TAC

(B) AAU and UAC   (E) UUC and CUA

(C) GGU and UGT

95.   The function of the ribosome is to:

(A) allow transcription between DNA and mRNA

(B) guide DNA along mRNA for duplication

(C) provide a meeting site for mRNA and tRNA

(D) transfer amino acids to DNA for ordering

(E) transport tRNA to DNA for translation

96.   The tRNA molecules that will bind to mRNA codons I and II will have which anticodons?

(A) UUA and CGC

(B) TTA and CGC

(C) CCG and TAT

(D) AAU and GCG

(E) GGC and ATA

Questions 97 - 98 refer to the following figure.

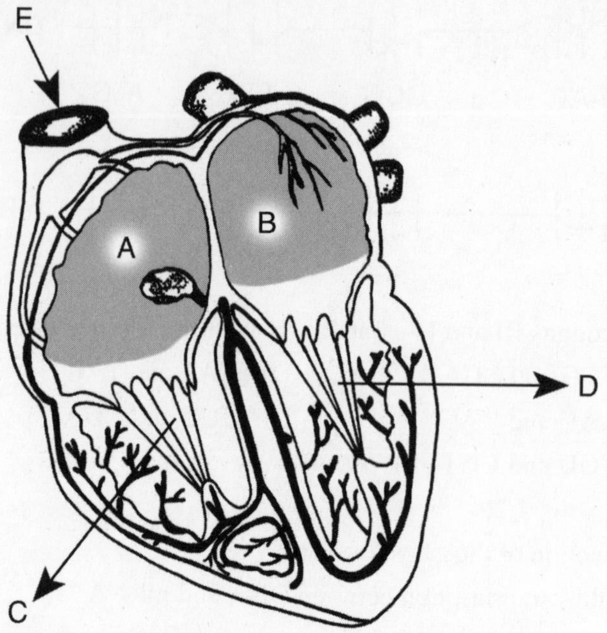

97. According to the figure, blood flows in the sequence:

(A) A-B-C-D-E

(B) A-C-B-D-E

(C) B-D-E-C-A

(D) B-C-A-B-E

(E) E-B-D-C-A

98. The region that directly sends blood to the lungs is:

(A) A

(B) B

(C) C

(D) D

(E) E

Questions 99 - 100 refer to the graph below.

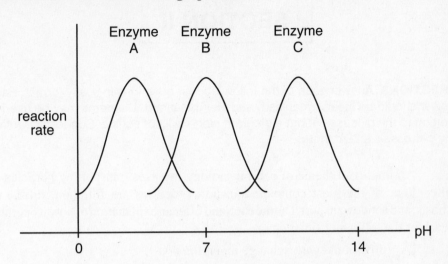

99.   Select the correct statement about the graph of enzyme activities.

    (A) All three enzymes work best at the same pH.

    (B) Enzyme C works best at the most acid pH.

    (C) Enzyme C works best at the most alkaline pH.

    (D) Enzyme A works best at the most basic pH.

    (E) Each enzyme works over pH values 0 to 14.

100.   Enzyme B could be which human enzyme?

    (A) amylase   (D) trypsin

    (B) pepsin   (E) maltase

    (C) sucrase

SECTION II

DIRECTIONS: Answer each of the following four questions in essay format. Each answer should be clear, organized, and well-balanced. Diagrams may be used in addition to the discussion, but a diagram alone will not suffice. Suggested writing time per essay is 22 minutes.

1.   An important theme of cell physiology involves transporting particles of matter. Four of the most common transport processes are filtration, diffusion, osmosis, and active transport. Define each and offer an explanation of how it operates in each of the following situations.

   (A) diffusion – gas exchange in an *Amoeba*

   (B) filtration and osmosis – fluid exchange in a capillary

   (C) active transport and diffusion – electrical membrane potential in a neuron

2.   How does Darwin's explanation of natural selection complement modern genetic knowledge to produce the current model of evolution? Offer an example of how this model could explain the change of a population characteristic through time: e.g., eye color, limb length, etc.

3.   Plant and animal cells reproduce by two patterns: mitosis and meiosis. Compare and contrast the two by:

   (A) contribution to plant and animal life cycles

   (B) manipulation of chromosome number in cells

   (C) roles in growth and development

   (D) relationship to each other in sexually reproducing organisms

4.   Compare water balance problems dealt with by a saltwater and freshwater fish. What adaptions have they evolved to solve these problems? How do these mechanisms compare to solutions evolved by terrestrial mammals, particularly to their kidney structure and function?

ADVANCED PLACEMENT BIOLOGY EXAM III

ANSWER KEY

1.	(B)	26.	(B)	51.	(E)	76.	(A)
2.	(E)	27.	(C)	52.	(D)	77.	(E)
3.	(A)	28.	(B)	53.	(A)	78.	(E)
4.	(D)	29.	(D)	54.	(E)	79.	(C)
5.	(C)	30.	(A)	55.	(B)	80.	(A)
6.	(C)	31.	(D)	56.	(E)	81.	(D)
7.	(E)	32.	(C)	57.	(D)	82.	(C)
8.	(A)	33.	(C)	58.	(B)	83.	(E)
9.	(E)	34.	(C)	59.	(A)	84.	(D)
10.	(B)	35.	(E)	60.	(E)	85.	(A)
11.	(D)	36.	(D)	61.	(C)	86.	(B)
12.	(E)	37.	(B)	62.	(B)	87.	(E)
13.	(A)	38.	(A)	63.	(C)	88.	(E)
14.	(C)	39.	(D)	64.	(B)	89.	(C)
15.	(B)	40.	(B)	65.	(D)	90.	(B)
16.	(C)	41.	(B)	66.	(B)	91.	(B)
17.	(D)	42.	(B)	67.	(C)	92.	(B)
18.	(D)	43.	(D)	68.	(E)	93.	(D)
19.	(E)	44.	(B)	69.	(A)	94.	(B)
20.	(D)	45.	(D)	70.	(E)	95.	(C)
21.	(A)	46.	(A)	71.	(C)	96.	(D)
22.	(B)	47.	(A)	72.	(B)	97.	(B)
23.	(D)	48.	(E)	73.	(A)	98.	(C)
24.	(E)	49.	(A)	74.	(D)	99.	(C)
25.	(D)	50.	(A)	75.	(B)	100.	(A)

ADVANCED PLACEMENT
BIOLOGY EXAM III

DETAILED EXPLANATIONS
OF ANSWERS

SECTION I

1.   **(B)**

Heat capacity is the amount of heat energy required to separate a given amount of molecules. The higher the heat capacity, the more stable the set of molecules is. Water has a high heat capacity (1 cal/gm/^{0}C), therefore, it is highly stable and relatively unaffected by large changes in environmental temperature. Water is not a universal solvent because it is a polar molecule and will, therefore, only dissolve other polar (mostly inorganic) molecules. Viscosity refers to the rate at which a liquid flows and does not pertain to this question.

2.   **(E)**

The virtual absence of atmospheric oxygen allowed organic molecules in Earth's prebiotic areas to exist without undergoing oxidation. Had oxygen been present in appreciable concentrations, early organic molecules would have been oxidized and would therefore have been rendered unable to form macromolecules, the formation of which represented the next step towards "life." Simple amino acids were present, but they did not contribute to their own survival. Atmospheric ammonia was present in high concentrations, as was atmospheric methane. Rudimentary enzymes were not present at first, and could not have contributed to the prolongation of the molecules' existences.

3.   **(A)**

The humerus, or the upper arm bone, articulates with the radius and ulna (forearm bones) at its distal end. Its other end fits into the lateral socket of the scapula, or shoulder blade. It does not articulate with the clavicle, or collarbone.

4.   **(D)**

The nucleolus is a dark-staining spherical body inside the cell's nucleus. It is not associated with an organelle nor is it in the cytoplasm.

5.   **(C)**

Lysine is an amino acid, a subunit of proteins. Ribosomes are the sites of protein synthesis in a cell. By their loss, a cell would lose its ability to incorporate incoming amino acids into the proteins that it builds.

6.   **(C)**

Pepsin is a protease. This enzyme catalyzes chemical breakdown of proteins. The other four choices belong to the enzyme class of carbohydrases. They catalyze carbohydrate digestion. Amylase, also known as ptyalin, catalyzes the digestion of the polysaccharide starch into the sugar maltose. Sucrase and maltase break down the carbohydrate disaccharides sucrose and maltose, respectively.

7.   **(E)**

Somatic cells are diploid. In this species the diploid (di = 2) chromosome number is 80. A tetraploid (tetra = 4) chromosomal would contain 160 chromosomes, because there would be four, instead of two, choices of each chromosome.

8.   **(A)**

A diploid cell proceeding through meiosis yields haploid daughter cells with a halved chromosome number. A cell with a diploid chromosome number of 42 has 21 pairs of homologous chromosomes. If all twenty-one pairs undergo normal disjunctions, then each daughter cell will contain twenty-one chromosomes. If only twenty pairs do so, then one daughter cell will have twenty chromosomes and one will have twenty-two chromosomes.

9.   **(E)**

Wandering to other body sites from point of production is a characteristic of cancer cells. This traveling seeds other body regions with the rapidly-dividing cells, thus spreading the cancer.

10.   **(B)**

The insertion is the more moveable of the two locations to which a muscle is attached. The origin is the anchored end toward which the movable end moves to produce movement. Prime mover refers to the main muscle contracting to produce a movement. Its opposing antagonistic muscle must yield by stretching or relaxing. The synergist is a muscle that aids the prime mover in its action.

11.   **(D)**

In a cell cycle, the S phase is characterized by DNA synthesis prior to the active stages of mitosis. Chromosomes must duplicate at this stage or there will be an absence of chromosome duplicates to separate into daughter cells during division.

12. **(E)**

Three DNA nucleotides code for one amino acid in a protein. The ratio is 3 to 1, or 450 to 150.

13. **(A)**

Rods and cones are retinal cells lining the eye's inner surface. Cones are specialized for color discrimination or visual activity. Rods are utilized in dim light.

14. **(C)**

Normally, genetic information is transferred from DNA to RNA; RNA then provides the necessary information for protein synthesis. A few oncogenic (cancer-causing) viruses are known to transfer information from RNA to DNA; the DNA then directs protein synthesis.

15. **(B)**

In the lac operon model, the sugar, lactose, is the inducer. It will bind to the repressor produced by the regulator gene. Unable to bind to and inhibit the operator gene, the repressor is inhibited. This allows the operator gene to activate the cistrons. These structural genes synthesize the enzymes that metabolize the substrate lactose.

16. **(C)**

During mitotic metaphase, the chromosomes align in the equatorial plane of the cell's mitotic spindle. In anaphase, the centromeres split and chromosome duplicates are pulled apart. The cell divides into two daughter cells in the next stage, telophase. Prophase precedes metaphase.

17. **(D)**

The number of permutations is 4^3, or 64.

18. **(D)**

If a uracil-containing nucleotide is added, then the DNA nucleotide on the strand that is being transcribed must contain adenine. Therefore, the base on the strand of DNA that is not being transcribed must contain thymine.

19. **(E)**

A and C are farthest apart. B, which is 10 units from A and 5 units from C, is in between. Thus, ABC or CBA are the only choices compatible with the data.

20. **(D)**

Pith is the core, with xylem placed around it by the cambial growth layer. Phloem is deposited to the outside, with the cortex external to it.

21.   **(A)**

Each year the cambium puts down a new xylem layer, pushing older ones progressively toward the center. As xylem ages and matures, it becomes the stem's wood.

22.   **(B)**

Lactase is the enzyme that catalyzes the hydrolysis of the disaccharide lactose into its monosaccharide components, galactose and glucose. Glucose and glucose are the monosaccharide components of the disaccharide maltose. Glucose and fructose compose the disaccharide sucrose.

23.   **(D)**

The father could not have had a blood-type with a negative Rh-factor, because the trait for a negative Rh-factor is recessive. The father must also have blood-type O or, heterozygously, have blood type A or B, in order for him to have donated a recessive i (blood-type O) gene. Therefore, the father must have blood-type A^+, B^+ or O^+. Only A-positive is listed as a choice.

24.   **(E)**

Among mammals, the smaller the organism, the greater its surface-to-volume ratio and coupled metabolism. The shrew is the smallest mammal among the choices and shows these characteristics.

25.   **(D)**

The probability of independent events occurring in succession is the product of their separate probabilities. Births are independent events. 1/2 to the fifth power equals 1/32.

26.   **(B)**

Populations have a tremendous capacity to increase their numbers. There is competition for resources in short supply. Genetic variations best equipped to survive will do so at a higher probability. Their chance to reproduce and contribute genes to the next generation is also more likely.

27.   **(C)**

This is an example of a dihybrid cross. Phenotypically, 9/16 of the offspring express the dominant allele of both genes, 3/16 of the offspring express the dominant allele of the first gene and the recessive allele of the second gene, 3/16 of the offspring express the dominant allele of the second gene and the recessive allele of the first gene, and 1/16 of the offspring will express the recessive alleles of both genes.

28.   **(B)**

A person of blood-type AB has no anti-A and no anti-B antibodies in his blood plasma. Therefore, there will be no antibodies present that would attack foreign red blood cells that enter the bloodstream during transfusion. A person whose blood has a positive Rh-factor also has no antibodies that attack Rh antigens present on red blood cells. Therefore, a person of blood-type AB+ would have no trouble in receiving any type of blood during a transfusion.

29.   **(D)**

The formula for this is 2^n, in which n equals the number of heterozygous gene pairs. $2 \times 2 \times 2 = 8$.

30.   **(A)**

Viruses are incredibly small (nanometers). They lack normal cellular structures and thus need a host organism to grow and reproduce. They consist of protein coats surrounding nucleic acid cores.

31.   **(D)**

All are members of the order of Primates.

32.   **(C)**

The zygote is the fertilized egg, or first cell. Five divisions of mitosis will increase the early embryo cell number to 32.

33.   **(C)**

Crossing-over, the exchange of corresponding regions of homologous chromosomes, could occur between the two medial chromosomes (EFGH and IJKL) to produce many possible new chromosomes, one of which is EFKL.

34.   **(C)**

This is the photosynthetic layer saturated with water vapor found between the upper and lower epidermis. The high water vapor content usually assures 100% humidity.

35.   **(E)**

Pruning a flowering plant, that is, cutting off the bud at the plant shoot apex, removes the source of the plant hormone that would travel vertically down the plant and inhibit lateral bud growth. In its absence, lateral bud growth from the shoot increases. The growth hormone traveling most often through the plant is of a family termed the auxins.

36.　　**(D)**

Working backwards from offspring to parents, an Aa x aa cross is the only possible one producing a 50-50 ratio in offspring variability. Consider the genetic grid:

	A	a
a	Aa	aa
a	Aa	aa

37.　　**(B)**

The concentration of follicle-stimulating hormone, FSH, increases following menses. Thus, the menstrual cycle continues. It is secreted by the pituitary gland and serves to increase follicle growth around a selected sex cell in the ovary.

ACTH　=　adrenocorticotrophic hormone

LH　　=　luteinizing hormone

GnRH　=　gonadotrophin-releasing hormone

GH　　=　growth hormone

38.　　**(A)**

In renal physiology, the volume eliminated equals the volume filtered minus the volume reabsorbed. $X - 1.5l = 188l$ eliminated. The unknown amount equals $189.5l$.

39.　　**(D)**

Morphology refers to body structure and form while phylogeny represents evolutionary history. The two are related. For example, a chimpanzee is the most humanlike animal because of the recent common evolutionary ancestor of chimp and human, revealed by the fossil record.

40.　　**(B)**

The genetic cross is $I^A i$ dd (blood-type A and Rh-negative, which is a recessive condition) x $I^B i$ Dd. In summary:

	I^B D	I^B d	i D	i d
I^A d	$I^A I^B$ Dd	$I^A I^B$ dd	$I^A i$ Dd	$I^A i$ dd
i d	$I^B i$ Dd	$I^B i$ dd	ii Dd	ii dd

Note: Only the recombination in the lower right corner yields a completely recessive genotype, indicative of blood-type O, Rh-negative offspring. This is only one of the eight possible recombinations.

41. **(B)**

Auxin, the very hormone that stimulates shoot growth, seems to have an inhibitory effect on the specialized cells of the plant root at high concentrations. It inhibits their mitosis rate which is responsible for vertical elongation.

42. **(B)**

"Trachea" means tube, the key to the success of this group of land plants. Their vascular tissue is composed of xylem and phloem. Fungi and mosses do not belong to this phylum. Tracheophytes are autotrophs (self-nourishing) due to their photo-synthetic ability.

43. **(D)**

Insulin, as well as growth hormone and interferon, are now synthesized by bacteria. Actin and myosin, muscle contractile proteins, plus the red blood cell protein for gas transport, hemoglobin, are proteins, but cannot be synthesized as yet by such methods.

44. **(B)**

DNA makes RNA during genetic transcription. DNA's base sequence determines RNA nucleotide sequence. RNA polymerase is the enzyme that catalyzes the assemblage of these subunits into a polymer, RNA.

45. **(D)**

Pulse pressure is the difference between an artery's high (systolic) and low (diastolic) pressures. The pressure in all major arteries is pulsatile.

$$\text{(Systolic pressure)} - \text{(Diastolic pressure)} = \text{(Pulse pressure)}$$
$$x - 90 \text{ mmHg} = 30 \text{ mmHg}$$
$$x = 120 \text{ mmHg}$$

The systolic pressure is 120 mmHg.

46. **(A)**

The invertebrate was removed from a freshwater environment and therefore could not have been an Echinoderm, because echinoderms live only in marine environ-ments. Poriferans and Coelenterates do not have mesodermal germ layers. Annelids do not have an outer cuticle.

47. **(A)**

Lymphocytes are white blood cells that attack foreign, invasive agents in the body.

T-lymphocytes change to plasma cells that produce humoral antibodies. These molecules react against foreign chemical agents, antigens in the blood. B-lymphocytes attack cellular invaders, such as the foreign cells in a tissue graft.

48.   **(E)**

Acetylcholine is a neurotransmitter, which is a class of molecules that traverse synaptic clefts in order to perpetuate a neural impulse. Any drug that inhibited the action of acetylcholine would have to act on the synapse.

49.   **(A)**

This is a snail shell-shaped structure in the inner ear. The semicircular canals (dynamic equilibrium) and vestibule (static equilibrium) are there to control body balance. The pinna, outer ear cartilage flap, and tympanum (eardrum) transmit sound waves from the outer ear through the middle ear and on to the inner ear.

50.   **(A)**

Arteries take blood away from the heart, dividing into smaller, more numerous arterioles. They divide to become numerous, microscopic capillaries for exchange with cells. They collect into venules, which merge to form larger veins. Venules and veins return blood to the heart.

51.   **(E)**

Primates, as one order of mammals, have four-chambered hearts. All other listed choices are characteristics that describe primates, a taxonomic order that humans share with the great apes, monkeys, and prosimians.

52.   **(D)**

The population is mating randomly, so the Hardy-Weinberg formula may be used:

$$p^2 + 2pq + q^2$$

in which p is the dominant allele's frequency and q is the recessive allele's frequency. It is given that q^2, the frequency of organisms that express the homozygous recessive alleles, is 36%. Since $q^2 = .36$, then q = .6.

53.   **(A)**

This gas constitutes 79% of the atmosphere. Soil-dwelling bacteria fix it in the soil in a chemical form for plant use — nitrogen fixation.

54.   **(E)**

Herbivores are plant-eaters and are first to feed in a food chain.

55.   **(B)**

Carbon monoxide is a colorless, odorless gas that can bind to hemoglobin without the subject's awareness. As hemoglobin in red blood cells transports oxygen, oxygen's unavailability due to CO binding causes internal suffocation, or asphyxiation.

56.   **(E)**

Translocation is the attachment of a chromosome fragment to a nonhomologous chromosome. Duplication is the attachment of the fragment to the homologous chromosome's counterpart, thus repeating gene types already there. Inversion is the reattachment of the fragment to the original chromosome, but in a reversed orientation, resulting in a reversed gene order. In a deletion, the chromosome fragment does not reattach. Diversion does not refer to chromosomal mutations.

57.   **(D)**

The seminal vesicle adds fluid in the vas deferens prior to the fluid's entrance into the prostrate gland beneath the bladder. The Cowper's gland adds a small final amount to the urethra prior to the fluid's entrance into the penis.

58.   **(B)**

In general, there is a decreased amount of energy at each successive trophic level of an energy chain. Producers are found at the base of this chain and thus harbor most of the energy in the chain.

59. **(A)**   60. **(E)**   61. **(C)**   62. **(B)**

Choice (A), NH_2, is the amino group. Along with an acid group, COOH, not shown, it bonds to the central carbon of an amino acid to derive its name. A nucleotide, the building block subunit of a nucleic acid, has three components: a pentose (five carbon) sugar, a nitrogen base, and a phosphate group as shown in choice (B). Choice (C) is the aldehyde group found on the number one carbon of the hexose chain of the monosaccharide glucose. (E) is the ketone group, denoting the number two carbon in the hexose chain of the monosaccharide fructose.

63.   **(C)**

This organelle is the mitochondrion, the site of cellular respiration. Pyruvic acid enters the Krebs cycle (citric acid cycle) here, where energy released by oxidation reactions performed on pyruvic acid is stored in the high-energy phosphate bonds of ATP. ATP, adenosine triphosphate is the molecule used by all cells to store energy.

64.   (B)

The inner surface of a mitochondrion's inner membrane has bound to it molecules that take part in oxidative phosphorylation. These molecules are alternately reduced and oxidized, which releases energy that can be used to synthesize ATP.

65.   (D)

The anaerobic metabolism of glucose is known as glycolysis. Unlike the aerobic phase of metabolism in the mitochondrion, the team of enzymes running the glycolytic pathway are found in the cytoplasm near the mitochondrion.

66. (B)   67. (C)   68. (E)   69. (A)

$$\underset{\text{glucose}}{6CO_2 + 12H_2O \xrightarrow{\text{light}} 1C_6H_{12}O_2 + 6H_2O + 6O_2}$$

In the light reactions of photosynthesis (photosystems I and II), light causes the excitation of electrons in chlorophyll. These excited electrons are passed from one acceptor molecule to another, and finally are accepted by NADP. However, since a chlorophyll molecule must give up its electrons, they must be replaced. According to the equation

$$2H_2O \rightarrow 4H^+ + 4e\text{-} + O_2,$$

water donates the electrons that are needed by the now electron-poor chlorophyll molecule. Oxygen gas is also a product of this reaction.

CO_2 enters the dark reactions of photosynthesis (Calvin-Benson cycle), and is used to synthesize glucose, the final product of the Calvin-Benson cycle.

Choice (D) could refer to electrons or even to light energy, but these were not listed in the questions. Hence, (D) is an incorrect choice.

70.   (E)

The I-band is the region of the sarcomere that contains actin only. (A) designates the Z-line. (B) specifically points out groups of actin. (C) designates a bundle of myosin molecules. (D) designates the A-band, which contains bundles of myosin, and the region of overlap of actin and myosin.

71.   **(C)**

The thicker myosin protein filaments have cross-bridges coming off of them at right angles. These crossbridges can bind to actin.

72.   **(B)**

The crossbridges, which are actually the heads of individual myosin molecules, temporarily bind to nearby actin molecules. The bridges then bend; this causes the actin filament to move along the myosin filament. The movement of many actin filaments causes the region between the Z-lines, the sarcomere, to shorten. The shortening of many sarcomeres results in a muscle contraction.

73.   **(A)**

(A) represents the nonconducting pith while (D), (C), and (B) respectively represent first-, second-, and third-year xylem growth. (E) designates phloem, another conductive tissue type laid down outside of the other layers.

74.   **(D)**

Xylem is pushed from the growth layer inward. Thus, the more central the xylem layer, the older it is. (D) thus designates the newest layer (third layer) of xylem.

75. **(B)**   76. **(A)**   77. **(E)**

Each choice is descriptive of its matched invertebrate phylum.

78. **(E)**   79. **(C)**   80. **(A)**   81. **(D)**

The *Paramecium* is a freshwater protozoan that has numerous hairlike cilia on its cell membrane. They beat in synchrony to propel the organism. Mastigophorans whip a flagellum to produce movement, as does the *Euglena*. Sarcodinians, such as the *Amoeba,* project protoplasmic extensions, pseudopodia, to move along. Sporozoans, immobile as adults, cause harm to their hosts. Generic member *Plasmodium* is the best known; it causes malaria. A bacteriophage is a virus parasitizing a bacterium.

82. **(C)**   83. **(E)**   84. **(D)**   85. **(A)**

Chordates have supportive dorsal structures, either notochords or vertebral columns. Coelenterates, such as jellyfish, have saclike bodies and radial symmetry. All coelenterates have specialized stinging cells, nematocysts, in their external cell layers. Platyhelminthians, such as members of genus *Dugesia* (commonly called planaria), lack the true body segmentation of annelids, the segmented worms. They are dorsoventrally flattened and have gastrovascular cavities. Poriferans are sponges, which have retained many primitive animal characteristics. They greatly (but not totally) resemble their distant ancestors, who, quite early in animal evolution, diverged from the evolution of the other animal phyla.

86. **(B)**

This structure is the medulla, at the base of the brainstem. It controls blood pressure by gauging the sizes of blood vessels and their resistance to blood flow. Cardiac and respiratory centers are also found here.

87. **(E)**

This is the temporal lobe of the cerebral cortex. Mapped regions for taste (gustation), smell, and hearing are found here. Vision is the domain of the occipital lobe (D).

88. **(E)**

The pons is a hindbrain structure above the medulla. It contains ascending and descending tracts.

89. **(C)**

Autotrophs make their own food. As producers such as the oak tree, they synthesize organic nutrients such as sugars. Heterotrophs depend on producers for their food in a ready-made form. They are consumers and represent successive links of the food chain.

Since only about 10% of the energy made available to members of one trophic level can be acquired by members of the next trophic level, it stands to reason that the heterotrophs (of any food chain) that are members of the trophic level closest to the producers' (autotrophs') trophic level will have more energy available for them. Therefore, in this food chain, the insects, of the second trophic level, are the heterotrophs with the most useful energy available to them.

90. **(B)**

Omnivores (omni=all) feed on both plant and animal matter. Of the organisms that are listed, only the human qualifies as an omnivore. Both the bird and the pike are carnivores, and the insect is an herbivore.

91. **(B)**

The ten chromosomes contain two chromatids each, for a total of twenty chromatids. For each of the five kinds of chromosomes, another one in the group exists that is similar in size, shape, and structure: a homologue.

92.   **(B)**

The cell that contains these chromosomes is diploid, because there are two copies of each type of chromosome, each of which contains two chromatids. The two copies of each type of chromosome are homologous. If the cell completes mitosis, there will be <u>ten</u> chromosomes in each daughter cell (each daughter cell will receive one chromatid of each chromosome). Meiosis results in haploid gametes. The haploid number in this case is half of ten, or five.

93.   **(D)**

A karyotype is a categorization of the chromosomes in a cell based on chromosomal similarities and differences. For example, human chromosomes, of which there are 23 pairs, are karyotyped into seven groups.

94.   **(B)**

The base-pairing rules between DNA and RNA for DNA transcription are:

DNA	RNA
Adenine	Uracil
Cytosine	Guanine
Guanine	Cytosine
Thymine	Adenine

95.   **(C)**

The ribosome is the site at which a given mRNA molecule is "read." During this decoding, a tRNA molecule with a complementary anticodon carries an amino acid to the C-terminus of the protein that is being synthesized.

96.   **(D)**

The anticodons that will bind to the mRNA are determined by the mRNA codons, which in turn are determined by the DNA sequence:

DNA	mRNA	tRNA
Adenine	Uracil	Adenine
Cytosine	Guanine	Cytosine
Thymine	Adenine	Uracil
Guanine	Cytosine	Guanine

97. **(B)**

If one chooses to start with the right atrium, (A), blood next moves through the right ventricle, (C). It then flows to the lungs in the pulmonary artery, not shown, and returns to the left atrium (B) in pulmonary veins. This atrium primes the left ventricle, (D), and the ventricle in turn pumps blood out through the ascending aorta, (E).

98. **(C)**

According to the previous explanation, this is the right ventricle's role.

99. **(C)**

Each enzyme works best in a unique range within 0-14. Enzyme C is farthest to the right for the highest number, most alkaline pH.

100. **(A)**

Amylase, in the saliva, works optimally in the oral cavity's neutral pH.

SECTION II

ESSAY I

The *Amoeba* is a freshwater protozoan. Its entire makeup consists of one cell. All regions of the organism are in close proximity to the external environment. Under these conditions, diffusion can account for all local transport of substances.

Diffusion is the movement of matter's particles from a region of higher concentration to a region of lower concentration. Be they atoms, ions, or molecules, particles of matter have a tendency to spread out by virtue of their randomized, colliding motion. A bottle of perfume molecules, opened in a room, will release molecules that spread out as they diffuse through the room. If the room is sealed off, the vaporized molecules become equally distributed. Diffusion, therefore, tends toward a balanced concentration of matter's particles, or equilibrium.

In *Amoeba*, oxygen will diffuse from the outside pond water into the cell. Relatively less is in the cell because it is consumed by the cell. Extracellular oxygen moves toward this deficit. Carbon dioxide is produced in the cell. Its concentration gradient forces CO_2 outward. Nutrient molecules will also move in, whereas accumulated intracellular waste diffuses outward. The cell membrane must be permeable to these substances to allow free transport along their concentration gradients.

Osmosis is the diffusion of water through a permeable membrane. Another description of osmosis is the movement of water into a hypertonic environment. Hypertonic means a higher solute (dissolved substance) concentration. If solute levels are higher, water concentration is lower. The moving water comes from a hypotonic setting (lower solute concentration, higher water levels). Filtration is the movement of materials by bulk flow. The mere mechanical pressure of a moving substance accounts for particle transport rather than natural, randomized movement. The impact of water coursing through a garden hose will cause its escape if the hose wall is punched full of holes.

Both osmosis and filtration explain substance movement in the circulatory system vessel exchanging contents with body cells, the capillary. Arterial blood flow at the capillaries' input end is under high filtration pressure from heart pumping action. At the venous end, this pressure has been weakened by the frictional resistance to blood flow of the small-diametered capillary. Both end pressures, as with water in the garden hose, force fluid outward. High concentrations of plasma proteins remain in the blood, as they are too large to pass through the capillary membrane pores. They keep the inside blood hypertonic to the outside and thus draw fluid into the blood by osmosis uniformly along the capillaries' length.

At the arterial end, blood fluid (plasma) moves out to cells as the strong filtration pressure overcomes osmosis. At the venous end, the weakened filtration pressure succumbs to the stronger, uniform osmotic pressure. Therefore, fluid with materials is drawn from the cells back into the blood as it flows from the capillary.

Active transport is the opposite of diffusion. Matter moves from areas of <u>lower</u> concentration to those of <u>higher</u> concentration as the cell expends energy to transport. Along a nerve cell's membrane, extracellular sodium ions diffuse in due to their high outside concentration. Potassium ions diffuse to the outside. An active transport mechanism, however, pumps sodium back to the outside and potassium to the inside. This keeps each poised higher at their respective extracellular and intracellular levels. As charged particles, ions, they maintain regionally a constant electrical-like character along the neuron's membrane.

ESSAY II

Darwin's principle of natural selection accounts for the force of the environment in the evolution of a population. The major points of his premise are as follows:

1. Populations have a tremendous biotic potential to increase their numbers. As an example of the possibility of growth rate, consider a female sunfish in a pond. It can lay 200,000 eggs per reproductive cycle. About one-half of these eggs could develop into female sunfish. Each of these 100,000 females could lay 200,000 eggs as this trend multiplies to astronomical figures after very few generations of sunfish. However, only two or three of the hatched sunfish may survive. Among wild populations, high death rates among the young is the rule. This leads to the next point.

2. Darwin was influenced in his thinking by an economist named Malthus. Taking a page from supply-side economics, Darwin concluded that the amount of resources to support a population is limited. There is just so much oxygen, food, space, etc., in the pond to support a maximum number of fish. With the tremendous biotic potential of a species, competition for resources is inevitable.

3. By studying populations of reptiles and birds of the Galapagos Islands off the coast of South America, Darwin concluded that variation, genetic difference, is a characteristic of any population. During his study in the mid-nineteenth century, however, he did not know the basis for the variation, the actions of genes, yet undiscovered.

4. Those with adaptive variations favorable in the given environment have better probabilities of surviving and leaving offspring. Thus, broader leaves, taller giraffes, faster predators, or better-camouflaged prey all have adaptions to promote survival. This survival power for increased life span yields increased reproductive fitness, the individual's ability to pass its genes on to future generations.

5. This higher probability of survival and reproductive fitness allows affected members to have more of an effect on the gene pool of the next generation. Thus, a superior gene for tallness, among more surviving members possessing it, leads to higher odds that it will be genetically passed on and lead to a higher percentage of tall members in the next generation.

The merger of these principles with genetics came with the understanding of mutations. Mutations are changes in a gene and the raw material for evolution. Without a source of change, a population cannot change or evolve. For example, if the only form of an eye color gene were dark, "B," all members of the population would be homozygous for "B," BB. All mating, would be BBxBB and produce homozygous organisms with dark eye color. If the "B" dominant gene mutates to a recessive "b," then there is an eye color alternative. A mating of two heterozygous organisms, BbxBb, can produce blue-eyed offspring, bb, with a 25% chance. If blue eyes is adaptive against the environment, more blue-eyed individuals will survive longer. Over time they will leave their blue eye genes hereditarily and gradually increase the frequency of blue-eyed individuals in the future gene pool.

ESSAY III

Mitosis is cell reproduction: one parent cell divides to form two daughter cells and each daughter cell is genetically identical to the parent cell. The genetic constancy includes chromosome number and combination as well as gene-by-gene content on each chromosome. For example, an onion cell normally has a full complement of 24 chromosomes. During its cell cycle, each chromosome duplicates and becomes double-stranded. With the onset of mitosis, the duplicates (chromatids) of each chromosome are separated in orderly fashion at the same time. The duplicates of each are finally separated and segregated into separate daughter cells as the cell splits into two.

Mitosis is more than just a mere splitting. Its preservation of the genetic picture is also paramount. Mitosis functions in the growth and development of the organism of a species. In its life cycle, for example, a frog begins as a zygote, the fertilized egg. Mitosis multiplies the original cell, numbering from one to two - four - eight - sixteen, etc. Eventually, cell number reaches the millions, billions, and trillions. The human body is estimated to have 75 trillion cells.

Even when growth of cell number ceases, mitosis continues to function in replacement of worn-out cells. Outer layers of skin cells are constantly dying. A human red blood cell normally has a life span of 120 days. Mitosis balances rates of cell death with rates of cell reproduction to retain the needed number of cell types. Cancer is an affliction in which cell production is too rapid. Specific cells become too numerous and compete with other cells for nutrients and space.

Meiosis, on the other hand, changes the genetic picture by producing cells with one-half the chromosome number of the full species complement. Two successive divisions of a parent cell produce daughter cells that are <u>haploid</u>. In other words, they possess one-half the species' chromosome number. In the division process, chromosomes in a pair are separated. Thus if an organism has 64 chromosomes, or 32 pairs, meiosis separates chromosomes in each pair to cut the number to one-half by a very specific pattern. In mitosis, chromosome pairs are not separated, as the full complement is preserved from parent to daughter cells. For example, human cells produced mitotically receive 23 chromosome pairs and a full complement of 46. Generally, mitosis produces <u>diploid</u> cells ("di" = two).

In most animals, meiosis produces sex cells, or gametes. During fertilization, two gametes from opposite sexes recombine to reestablish a full chromosome complement in the zygote. Meiosis produces great variety during sex-cell production. Mathematically, sorting one chromosome per pair, randomly, from all pairs yields a tremendously large number of sex cell identities. For example, in humans, the number of genetic variations in sex cells is 2^{23}, or over 8 million. The exponent 23 comes from the number of chromosome pairs.

In the life cycle of many sexually-reproducing plants, both processes of cell production figure into the plant's alternation of generations. A diploid sporophyte reproduces spores by meiosis. These haploid products develop into a smaller gametophyte. Haploid gametophytes produce haploid cells by <u>mitosis</u>, thus preserving the haploid chromosome number. Fusion of some of these haploid cells founds a diploid sporophyte after mitosis for its growth and development.

ESSAY IV

Ironically, a marine fish such as a tuna or marlin faces potential body water loss. This is because their body fluids are hypotonic to the extracellular salt water. Apparently, marine fish evolved from freshwater, inland ancestors and retained the dilute body fluids that matched that environment. The hypertonic outside environment thus draws water from the fish by osmosis. To some degree, they can prevent water loss in their scaly, impermeable body coverings. Certain permeable surfaces, such as the gill areas, however, are vulnerable.

Marine fish tend to lose water by osmosis and take in the outside salt by diffusion. They solve this potential problem of imbalance by drinking continuously and excreting salt through specialized cells in their gills. They have not evolved a kidney powerful enough to concentrate entering salts into the urine as another salt elimination route.

Freshwater fish face the opposite problem. Their body fluid solute levels are higher than an extracellular setting relatively devoid of such dissolved solids. Their body fluids, therefore, attract outside water osmotically and lose solutes to the outside by diffusion across vulnerable body surfaces. Their kidneys excrete dilute urine. They seldom drink and actively absorb lost salts through specialized transporting cells.

The main water-balance problem faced by terrestrial organisms, including mammals, is desiccation. Mammals have evolved a remarkable kidney to combat this potential problem. Physiologically, the kidney works by at least two processes: filtration and reabsorption.

The kidney is a good example of a whole organ whose activity is determined by the collective action of its individual parts. The kidney parts are microscopic units termed nephrons. A typical mammalian kidney has at least one million of such nephrons. The nephrons conduct the two processes of renal physiology.

Imagine the nephron as a smoking pipe with a bowl and a stem. The nephron's bowl is a cuplike section termed the Bowman's capsule. A specialized capillary tuft, the glomerulus, is housed inside of it. This region is the site of renal filtration. Filtration is the movement of blood plasma materials from the blood into the Bowman's capsule. Filtration is a very unselective, nondiscriminating process. Most all soluble blood plasma components move into the nephron initially by substantial amounts.

Step two is reabsorption. This involves the tubular portion of nephrons that relate to another capillary network surrounding them, the peritubular capillaries. Here, components in the initial filtration move from capsule to tubule and return from the microscopic nephron tracts, tubules, back into the blood. Substances returned to the blood flow away and are thus retained. Reabsorption rates are usually very high. For example, a pair of human kidneys can filter 190 liters of recycled body water per day. However, 187 to 189 liters are returned to the blood once the kidneys have monitored levels and returned water as needed. In spite of the high reabsorption rates, there is some latitude for control and fine tuning. The antidiuretic hormone from the posterior pituitary gland works in the kidney to oppose diuresis and facilitate water reabsorption. If 187 liters of 190 are reabsorbed, 3 liters is eliminated. If 189 liters are taken back, only 1 liter is eliminated. Aldosterone, a hormone from the adrenal cortex, works on tubular permeability to increase sodium reabsorption as needed.

Thus, final reabsorption rates work to meet body needs for chemical components.

THE ADVANCED PLACEMENT EXAMINATION IN

BIOLOGY

TEST IV

ADVANCED PLACEMENT
BIOLOGY EXAM IV

SECTION I

100 Questions
80 Minutes

DIRECTIONS: For each question, there are five possible choices. Select the best choice for each question. Blacken the correct space on the answer sheet.

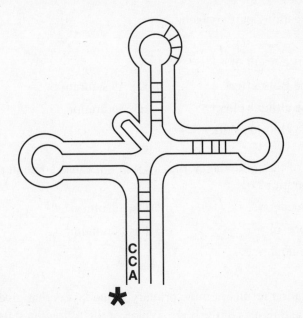

1. In the tRNA molecule above, the asterisk at the CCA-terminal represents

(A) the anticodon loop.

(B) the site of amino acid attachment.

(C) the binding site for mRNA.

(D) a bond between base pairs.

(E) the codon.

Questions 2- 3 refer to the oxyhemoglobin dissociation curve.

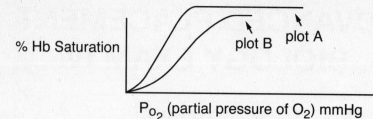

% Hb Saturation

plot B   plot A

P_{O_2} (partial pressure of O_2) mmHg

2.   Plot A depicts hemoglobin under normal conditions. Plot B shows that the curve has shifted to the right and down. This may occur under conditions of

   (A) increased pH.

   (B) decreased temperature.

   (C) exercise.

   (D) hyperventilation.

   (E) breathing pure oxygen.

3.   Plot B is a result of

   (A) the Bohr effect.   (D) desaturation.

   (B) the altitude effect.   (E) saturation.

   (C) the chloride shift.

4.   Which of the following hormones will <u>not</u> cause a rise in plasma glucose concentration?

   (A) glucagon   (D) insulin

   (B) cortisol   (E) adrenaline

   (C) epinephrine

5.   Gastrulation results in three primary tissue layers that give rise to all the organs and tissues of the body. Which of the following statements is true?

   (A) Endoderm gives rise to muscle.

   (B) Epiderm gives rise to skin.

   (C) Mesoderm gives rise to bone.

   (D) Ectoderm gives rise to the gut lining.

   (E) Periderm gives rise to skin.

6.   Industrial melanism refers to the process whereby

   (A) light moths became dark moths.

   (B) dark-colored moths became favored by the environment.

(C) a mutant gene for dark wings evolved.

(D) dark moths had a survival advantage on both light and dark tree trunks.

(E) skin cancer abounded due to industrial hazards.

7. The only molecule not found in DNA is

(A) deoxyribose   (D) phosphate

(B) uracil   (E) thymine

(C) cytosine

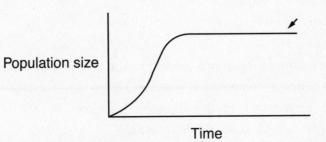

Population size

Time

8. In the graph above, the arrow indicates specifically

(A) the biotic potential.

(B) the density-dependent effect.

(C) the sigmoid growth curve.

(D) the carrying capacity.

(E) the density-independent effect.

9. Which of the following conditions is due to the effects of a dominant allele?

(A) Albinism   (D) Polydactyly

(B) Hemophilia   (E) Color-blindness

(C) Sickle-cell anemia

10. Facilitated diffusion

(A) requires ATP.

(B) requires a protein carrier.

(C) refers to the osmosis of water.

(D) moves substances against a concentration gradient.

(E) is diffusion that occurs easily.

11.   Examples of fungi include all of the following EXCEPT
(A) yeasts   (D) mushrooms
(B) molds   (E) algae
(C) mildews

12.   In base pairing within DNA molecules,
(A) adenine is bound to thymine by hydrogen bonds.
(B) adenine forms a peptide bond with thymine.
(C) adenine bonds ionically to thymine.
(D) guanine binds to uracil.
(E) adenine binds to uracil.

13.   All of the following statements concerning leaf anatomy are true EXCEPT
(A) The cuticle is composed of waxes and helps in water retention.
(B) The stomata are pores that allow gas diffusion.
(C) The mesophyll contains chloroplasts.
(D) The xylem conducts water.
(E) The palisade layer is adjacent to the lower epidermis.

14.   Radial body symmetry is present in
(A) cnidarians.   (D) annelids.
(B) flatworms.   (E) mollusks.
(C) arthropods.

15.   An example of a mechanism of post-mating reproductive isolation is
(A) mechanical isolation   (D) behavioral isolation
(B) hybrid sterility   (E) geographical isolation
(C) seasonal isolation

16.   What would the probable ratio of the number of brown-eyed children to the number of blue-eyed children be if their parents were both brown-eyed and both heterozygous for the allele for brown eyes?
(A) 3:1   (D) 1:0
(B) 1:2:1   (E) 1:1
(C) 1:3

17. Punctuated equilibrium refers to which of the following?

    (A) Short periods of rapid speciation separated by periods of slower evolutionary change

    (B) Adaptive radiation

    (C) Convergent evolution

    (D) Gradualism

    (E) Catastrophism

18. The pelagic province of the open ocean is divided into several different regions. The uppermost epipelagic region has more life than the deeper ones because

    (A) it receives the fresh rainfall

    (B) light penetration allows for photosynthesis

    (C) light penetration allows for respiration

    (D) warmer temperatures allow for growth

    (E) tidal action keeps the nutrients suspended

19. The replication fork

    (A) is the site at which the single-stranded regions emerge.

    (B) refers to the lagging strand.

    (C) refers to the leading strand.

    (D) refers to the site of base pair formation.

    (E) is seen in transcription.

20. Synapsis

    (A) occurs during the second meiotic division.

    (B) refers to the pairing between homologous chromosomes.

    (C) is synonymous with chiasmata.

    (D) refers to the tetrad of chromatids.

    (E) are the junctions between neurons.

21. The cell types found in phloem are

    (A) sieve tube members and vessels.

    (B) sieve tube members and tracheids.

    (C) tracheids and vessels.

    (D) companion cells and vessels.

    (E) sieve tube members and companion cells.

22.   The cell organelles that are most similar to prokaryotes are
        (A) the mitochondria and chloroplasts.
        (B) the rough and smooth endoplasmic reticula.
        (C) the rough endoplasmic reticula and ribosomes.
        (D) the rough endoplasmic reticula and Golgi apparatuses.
        (E) the lysosomes and ribosomes.

23.   The notochord is the forerunner of which vertebrate structure?
        (A) spinal cord   (D) gill
        (B) vertebral column   (E) gill slits
        (C) brain

24.   Because fungi can obtain nutrients from nonliving organic matter, they are
        referred to as
        (A) parasitic   (D) heterotrophic
        (B) saprophytic   (E) pathogenic
        (C) eukaryotic

25.   The founder effect
        (A) is a direct effect of mutation.
        (B) is an extreme case of gene flow.
        (C) is an extreme case of genetic drift.
        (D) occurs by natural selection.
        (E) is an extreme case of natural selection.

26.   Which of the following is the female reproductive organ of a flower?
        (A) stamen   (D) receptacle
        (B) anther   (E) carpel
        (C) petal

27.   The anticodon is found on
        (A) mRNA   (D) DNA
        (B) rRNA   (E) ATP
        (C) tRNA

28. Gastrulation refers to

(A) fusion of the sperm and egg nuclei

(B) embryonic cell division with no increase in embryo size

(C) differentiation of body parts as signaled from an adjacent part

(D) the development of the notochord and dorsal hollow nerve cord

(E) the migrations of cells into three primary germ layers

29. All of the following events occur in a flower EXCEPT

(A) pollination

(B) fertilization

(C) megaspore formation

(D) pollen tube growth

(E) photosynthesis

30. Double fertilization

(A) results in fraternal twins.

(B) results in identical twins.

(C) results in Siamese twins.

(D) is unique to angiosperms.

(E) occurs in all seed-producing vascular plants.

31. Decomposers feed on

(A) producers.

(B) herbivores.

(C) primary carnivores.

(D) consumers.

(E) dead organic matter.

32. Terms referring to the hydrologic (water) cycle include ALL of the following EXCEPT

(A) transpiration

(B) evaporation

(C) fixation

(D) precipitation

(E) runoff

33. Mating between a blue-eyed woman and a heterozygous brown-eyed man would result in a ratio of brown-eyed to blue-eyed children of

(A) 1:1

(B) 1:2

(C) 2:1

(D) 1:0

(E) 0:1

34.　A phenotype refers to

(A)　the genetic makeup of an individual.

(B)　the expression of dominant traits.

(C)　the expression of recessive traits.

(D)　the manifest expression of the genotype.

(E)　the heterozygous condition.

35.　All of the plant groups below are vascular EXCEPT

(A)　mosses

(B)　ferns

(C)　horsetails

(D)　gymnosperms

(E)　seed plants

36.　A bacteriophage

(A)　is a bacterium that phagocytoses other organisms.

(B)　is a bacterium that becomes phagocytosed by other organism.

(C)　is a virus that infects bacteria.

(D)　is a fragment of DNA.

(E)　lives in a lysogenic cell.

37.　The reduced form of the coenzyme in the dehydrogenase enzymes is

(A)　NADH

(B)　FAD

(C)　ADH

(D)　NAD^+

(E)　ACTH

38.　In the first step of glycolysis, the phosphorylation of glucose is coupled to

(A)　the production of carbon dioxide

(B)　the reduction of NAD^+

(C)　the synthesis of ATP

(D)　the hydrolysis of ATP

(E)　the loss of electrons

39.　The active portion of the cytochrome enzymes is a heme group. It contains a mineral element which can exist in the oxidized or reduced state. This element is

(A)　sodium

(B)　iodine

(C)　iron

(D)　potassium

(E)　calcium

40.   Chemiosmosis refers to the idea that an ion flowing down its electrochemical gradient drives ATP synthesis. This ion is

(A) Phosphate ion, thus the term oxidative phosphorylation

(B) Sodium ion

(C) Iron ion

(D) Hydrogen ion

(E) Calcium ion

Directions: The following groups of questions have five lettered choices followed by a list of diagrams, numbered phrases, sentences, or words. For each numbered diagram, phrase, sentence, or word choose the heading which most directly applies. Blacken the correct space on the answer sheet. Each heading may be used once, more than once, or not at all.

Questions 41 - 43 describe the basic functional units of organs or systems.

(A) Nephron   (D) Alveolus

(B) Neuron   (E) Villus

(C) Sarcomere

41.   Functional unit of the kidney, it produces urine.

42.   As the functional unit of a muscle, it contracts.

43.   This cell transmits messages.

Questions 44 - 46 refer to events dealing with DNA.

(A) Transcription   (D) Translocation

(B) Translation   (E) Transduction

(C) Transformation

44.   The process by which a cell takes up DNA from its immediate environment and incorporates that DNA into its genome.

45.   The process of linking amino acids together to form a protein.

46.   The transfer of bacterial DNA from one organism to another by way of a viral vector.

Questions 47 - 50 distinguish different terms relating to the alternation of generations in plant life cycles.

(A) Sporophyte   (D) Sporangia

(B) Spore   (E) Spore mother cell

(C) Homosporous

47.   Plant that produces only one type of spore

48.   The haploid product of a sporophyte

49.   The diploid generation, it becomes more dominant in the evolution of plants

50.   The multicellular structure that produces megaspores and microspores

Questions 51 - 54 refer to animal cell organelles and their functions.

   (A) Mitochondrion

   (B) Lysosome

   (C) Ribosome

   (D) Smooth endoplasmic reticulum

   (E) Microfilament

51.   Functions in protein synthesis

52.   Functions in the cytoskeleton

53.   Fuses with phagocytic vesicles

54.   Synthesizes lipids

Questions 55 - 58 list enzymes that function in the key metabolic processes involved in complete glucose oxidation.

   (A) Krebs Cycle

   (B) Electron transport chain

   (C) Glycolysis

   (D) Formation of acetyl CoA

   (E) Chemiosmosis

55.   Hexokinase

56.   Cytochrome oxidase

57.   Pyruvate dehydrogenase

58.   Succinate dehydrogenase

Questions 59 - 61 refer to plant hormones and their functions.

   (A) Gibberellins   (D) Auxins

   (B) Abscisic acid   (E) Cytokinins

   (C) Ethylene

59.   Stimulates fruit ripening

60.   Promotes closure of the stomata

61.   Terminates seed dormancy.

Questions 62 - 65 describe distinguishing characteristics of major animal phyla.

(A) Mollusca   (D) Annelida

(B) Chordata   (E) Arthropoda

(C) Echinodermata

62.   Members of this phylum have dorsal body walls called mantles; each organism has a muscular organ called a foot

63.   These segmented worms include the earthworms

64.   Members of this phylum have hardened exoskeletons and jointed appendages

65.   Locomotion in members of this phylum is based on a water-vascular system

Questions 66 - 70 refer to the diagram below which shows the secondary growth of a woody stem.

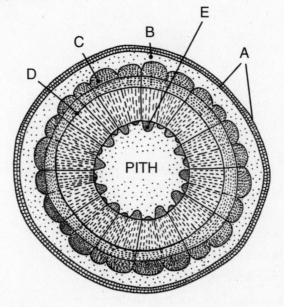

66.   Vascular cambium

67.   Primary phloem

68.   Primary xylem

69.   Epidermis

70.   Cortex

Directions: The following questions refer to experimental or laboratory situations or data. Read the description of each situation. Then choose the best answer to each question. Blacken the correct space on the answer sheet.

Questions 71 - 73 refer to the pedigree below.

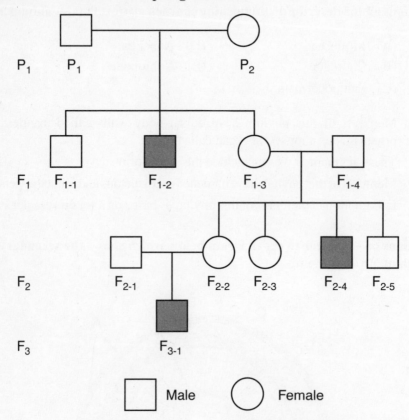

Male   ◯ Female

Shading indicates the presence of a disease.

71.   With reference to the above figure, all of the following statements concerning the disease in question are true EXCEPT

(A) It is sex-linked.

(B) It is caused by a recessive gene.

(C) It may be hemophilia.

(D) It is passed from mothers to their sons.

(E) It is expressed only in the homozygous recessive state.

72.   If the disease were colorblindness, the genotype of P_1 must be

(A) X^CX^c (D) X^CY

(B) X^CX^C (E) X^cY

(C) X^cX^c

73. If F_{2-5} were to marry a woman homozygous dominant for the trait in question, the probability that they would have a child afflicted with the disease is

(A) 0%

(B) 25%

(C) 50%

(D) 100%

(E) unknown; cannot be determined from information given.

Questions 74 - 77 refer to the graph below, which represents data obtained from a spirometer, an instrument that measures the volume of air moved into and out of the lungs during breathing. The volume of air moved into the lungs during a normal quiet inpiration is called the tidal volume. This same volume will be moved out of the lungs during a normal quiet expiration. One tidal inspiration is labeled on the graph (see bar).

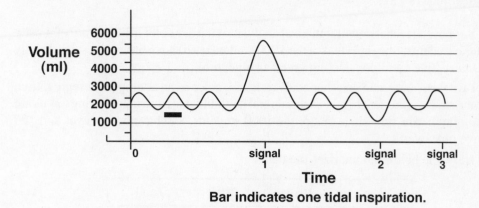

Bar indicates one tidal inspiration.

74. At the time of signal 1, the subject has inspired maximally. What is the subject's inspiratory reserve volume?

(A) 6500 ml

(B) 3500 ml

(C) 3000 ml

(D) 2500 ml

(E) 2000 ml

75. Just before signal two, the subject

(A) inspired maximally

(B) expired forcefully

(C) increased his breathing rate

(D) decreased his breathing rate

(E) stopped breathing

76.   What is the subject's vital capacity?

(A) 5500 ml   (D) 2500 ml

(B) 4500 ml   (E) 2000 ml

(C) 3500 ml

77.   Assuming that the time span between signals two and three represents 30 seconds, this subject's respiratory rate is

(A) about 6 breaths/minute

(B) about 24 breaths/minute

(C) 12 breaths per 30 second interval

(D) about 12 breaths per minute

(E) None of the above

Questions 78 - 81.

Suppose a teacher does a statistical analysis of the eye color in her school of mostly black students. She finds that of the 1000 students, 910 have brown eyes, while only 90 have blue eyes (considering green as blue, too).

Five years later, she does her analysis again, since as an attempt at desegregation, some students are sent to other schools and new students from neighboring towns are brought in. She now finds that of the 1000 students, 840 have brown eyes and 160 have blue eyes.

Her table below summarizes the data.

Year	Brown	Blue	Total
1981	910	90	1000
1986	840	160	1000

78.   In the original sample (1981), the frequency of the allele for brown eyes (B) is

(A) .7   (D) .3

(B) .49   (E) .91

(C) .9

79.   The number of students in the original sample that are heterozygous for brown eyes is

(A) 910

(B) 490

(C) 420

(D) 90

(E) cannot be determined by the data given

80.   The deviation from the Hardy-Weinberg equilibrium, as exemplified by the
        new data in 1986, is due to

(A)   mutation   (D)   selection

(B)   migration   (E)   chance

(C)   smaller sample size

81.   In the second sample, the frequency of the allele for blue eyes (b) is

(A)   .84   (D)   .16

(B)   .6   (E)   .4

(C)   .04

Questions 82 - 85 refer to responses to receptor stimulation and blockade.

The autonomic nervous system is the involuntary nervous system which inner-vates smooth muscle, cardiac muscle and glands. There are two divisions: the sympathetic division is stimulated by the release of the neurotransmitter chemical norepinephrine. Sympathetic stimulation causes the "fight or flight" reaction: it readies the body for action. It causes pupillary dilation, increases in heart and respiratory rates and vasoconstriction of many blood vessels to increase blood pressure. The parasympathetic division is stimulated by the release of the neurotrans-mitter acetylcholine. It allows the body to rest and recuperate, and as such, stimulates digestive activities. It has opposing effects from the sympathetic division on the pupil, heart and many other organs.

In the following experiment, a frog was used. A few drops of various chemicals were placed on appropriate organs or tissues in or on the frog and the responses were observed or measured. The responses listed below are all relative to the unstimulated state.

Chemical:	Atropine	Propranolol	Curare
Response:	pupil dilation	decreased heart rate	Paralysis of skeletal (voluntary) muscle

82. Given that atropine has no direct effect on the receptors for norepinephrine, the mechanism of action for atropine is

   (A) stimulation of the sympathetic nervous system

   (B) inhibition of the sympathetic nervous system

   (C) stimulation of the parasympathetic nervous system

   (D) inhibition of the parasympathetic nervous system

   (E) not suggested by the information given

83. Given that propranolol has no direct effect on the receptors for acetylcho-line, it may be concluded that it

   (A) stimulates norepinephrine releasing cells

   (B) blocks the action of norepinephrine

   (C) stimulates sympathetic nerves

   (D) stimulates parasympathetic nerves

   (E) inhibits parasympathetic nerve activity

84. If one were to cut the parasympathetic nerve (vagus) which innervates the heart, one would expect to see

(A) an increase in heart rate, due to increased sympathetic activity

(B) an increase in heart rate due to decreased parasympathetic activity

(C) a decrease in heart rate due to decreased parasympathetic activity

(D) a dead heart, as a heart requires innervation for function

(E) a decrease in heart rate, since that is the effect of parasympathetic stimulation

85.   Curare acts via

(A) stimulating sympathetic activity

(B) stimulating parasympathetic activity

(C) inhibiting parasympathetic activity

(D) inhibiting sympathetic activity

(E) none of the above.

Questions 86 - 88 refer to the fates of pyruvate. Pyruvate is placed into three different chambers that contain various substances. Pyruvate is converted to the substances listed.

Chamber:	A	B	C
Product:	lactate	alcohol	CO_2 and water

86.   Which tube(s) lack(s) oxygen?

(A) A and B   (D) A, B, and C

(B) B and C   (E) A only

(C) A and C

87.   Which tube(s) contain(s) yeast cells?

(A) A   (D) A and B

(B) B   (E) A, B, and C

(C) C

88.   Which tube mimics the biochemical events that occur in the cells of a sprinter?

(A) A   (D) A and B

(B) B   (E) B and C

(C) C

Questions 89 - 91 refer to the graphs below. Two species of *Paramecium* (A and B) are grown separately and together. The growth curves of their populations are depicted below.

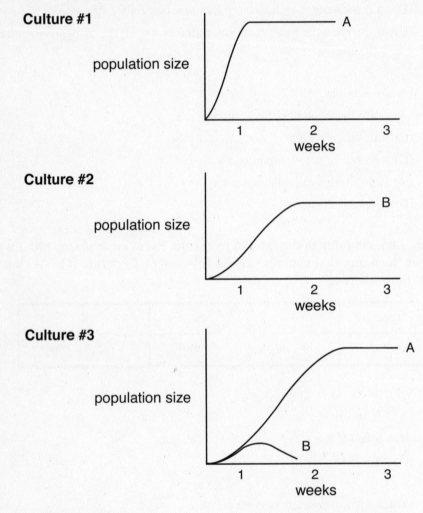

89. The type of interaction between species A and B is described as

    (A) mutualistic   (D) a survivorship curve

    (B) protocooperative   (E) symbiotic

    (C) competitive exclusion

90. In the culture #3, the population size of species A when compared to its size in culture #1

    (A) is less than it is in culture #1

    (B) is the same as in culture #1, but it takes longer to reach maximum size

    (C) is greater than it is in culture #1.

    (D) is the same as it is in culture #1, but it reaches maximum faster

    (E) is unaffected by the presence of species B

91.   When comparing the maximum population sizes for species B in the mixed culture vs. solo culture, it is evident that

    (A) B reaches its maximum faster in the mixed culture

    (B) The maximum population size for B in the solo culture is twice that of B in the mixed culture

    (C) The maximum population size for B is reached fastest in the solo culture

    (D) In the solo cultures, B's population size surpasses that of A

    (E) B does not have a maximum population size in the mixed culture

Questions 92 - 93 refer to the experiment using glycerinated skeletal muscle.

A rabbit psoas muscle is teased apart into individual fibers, some of which are maintained in glycerol solution under standard conditions at 25°C and pH 7. The length of the resting fibers are measured as 2 mm. Various solutions are added to the cerol solutions and the fibers are remeasured under the dissecting microscope. The results are listed in Table A. The solution in Experiment A that caused maximum contraction is then used in experiment B and experiment C and the results are depicted in Tables B and C, respectively.

Table A
Standard conditions
(25°C, pH 7)

Solution:	Glycerol	Glycerol + ATP	Glycerol + Salts (KCl, $MgCL_2$)	Glycerol + ATP + Salts
Length of fiber (mm):	2	1.75	2	.75

Table B
Optimal solution from experiment A

Conditions:	25°C, pH 7	37°C, pH 7
Length of fiber (mm):	.70	.50

Table C
Optimal solution from experiment A

Conditions:	25°C, pH 7	25°C, pH 4
Length of fiber (mm):	.65	1.00

92. In experiment A, contraction of skeletal muscle occurred most readily in the presence of

   (A) glycerol.

   (B) glycerol and ATP.

   (C) glycerol and salts.

   (D) glycerol, ATP, and salts.

   (E) nervous stimulation.

93. Considering experiments B and C, skeletal muscle contraction is optimal under the conditions of

   (A) standard conditions, by definition.

   (B) room temperature and acidic environment.

   (C) body temperature and neutral pH.

   (D) freezing temperature and neutral pH.

   (E) room temperature and neutral pH.

Questions 94 - 95 refer to an experiment in polypeptide hydrolysis.

   Polypeptides are placed into warm watery solutions in separate beakers, each containing a different substance that has been isolated from pancreatic juice or intestinal tissue. After two hours, the contents of the individual beakers are analyzed. The results are below.

Substance Present in Beaker:	Mucus	Trypsin	Chymotrypsin	Carboxypeptidase	Aminopeptidase
Results:	Poly-peptides	Dipeptides Tripeptides	Dipeptides Tripeptides	Amino Acids Dipeptides Tripeptides	Amino Acids Dipeptides

94. It appears that the only substance that has no enzymatic activity is

   (A) mucus

   (B) typsin

   (C) chymotrypsin

   (D) carboxypeptidase

   (E) aminopeptidase

95.   The only substances that act on the terminal residues of the polypeptide are

(A) carboxypeptidase and chymotrypsin

(B) mucus and trypsin

(C) trypsin and chymotrypsin

(D) carboxypeptidase and aminopeptidase

(E) polypeptides and aminopeptidase

Questions 96 - 97 refer to an experiment that concerns cell poisons. The cell is viewed with a powerful microscope under normal conditions and again in the presence of a cell poison. The activity of the cell is noted in the chart below.

Poison:	None	Cytochalasin B	Colchicine
Cell Activity:	normal	No movement of vesicles and other organelles No contraction in skeletal muscle fibers	No chromosome movement

96.   The organelles that cytochalasin B must act on are

(A) actin and myosin   (D) mitochondria

(B) microtubules   (E) nucleus

(C) microfilaments

97.   The protein that colchicine binds to is

(A) actin   (D) histone

(B) myosin   (E) chromatin

(C) tubulin

Questions 98 - 100 refer to the table below, in which the presence (+) or absence (-) of certain types of organelles in five sample human cells is indicated. A blank does not signify the absence of an organelle, just its relative lack of importance when compared to the importance of other organelles.

	Nucleus	Flagellum	Lysosome	Mitochondria	Golgi Apparatus
Cell A	–	–		–	
Cell B	+	–	+	+ +	
Cell C	+	+	+	+	
Cell D	+	–	+ +		
Cell E	+	–		+	+

98. Which cell is most likely to be one that is secreting proteins?

   (A) Cell A   (D) Cell D

   (B) Cell B   (E) Cell E

   (C) Cell C

99. Which cells would most likely be found in blood?

   (A) A and B   (D) D and E

   (B) B and E   (E) C and D

   (C) A and D

100. Cell C is

   (A) a muscle cell, due to the presence of mitochondria.

   (B) an egg cell.

   (C) a neuron.

   (D) prokaryotic.

   (E) haploid.

SECTION II

DIRECTIONS: Answer each of the following four questions in essay format. Each answer should be clear, organized and well-balanced. Diagrams may be used in addition to the discussion, but a diagram alone will not suffice. Suggested writing time per essay is 22 minutes.

1.   Describe the four major groups of organic compounds that compose the human body. Include their functions in your essay, but focus on their chemical constitutions.

2.   Describe the major steps of translation: initiation, elongation, and termination. Describe also the basic structure of a ribosome and the activation step required before translation can occur.

3.   Discuss the levels of organization in an organism and the major systems in the human body, including their organs and functions.

4.   Define and explain the three major plant tropisms: phototropism, gravitropism, and thigmotropism.

ADVANCED PLACEMENT
BIOLOGY EXAM IV

ANSWER KEY

1.	(B)	26.	(E)	51.	(C)	76.	(B)
2.	(C)	27.	(C)	52.	(E)	77.	(E)
3.	(A)	28.	(E)	53.	(B)	78.	(A)
4.	(D)	29.	(E)	54.	(D)	79.	(C)
5.	(C)	30.	(D)	55.	(C)	80.	(B)
6.	(B)	31.	(E)	56.	(B)	81.	(E)
7.	(B)	32.	(C)	57.	(D)	82.	(D)
8.	(D)	33.	(A)	58.	(A)	83.	(B)
9.	(D)	34.	(D)	59.	(C)	84.	(B)
10.	(B)	35.	(A)	60.	(B)	85.	(E)
11.	(E)	36.	(C)	61.	(A)	86.	(A)
12.	(A)	37.	(A)	62.	(A)	87.	(B)
13.	(E)	38.	(D)	63.	(D)	88.	(A)
14.	(A)	39.	(C)	64.	(E)	89.	(C)
15.	(B)	40.	(D)	65.	(C)	90.	(B)
16.	(A)	41.	(A)	66.	(D)	91.	(A)
17.	(A)	42.	(C)	67.	(C)	92.	(D)
18.	(B)	43.	(B)	68.	(E)	93.	(C)
19.	(A)	44.	(C)	69.	(A)	94.	(A)
20.	(B)	45.	(B)	70.	(B)	95.	(D)
21.	(E)	46.	(E)	71.	(E)	96.	(C)
22.	(A)	47.	(C)	72.	(D)	97.	(C)
23.	(B)	48.	(B)	73.	(A)	98.	(E)
24.	(B)	49.	(A)	74.	(C)	99.	(C)
25.	(C)	50.	(D)	75.	(B)	100.	(E)

ADVANCED PLACEMENT
BIOLOGY EXAM IV

DETAILED EXPLANATIONS
OF ANSWERS

SECTION I

1.   **(B)**

A tRNA (transfer RNA) molecule is a small RNA molecule (see figure). There are specific tRNAs for specific amino acids. One end of the molecule binds to the amino acid that is to be added to the growing polypeptide chain. This end always has a terminal CCA (cytosine, cytosine, adenine) sequence.

The other end has the anticodon, which can bind to codons on mRNA. Thus the codon ultimately calls for a specific amino acid in the medium. Note that the binding between tRNA and mRNA is via hydrogen bonds of the base pairs.

The shape of the tRNA molecule is maintained by hydrogen bonds between complementary base pairs within the molecule itself.

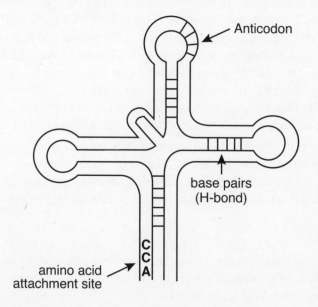

2.   **(C)**

The curve shows the relationship between the percent saturation of hemoglobin versus the partial pressure of oxygen (P_{O2}) measured in mmHg. As P_{O2} increases, there is an increased saturation of hemoglobin by oxygen. Several physiological parameters affect the desaturation of hemoglobin; these factors ease the dissociation of oxygen from hemoglobin so that the oxygen may diffuse into the cells in need. This increased unloading of oxygen from hemoglobin is represented by a curve that has shifted to the right and down (plot B). Note that at any given P_{O2}, hemoglobin is less saturated with oxygen. This shift is called the Bohr effect. The primary factors responsible for the shift are an increase in P_{CO2} (partial pressure of carbon dioxide) and an increase in acid (H^+) levels, which is a decrease in pH. Increased temperature will also shift the curve.

During exercise, when the active cells need more oxygen, hemoglobin will unload the oxygen due to three combined factors: increased temperature, increased carbon dioxide pressure, and decreased pH. Hypoventilation can also induce this change since carbon dioxide is retained in the body, whereas in hyperventilation, excess carbon dioxide is expelled, thus decreasing the concentration of this gas.

A decrease in carbon dioxide concentration or an increase in pH would cause the curve to shift to the left. Breathing pure oxygen would certainly not indicate an oxygen shortage and thus the curve would not shift to the right under such circumstances.

3.   **(A)**

The shift of the oxyhemoglobin dissociation curve to the right due to the presence of increased levels of hydrogen ion (H^+) or carbon dioxide (CO_2) is called the Bohr effect. At high altitude, the Bohr effect comes into play due to the build-up of a substance called 2,3-diphosphoglycerate (DPG). While DPG is a normal constituent of red blood cells, its concentration nearly doubles within two days of exposure to the environmental conditions present at high altitudes. Consequently, there is a decrease in the saturation of hemoglobin by oxygen, allowing increased delivery to the tissues since the shift to the right represents a desaturation of hemoglobin. A shift to the left would indicate increased saturation, although under sea level conditions, hemoglobin is already about 97% saturated in arterial blood.

The chloride shift refers to the diffusion of chloride ions from the plasma into red blood cells to compensate for the diffusion of bicarbonate ions in the reverse direction. Thus ionic balance is maintained. Sodium bicarbonate is formed in the extracellular fluid, while potassium is formed within the red blood cell.

4.   **(D)**

Plasma glucose concentration is regulated and often falls between a fasting level of 80 mg/dl and a post-absorptive level of 130 mg/dl. Many hormones participate in the regulation of plasma glucose levels.

Insulin is a hypoglycemic hormone; in other words it is secreted from the pancreas after a meal and stimulates the uptake of glucose by fat and muscle cells, hence lowering blood glucose concentration. In contrast, glucagon, another pancreatic hormone, is secreted when plasma glucose concentration is low. It increases plasma glucose levels by stimulating the breakdown of glycogen into glucose by hepato-cytes (liver cells). This process is called glycogenolysis. The glucose then diffuses into the blood. This hormone is an important regulator of plasma glucose between meals.

Cortisol is one of the group of glucocorticoids that is released from the adrenal cortex. As suspected by its classification, it affects glucose metabolism. Cortisol increases blood glucose concentration mainly by inhibiting its peripheral utilization at the expense of fatty acids. In addition, it stimulates liver gluconeogenesis, the production of glucose from amino acid precursors.

Epinephrine, also called adrenaline, is a hormone that is released from the adrenal medulla. It assists the sympathetic nervous system and prolongs the "fight or flight" syndrome, which prepares an animal to escape or confront a stress. Among other things, plasma glucose levels are increased to supply energy to deal with the stress. Once again, the liver is stimulated to release glucose from its storage supply.

5.   **(C)**

Gastrulation occurs early in embryonic life. It refers to the process whereby the single-layered blastula is transformed into a three-layered gastrula. The three germ layers are the ectoderm (outer layer), mesoderm (middle layer), and endoderm (inner layer). There is no epiderm or periderm.

The ectoderm will become the epidermis of the skin and all neural tissue. The mesoderm becomes the connective tissue (including blood and bone), muscle, and organs of the circulatory, reproductive, and excretory systems. The endoderm is destined to line the gut and to form accessory glands of the gut. It also forms the lung epithelium.

6.   **(B)**

The peppered moth, *Biston betularia*, can be either light- or dark-colored. Dark color is controlled by a dominant allele, but was rare in the European population prior to the Industrial Revolution in the mid-1800s. In the early part of the century, the light moths were predominant; they camouflaged well with the tree trunks, and hence were less likely to be eaten by their predators, birds.

The pollutants of the Industrial Revolution settled on the tree trunks; the soot made the trunks dark. Now the dark moths would have the selective advantage due to camouflage.

It is important to realize that light moths do not "become" dark, or vice versa. Both already existed in the environment, perhaps due to an earlier mutation. Natural selection was at work here; those moths that had the gene for dark color would be more likely to survive and hence pass their genes on. Thus, industrial melanism refers to the evolutionary change whereby the dark moths had a selective advantage in their changing environment. Whether or not skin cancer developed is immaterial to this question.

7.   **(B)**

DNA (deoxyribonucleic acid) is a polymer of nucleotides. It is the substance of variety in life, since our genes are made of DNA. The nucleotides that comprise nucleic acids consist of a nitrogenous base, a pentose sugar, and a phosphate group.

The nitrogenous bases are classified as purines (double-ringed structures), such as adenine and guanine, or pyrimidines (single-ringed structures), such as thymine or cytosine. In RNA, the pyrimidine base uracil replaces thymine.

Pentose sugars are five-carbon sugars, as opposed to the hexoses (six-carbon sugars) in the food we eat, The pentose in DNA is deoxyribose, but it is ribose in RNA.

A base and a sugar chemically linked is called a nucleoside. When a phosphate attaches to it, the resulting structure is a nucleotide. Nucleotides bond together to form long strands of nucleic acid, either DNA or RNA.

8.   **(D)**

There are several terms used to describe aspects of population growth. No population can show infinite growth; they stabilize at a certain size, despite early rapid growth. This stable number is called the carrying capacity. Of course, there are small fluctuations about this value; when the population exceeds its capacity, the death rate will exceed the birth rate and bring the population back down to capacity.

The biotic potential refers to the rate at which a population will grow, when growth is uninhibited, such as in the early growth of a population. The slope indicating biotic potential is exponential - it has a very sharp slope.

The ultimate graph of population growth is sigmoid (S-shaped) because as the carrying capacity is approximated, the slope flattens considerably, indicating a decreased rate of growth.

Limitations on population growth can be density-dependent or density-independent. Density-dependent factors may include limited resources such as food, water, and space, or behavioral factors.

Density-independent factors do not involve population size. For instance, cold spells or other climate changes can affect the population size.

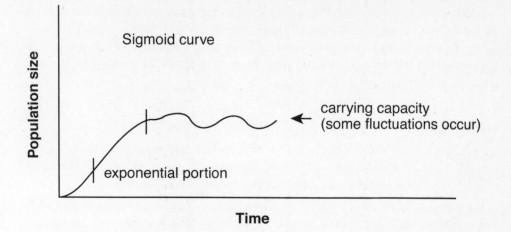

9.   **(D)**

Polydactyly, a condition in which the afflicted has six fingers, is due to the effects of a dominant gene. Both hemophilia and colorblindness are sex-linked traits. The genes are on the X-chromosome and are recessive. While color-blindness is more a condition than a disease, hemophilia is a dangerous disease, in which the blood clotting mechanism is faulty. The alleles for albinism and sickle-cell anemia are both recessive and are both located on autosomes (chromosomes other than the sex chromosomes). Albinos cannot produce melanin and hence have no color in their skin, hair, and eyes. They are very susceptible to the sun's rays and must protect themselves against the sun. Sickle-cell anemia is a type of anemia in which the distorted hemoglobin disrupts the shape of the red blood cell and hence limits its oxygen carrying capacity. Unlike other recessive diseases, in this case, a heterozygote (one with both the normal dominant and abnormal recessive allele) may show symptoms of sickle cell anemia under conditions of low oxygen tension, such as occur during severe exercise or at great altitudes.

10.   **(B)**

There are many types of cellular transport mechanisms. Diffusion is the net movement of molecules down their concentration gradient. For example, potassium is in high concentration inside a cell, so it diffuses to the outside of the cell, where it is in lower concentration. Of course, some potassium can diffuse into the cell, but the <u>net</u> movement is out of the cell. Osmosis is simply the diffusion of water; water moves from a region of high concentration (more dilute solution) to a region of lower concentration (more concentrated solution). In facilitated diffusion, the movement is still down its concentration gradient, but it is facilitated by protein carriers that span cell membranes. This mechanism may function in the diffusion of larger polar molecules, such as amino acids and glucose. The three transport mechanisms discussed above are said to be passive, i.e. they do not require the expenditure of cellular energy (ATP) because they move substances down concentration gradients.

Active transport requires ATP, as it moves substances against their concentration gradients. An important example of this is the Na^+/K^+ ATPase pump. This pump pumps K^+ into the cell in which the concentration of K^+ is already high. It also pumps sodium out of the cell, despite the high concentration of Na^+ outside of the cell already.

11.   **(E)**

Fungi are eukaryotic cells. Most are multicellular, except the unicellular yeasts. Fungi have cell walls composed of chitin. Their nutritional needs are met primarily by decomposition, although a parasitic mode of life is possible too.

There are four divisions of fungi. The Oomycota, or egg fungi, include water molds and mildews; the Zygomycota include bread molds; the Ascomycota are the sac fungi (these are the molds responsible for most food spoilage). Yeasts fall into this category as well. The Basidiomycota, or club fungi, include mushrooms, both edible and poisonous.

Algae are classified as plants (green, brown, and red algae), moneras (blue-green algae), or protists (diatoms, dinoflagellates, euglenoids, and golden-brown algae) depending how closely they resemble the members of a particular kingdom.

12.   **(A)**

In DNA molecules, there are specific rules that dictate which base will bond with which base. Adenine and guanine are both classified as purines, which are large, double-ringed nitrogenous bases. Thymine and cytosine are both pyrimidines, the smaller, single-ringed nitrogenous bases. A purine must pair with a pyrimidine due to the limited amount of space in the interior of the DNA molecule. The number of adenines in a DNA molecule is equal to the number of thymines; this is because they are always bound to each other. The same story holds for guanine and cytosine.

Bonding between base pairs occurs via hydrogen bonds. There are two hydrogen bonds between every adenine and thymine, and three between every guanine and cytosine. Although hydrogen bonds are not individually very strong, collectively they are quite strong. Yet the hydrogen bonds must easily break, whenever replication or transcription occurs.

Note that uracil is a pyrimidine base that replaces thymine in RNA molecules. Hence in transcription (synthesis of mRNA), adenine will bond with uracil.

13.   **(E)**

The leaf functions in photosynthesis, so its structure provides a large surface area in order to capture the sun's energy. The layers of a leaf include a mesophyll layer sandwiched between the epidermal layers.

The upper epidermis is covered by a waxy cuticle to afford protection by minimizing water loss. The mesophyll consists of loosely packed tissue with many chloroplasts in each cell and hence is the site of photosynthesis. The palisade mesophyll is adjacent to the upper epidermis, while the spongy mesophyll below, which contains much air space, is adjacent to the lower epidermis. The lower epidermis is also covered by a cuticle. This layer also has stomata, or pores, which regulate the movement of gases (oxygen, carbon dioxide, and water vapor) into and out of the leaf.

The vasculature of the leaf includes the xylem and phloem. Xylem brings water to the leaf while the phloem carries the photosynthetically produced sugars away.

14.   **(A)**

One major comparison between invertebrate animal phyla that can be observed is the type of body symmetry. The cnidarians, primitive invertebrates, have radial symmetry, as exemplified by the jellyfish. Their parts are arranged about a central axis.

Flatworms, mollusks, annelids, and arthropods are all bilaterally symmetrical: their bodies can be divided into similar right and left halves. They also have dorsal and ventral surfaces, and anterior and posterior ends.

It might seem surprising that echinoderms, rather advanced invertebrates, share the same type of symmetry as the cnidarians, radial symmetry. However, the larvae of echinoderms are bilaterally symmetrical and hence, echinoderms most likely evolved from bilaterally symmetrical ancestors.

15.   **(B)**

One type of phenomenon that limits evolutionary outcomes consists of reproductive isolating mechanisms, the barriers to successful mating. In this case, success means not simply producing viable offspring, but fertile ones as well.

Isolating mechanisms can be categorized as pre-mating or post-mating; the former indicates that no mating will occur, and the latter indicates that while mating occurs, it is unsuccessful.

Premating mechanisms are the more common at work in nature. Types of pre-mating mechanisms include, but are not limited to, the following. Geographical isolation refers to the separation of species due to their land and climate preferences/needs. Seasonal isolation occurs when the breeding seasons of two species do not overlap. Behavioral isolation indicates that communication is species-specific. A bird of one species may not respond to a mating call of another. Mechanical isolation indicates that the structures used in mating are incompatible due to size or shape.

Post-mating isolating mechanisms include hybrid sterility, in which an offspring is produced but is not fertile. For instance, a male donkey and a mare produce a mule, which is sterile. Other examples of post-mating mechanisms include the failure of the gametes to fuse and the abnormal development and early death of the hybrid after birth.

16.   **(A)**

Two people heterozygous for the allele for brown eyes carry one dominant and one recessive allele, by definition. Hence, their genotype would each be Bb. The best way to see the probability of the genotypes of their offspring is by using a Punnett square.

	B	b
B	BB	Bb
b	Bb	bb

The results of the Punnett square show that the genotypes of the offspring would be 25% homozygous dominant (BB), 50% heterozygous dominant (Bb), and 25% homozygous recessive (bb). The phenotypic ratio would be 75% brown-eyed (BB or Bb) and 25% blue-eyed (bb). The genotypic ratio is 1:2:1, but the phenotypic ratio, the question of interest, is 3:1. A ratio of 1:0 implies that only brown-eyed babies would be produced; a ratio of 1:1 implies an equal probability of brown-eyed and blue-eyed babies.

17.   **(A)**

There are two major patterns of evolution that may explain the changes that occur. When Darwin proposed his theory of evolution based on natural selection, he implied a mechanism of gradualism, whereby changes were continual and gradual, the sum of many small changes. More recently, another mechanism has been proposed, though it is still consistent with Darwin's theory of natural selection. In punctuated equilibrium, evolutionary changes occur during short periods of rapid change that are separated by long periods of little change. There is a minimum of transitional states.

Adaptive radiation refers to the emergence of several species from one species, due to the segregation of their habitats. For instance, the finches that Darwin described on his famous voyage on *The Beagle* may have all radiated from one original species of finch.

In a sense, convergent evolution appears to be the opposite of adaptive radiation. It describes the appearance of similar adaptations to the environment amongst different species, despite the lack of a common ancestor.

Catastrophism, proposed by George Cuvier, states that the seeming appearance of new species is due to events of mass destruction that left only a few survivors. The survivors repopulated the environment and appeared as new species. In his beliefs, there was only one time of creation.

18.   **(B)**

The ocean is itself an ecosystem. It is divided into many different regions. The pelagic province refers to the open ocean away from the continental shelf. There are various regions to this province based on the depth of the water. The epipelagic region is the uppermost one extending 200 meters, and while it does not have as much life as the waters nearest the shores, there is more life here than in the deeper zones.

Life can continue in the epipelagic region because there is enough light allowing for photosynthetic reactions. However, moving away from the surface, one reaches the mesopelagic region, which extends 800 meters. The decreasing light forbids photosynthesis. There is total darkness at the deeper bathypelagic region. Only decomposers, scavengers, and dead organisms from above are found here.

Of course, aside from light penetration, there are gradients in temperature and salinity. However, light is a direct requirement for photosynthesis.

There is no tidal action in the pelagic province since this is not the intertidal region which occurs in the shallow ocean.

19.   **(A)**

In order for replication to occur, the DNA double helix must separate. The site of separation, where the hydrogen bonds between base pairs break, is called the replication fork; the single-stranded regions emerge here.

Each of the parent strands serves as a template for DNA replication. The DNA polymerase enzyme that catalyzes the addition of nucleotides to the growing daughter strands can only read the parent chain in the 3' - to - 5' direction and hence synthesize the daughter strand in the 5' - to -3' direction. Since the original DNA duplex is antiparallel, i.e. the strands have their 3' and 5' ends oriented in opposite directions, the DNA polymerase will add nucleotides continuously on one strand and in discontinuous bursts on the other. The strand that shows continuous replication is designated the leading strand. Synthesis occurs in the direction of the replication fork. The other strand, the lagging strand, shows short bursts of replication away from the replication fork, but in the proper 5' - to - 3' direction.

There is no replication fork in the transcription of DNA to RNA, because only a central portion of one DNA strand unwinds and serves as a template.

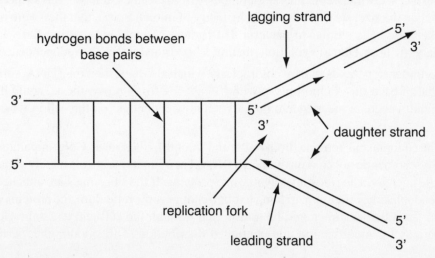

20.   **(B)**

In the first meiotic prophase, many events occur that provide the basis for variation even between offspring of the same parents.

First, the homologous chromosomes pair up in a process called synapsis. Since each homologous chromosome has already replicated, it exists as two sister chromatids joined together by a centromere. The paired chromosomes hence now exist as a tetrad of chromatids. Now crossing-over, the exchange of segments between homologous non-sister chromatids, can occur. The site of cross-over is called a chiasma (pl. chiasmata). Since the chromosomes and later the chromatids will ultimately segregate randomly and independently, and since they contain recombined chromosome segments and hence, recombined genetic traits, the foundation for variation is laid down.

The junctions between neurons are called synapses; the cells are separated by a synaptic cleft.

21.   **(E)**

Phloem is a vascular tissue that is continuous from the leaf to the stem to the root. It contains photosynthetically derived sugars and transports them from the site of origin in the leaf to other parts of the plant. The cells of phloem are the sieve tube members, which function in conduction, and the companion cells, which aid in the metabolic needs of the sieve tube members, since only the companion cells have nuclei.

The xylem transports water from the roots up to the top of the plant. In angiosperms, the vessel elements function primarily in conduction. The tracheids, while able to conduct, primarily give strength to the tissue.

22.   **(A)**

A mitochondrion is a cellular organelle that utilizes oxygen to produce ATP. It has its own DNA, which replicates autonomously from the nuclear DNA. It is suspected, based on the size, structure, and biochemistry of mitochondria, that they were once prokaryotic cells similar to bacteria that formed a symbiotic relationship with a eukaryotic host. Due to evolution, the mitochondrion has lost its independence.

A similar story holds true for chloroplasts, which also have their own DNA, similar to that of bacteria. A chloroplast, with its capacity for photosynthesis, could have originally been an independent prokaryote, now dependent on the cell in which it lives.

The endoplasmic reticula (both rough and smooth), ribosomes, Golgi apparatuses, and lysosomes do not contain their own DNA. Their functions are ultimately dictated by the nucleus. The ribosomes synthesize proteins. If the ribosomes are attached to the endoplasmic reticulum, making it rough endoplasmic reticulum, the proteins will enter the reticular lumen and be transported through the cell and reach the Golgi apparatus for modification and continued distribution. The smooth endoplasmic reticulum functions primarily in lipid synthesis. The lysosomes contain hydrolytic enzymes that can digest cell debris or the contents of endocytotic vesicles.

23.　　**(B)**

There are three distinguishing features of phylum Chordata, of which all vertebrates are members, although these features need not persist throughout life.

The presence of a notochord (hence the name Chordata) is prerequisite. This is a flexible rod that develops into a cartilaginous or bony vertebral column in vertebrates. The dorsal hollow nerve cord differentiates into the brain and spinal cord of vertebrates. Finally, the pharyngeal gill slits become the gills of fish, yet serve other, seemingly unrelated functions in higher vertebrates, due to modifications that occur during embryological development.

24.　　**(B)**

The fungi encompass an entire kingdom in the classification scheme. They function as decomposers of organic matter and hence aid in the carbon, nitrogen and phosphorus cycles. Of interest, fungi decompose both living and nonliving matter. The term saprophytic refers to its ability to decompose dead matter. This is in contrast to parasitic behavior, exhibited by some fungi, which refers to decomposition of living matter.

All fungi are eukaryotic. The eukaryotes, which means literally, "true nucleus" includes all organisms in kingdom Fungi, Animalia, Plantae, and Protista. They have a distinct nucleus enclosed in a membrane and many organelles. Only organisms of kingdom Monera (bacteria and cyanobacteria) are prokaryotic.

Prokaryotes do not have a distinct nucleus. Rather their DNA is in a nucleoid region.

The term heterotrophic refers to the inability to manufacture one's own food. Fungi secrete digestive enzymes onto their food substrate, and then absorb it. Animals are also heterotrophic, although animals ingest their food prior to digestion and absorption. In contrast, autotrophic organisms can produce their own food. For instance, plants produce food by photosynthesis. The monerans and protists are autotrophic or heterotrophic.

Some fungi are pathogenic, i.e. cause disease. Fungi can cause disease in animals (ringworm) and plants (potato blight). However, most fungi are not pathogenic and may even serve specific benefits for mankind. For instance the antibiotic penicillin is produced by a fungus.

25.　　**(C)**

There are many factors that participate in evolutionary change. Mutation refers to random, but inheritable changes in DNA. Natural selection refers to the idea that some genotypes will be selected by the environment for survival and propagation. Gene flow implies that allele frequency can change due to migration in or out of the population. Genetic drift refers to random fluctuations in the frequencies of alleles. An extreme case of genetic drift is called the founder effect. It is known that genetic drift is especially important in small populations. When only a few individuals become separated from the main population, they, in essence, are the founders of a new population. The genotype frequency of this new population may differ markedly from the original population from which these founders emerged, because they represent only a small sample of all the genotypes that are present in the main population.

26.   **(E)**

The sexual reproductive structures of angiosperms are in the flower (see figure). The female reproductive organ is the carpel, which has three parts. The base of the carpel is the ovary. It contains the ovule within. The ovary may develop into a fruit. A stalk called a style extends from the ovary. The sticky cap of the style is the stigma. It is the site that receives pollen.

The male reproductive organs are the stamens, which consist of pollen-bearing, two-lobed anthers atop single stalks called filaments.

The non-reproductive portions of the flower include the receptacle, which functions as a stem. The outermost whorls are the green sepals. The inner whorls are the colorful petals, which attract insects and other pollinators.

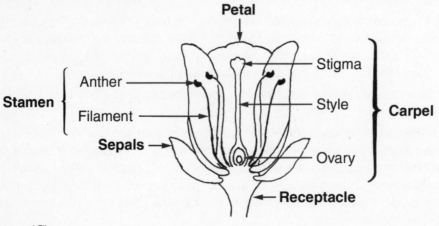

27.   **(C)**

DNA contains the codes for all the proteins that we need. DNA is transcribed by mRNA (messenger RNA). There are other RNAs also made from DNA: tRNA and rRNA (transfer RNA and ribosomal RNA, respectively). Different types of RNA polymerase molecules aid in the synthesis of different types of RNA.

mRNA aligns with ribosomes and contains the codons (sequences of three nucleotides) that represent specific amino acids and stop signals.

The rRNA and ribosomal proteins are the structural components of ribosomes.

tRNAs are small RNAs. They are specific for amino acids and carry the amino acid to the growing polypeptide chain on the ribosome. tRNAs have anticodons, triplets of nucleotides, that bind to the codons on mRNA. Therefore, mRNA determines which amino acids are added to the polypeptide, because each codon calls for a certain amino acid.

ATP (adenosine triphosphate) is a nucleotide that fuels the energy-requiring reactions of the body. Important functions of ATP include active transport and muscle contraction.

28.　　**(E)**

Embryological development in vertebrates follows an orderly sequence of fertilization, cleavage, gastrulation, and neurulation.

Fertilization refers to the process whereby a haploid sperm cell penetrates a haploid egg cell and their nuclei fuse, forming the diploid zygote (fertilized egg).

Cleavage begins immediately: it refers to the series of cell divisions which produces many smaller cells. It results in a solid ball of about 32 cells called a morula, which continues division to form a hollow ball of cells called a blastula. Despite the many cell divisions, there is no change in overall size.

Next, cells migrate in a particular pattern. These changes in the embryo are called gastrulation and result in three cell layers: ectoderm, mesoderm, and endoderm. All organs are derived from these layers. For example, the ectoderm gives rise to the skin and nervous system, the mesoderm gives rise to the skeleton and muscles, and the endoderm gives rise to the digestive tract and lungs.

The differentiation of the layers into organs follows a specific time sequence. The first organs which develop are the notochord and dorsal hollow nerve cord, in a process called neurulation. These organs need only be present in vertebrate embryos, but they may not necessarily persist into post-gestational life, depending upon the organism in question.

Induction refers to the event whereby one tissue determines the course of development of adjacent tissue. It is best exemplified by the development of the lens of the eye from epidermal tissue upon contact with the optic stalk.

29.　　**(E)**

The flower is the reproductive organ of the angiosperms, or flowering plants. The gametes form in the flower. In the male organ, specifically the anther, microspore mother cells that are produced mitotically undergo meiosis to form microspores, which develop into binucleate pollen grains, the immature male gametophyte. In the female organ, specifically the ovary, megaspore mother cells that are produced mitotically undergo meiosis to form megaspores, one of which develops into the female gametophyte, which will divide mitotically and ultimately produce the egg, and other non-functional cells.

Pollination refers to the transfer of pollen grains from the male organ to the sticky surface of the stigma, the most exposed portion of the female organ. This initiates the growth of the pollen tube from the stigma down through the style to reach the ovary.

During pollen growth, one of the nuclei of the pollen grains will mitotically divide and produce two sperm cells. The male gametophyte is now mature. The sperm are delivered directly to the egg. The nuclei fuse and fertilization is complete.

Photosynthesis is a non-reproductive process. It occurs in the organs that have cells with chloroplasts, such as leaves, which have mesophyll cells rich in chloroplasts.

30.   **(D)**

Double fertilization is unique to the angiosperms, or flowering plants.

A pollen grain, the immature male gametophyte, has two nuclei. During pollen tube growth, one of the nuclei divides mitotically to produce two sperm nuclei. It is now a mature male gametophyte.

The megaspore that develops into the female gametophyte divides mitotically to produce eight haploid nuclei. One will become the egg, two will become polar nuclei, and the other five serve no known function and disintegrate.

When fertilization occurs, not only does a sperm nucleus fuse with the egg nucleus to produce the zygote, but the second sperm nucleus fuses with both polar nuclei to form the endosperm cell. Since the gametes are all haploid, the zygote is diploid as expected, and the endosperm is triploid. The zygote will develop into the embryo; the endosperm functions to store food.

The other group of seed-producing vascular plants are the gymnosperms, which, like angiosperms, rely on pollination for reproductive success. Gymnosperms do not display double fertilization. The sperm cells just fuse with egg cells.

There are different ways in which twins can be produced. Fraternal twins are not identical, because they result from the fusion of two distinct sperm cells and two distinct egg cells. In contrast, identical twins result from post-zygotic events. A single sperm fertilizes a single egg. The resultant zygote splits into two embryos early in development. Their genetic constitution is exactly alike and of course they are always the same sex. Siamese twins, those born attached at some point on their bodies, are always identical twins that have not separated completely. Surgical separation is usually performed shortly after birth.

31.   **(E)**

The decomposers are important parts of the food chain. They are usually bacteria and fungi. They occupy no particular trophic level, because they feed on organisms of all levels. In general, they feed on dead organic matter, whether it came from a producer or a consumer (herbivores and carnivores) or even another decomposer.

The function of decomposition is to return gases and minerals, which contain vital elements like carbon, nitrogen, oxygen, and phosphorus, to the biosphere to be recycled. The elements are now available to the producers.

32.   **(C)**

Biogeochemical cycles exist for the elements carbon, hydrogen, oxygen, and nitrogen, which cycle between the earth, living organisms, and the atmosphere.

The water cycle is relatively simple to follow. Water can enter the atmosphere via various sources. Water evaporates as vapor from the land. Respiration of animals and plants produces water vapor. Plants lose water by evaporation through openings in the leaves by a process called transpiration.

Water returns to the earth as precipitation (rain or snow). Most of this water falls on oceans and other bodies of water. A small percentage of the precipitation falls on the land. This water can percolate into the soil and eventually reach the groundwater which will eventually drain into a larger body of water. The surface water is also transported as runoff. And of course some of the precipitate will evaporate.

The term fixation can be applied in both the nitrogen and carbon cycles. Carbon dioxide fixation occurs during photosynthesis, where it is incorporated into carbohydrate. Nitrogen fixation refers to the process whereby atmospheric molecular nitrogen is incorporated into nitrogen-containing compounds. Some microorganisms carry out this process.

33.   **(A)**

A blue-eyed woman is homozygous recessive (bb). A heterozygous man is Bb. The cross is best seen with a Punnett square:

	B	b
b	Bb	bb
b	Bb	bb

The proportions of the offspring are half heterozygous (Bb) and thus brown- eyed, and half homozygous recessive (bb) and thus blue-eyed. An equal proportion of brown- and blue-eyed offspring is a 1:1 ratio.

A 1:2 ratio would indicate that for every brown-eyed child, there are two blue-eyed children. A 2:1 ratio would be the reverse. A 1:0 ratio would mean that all the offspring are brown-eyed and none are blue-eyed. A 0:1 ratio is the reverse.

34.   **(D)**

The genotype is the actual genetic constitution of the individual, but the phenotype is the expression of those genes. For instance, the genotypes that code for eye color are BB (homozygous dominant), Bb (heterozygous) and bb (homozygous recessive). There are thus three genotypes. But there are only two phenotypes: Bb and BB both code for brown eye color, as the allele for brown eyes (B) is dominant to that for blue eyes (b). Blue eyes are only possible with the genotype bb. (Note that green eyes are considered as blue, genotypically and phenotypically). Thus a blue-eyed person knows his genotype immediately, but a brown-eyed person needs to look at his lineage to possibly figure out his genotype.

Phenotype includes all physical characteristics of an organism that are the results of genotype. A characteristic need not be seen by an observer to be included in an organism's phenotype; e.g. one's blood type is part of one's phenotype.

35.   **(A)**

The ancestors of modern bryophytes were the first land plants. However, lacking vascular tissue, which transports water and food throughout the plant, bryophytes must live in moist areas. They are anchored to the ground by rhizoids, which function as roots. Sexual reproduction requires water: the antheridia release sperm in the water and they must swim to the eggs that are produced by the archegonia. Classes of bryophytes include liverworts, hornworts, and mosses, of which the last is the most well-known.

Vascular plants show a definite evolutionary advancement. The vascular tissue includes xylem, which transports water from the roots to the leaves via the stem, and phloem, which transports food to all parts of the plant.

The lower vascular plants, such as the horsetails and ferns, require water for sexual reproduction. Like the bryophytes, the sperm that are produced by the antheridia must swim to the eggs that are produced by the archegonia. However, unlike the bryophytes, these plants have vascular tissue and true stems. Some lower vascular plants also have true roots + leaves.

The most advanced of the vascular plants are the seed plants: the gymnosperms (cone-bearing plants) and the angiosperms (flowering plants). Their reproduction is independent of water. Seeds can be dispersed by many media (aside from water), including wind and animal vehicles. The reproductive structures of the gymnosperms are cones; the reproductive structures of the angiosperms are flowers.

36.   **(C)**

Viruses are very small structures. They are not organisms in the true sense because they cannot reproduce. They require hosts for their metabolic and reproductive needs. Virus consists of a single strand of DNA or RNA enclosed in a protein sheath called a capsid, and may or may not have a surrounding envelope. Viruses can specifically attack plants, animals, or bacteria.

A bacteriophage is a virus that attacks bacteria. It is sometimes simply called a phage. Bacteriophages always contain DNA as their nucleic acid. The phage injects its nucleic acid into the host cell, leaving its protein coat outside. The phage now begins to control the host cell activity by directing the synthesis of more viruses. The phage kills the host cell by lysing it, releasing the newly formed viruses. Sometimes, the phage does not cause lysis. Rather, the viral DNA becomes incorporated into the host's single chromosome; there it lies latent. The term prophage refers to the fragment of vital DNA that is inserted into the bacterial chromosome. The virus is referred to as a lysogenic, or temperate, phage (as opposed to a virulent one), and the host cell is called a lysogenic cell, since it has the ability to lyse in the future.

37.   **(A)**

Dehydrogenases are a class of enzymes which catalyze oxidation/reduction reactions. Literally, the term means take hydrogens away. It does this by removing electrons and hydrogen ions from a substrate.

The active portion or coenzyme of the dehydrogenases can exist in the oxidized form (FAD, NAD^+). The reduced form has gained the electrons and hydrogen ions and thus forms NADH and $FADH_2$. When NAD^+ is reduced to NADH, it is coupled to the oxidation of a substrate. For instance, in the Krebs cycle, isocitrate is oxidized to alpha-ketoglutarate concomitant with the reduction of NAD^+ to NADH. Many of the steps in the Krebs cycle are catalyzed by dehydrogenases: three of the steps use NAD^+ and one uses FAD.

Conversely, when NADH is oxidized to NAD^+, it is coupled to the reduction of a substrate. For instance, the reduction of pyruvate to form lactate occurs concomitantly with the oxidation of NADH to NAD^+. (This regeneration of NAD^+ allows glycolysis to continue.)

ADH and ACTH are hormones. ADH (antidiuretic hormone) acts on the kidney to increase water reabsorption back into the blood (hence it counteracts a diuresis). ADH is released from the posterior pituitary gland.

ACTH (adrenocorticotrophic hormone) is released from the anterior pituitary gland. Its target is the adrenal cortex and it stimulates the release of glucocorticoids such as cortisol from that gland.

38.   **(D)**

Glycolysis is the first of a sequence of reactions dealing with the complete oxidation of glucose as described by the following equation:

$$\text{Glucose} + 6\,O_2 \rightarrow 6\,CO_2 + 6\,H_2O + 38\,\text{ATP}.$$

This complete oxidation requires the enzymatic reactions of glycolysis, the Krebs cycle, and the electron transport chain. Glycolysis functions to convert the six-carbon glucose molecule into two three-carbon pyruvate molecules. Pyruvate is converted to acetyl CoA, which then enters the Krebs cycle.

While much ATP can be produced ultimately from glucose oxidation, some ATP must be initially "invested." This investment occurs in the first and third steps of glycolysis, each of which requires one ATP molecule. In the first step of glycolysis, glucose is phosphorylated to form glucose-6-phosphate. The energy for this step comes from the hydrolysis (breakdown) of ATP to ADP. The phosphate group is transferred from ATP to glucose.

The production of carbon dioxide occurs primarily in the Krebs cycle. The Krebs cycle is also the site of many oxidation reactions, where the intermediates lose their electrons and hydrogen ions, which are transferred to NAD^+ and FAD, reducing them to NADH and $FADH_2$. These reduced forms donate their electrons to the electron transport chain. Electron transport is associated with the production of 36 of the ATP molecules. The other two are produced in glycolysis (actually, four ATPs are produced in glycolysis but two are used, so there is a net production of two ATPs in glycolysis).

39.   (C)

The active portion of the cytochrome enzymes is a heme group which is an iron-containing pigment. The cytochromes function in many of the oxidation-reduction reactions of the electron transport chain. They are pure electron carriers. The iron can exist in the oxidized state (Fe^{3+}) or the reduced state (Fe^{2+}). Note that the reduced form has gained an electron and is thus less positively charged. Heme is also found in the oxygen transporting protein hemoglobin.

Sodium (Na^+) is the major cation of the extracellular fluid, while potassium (K^+) is the major cation of the intracellular fluid. Calcium (Ca^{++}) is stored in bone tissue. These three cations are very important in nerve and muscle activity. Iodine is taken up by the thyroid gland and is essential in the synthesis of thyroid hormones.

40.   (D)

In the mitochondrion, as electrons are being transferred along the electron transport chain of the inner mitochondrial membrane, hydrogen ions are being pumped from the mitochondrial matrix to the intermembrane space (the space between the inner and outer mitochondrial membranes). (See figure.) For each NADH which donates its electron pair, three pairs of hydrogen ions are extruded into the space, while for $FADH_2$, donating its electrons, only two pairs of hydrogen ions are extruded.

The inner mitochondrial membrane also has ATP synthetase enzymes. A channel spans the membrane and the enzymatic head faces the matrix side. Hydrogen ions accumulate in the space and hence flow down their gradient through the channel back into the matrix. The dissipation of the gradient is associated with ATP synthesis. (Of course, the gradient is not dissipated since more hydrogen ions are being pumped into the space.) For every pair of hydrogen ions flowing back into the matrix, one ATP molecule is synthesized. Thus, three ATPs are synthesized for each NADH, while only two ATPs are synthesized for each $FADH_2$.

A chloroplast is a double-membraned organelle which contains many thylakoid (flattened sacs) within the stroma (matrix). A similar principle explains ATP synthesis in chloroplasts. In this case, hydrogen ions flow down their gradient from the interior of the thylakoid back to the stroma.

Mitochondrion

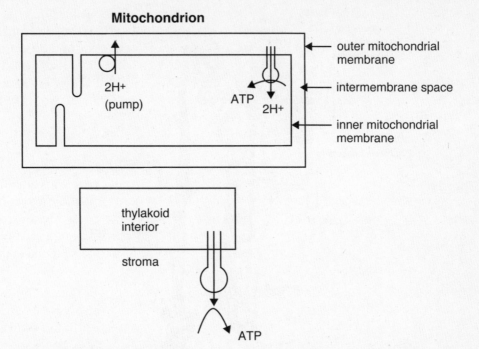

The term oxidative phosphorylation refers to the coupling of oxidation in the respiratory (electron transport) chain to the phosphorylation of ADP to form ATP. However, it is the H^+ not the phosphate group which travels through the channel protein. Sodium ion is the major cation of the extracellular fluid. Iron is found in the cytochrome enzymes of the electron transport chain. Calcium is an important cation in nerve and muscle activity.

41. (A)   42. (C)   43. (B)

Each kidney contains about one million nephrons (see Figure 1). A nephron is a renal tubule and the associated vascular component. The tubule consists of Bowman's capsule, the proximal convoluted tubule, the loop of Henle, the distal convoluted tubule, and the collecting duct. Collecting ducts from many nephrons join together to carry urine out of the kidney into the ureter. The vascular component includes the afferent arteriole, the glomerular capillaries, the efferent arteriole, and the peritubular capillaries. The plasma in the glomerular capillaries is filtered by Bowman's capsule. The filtrate moves through the tubules, in which reabsorption (movement of solutes and water from tubular lumen to blood) or secretion (movement of solutes and water from the blood into the tubular lumen) may occur. By the time the fluid leaves the collecting duct, no changes in urine composition can occur.

A sarcomere is the functional contractile unit of a muscle (see Figure 2). It consists of thick and thin filaments. The thick filaments contain myosin, while the thin ones are composed primarily of actin. The Z lines divide individual sarcomeres, which line up sequentially along the length of the muscle cell. The dark staining region, called the A band, is due to the presence of the thick filament. The region between adjacent A bands is called the I band.

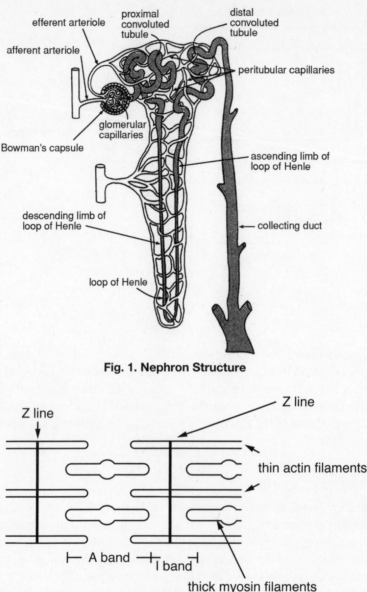

Fig. 1. Nephron Structure

Labels: efferent arteriole, proximal convoluted tubule, distal convoluted tubule, afferent arteriole, peritubular capillaries, glomerular capillaries, Bowman's capsule, ascending limb of loop of Henle, descending limb of loop of Henle, collecting duct, loop of Henle

Fig. 2. Sarcomere

Labels: Z line, Z line, thin actin filaments, A band, I band, thick myosin filaments

A neuron is a nerve cell. Neurons can electrically depolarize (decrease their membrane potential). When the wave of excitation reaches the end of this long cell, a chemical neurotransmitter is released into a space called a synapse. The neurotransmitter can then bind to the receptors of an adjacent neuron and excite it. In this manner, a message has been transmitted.

An alveolus is one of millions of small sacs in the lungs. Since each alveolus is covered with pulmonary capillaries, there is an immense surface area available for gas exchange between the lungs and the pulmonary blood. Hence, oxygen can diffuse into the blood and carbon dioxide can diffuse into the alveolus, where it will be exhaled.

A villus is a microscopic fold of the innermost lining (mucosa) of the small intestine. It has many microvilli on it, which contain digestive enzymes. Nutrients are absorbed through the villus into either the blood or lymphatic capillaries.

44. (C)   45. (B)   46. (E)

In transcription, the cell uses one strand of DNA as a template for the assembly of a messenger RNA molecule (mRNA). Like replication, transcription is based on complementary base pairing. RNA differs from DNA in having a different sugar in the backbone (ribose instead of deoxyribose) and having a different nitrogenous base to pair with adenine (uracil instead of thymine).

In translation, the second major step of the overall process called protein synthesis, mRNA aligns with a ribosome in the cytoplasm (either free or bound to rough endoplasmic reticulum). On the ribosome, anticodons of two tRNA molecules form complementary pairs with two codons of the mRNA. Each codon is a set of three bases coding for a single amino acid. Each tRNA has an anticodon at one end and an amino acid bound to its other end. Components of the ribosome catalyze the formation of a covalent bond between two adjacent amino acids.

Transformation is the process by which a cell takes up DNA from its immediate environment and incorporates that DNA into its genome, resulting in both phenotypic and genotypic changes. In this way, living bacteria can be "transformed" by the debris from dead bacterial cells. By observing this phenomenon and correctly interpreting it, British scientist Frederick Griffith showed that the hereditary material was a chemical. It took other scientists 14 years to identify that chemical as DNA. Transduction is a process whereby viruses specific to bacteria, called bacteriophages, transfer DNA from one bacterial cell to another. The virus may transfer random pieces of bacterial DNA (generalized transduction) or it may incorporate specific parts of bacterial DNA into its own genome, and subsequently cause its genome to be incorporated into the host bacterial genome (specialized transduction).

Transduction is a process whereby viruses specific to bacteria, called bacteriophages, transfer DNA from one bacterial cell to another. The virus may transfer random pieces of bacterial DNA (generalized transduction) or it may incorporate specific parts of bacterial DNA into its own genome, and subsequently cause its genome to be incorporated into the host bacterial genome (specialized transduction).

"Translocation" is used in three different ways in molecular biology: (1) To refer to the process in which a ribosome moves a tRNA from the first tRNA site to the second. (2) To refer to an exchange of portions of non-homologous chromosomes, due to breakage of chromosomes. (3) To describe a process in plants, in which food is transported from the leaves to the roots by way of the vascular phloem tissue.

47. (C)   48. (B)   49. (A)   50. (D)

All plants show an alternation of generations. The diploid (2n) generation is a sporophyte plant, a spore-producing plant. The haploid (1n) generation is the gametophyte plant, the gamete-producing plant. In the evolution of plants, the sporophyte generation becomes increasingly dominant.

The life cycle is illustrated starting with the sporophyte generation. The sporophyte plant has multicellular structures called sporangia. The spore mother cells within undergo meiosis andproduce haploid spores. If the plant can produce both types of spores (megaspores and microspores), it is heterosporous. If it produces only one type of spore, it is homosporous.

The spores are the first cells of the haploid generation and as such, they grow into the haploid gametophyte plant. Mitosis in the gametophyte results in production of haploid gametes, eggs, and sperm. Fusion of the gametes results in a diploid zygote that is a member of the sporophyte generation and grows into a sporophyte plant. The cycle repeats.

51. **(C)**   52. **(E)**   53. **(B)**   54. **(D)**

A "typical" animal cell, if there is such a thing, has many cell organelles, which carry out specific functions within their compartments.

Ribosomes are small organelles composed of rRNA (ribosomal RNA) and ribosomal proteins. They may occur free in the cytoplasm or bound to the endoplasmic reticulum. In the latter case, the endoplasmic reticulum is then referred to as rough endoplasmic reticulum. Ribosomes are the sites of protein synthesis, as they link up with mRNA. Free ribosomes synthesize cellular proteins; ribosomes on the rough endoplasmic reticulum synthesize proteins destined for export.

Microfilaments and microtubules are the constituents of the cytoskeleton — they are the framework upon which cell shape is maintained. They also function in cell movements. Actin is an example of a protein found in microfilaments; it has a specific function in skeletal muscle contraction. Tubulin is the protein in microtubules. Microtubules are components of cilia and flagella.

Lysomes are small membrane-bound spheres that contain hydrolytic enzymes. One function of lysosomes is the digestion of aged organelles. Lysosomes also fuse with vesicles formed by endocytosis. The phagocytic vesicle may contain "food" particles; alternatively, it may contain bacteria particles. In either case, the engulfed vesicle fuses with the lysosome for digestion.

The endoplasmic reticulum is a series of channels that originate near the nucleus and extend throughout much of the cell, serving as an intracellular circulatory system. Endoplasmic reticulum that has ribosomes attached is called rough endoplasmic reticulum. It functions in the transport of proteins synthesized on its ribosomes. Endoplasmic reticulum devoid of ribosomes is called smooth endoplasmic reticulum. It functions in lipid synthesis, including the synthesis of steroids. In muscle cells, the specialized smooth endoplasmic reticulum is called the sarcoplasmic reticulum: it stores and releases calcium, as dictated by the stimulus for muscle contraction.

Mitochondria are the sites of oxygen utilization and ATP (energy) production. Mitochondria are especially prominent in active cells, i.e., those that undergo contraction, active transport, and other metabolically active processes.

55. **(C)**   56. **(B)**   57. **(D)**   58. **(A)**

The enzymes in the questions all participate in the complete oxidation of the glucose. The metabolic process that initiates the total oxidation of glucose is glycolysis, which breaks glucose down into pyruvate. Pyruvate is then converted into acetyl CoA, which takes part in the Krebs cycle. Reducing equivalents formed from these processes transfer their electrons to the electron transport chain. The movement of electrons along the respiratory chain is prerequisite to the chemiosmotic synthesis of ATP.

Hexokinase catalyzes the first step of glycolysis, the entire process of which occurs in the cytoplasm. Although the net yield of glucose oxidation will be 38 ATPs, some energy must be initially invested. This will start the glucose "burning." A kinase is an enzyme that transfers a phosphate group. In this case, it transfers phosphate from ATP to a hexose (six-carbon sugar), glucose. The glucose is then sequentially broken down into two pyruvate molecules.

In the presence of oxygen, pyruvate enters the mitochondria, in which it is decarboxylated (loses a carbon dioxide) and oxidized (loses of pair of electrons and hydrogen ions) to form acetyl CoA. These two sequential steps are catalyzed by a single large enzyme complex (series of polypeptides) called pyruvate dehydrogenase.

Acetyl CoA is shuttled into the Krebs cycle, in which it combines with a four-carbon compound oxaloacetate, to regenerate the six-carbon citrate molecule. In this cycle, sequential oxidation steps (as well as two decarboxylation steps) that regenerate oxaloacetate occur. The oxidation steps are carried out by dehydrogenase enzymes that remove electrons and hydrogen ions from the substrates and transfer them to their own coenzymes, NAD^+ or FAD. For example, succinate dehydrogenase catalyzes the conversion of succinate to fumarate. Concomitantly, $FADH_2$ is formed.

The NADH and $FADH_2$, which are formed primarily in the Krebs cycle, but also in glycolysis and in the formation of acetyl CoA, now move to the electron transport chain, which is located in the inner mitochondrial membrane. Many of the participating enzymes which transfer the electrons along the respiratory chain are called cytochromes. They contain iron in the oxidized (Fe^{3+}) or reduced (Fe^{2+}) state. The final step, catalyzed by cytochrome oxidase, reduces oxygen to water as the reduced iron is oxidized by oxygen.

These oxidation steps are coupled to the phosphorylation of ADP, to form ATP. This complex process, called chemiosmosis, requires an ATP synthetase enzyme on the inner mitochondrial membrane facing the mitochondrial matrix. The ATP synthesized is now used to do work for the cell.

59. **(C)**   60. **(B)**   61. **(A)**

Ethylene is produced during plant respiration and is associated with fruit ripening. It has other functions, such as the abscission of leaves. Although, by name, it would appear that abscisic acid promotes the latter function just attributed to ethylene, this is of only minor importance. The major role of abscisic acid appears to be in promoting the closure of the stomata. The effects of abscisic acid oppose those of many of the hormones that aid in plant growth and development.

Gibberellins stimulate seed germination by activating enzymes of the seed. They also promote the elongation of stems, particularly in genetically dwarfed plants.

Cytokinins function in cell division; auxins function in stem elongation, particularly in response to light.

62. **(A)**   63. **(D)**   64. **(E)**   65. **(C)**

Mollusks, which include snails, clams, and scallops, have muscular mantles as a distinguishing feature. This mantle is a pair of folds on the dorsal body wall that envelopes and protects the visceral organs. In those mollusks that have shells, it is the cells of the mantle that secrete the chemical components required to produce a shell. A muscular foot on the ventral surface of a mollusk functions in locomotion.

The best-known species in the phylum Annelida is the earthworm. Annelids are segmented worms: their bodies are partitioned into segments that are lined by longitudinal and circular muscles.

There are nearly one million different species of arthropods. Among the distinguishing features of an arthropod are the hardened exoskeleton composed of protein and chitin and jointed appendages. Like the bodies of annelids, their bodies are segmented. Examples of arthropods are spiders, crabs, and centipedes, to name a few.

The echinoderms are all marine, in contrast to members of other phyla that were discussed, which live in marine, freshwater, and terrestrial environments. A unique feature of echinoderms is their method of locomotion. They have water-vascular systems in which seawater circulates through canals and tube feet. Sea stars (starfish) are echinoderms.

The chordates include fish, amphibians, reptiles, birds, and mammals. The distinguishing characteristic of this seemingly wide classification is the notochord, which functions as a skeletal framework at some time in embryonic or post-natal life. Other distinguishing characteristics include a dorsal hollow nerve cord, pharyngeal gill slits, and a postanal tail at some point during development.

66. **(D)**   67. **(C)**   68. **(E)**   69. **(A)**   70. **(B)**

Aerial stems are classified as woody or herbaceous. Since the stems of the latter types are annual, there is no secondary growth. The diagram shows secondary growth in a woody stem. The primary tissues develop in the first year of growth. All growth that occurs after the first year is called secondary growth.

Secondary growth arises from the vascular cambium, a continuous ring between the two types of vascular tissue, xylem and phloem. The cells of the vascular cambium divide, producing secondary tissues. Towards the end of every year, the cells that are produced by the vascular cambium are smaller, and the portion of vascular tissue that contains these smaller cells appears as a dark annual ring.

The phloem contains companion cells and sieve tubes that conduct food substances from the leaves down into the root. The primary phloem lies just external to the vascular cambium. During secondary growth, this primary layer moves outward, and secondary phloem then lies adjacent to the cambium.

The xylem contains tracheids and vessel members. It conducts water from the roots up to the leaves. The primary xylem is just internal to the vascular cambium. As secondary growth occurs, this layer is pushed inward, away from the cambium, by secondary xylem. The epidermis is the outermost single layer of cells. In the root, it functions in water and mineral absorption, but in the stem, it has a heavy cuticle layer that protects the tissues from desiccation.

The cortex is the ground substance consisting of widely spaced cells. It has a role in support and storage.

The tissue in the center of the stem is pith.

71. **(E)**   72. **(D)**   73. **(A)**

The transmission of the disease to the second and third filial (F_2 and F_3) generations are clearly from the mothers to their sons, since the fathers have simply married into the family. This suggests a sex-linked disease, which is in accordance with the transmission to the first filial generation, as well.

Sex-linked diseases are carried on the X chromosome. The Y chromosome is smaller than the X chromosome and contains genes that produce maleness. The X chromosome can carry the gene for color blindness, hemophilia, and baldness, all of which are conditions that can be seen more often in males.

The allele for the disease must be a recessive one, since all of the mothers in the pedigree are carriers, but not afflicted. In order for a female to be afflicted, she must be homozygous recessive. However, a male cannot have a homozygous recessive genotype for the disease, since he only has one X chromosome. In this case, the recessive allele is expressed when he contains only one "bad" X chromosome, since the Y chromosome contains a dominant allele whose effects could mask the effects of the recessive allele.

$X^C X^C$ normal female

$X^C X^c$ carrier female

$X^c X^c$ color-blind female

$X^C Y$ normal male

$X^c Y$ color-blind male

Since P_1 is a normal male, his genotype must be $X^C Y$.

A female can only be color blind if she inherits two recessive alleles, which means her father must be color blind, and her mother must be a carrier (or color blind herself). Of course, marriage between relatives increases this incidence.

$F_{2.5}$ is a normal male, since there is no carrier state for the male. His genotype is X^CY. If he marries a homozygous dominant woman, X^CX^C, she is normal and they cannot have an afflicted child.

74. **(C)**   75. **(B)**   76. **(B)**   77. **(E)**

A spirometer measures the volume of air moved into and out of the lungs during breathing. There are four basic lung volumes. The tidal volume is the volume of air moved in a standard breath. The subject's tidal volume is 500 ml. The inspiratory reserve volume (IRV) is the volume of air that one can inspire in addition to the tidal volume. In the figure, it is the volume between 5500 ml and 2500 ml, or 3000 ml. It is important NOT to include tidal volume in the IRV. The expiratory reserve volume (ERV) is the volume of air that one can exhale in addition to tidal volume; this is produced during a forced exhalation. In the figure, it is the difference between 2000 ml and 1000 ml, or 1000 ml. The subject performed a maximal expiration just before the second signal, as indicated by the downward deflection on the spirometer reading. The residual volume cannot be measured on a spirometer. It is the volume of air left in the lungs despite a maximal expiration. It is typically about 1000 ml.

Lung capacities are simply sums of the lung volumes. Inspiratory capacity is the sum of tidal volume and inspiratory reserve volume. Functional residual capacity is the sum of expiratory reserve volume and residual volume. Total lung capacity is the sum of all four volumes.

Vital capacity is the sum of tidal volume and both reserve volumes. This sum can be measured directly by inhaling maximally and then exhaling maximally, thus achieving in one breath the greatest deflections both upward and downward. However, the subject did not do this. The vital capacity is the difference between 5500 ml and 1000 ml, or 4500 ml. Note that this is the sum of tidal volume (500 ml), inspiratory reserve volume (3000 ml) and expiratory reserve volume (1000 ml).

None of the choices (A–D) for Item 77 fits because the breathing rate cannot be figured with the data provided. Spirometry measures the volume of air moved into the lungs in an inspiration and the volume of air moved out of the lungs in an expiration. (A spirometer does not measure the residual volume of the lungs.) Thus, the premise of the question—that one could find the subject's respiratory rate (including inspirations and expirations)—does not hold up, for the spirogram does not indicate a span of time across the full range of measurement. (Only two wave forms are shown between signals 2 and 3. The spirogram would need six to show a rate of 12 breaths per second.)

78. **(A)**   79. **(C)**   80. **(B)**   81. **(E)**

The Hardy-Weinberg equilibrium refers to an equilibrium in which the proportion of alleles at a given locus will remain constant. The requirements for such an equilibrium are: no mutation, no migration, no natural selection, and a large population size. In real populations, these factors are not usually all met and a change in the allele frequencies can occur.

Assuming a Hardy-Weinberg equilibrium, there are two mathematical statements that can describe it. If the trait, such as eye color, has only two alleles, p and q, then

$$p + q = 1$$

in which p is the frequency of one allele and q is the frequency of the other allele. (The sum of the frequencies must equal 1). Another mathematical equation is true under this equilibrium:

$$(p + q)^2 = p^2 + 2pq + q^2$$

If p represents the dominant allele, then p^2 is the frequency of homozygous dominants in the population. If q is the frequency of the recessive allele, the q^2 is the frequency of homozygous recessives in the population. Thus 2pq is the frequency of heterozygotes in the population. Note also that:

$$p^2 + 2pq + q^2 = 1$$

In the original sample, 91% of the students have brown eyes and 9% have blue eyes. Since 9% (or .09) is equal to q^2, then q must be .3. Therefore, p must be .7, which is (1-.3).

The 910 brown-eyed students consist of those that are homozygous and those that are heterozygous for the allele for brown eyes. The homozygous dominant population represents 49% ($p^2 = .7^2$) of the total population and the heterozygotes make up 42% of the total. (2pq = 2 x .7 x .3). 42% of 1000 students is 420 students.

The data for 1986 is significantly different. The change in allele frequencies can be accounted for by migration (immigration and emigration) during the attempt at desegregation.

The other factors that could disrupt a Hardy-Weinberg equilibrium are not pertinent here. For instance, the population size is the same.

In the second sample, blue eyes account for 16% of the population (160/1000). Thus, $q^2 = .16$ and q must equal .4. To verify this, note that p must equal .6. Therefore, the homozygous dominant population would account for 36%, or 360 students, and the heterozygotes would account for 48% (2 x .6 x .4), or 480 students. Indeed, there are 840 (which equals 360 + 480) brown-eyed students in the second population.

82. **(D)**   83. **(B)**   84. **(B)**   85. **(E)**

From the data given, pupillary dilation would seem to be caused by stimulating sympathetic nerves or inhibiting parasympathetic ones. Since atropine has no effect on receptors for norepinephrine, it has no sympathetic effect. Since parasympathetic stimulation causes pupillary constriction, atropine must block this effect, by blocking the receptors for acetylcholine.

Likewise, since propranolol causes a decrease in heart rate that is not due to parasympathetic (acetylcholine) stimulation, it must be due to sympathetic inhibition, by blocking norepinephrine activity.

The heart beats spontaneously, but its rate is modified by the combined effect of sympathetic and parasympathetic discharge. At rest, parasympathetic discharge is greater and causes an inhibitory tone. When the vagus nerve is cut, parasympathetic discharge to the heart is abolished. This will allow the heart rate to increase, because there is no counteraction to sympathetic discharge. However, note that sympathetic discharge is not increased; it is merely not counteracted. Also note that even if the heart were removed from the body and hence totally denervated, it could continue to beat for a while at its intrinsic rate.

Curare causes paralysis of the skeletal muscles.

Skeletal muscle is voluntary, as opposed to smooth and cardiac muscle. Hence it is not innervated by the autonomic nervous system. Instead it is innervated by the somatic motor nervous system.

86. (A)   87. (B)   88. (A)

During glycolysis, glucose is converted to pyruvate. Pyruvate has many fates in the cell, depending upon whether or not oxygen is available, and the type of cell that is involved.

Under aerobic conditions, i.e., when oxygen is present, pyruvate is transferred from the cytoplasm to the mitochondrial matrix. There, it is converted to acetyl CoA, which enters the Krebs cycle. Oxidative phosphorylation then occurs. The result is the production of carbon dioxide, water, and ATP, which occurred in test tube C.

Under anaerobic conditions, pyruvate has other fates. Fermentation occurs when an intermediate of carbohydrate metabolism acts as the final acceptor of electrons from NADH, as opposed to what occurs in the electron transport chain in which oxygen is the final acceptor of electrons and is reduced to water.

In lactate fermentation, pyruvate acts as the final electron acceptor and is converted to lactate. The importance of this step is that it regenerates the NAD^+ and allows glycolysis to continue. In animal cells, lactate fermentation occurs when oxygen is in short supply, as when sprinting. When lactate is formed and diffuses into the blood, it causes pain (usually in the calves of a sprinter), and causes the sprinter to slow down or stop. Thus the affected muscles will start to get more oxygen. In essence, this mechanism prevents him from accidentally suffocating himself!

Alcoholic fermentation occurs in yeast cells, which use acetaldehyde as the final electron acceptor. Pyruvate is converted to acetaldehyde, which is converted to ethyl alcohol (ethanol). Carbon dioxide gas is also produced. The gas is responsible for causing breads that are baked with yeast to rise. Alcoholic fermentation in yeasts is used to make beer. There are even rare cases of humans whose cells can perform alcoholic fermentation, causing the person to become spontaneously drunk!

89. (C)   90. (B)   91. (A)

The two species of *Paramecium* each survive in the culture dish alone, but when mixed together, species B succumbs to species A. The interaction between the two species is called competitive exclusion, because they are both competing for the same nutrients in the culture, but, due to limited resources, one must succumb. This interspecific competition is merely due to the overlap of their niches (in this case, a culture dish). Species that are very similar have similar requirements and hence are more likely to succumb to competitive exclusion.

A survivorship curve is a curve that describes the percentage of population at all gradations of age. By looking at a survivorship curve, one can easily see if age is correlated with mortality. For instance, some organisms are susceptible at birth, but if they survive that period, they may live for a long time.

Protocooperation refers to a mutually beneficial interaction between two species living together, but unlike mutualism, in protocooperation, the interaction is not obligatory. Symbiosis is a general term referring to all interactions between two species in a community.

The size of population A is ultimately the same whether it is living alone or with species B, as indicated by the growth curves. However, the initial growth period in the combined culture is greater; as species B dies off, the growth of species A picks up.

At one week in time, it is clear the size of the population of species A is still climbing toward its maximum, but the size of the population of species B has already peaked and is declining.

The graphs plot population size vs. time. Although the maximum population size of B in the mixed culture is very low and never stabilizes, its peak is reached in about a half a week vs. one and a half weeks in the solo culture. B shows its greatest numbers in the solo culture, but that value is still less than the size of A in either the solo or mixed cultures. Furthermore, it is about three times the size of B's size in the mixed culture.

92. **(D)**   93. **(C)**

Glycerinated skeletal muscle is used to examine the striations of skeletal muscle. The lengths of the fibers can be measured with a millimeter ruler. If a fiber becomes shorter upon application of a chemical, it has contracted. It usually appears darker as well, because the cross striations (dark and light bands) get closer together as the microscopic sarcomeres shorten.

In Experiment A, the muscle fiber that is shortest is the one that is in the presence of ATP and salts ($KC1$ and $MgC1_2$), in addition to the glycerol solution. While ATP is of course required to provide the energy for contraction, the salts are necessary as activators of the ATPase enzyme. The slight contraction that occurred in the fiber that was in contact with glycerol and ATP alone is probably an error due to contamination by salts. For instance, there are many salts on the skin. Touching the fiber can contaminate it.

Standard conditions are pH 7 and room temperature (25°C). However, in vivo, the muscle tissues are bathed in extracellular fluid with a pH of about 7.4 (plasma) and body temperature is warmer than room temperature. Body temperature is about

37°C. Experiment B shows that a rise in temperature increased the amount of contraction, as indicated by the decrease in fiber length. When the length of a fiber in a neutral solution is compared with that of a fiber in an acidic solution (pH 4), it is clear that contraction occurs more readily in the neutral solution. Freezing temperatures (0°C) were not measured, but they would probably be inhibitory to muscle contraction. However, glycerinated muscle can be stored in a frozen or very cold state.

94. (A)   95. (D)

Mucus is produced throughout much of the digestive tract, including the stomach, esophagus, and large intestine. It serves as a lubricant. Mucus had no effect on the polypeptide, as it remained intact after two hours.

Peptidases can be classified as endopeptidases or exopeptidases. The former type breaks peptide bonds in the middle of the chain, yielding shorter fragmented chains. The latter cleaves off the terminal amino acid, yielding a free amino acid.

Chymotrypsin and trypsin are pancreatic endopeptidases. Their actions result in the formation of shorter peptides called dipeptides and tripeptides (peptides having two and three amino acids, respectively). Carboxypeptidase is an exopeptidase that is produced in the pancreas. It cleaves the peptide bond at the C-terminus of a polypeptide. It thus yields free amino acids as well as the short peptides. Aminopeptidase is an exopeptidase that is attached to the small intestinal brushborder, and usually is active as the short peptides are being absorbed by the intestinal epithelium. Aminopeptidase cleaves the peptide bond at the N-terminus, also yielding free amino acids and very short peptides.

96. (C)   97. (C)

There are two organelle components of the cell's cytoskeleton that control cell movements and cell shape. Microfilaments are composed primarily of the protein actin. (Myosin, which functions with actin in muscle contraction, is larger than true microfilaments). Aside from muscular contraction, microfilaments are responsible for cytoplasmic streaming, in which organelles are in continual motion.

Microtubules have larger diameters than microfilaments do. They are composed of the protein tubulin, in a polymerized form. Unlike microfilaments, these are hollow cylinders. Microtubules are very active in mitosis, in which they are responsible for chromosome movement.

There are many chemicals that are poisonous to certain organelles in the cell. For instance, ouabain inhibits the Na^+-K^+ ATPase pump. Cyanide binds to a cytochrome in the electron transport chain and prohibits oxygen utilization.

Cytochalasin B binds to actin and inhibits its interaction with myosin to produce muscular contractions. It also inhibits vesicular and organelle movements. Note that the organelle is a microfilament whereas actin is a protein.

Colchicine inhibits microtubular activity by binding to tubulin. Thus chromosome movement is prevented.

Histones are the proteins that, with DNA, comprise chromosomes. Chromatin is basically synonymous with chromosomes; however, the term is reserved for the long thread-like appearance of the chromosomes just before mitosis begins.

98. **(E)**   99. **(C)**   100. **(E)**

Secretory cells are specialized for the production and secretion of proteins or other substances that are produced within. If a cell is to produce protein, it must be equipped with a rich supply of rough endoplasmic reticulum and Golgi apparatuses. Protein synthesis occurs on the ribosomes. The proteins are inserted into the reticular lumen as they are being synthesized. Protein is then circulated through the reticulum and reaches the Golgi apparatus, in which chemical modifications, such as glycosylation (addition of sugars to form glycoproteins) may occur. Vesicles pinch off, move to the plasma membrane, and the contents of the vesicles are extruded by exocytosis. Secretory cells must also have many mitochondria in order to supply the energy for exocytosis. Cell E is secretory.

Cell A must be a red blood cell, since it is anucleate and has no mitochondria. It is believed that the lack of a nucleus provides more space for hemoglobin. Certainly, red blood cells cannot have mitochondria, since mitochondria utilize oxygen, and the purpose of the cell is to transport oxygen.

Cell D is probably a white blood cell, as indicated by the significant amount of lysosomes. There are many types of white blood cells; all have distinct nuclei. Some white blood cells are phagocytic, especially the neutrophils and the monocytes (after they become wandering macrophages). As phagocytes, they need high numbers of lysosomes to digest whatever they ingest, such as bacteria.

Cell C must be a sperm cell, because it is the only cell in the human body that has a flagellum. The flagellum is the tail of the cell; its beating movements cause the cell to swim. This activity requires high numbers of mitochondria. The head of the sperm contains acrosomal enzymes, which are basically like extracellular lysosomes: they digest the outer layers of the egg in order to allow the sperm nucleus to penetrate it. The gametes (eggs and sperm) are haploid. All animal cells are eukaryotic. Of course, in prokaryotes, flagella are much more common, as many bacteria have flagella.

Cell B may be a skeletal muscle cell, which has many mitochondria and many peripheral nuclei.

SECTION II

ESSAY I

Organic compounds contain carbon. Since carbon is tetravalent (able to make four bonds), it tends to form large compounds (when compared to inorganic compounds). Organic compounds form the primary structural and functional components of living cells, and hence of the entire organism. Large organic molecules are usually synthesized from smaller monomers, or building blocks. Aside from carbon, the elements found most often in organic compounds are hydrogen, oxygen, nitrogen, phosphorus, and sulfur. The four major classes of organic compounds are the carbohydrates, lipids, proteins, and nucleic acids.

Carbohydrates function as the most readily available energy source. The empirical formula of all carbohydrates is $C_nH_{2n}O_n$. They provide 4 calories per gram when consumed in the diet.

The building blocks for the larger carbohydrates are the monosaccharides, or simple sugars. Trioses are sugars that have three carbons. The pentoses, or five-carbon sugars, include ribose and deoxyribose, which are found in nucleic acids. The hexoses are the sugars in the foods we eat. These six-carbon sugars include glucose, fructose, and galactose.

Two monosaccharides chemically combined by dehydration reactions produce a disaccharide. Sucrose, table sugar, is a combination of glucose and fructose. Lactose, or milk sugar, is a combination of glucose and galactose. Maltose, a product of the degradation of starch, is the combination of two glucose molecules.

The polysaccharides are primarily polymers of glucose only. They are long chains containing hundreds of glucose molecules in them. Glycogen is the storage form of glucose in animal liver and muscle cells. The glycogen can be hydrolyzed when glucose is needed, such as during exercise. Starch is the storage form of glucose in plant cells. Plants produce glucose by photosynthesis and then store it as starch. We eat the starch. Cellulose is the structural component of plant cell walls. It is indigestible by humans, although ruminants such as cows and sheep have bacteria in their rumens that can digest it. Although cellulose and starch both occur in plants, the linkages between the glucose subunits are different and thus the molecules are very different and we can only digest starch.

Lipids are nonpolar compounds that can dissolve in substances like benzene or ether, but not in water. There are many types of lipids, including the fatty acids, which are long hydrocarbon chains with acid (carboxyl) groups at one end. Fatty acids may be saturated or unsaturated, where the former indicates that the acid is carrying all the hydrogens possible. A triacylglycerol (triglyceride) molecule is the fat that we eat and the fat that we store subcutaneously for insulation and protection. As an energy source, triglycerides provide 9 calories/gram. A monoglyceride is one glycerol molecule, attached to one fatty acid. A diglyceride has two fatty acids attached and a triglyceride has three fatty acids attached to the glycerol. Glycerol is a triol, i.e. it has three alcohol groups. In a triglyceride, the three acid groups from the fatty acids bind to the three alcohol groups due to dehydration reactions. Since the acids can no longer ionize and become charged, triglycerides are also called neutral fats.

Another type of lipid is the phospholipid, which is a diglyceride with a phosphate group attached to the third carbon of the glycerol. The phosphate group is charged, but the fatty acid chain components of the diglyceride are not. Hence, the molecule is amphipathic: it has both polar and non-polar portions. For this reason, it functions in the cell membrane, forming the lipid bilayer, in which the polar phosphate heads are oriented toward the aqueous fluids (intracellular and extracellular fluids), and the fatty acid tails are oriented inward to the center of the lipid bilayer. Phospholipids also form micelles, which are used in the digestive tract to transport fats to the intestinal epithelium. They also form surfactants, used in the respiratory system to decrease the surface tension of the alveoli and prevent their collapse.

Steroids are another class of lipids. They have four-ringed structures. Examples of steroids are cholesterol, vitamin D, bile salts, and the hormones of the adrenal cortex and the gonads (ovaries and testes).

The basic building blocks of proteins are the amino acids. There are twenty amino acids used in protein synthesis. Amino acids consist of a central carbon attached to a hydrogen, amino group (NH_2), carboxylic acid group (COOH), and an R group. The R group is a collection of atoms that differs from one amino acid to the next.

A dipeptide is the union of two amino acids by a peptide bond. The amino terminus of one amino acid links up with the carboxyl terminus of the previous one in a condensation reaction.

A polypeptide is a polymer of amino acids. It may contain 10 amino acids or more than 100. Proteins are arbitrarily defined as polypeptides with over 50-100 amino acids. Proteins may consist of 1 or more polypeptide chains.

Proteins function as enzymes, antibodies, hormones (insulin) muscle proteins (actin and myosin), structural proteins (collagen and keratin), clotting proteins (fibrinogen), etc.

Ingested protein supplies 4 calories/gram, but is not a major energy source for the body. Proteins are major sources of energy only during periods of starvation, during which no fats or carbohydrates are ingested.

Nucleic acids are polymers of nucleotides. Each nucleotide contains a nitrogenous base, which may be a purine or a pyrimidine. The purine bases are double-ringed structures, such as adenine or guanine. The pyrimidine bases are single-ringed structures such as cytosine, thymine, and uracil. Nucleotides also must contain pentose sugars, such as deoxyribose or ribose. Finally, a nucleotide has one or more phosphate groups attached.

The nucleic acid DNA (deoxyribonucleic acid) contains the genetic codes for proteins that are necessary for life. The sugar in DNA is deoxyribose and the bases may be adenine, thymine, cytosine, or guanine. The nucleic acid RNA (ribonucleic acid) transfers the code in DNA to make protein. It contains the sugar ribose and may have the bases adenine, uracil, cytosine, and guanine.

While the other three organic compounds provide calories in the diet, nucleic acids do not.

ESSAY II

Translation is the process of protein synthesis. The codon on mRNA recognizes and binds to the anticodon on tRNA, which recognizes and binds to a specific amino acid. Note that there is no direct recognition between the codon on mRNA and its amino acid. For instance, a codon UUC on mRNA will bind to the anticodon AAG on a tRNA, which specifically binds to the amino acid phenylalanine; hence UUC is a codon for phenylalanine.

Before translation can occur, the tRNAs must become attached to their appropriate amino acids in an activation step, which requires the expenditure of ATP.

A ribosome, which consists of protein and rRNA (ribosomal RNA), has two sites on it (see figure). The A site is closer to the 3' end of the mRNA and the P site is closer to the 5' end of the mRNA. During translation, the ribosome moves toward the 3' end.

There are three stages of translation: initiation, elongation, and termination.

Translation is initiated by an initiating codon AUG. The small subunit of the ribosome attaches to the mRNA at that site (see figure). The initial tRNA, which always carries methionine, binds to the codon at the P site. A large subunit of the ribosome now attaches, and the ribosome is fully functional.

There are several steps in the elongation phase. The tRNA that is capable of bonding to the next mRNA codon now arrives at the A site. This tRNA molecule is also attached to an appropriate amino acid. The preceding amino acid at the P site is linked to the new one by a peptide bond. The peptide chain on the P site (which at this point is just a single amino acid) is transferred to the A site, and the tRNA at the P site is released to be used again. Translocation follows, whereby the new tRNA with its attached chain (or in this case just a dipeptide) moves to the P site, since the ribosome has moved one codon toward the 3' end of the mRNA. The A site is now available and binds the third tRNA which is carrying the next amino acid with it. Elongation continues, as hundreds of amino acids can be added.

Termination is marked by the presence of "stop" codons of mRNA: UAA, UAG, and UGA. There are no tRNAs for these codons. Instead, a protein is bound at the A site, causing the polypeptide and mRNA to be released from the ribosome. In addition, the polypeptide is released from the last tRNA. The ribosomal subunits then dissociate.

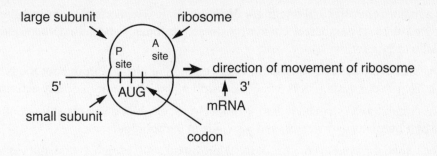

ESSAY III

There are many levels of organization of the human body, and thus there are many approaches to the study of human anatomy and physiology. The chemical level is a reminder that the human body is ultimately a collection of chemicals.

Even at this level, there are many sublevels: The subatomic level, the atomic level, the molecular level, and the macromolecular level.

Above the macromolecular level is the cellular level. The cell is the basic structural and functional unit of life. Within cells are organelles, each of which has a special function.

A tissue is a group of similar cells. There are four basic tissues that compose the human body: muscle tissue is specialized for generating force and movement; nerve tissue is used for communication; connective tissue plays a supportive role (blood and bone are both example of connective tissue); epithelial tissue is used in protection, secretion, and absorption.

An organ is composed of two or more tissues performing a single function. Many organs have all four types of tissue within them.

An organ system is a group of organs whose functions are closely linked in some way.

Finally, an organism, such as man, is a group of organ systems interacting together in life.

Systemic anatomy, or physiology, is a study at the level of the organ system.

The integumentary skin, which includes the skin and its derivatives (hair, nails) functions in protection (from dehydration, bacteria), thermoregulation, and vitamin D production. In addition, wastes can be eliminated through the skin. The skin contains many sensory receptors.

The skeletal system consists of bone and cartilage. It functions in support and protection, blood cell production, and mineral storage. Bones also provide sites of attachment for muscles.

The muscular system includes skeletal muscle attached to the bones, cardiac muscle in the heart, and smooth muscle in the vessels and visceral organs. All muscle types can contract, and thus pump blood, perform peristalsis, or cause the body to move. In addition, skeletal muscle functions in posture and heat production (shivering produces heat).

The nervous system consists of the brain, spinal cord, nerves, and sensory organs.

It is a major controller and integrator of activities. It is responsible for thought and consciousness. It can detect changes in the environment and initiate appropriate somatic responses.

The endocrine system consists of many endocrine glands throughout the body. With the nervous system, it is a major controller and integrator of bodily activities.

The circulatory system includes the blood, heart, and blood vessels. It functions to transport nutrients and wastes, and also aids in thermoregulation.

The lymphatic system consists of the white blood cells, lymph, lymphatic vessels, and lymphatic organs (tonsils, spleen, etc.). It functions in the transport of fats from the gastrointestinal tract to the blood and in the return of proteins and fluids to the blood. It also functions in immune reactions.

The respiratory system includes the nose, trachea, and lungs (and the subdivisions within, such as the bronchioles and alveoli). It functions in gas exchange and acid-base balance.

The digestive system includes the mouth, esophagus, stomach, intestines, and accessory structures such as the pancreas, liver, gallbladder, and salivary glands. It functions in mechanical and chemical digestion, absorption, and elimination.

The urinary system includes the kidneys, ureters, bladder, and urethra. It regulates the volume and composition of blood by regulating the fluid and electrolyte balance. It aids in acid-base balance and in the elimination of wastes.

The reproductive system includes the testes, ovaries, and many other organs. However, the gonads (testes and ovaries) complete certain functions, which include the production of gametes (eggs and sperm) and the secretion of hormones. However, unlike the other systems, a functional reproductive system is not necessary for life, though, it is necessary for the continuity of the generations.

ESSAY IV

Tropisms are growth responses to external stimuli. A positive tropism is a response toward a stimulus; a negative tropism is a response away from a stimulus.

The most understood tropism is phototropism, in which stems bend towards a light source. In addition, the leaves of a plant turn their surfaces toward the light source. This positive phototropic response is mediated by the plant hormone auxin. Auxin migrates and accumulates in the shaded side of the stem and promotes cell elongation oriented horizontally. The asymmetric growth causes the stem to bend away from the shaded side and hence toward the light.

Gravitropism is a response to gravity. It was previously called geotropism. Stems display a negative gravitropic response and roots show a positive response. In other words, if a shoot is placed horizontally, the stems will grow upward, against gravity, and the roots will grow downward, in the direction of gravity's force. The response in the stem is probably due to auxin. If a stem is oriented horizontally, auxin will accumulate on the lower side of the stem and stimulate cell elongation. The rapid growth on the underside will cause the stem to grow upward. In the root, the response may not be mediated by a hormone. The root cap has an inhibitory substance. If a root is oriented horizontally, the substance will accumulate on the lower side and inhibit or slow down cell elongation. Hence the more rapid growth on the upper surface will cause the root to bend down.

Thigmotropism is a response to touch. It is seen, for instance, in vines that curl around contacted objects. It appears that cell elongation stops on the contacted side; however, the mechanism by which this occurs has not be elucidated. This type of growth is due to a mechanical stimulus and is aided by the hormone auxin.

Besides these types of tropisms, there are some that are caused by various stimuli in the environment such as water, temperature, chemicals, and oxygen. These factors, in combination with plant hormones (like auxin and gibberellins), control the growth response of a plant at various stages. The cellular response during tropism is now being studied.

THE ADVANCED PLACEMENT EXAMINATION IN

BIOLOGY

TEST V

ADVANCED PLACEMENT BIOLOGY EXAM V

SECTION I

100 Questions
80 Minutes

DIRECTIONS: For each question, there are five possible choices. Select the best choice for each question. Blacken the correct space on the answer sheet.

Question 1 refers to the following diagram.

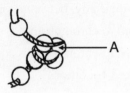

1. The structure labelled A is

   (A) DNA

   (B) RNA

   (C) a histone protein

   (D) a prokaryote

   (E) a flagellum

2. Laboratory procedures used to form hybrid nucleic acids depend on the fact that:

   (A) hydrogen bonds will not be broken when gentle heat is applied

   (B) denaturation of nucleic acids is irreversible

   (C) strands that are complementary will find each other

   (D) nitrogenous bases will repel each other

   (E) DNA will associate only with DNA, not RNA

3. In DNA, hydrogen bonding joins:

   (A) two strands of the helix

   (B) nearby pyrimidine bases

   (C) five-carbon sugars

(D) phosphate groups

(E) purine bases

4. In bryophytes, the zygote divides mitotically to become a structure called the:

(A) haploid sporophyte

(B) archegonium

(C) diploid sporophyte

(D) antheridium

(E) protonema

5. In conifers, microsporangia:

(A) produce cones

(B) contain the ovule

(C) release spores

(D) contain pollen tubes

(E) contain endosperm

6. What is the relationship, if any, between color blindness and hemophilia?

(A) Both are restricted to chromosomes coming from the father

(B) Both are restricted to chromosomes coming from the mother

(C) Both are sex-linked conditions

(D) Both are caused by dominant genes

(E) Both are present on the Y-chromosome

7. A mother with Rh-negative blood had a baby with Rh-positive blood. The father of the baby must have been:

(A) Rh-negative

(B) homozygous Rh-positive or heterozygous Rh-positive

(C) homozygous Rh-positive

(D) heterozygous Rh-negative

(E) heterozygous Rh-positive or homozygous Rh-negative

8. Which of these statements about DNA in eukaryotic cells is not true?

(A) Most of the DNA of the cell is used for gene expression

(B) The amount of DNA per diploid cell is the same for every diploid cell of a species

(C) There is much variation in the amounts of DNA among different species

(D) DNA is frequently redundant and repetitive

(E) About half of the weight of a chromosome is contributed by DNA

9.   Restriction enzymes are used in genetic research to:
      (A) cleave DNA molecules at certain sites
      (B) produce individual nucleotides from DNA
      (C) slow down the reproductive rate of bacteria
      (D) remove DNA strands from the nucleus
      (E) prevent histones from reassociating with DNA

10.   The nitrogenous base that is complementary to uracil is:
      (A) thymine   (D) adenine
      (B) guanine   (E) uracil
      (C) cytosine

11.   Mutations are caused by:
      (A) base changes in DNA
      (B) base changes in RNA
      (C) changes in the sugars of DNA
      (D) changes in the phosphates of RNA
      (E) deletions of a codon on RNA

12.   What change in the normal structure of hemoglobin results in sickle-cell anemia?
      (A) There is a change in the sequence of the amino acids
      (B) There is a substitution of one amino acid for another
      (C) There is a change in the number of nucleotides
      (D) The peptide bonds are broken in the sickle-cell hemoglobin molecule
      (E) The hydrogen bonds are weaker in the sickle-cell hemoglobin molecule than in the normal hemoglobin molecule

13.   All of the following are components in animal membranes EXCEPT:
      (A) nucleotides   (D) microtubules
      (B) carbohydrates   (E) polysaccharides
      (C) proteins

14.   Assume that clover has a (hypothetical) critical photoperiod of 14 hours. Clover should then flower if it is exposed to uninterrupted _____ for a period of _____.
      (A) light; 10 or less hours

(B) light; 14 or less hours

(C) darkness: 14 or more hours

(D) darkness; 10 or more hours

(E) darkness; 10 or less hours

15. What characteristic is found in all echinoderms?

(A) They are bilaterally symmetrical as adults

(B) They are protostomes

(C) They are deuterostomes

(D) They are pseudostomes

(E) They possess nematocysts

16. What would happen if acetylcholine were released by the vesicles in the axon terminals of a nerve cell and <u>no</u> cholinesterase were present?

(A) The acetylcholine would not diffuse across the synapse

(B) The impulse would shut down

(C) The postsynaptic membrane would become refractory (hyperpolarized)

(D) The resting potential would increase

(E) Constant uncontrolled firing at the post-synaptic membrane would occur

17. Two one-celled organisms oxidize glucose as their principal source of nutrition. One organism oxidizes glucose under anaerobic conditions and the other organism oxidizes glucose under aerobic conditions. After one day, the amount of ATP produced by both organisms was the same. Which organism probably consumed the <u>most</u> glucose?

(A) Aerobic organism

(B) Anaerobic organism

(C) Both organisms used approximately the same amount

(D) It depends on whether the two organisms oxidize glucose in the light or dark

(E) It depends on how much ATP is used to initiate the reaction

18. Fermentation:

(A) results in the formation of lactic acid

(B) does not require oxygen

(C) does require oxygen

(D) produces large amounts of energy

(E) occurs only in bacteria

19. In the Krebs cycle, the electron acceptor (of those listed) in the electron transport chain with the highest potential energy is:

(A) water

(B) oxygen

(C) cytochromes

(D) ADP

(E) NAD^+

20. Which of the following processes produces the maximum energy yield when one molecule of glucose is oxidized?

(A) Oxidative phosphorylation

(B) Oxidation of pyruvic acid

(C) Glycolysis in the mitochondria

(D) Glycolysis in the cytoplasm

(E) Formation of lactic acid

21. In humans, lymph is moved by:

(A) diffusion

(B) pressure from the heart

(C) a special lymph pump

(D) differing osmotic pressure in the capillaries

(E) active transport

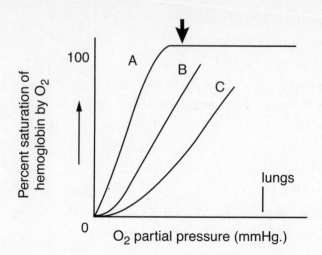

22. The three lines in the above graph represent the dissociation curves for the hemoglobin of a cat, mouse, and elephant. Which animal is represented by the line farthest to the left (see the arrow) and <u>WHY?</u>

    (A) A cat because it has the highest metabolic rate of the three and needs much oxygen

    (B) An elephant because its metabolic rate is low and it takes up and gives up oxygen most readily

    (C) An elephant because its metabolic rate is low and it takes up and gives off oxygen less readily

    (D) A mouse because it has a high metabolic rate and low oxygen requirements; therefore, hemoglobin unloads less readily

    (E) A mouse because it has a high metabolic rate and high oxygen requirements; therefore, hemoglobin hangs on to the oxygen at higher levels

23. Which of the following tissues is <u>not</u> related to connective tissue?

    (A) blood   (D) lymph

    (B) bone   (E) collagen

    (C) cartilage

24. Which functions as an enzyme by breaking down ATP to ADP during the contraction of a muscle?

    (A) calcium   (D) myosin

    (B) actin   (E) sarcomere

    (C) myofibril

25. Leaves develop from the:
    (A) apical meristem of the shoot
    (B) lateral meristem of the shoot
    (C) radicle
    (D) area of cell elongation
    (E) internodes

26. In angiosperms, photosynthesis takes place primarily in the:
    (A) guard cells   (D) palisade parenchyma
    (B) stomata   (E) spongy parenchyma
    (C) epidermal layer

27. A respiratory system does not necessarily need:
    (A) an exchange surface with an adequate area
    (B) a means to transport gases to internal areas
    (C) a means of protecting exchange surfaces
    (D) moist gas exchange surfaces
    (E) a location deep inside an organism

28. The pollen grains of angiosperms:
    (A) contain two sperm cells
    (B) contain pollen tubes
    (C) contain one polar body each
    (D) have a fragile outer coating
    (E) contain fusion nuclei

29. In angiosperms, what structure develops from the outer layer of the ovule after double fertilization has taken place and the seed is being produced?
    (A) endosperm   (D) embryo
    (B) fruit   (E) carpel
    (C) seed coat

30. T-cells are generally not involved in fighting:
    (A) cancer cells
    (B) transplanted foreign tissue
    (C) viral infections
    (D) bacterial infections
    (E) parasitic infections

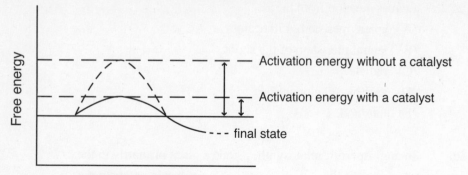

Reaction progress

31. What conclusions can be drawn after studying the above energy diagram for an exergonic reaction?

   (A) An uncatalyzed reaction requires less activation energy than a cata-lyzed reaction does

   (B) The initial state contains less free energy

   (C) Overall free energy is unchanged by the presence of a catalyst

   (D) Activation energy is unchanged with or without a catalyst

   (E) A catalyst decreases D G

32. The number of codons that can be translated into amino acids is:

   (A) 4   (D) 61

   (B) 16   (E) 64

   (C) 24

33. Which statement about respiration is <u>incorrect</u>?

   (A) Humans use positive-pressure breathing

   (B) When exhaling, the position of the diaphragm and ribs in humans is: ribs lowered, diaphragm raised

   (C) Abdominal breathing in humans does not depend on active transport of air

   (D) Frogs use positive-pressure breathing

   (E) Air flow in the lungs of birds is unidirectional

34. Which of the following does <u>not</u> have an open circulatory system?

   (A) clam   (D) earthworm

   (B) grasshopper   (E) crayfish

   (C) snail

35. In animals that have three-chambered hearts, there is mixing of blood with oxygen and blood without oxygen in the ventricle. These animals are referred to as being:

    (A) warm-blooded   (D) isotherms

    (B) homotherms   (E) heterotherms

    (C) poikilotherms

36. Countercurrent exchange as applied to gills means that:

    (A) blood with oxygen and blood without oxygen flow in opposite directions

    (B) oxygen and carbon dioxide flow in opposite directions

    (C) oxygen and carbon dioxide enter the gills from opposite directions

    (D) water and blood move in opposite directions

    (E) water moves into the gills in a direction opposite to that of the current of the stream

37. In the two-chambered heart of a fish,

    (A) the heart has two atria

    (B) the heart pumps blood into two ventricles

    (C) there is a clear division between pulmonary and systemic circulations

    (D) blood goes directly from the heart to the gills and systemic capillary beds

    (E) there is a mixing of oxygenated blood and deoxygenated blood

38. In capillary exchange:

    (A) proteins in the blood and tissue help to determine osmotic pressure

    (B) osmotic pressure moves water outside the capillaries only

    (C) blood pressure is greater than osmotic pressure at the venous end of the capillaries

    (D) blood pressure is less than osmotic pressure at the arterial end of the capillaries

    (E) the pressure of tissue fluid is greatest at the arterial end of the capillaries

39. Which of the following is <u>not</u> a cofactor?

    (A) Mn^{2+} (D) FAD

    (B) NAD^+ (E) ascorbic acid

    (C) ATP

40.   Glycolysis is most closely linked with what part of the cell?

    (A) nucleolus   (D) cytoplasm

    (B) mitochondria   (E) endoplasmic reticulum

    (C) plasma membrane

41.   Photosynthetic guard cells can increase their turgor pressure by taking in water which causes them to swell , and, therefore, causes the opening of the stoma that they regulate. This intake of water is caused by:

    (A) converting sugar to starch during the night

    (B) the hydrolysis of ATP

    (C) the active transport of potassium ions into the guard cells

    (D) converting starch to sugar in darkness

    (E) synthesis of intracellular proteins

For Question 42, refer to the following list of terms that may be in the basic body plan of acoelomates and/or pseudocoelomates:

    1. ectoderm   4. digestive cavity

    2. endoderm   5. coelom

    3. mesoderm   6. pseudocoelom

42.   Starting with the <u>outside</u> layer, include all structures that would be seen in a cross section of a round worm (phylum Nematoda).

    (A) 1, 6, 3, 4, 2   (D) 6, 4, 1, 2, 3

    (B) 2, 3, 4, 1, 5   (E) 3, 2, 1, 4, 6

    (C) 1, 3, 6, 2, 4

Directions: The following groups of questions have five lettered choices followed by a list of diagrams, numbered phrases, sentences, or words. For each numbered diagram, phrase, sentence, or word choose the heading which most directly applies. Blacken the correct space on the answer sheet. Each heading may be used once, more than once, or not at all.

Questions 43 - 44

    (A) exons   (D) euchromatic

    (B) nucleosome   (E) nucleolus

    (C) heterochromatin

43. Region that is associated with active transcription of RNA.

44. The place where ribosomes are produced.

Questions 45 - 47

(A) Meiosis   (D) Replication

(B) Mitosis   (E) Both Meiosis and Mitosis

(C) Metaphase II

45. At the end of this process, each nucleus has the haploid number of chromosomes.

46. Cytokinesis occurs in this process.

47. The products that result at the end of this process are diploid.

48. This process requires two complete cellular divisions.

Questions 49 - 52

(A) glucagon   (D) lipase

(B) pepsin   (E) bile salts

(C) salivary amylase

49. Which hormone or enzyme starts the breakdown of starch?

50. Which enzyme digests proteins?

51. This enzyme, secreted by the pancreas, breaks down fats.

52. This hormone, produced by the pancreas, helps to break down glycogen.

Questions 53 - 55

(A) density dependent factor

(B) density independent factor

(C) J-shaped curve

(D) S-shaped curve

53. Within the context of population growth, competition, parasites, and predators are examples.

54. Exponential growth of a population is best represented by this.

55. This is the most likely representation of growth in a population. The rate of increase is exponential then changes as the carrying capacity is reached.

Questions 56 - 57 refer to the diagrams below that demonstrate three general types evolutionary trends on a population.

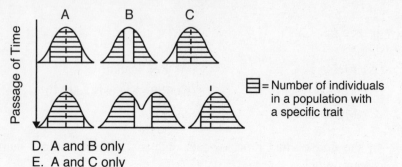

D. A and B only
E. A and C only

56. Which is an example of disruptive selection?

57. An insect population that develops resistance to insecticides, can be represented by which graph?

Questions 58 - 59

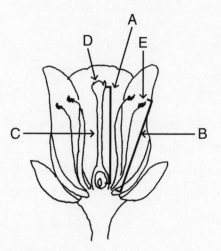

58. The male reproductive structure.

59. Location at which pollen grains attach, germinate, and produce pollen tubes.

Questions 60 - 62 refer to characteristics of the following organisms.

(A) acoelomates

(B) pseudocoelomates

(C) coelomates

(D) acoelomates and pseudocoelomates

(E) acoelomates, pseudocoelomates, and coelomates

60. Triloblasty is characteristic of members of this group.

61. A digestive cavity is characteristic of members of this group.

62.   Members of this group have fluid-filled cavities within their mesodermal cavities that contain the digestive tract and other internal organs.

Questions 63 - 65 refer to the action potential curve of a neuron as it carries an impulse.

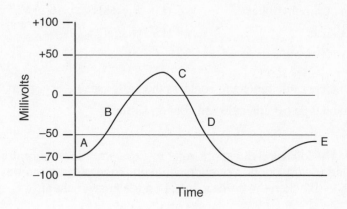

63.   Which letter represents the time at which the potassium ions rush out of the neuron?

64.   Which letter represents the place at which the nerve fiber is stimulated?

65.   Which letter represents the place at which Na ions are actively pumped out of the membrane to re-establish the balance of Na^+ and K^+ ions?

Questions 66 to 69

   (A) secondary xylem   (D) bark
   (B) phloem   (E) vascular cambium
   (C) cork

66.   Which structure transports water and solutes upward in angiosperms?

67.   Sugar can move upward or downward in this structure.

68.   In dicots this tissue is actively growing and dividing.

69.   The growth rings found in the cross section of a tree trunk are made up primarily of this.

Questions 70 - 71 refer to photosynthesis.

   (A) C_3 (D) Photosystem II
   (B) C_4 (E) Photophosphorylation
   (C) Photosystem I

70.   The first step in the Calvin Cycle is the fixation of carbon by the binding of CO_2 to ribulose bisphosphate (RuBP).

71.   Adaptation to hot, dry environments.

Questions 72 and 73

(A) Carbohydrates   (D) Steroids

(B) Fats   (E) Nucleic acids

(C) Proteins

72.   Which organic molecule contains the most useable energy per mole?

73.   Which type of molecule can contain sulfur?

Directions: The following questions refer to experimental or laboratory situations or data. Read the description of each situation. Then choose the best answer to each question. Blacken the correct space on the answer sheet.

Questions 74 - 76 refer to a set of experiments.

This set of experiments shows the influence of environmental factors on enzyme action. The materials used are an enzyme naturally found in potatoes and a clear substrate which forms an end product with a yellowish-brown color which indicates that a reaction between the substrate and the enzyme has occurred.

Experiment 1 - Effect of heat on enzyme action. Three tubes are filled 3/4 of the way with distilled water. Tube 1 is placed in crushed ice (0°c). Tube 2 is placed in a beaker of boiling water (100 °c), and tube 3 is kept at room temperature. After ten minutes, ten drops of potato extract (which contains the enzyme) and ten drops of substrate are added to each tube. The tubes are shaken and returned to their original temperature condition. The color of each tube is recorded after ten minutes using the grading scale of : 0, 1, 2, 3 (where 0 indicates no color change and 3 indicates intense color change).

Experiment 2 - The effect of substrate specific activity. Ten drops of the substrate for the potato enzyme are added to tube 1. Ten drops of a compound, similar in shape to the substrate are added to tube 2. Ten drops of yet another isomer of the substrate are added to tube 3. Then, ten drops of the potato enzyme are added to each of the 3 tubes. The three tubes are shaken, placed in a warm bath (35° c), and color formation is observed after ten minutes, as shown by this table:

Tube	Color after 10 minutes (Enzyme Activity)
1	3
2	1
3	0

74. What would be the most likely representation of the effect of temperature on the turnover rate of the enzyme based on Experiment 1?

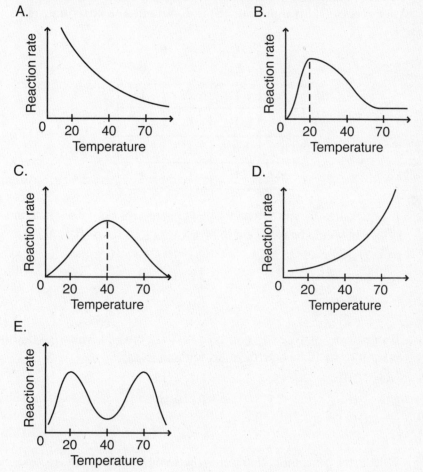

A.

B.

C.

D.

E.

75. The results in experiment 2 indicate that:

(A) enzymes are highly specific for their substrate

(B) enzymes are only moderately specific for their substrate

(C) enzymes can distinguish among closely related components

(D) enzymes cannot distinguish among isomers

(E) A and C are true

76.   Which of the following might occur if more of the substrate in tube 2 from experiment 2 were added and the temperature was increased to 40°C?

(A) The results would not change

(B) The enzyme activity would decrease

(C) The enzyme would become denatured

(D) The enzyme activity would increase slightly

(E) Such a prediction cannot be made

Questions 77 - 79 refer to the Punnett Square. It represents possible patterns of inheritance in dihybrid crosses. Brown eyes (B) are dominant and Blue eyes (b) are recessive. Straight hair (S) is dominant and curly hair (s) is recessive.

	BS	Bs	bS	bs
BS	A	B	C	D
Bs	E	F	G	H
bS	I	J	K	L
bs	M	N	O	P

77.   If organisms of type "J" and type "O" are crossed, what fraction of the offspring would be expected to be <u>homozygous</u> for <u>both</u> <u>traits</u>?

(A) 1/16   (D) 7/16

(B) 3/16   (E) 9/16

(C) 4/16

78.   If organisms of type "J" and type "O" are crossed, what fraction of the offspring would be <u>heterozygous</u> for <u>both</u> <u>traits</u>?

(A) 1/16   (D) 7/16

(B) 3/16   (E) 9/16

(C) 4/16

79.   What is the probability that a cross between a homozygous recessive male and a heterozygous female will produce offspring with brown eyes and curly hair?

(A) three-sixteenths   (D) three-fourths

(B) one-fourth   (E) one

(C) one-half

Questions 80 - 82 refer to these generalized survivorship curves:

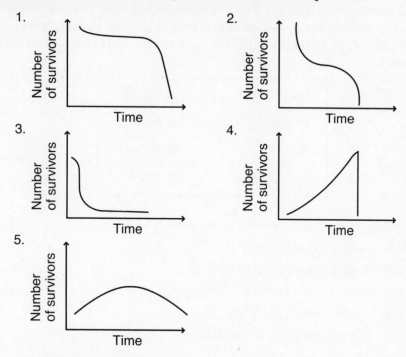

80.   What is probably true about a species represented by graph #3?

(A) They have a slower development

(B) They have many offspring during a period of time

(C) They have a low mortality early in life

(D) They are as likely to die early in life as late in life

(E) They are not well adapted for dispersal in the environment

81.   How is curve #1 different from curve #2?

(A) Curve #1 shows exponential growth, while curve #2 does not.

(B) Curve #1 is more representative of small offspring than large offspring.

(C) Curve #1 favors offspring which have much parental care.

(D) For curve #1, the mortality rate at all ages is more or less constant compared to curve #2.

(E) Only (A) and (D).

82.   Which graph indicates an overshooting of the carrying capacity?

(A) 1   (D) 4

(B) 2   (E) 5

(C) 3

Questions 83 - 85 are based on the following information and chart.
Both the Smith family and the Jones family had babies at the same time.
There was a mix-up in the hospital nursery; but luckily, the hospital had the
blood groups of the Jones' and the two babies. The chart below gives that
information.

Mr. Jones	-	group AB
Mrs. Jones	-	group B
Baby 1	-	group A
Baby 2	-	group O

83. Which of the babies belongs to the Joneses?

    (A) Baby 1 (Blood group A)

    (B) Baby 2 (Blood group O)

    (C) Either Baby 1 or Baby 2

    (D) Neither Baby 1 nor Baby 2

    (E) None of the answers are correct.

84. If Mr. Jones had group O blood, which child would have belonged to the Joneses?

    (A) Baby 1 (Blood group A)

    (B) Baby 2 (Blood group O)

    (C) Either Baby 1 or Baby 2

    (D) Neither Baby 1 nor Baby 2

    (E) None of the answers are correct.

85. If Mrs. Jones had group A blood, which child would have belonged to the Joneses?

    (A) Baby 1

    (B) Baby 2

    (C) Either Baby 1 or Baby 2

    (D) Neither Baby 1 nor Baby 2

    (E) None of the answers are correct.

Questions 86-88. The following time plot represents a predator and prey
population. The predator is the lynx and the prey is the snowshoe hare. The
letters refer to growth rates for the populations.

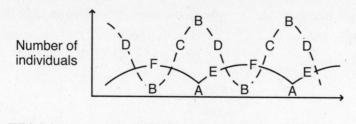

Number of individuals

86.   Which letter represents the prey increasing?

(A) A   (D) D

(B) B   (E) E

(C) C

87.   Which letter(s) represent zero population growth?

(A) A and B   (D) D and E

(B) B and C   (E) A and E

(C) C and D

88.   What is the most common explanation for why prey populations are limited below their carrying capacity?

(A) The age of the prey makes them susceptible to predators

(B) Prey in poor physical condition are taken by predators

(C) The existence of only one species that is prey to a predator means that the species will be preyed on to extinction

(D) The availability of food is the limiting factor

(E) None of the above

Questions 89 - 91 are based on the simplified diagram which represents a nephron. The numbers represent the different structures of the nephron.

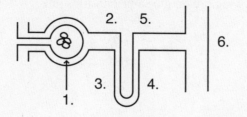

89.   Chloride ions are actively pumped out of this structure.

(A) 1   (D) 4

(B) 2   (E) 5

(C) 3

90.   At which structures are the walls of the tubules freely permeable to water?

    (A) 1, 2, 3, 4   (D) 1, 2, 4, 6

    (B) 2, 3, 5, 6   (E) 1, 3, 5, 6

    (C) 1, 3, 4, 5

91.   Where does filtration take place in the nephron?

    (A) 1   (D) 4

    (B) 2   (E) None of the above.

    (C) 3

Questions 92 - 93 refer to a female *Drosophila* heterozygous for ebony body color (recessive) and curly wings (recessive) that was mated to an ebony-bodied, curly-winged male resulting in the following offspring:

    200   ebony body, normal wing

      10   normal body, normal wing

       5   ebony body, curly wing

    150   normal body, curly wing

92.   Choose the correct statement(s).

    1.   The genes are linked. In the female, the alleles for normal body and normal wing are on the same chromosome.

    2.   The genes are linked. In the female, the alleles for normal body and curly wing are on the same chromosome.

    3.   The genes are unlinked.

    4.   The genes are linked. In the female, alleles for ebony body and curly wing are on the same chromosome.

    5.   The genes are linked. In the female, the alleles for ebony body and normal wing are on the same chromosome.

    (A) 1, 2   (D) 2, 5

    (B) 2, 4   (E) 1, 5

    (C) 3

93.   Which process must occur in order to obtain ebony body, curly wing phenotype in the offspring?

    (A) Nondisjunction during meiosis in the female

    (B) Crossing over during gamete formation in the female

    (C) Crossing over during gamete formation in the male

    (D) A mutation in the female

    (E) A mutation in the male

Questions 94 - 97. The following shows the change, over time, in the vegetation of a farmed area which was left alone for many years.

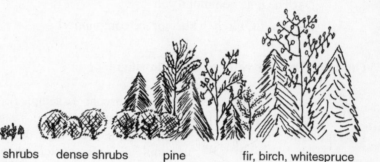

| abandoned field | herbs, shrubs (weeds) | dense shrubs | pine | fir, birch, whitespruce |

year 0   **year 150**

94.   The above diagram illustrates

        (A) Primary Succession   (D) Pioneer Plants

        (B) Secondary Succession   (E) Evolution of pine trees

        (C) Tertiary Succession

95.   The stage which is most likely to be the most stable is

        (A) the herb community

        (B) the shrub community

        (C) the dense shrub community

        (D) the pine community

        (E) the fir, birch, white spruce community

96.   The most diversity would be expected to be in the

        (A) herb community

        (B) shrub community

        (C) dense shrub community

        (D) pine community

        (E) fir, birch, white spruce community

97.   Which of the following tends to produce more organic material than it uses?

(A) The herb community

(B) The shrub community

(C) The dense shrub community

(D) The pine community

(E) The fir, birch, white spruce community

Questions 98 - 100 refer to the following:

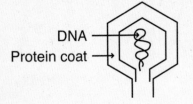

DNA

Protein coat

The protein coat of a sample *E. coli* bacterio-phage (virus that attacks bacteria) is labelled with radioactive sulfur. In addition, the DNA core of another sample *E. coli* bacteriophage is labelled with radioactive phosphorus. The two phages are then added to two different colonies of bacteria grown in nonradioactive media.

98.   Analysis showed that:

(A) the host cell had both radioactive sulfur and phosphorus

(B) the host cell had only radioactive sulfur

(C) the host cell had only radioactive phosphorus

(D) the host cell had neither radioactive sulfur nor radioactive phosphorus

(E) viral infection cannot take place in a nonradioactive medium

99.   In the bacteriophage infection cycle described in the experiment,

(A) the entire virus particle enters the host cells

(B) the protein coat of the bacteriophage enters the host cell

(C) the viral DNA is left outside the host cell

(D) the viral DNA replicates within the host cell

(E) the viral protein coat replicates within the host cell

100.   The Hershey and Chase experiment was used to prove that:

(A) proteins contain the genetic material

(B) DNA is the genetic material

(C) viruses cannot reproduce in a radioactive medium

(D) viruses cannot infect a host which is radioactive

(E) bacteriophages reproduce only the DNA inside the host cell

SECTION II

DIRECTIONS: Answer each of the following four questions in essay format. Each answer should be clear, organized, and well-balanced. Diagrams may be used in addition to the discussion, but a diagram alone will not suffice. Suggested writing time per essay is 22 minutes.

1.   Nitrogen, phosphorus, and carbon are recovered through biogeochemical cycles in which matter flows in a cyclical pathway. Describe each cycle, including the effects humans have had on each.

2.   Chromosomes pass genetic information through generations. Explain how this occurs in three phases:

   (A) Explain the structure, function, and location of DNA.

   (B) Detail DNA replication. State specifically where this process occurs.

   (C) Describe protein synthesis at the ribosomal level.

3.   Development in flowering plants begins from a seed.

   (A) Describe the germination process. How can you tell if starch is present?

   (B) Some seeds contain substances similar to antibiotics. Design an experiment to detect such substances.

4.   The ATP/ADP energy system is used both by biological systems that require energy and ones that release it. Relate each of the following, giving examples where appropriate, to the transformation of energy and/or ATP formation:

   (A) First and Second Law of Thermodynamics

   (B) Anabolism and catabolism

   (C) Phosphorylation of ADP to ATP

   (D) Coupled reactions

ADVANCED PLACEMENT BIOLOGY EXAM V

ANSWER KEY

1.	(C)	26.	(D)	51.	(D)	76.	(D)
2.	(C)	27.	(E)	52.	(A)	77.	(C)
3.	(A)	28.	(A)	53.	(A)	78.	(C)
4.	(C)	29.	(C)	54.	(C)	79.	(B)
5.	(C)	30.	(D)	55.	(D)	80.	(B)
6.	(C)	31.	(C)	56.	(B)	81.	(C)
7.	(B)	32.	(D)	57.	(B)	82.	(D)
8.	(A)	33.	(A)	58.	(B)	83.	(A)
9.	(A)	34.	(D)	59.	(D)	84.	(B)
10.	(D)	35.	(C)	60.	(E)	85.	(A)
11.	(A)	36.	(D)	61.	(E)	86.	(C)
12.	(B)	37.	(D)	62.	(C)	87.	(A)
13.	(A)	38.	(A)	63.	(C)	88.	(D)
14.	(E)	39.	(C)	64.	(B)	89.	(D)
15.	(C)	40.	(D)	65.	(D)	90.	(B)
16.	(E)	41.	(E)	66.	(A)	91.	(A)
17.	(B)	42.	(C)	67.	(B)	92.	(D)
18.	(B)	43.	(D)	68.	(E)	93.	(B)
19.	(E)	44.	(E)	69.	(A)	94.	(B)
20.	(A)	45.	(A)	70.	(A)	95.	(E)
21.	(D)	46.	(E)	71.	(B)	96.	(E)
22.	(C)	47.	(B)	72.	(B)	97.	(A)
23.	(D)	48.	(A)	73.	(C)	98.	(C)
24.	(D)	49.	(C)	74.	(C)	99.	(D)
25.	(A)	50.	(B)	75.	(E)	100.	(B)

ADVANCED PLACEMENT
BIOLOGY EXAM V

DETAILED EXPLANATIONS
OF ANSWERS

SECTION I

1.   **(C)**

A nucleosome consists of a DNA double helix wound around a cluster of histone proteins.

2.   **(C)**

Hybridization is used to detect the presence of specific nucleic acids and to determine the similarity of two nucleic acid sequences. The double helix of DNA is broken into its complementary strands by gentle heating (denaturation). When the solution is cooled, the hydrogen bonds reform. If denatured DNA molecules from a variety of sources are mixed together and denatured, two strands with nearly complementary sequences will combine to form a double helix.

3.   **(A)**

Hydrogen bonds form between the complementary base pairs which are combinations of a pyrimidine and a purine. The complementary base pairs of nucleotides are 1) adenine and thymine, and 2) guanine and cytosine. Deoxyribose, the five-carbon sugar present in DNA and the phosphate groups are both bound covalently in DNA.

4.   **(C)**

Bryophytes such as mosses and liverworts have life cycles which display an alternation of generations. In this life cycle, the zygote is produced by the fusion of gametes from the antheridium (contains sperm cells) and the archegonium (contains the egg cell). The zygote, which stays inside the archegonium, becomes the mature diploid sporophyte.

5.   **(C)**

In the microsporangium located inside the pollen-bearing male cone, the microspores develop into pollen grains which are the young male gametophytes. The pollen grains containing the microspores are released and find their way to the female cone (gametophyte) containing the archegonium which, in turn, contains the egg cell. The sperm cells are carried to the archegonium by the pollen tube (produced by the male gametophyte) which grows through the tissue of the ovule. Fertilization then occurs.

6.   **(C)**

Both are examples of sex-linked conditions carried by recessive genes on X-chromosomes.

7.   **(B)**

An Rh-negative woman can bear an Rh-positive baby if the father is Rh positive (having the "antigen D" allele). If the father is homozygous for the Rh factor, all the children will be Rh positive. If the father is a heterozygote, about half the children will be Rh positive. The question asked for what the father's Rh factor <u>must</u> have been: he could not have been just homozygous Rh positive or heterozygous Rh negative. Option (B) contains both possibilities.

8.   **(A)**

DNA and histones, proteins that are closely associated with DNA, are present in approximately equal amounts in chromosomes. DNA contains both repetitive sequences that code for protein (gene expression), and sequences that are not translated into proteins. The amount of DNA used for gene expression is small compared to the total DNA of the cell. In fact, in humans only about one percent of the DNA codes for protein.

9.   **(A)**

Restriction enzymes cleave strands of DNA segments at certain sites, thus yielding uniform fragments to be studied in the laboratory. The DNA molecule is not cleaved straight across by restriction enzymes; rather, these enzymes leave "sticky ends" that are complementary to another molecule cleaved by the same enzyme.

10.   **(D)**

Uracil is the base in RNA that is substituted for the thymine in DNA. The uracil links up with adenine, forming a complementary base pair.

11.   **(A)**

Mutations can be caused by changes in the nitrogenous bases of DNA. One change can be the replacement of one base pair for another within a segment of DNA. Other changes can be the insertion of extra base pairs, or the deletion of one or more base pairs. A change in RNA nucleotide sequence may result in faulty translation of a gene, but RNA is constantly degraded and synthesized; as long as DNA remains unchanged, RNA will almost always be correctly synthesized.

12.　　**(B)**

The entire structural difference between a normal and a sickle-cell hemoglobin molecule consists of the substitution of the amino acid valine for the amino acid glutamic acid. This substitution occurs in the sixth position of each of the two B-chains in hemoglobin.

13.　　**(A)**

A nucleotide is composed of a sugar, a phosphate group, and a base containing nitrogen. Nucleotides are found in chromosomes (DNA), which are in turn found in the nucleus of the cell. All other options represent substances that can be found in the cell membrane.

14.　　**(E)**

Plants measure darkness rather than light, and may not flower if the darkness is interrupted. For example, assume that clover will flower only if the light periods are longer than the critical length that is specific for that species. If we use 14 hours as the critical period, then the dark period should be an uninterrupted 10 hours or less.

15.　　**(C)**

Echinoderms are named for their spiny internal skeletons. They show radial symmetry (but larvae show bilateral symmetry) and water vascular systems of canals that provide locomotion. Water creates a liquid skeleton that makes the tube feet rigid enough to walk on. Echinoderms also exhibit deuterostome development. A major characteristic of this development is the formation of the anus at or near the blastopore while the mouth forms elsewhere. They do not possess nematocysts (stinging cells); only coelenterates do. Protostomes include all animals except chordates, hemichordates, and echinoderms. There are no such things as pseudostomes.

16.　　**(E)**

Cholinesterase is an enzyme that decomposes acetylcholine so that it cannot bind permanently to the postsynaptic membrane. The impulse then ends. If cholinesterase is absent, the acetylcholine continues to be released into the synaptic cleft and binds to the receptors of the postsynaptic membrane. However, molecules of acetylcholine remain bound to the receptors indefinitely, because cholinesterase is not present. This leads to rapid uncontrolled firing of the impulses, which could lead to uncontrollable tremors, spasms, or even death for the organism.

17.   **(B)**

Anaerobic organisms can produce a yield of two ATPs per glucose molecule as a result of glycolysis, which takes place in the cytoplasm of the cell and does not require oxygen. If oxygen is not present, the organism produces two ATPs by fermentation (either lactate or alcoholic process). This process reduces the pyruvate to lactic acid and releases NAD for further use by the cell. The carbohydrates that enter the anaerobic pathway are not completely broken down and much energy is still contained in lactate and ethanol. Only two ATPs are formed compared to the 36 ATPs that are formed as a result of the aerobic pathway (Krebs cycle and electron transport chain). Therefore, the more inefficient anaerobic organism would have to use more glucose to produce the same amount of ATP as the aerobic organism.

18.   **(B)**

Fermentation is the production of ethanol from glucose as done by yeast cells. In glycolysis, one glucose molecule is converted to two molecules of pyruvic acid and also provides enough energy for the synthesis of two molecules of ATP and two molecules of NADPH. The pyruvic acid, still containing much potential energy, can next enter either the anaerobic pathway or the aerobic pathway. In one type of anaerobic pathway, pyruvic acid is converted to ethanol by the action of yeast cells on sugar.

19.   **(E)**

Both NAD^+ and FAD (not listed) are the electron acceptors with the highest potential energies. After completion of the Krebs cycle, the carbon atoms of glucose have been oxidized, and some of the energy of the glucose has been utilized to generate ATP and ADP. The remaining energy is in the electrons removed from carbon-carbon bonds and the carbon-hydrogen bonds. These electrons pass to the electron carriers NAD^+ and FAD. These electron carriers pass the electrons along to electron carriers with lower energy levels (cytochromes) and finally to the electron carrier, oxygen, which has the lowest energy level. The oxygen then combines with hydrogen ions (protons) to produce water.

20.   **(A)**

The energy yield from oxidative phosphorylation is 32 ATP molecules. The oxidation of pyruvic acid produces 6 ATP molecules. Glycolysis in the mitochondria yields 6 ATP molecules in most cells. Glycolysis in the cytoplasm yields 2 ATP molecules. The formation of lactic acid which takes place during anaerobic respiration yields 2 ATP molecules.

21.   **(D)**

In humans, the lymph is moved along by contractions of the skeletal muscles, through which the lymph vessels are located. Also, lymph vessels return 99% of the fluid that leaves the capillaries at their arterial end. The fluid is reabsorbed at the venous ends of capillaries, where the osmotic pressure in the capillaries is less than the osmotic pressure outside the capillaries.

22.   **(C)**

Smaller, active animals, such as mice, have high metabolic rates. The rate of demand for oxygen by their tissues is greater because they are releasing much carbon dioxide (ex. in the lungs). The pH then becomes lower, and the hemoglobin unloads its oxygen, since increased acidity causes hemoglobin to release oxygen. The opposite is true for larger warm-blooded animals such as elephants which have lower metabolic rates. The hemoglobin hangs on to its oxygen longer allowing the tissues deep inside the body to be exposed to oxygen as the blood carries it to these tissues.

23.   **(D)**

Connective tissue provides support for body parts and binds struc-tures together. Options A, B, and C are examples of connective tissue. Collagen (Option E) is a protein found in skin and bone and is secreted by the cells of connective tissue. Collagen provides a rigid matrix in which connective tissue cells exist.

24.   **(D)**

According to the sliding filament theory, myosin filaments have extensions called cross-bridges, which bind to thin actin filaments at receptor sites and pull actin filaments toward the center of the sarcomere, the contractile unit. The cross-bridges can only bind to actin when calcium ions are present. These ions set up "receptor" sites on the actin, to which the cross-bridge can attach. Energy is used by the myosin cross-bridge to attach to the actin, pull it toward the center of the unit, release it, and reattach to the actin at a new "receptor" site. This energy is provided by the hydrolysis of ATP by myosin.

25.   **(A)**

The apical meristem of the shoot contains the tissues that produce new leaves, branches, and flowers. The lateral meristem (Option B) produces tissues that increase the thickness of woody plants. Areas of cell elongation (Option D) are those in which cell division is slowed and the length of each cell increases, hence the shoot length increases. Internodes are portions of the stem between locations at which leaf primordia and leaves arise from the stem. The radicle is the embryonic root of a plant.

26.   **(D)**

The palisade parenchyma consists of many-sided thin-walled cells that are long and narrow. Chloroplasts are located in these cells and most photosynthesis takes place therein. Below the palisade parenchyma is the spongy parenchyma (Option E), which has cells with irregular shapes that have some chloroplasts. Guard cells regulate transpiration and the entry of air into leaves by regulating the size of small openings (stomata) on the undersides of leaves.

27. **(E)**

Options (A) through (D) refer to characteristics of the respiratory system of both unicellular and multicellular organisms. In single-celled or simple organisms such as algae and flatworms, oxygen diffuses directly through cell membranes. Thus, location deep inside an organism is not a requirement of a respiratory system.

28. **(A)**

In angiosperms, the pollen grain is the male gametophyte stage in the alternation of generations life cycle. When a pollen grain lands on the stigma of a pistil, it germinates and generates a pollen tube. Two sperm cells, which were part of the pollen grain as a bi-nucleate structure, move into the pollen tube as it grows toward the ovary. Each pollen grain contains a tube nucleus, not a pollen tube. Polar bodies are associated with angiosperm ova, and fusion nuclei are cells that give rise to the endosperm.

29. **(C)**

In the process of double fertilization, one sperm nucleus from the pollen grain fertilizes the egg nucleus in the ovule forming a zygote that divides mitotically to produce the embryo (Option D). The other sperm nucleus from the pollen grain fertilizes the two central nuclei in the ovule resulting in a triploid nucleus. This triploid nucleus divides producing the endosperm, a tissue that surrounds the embryo and contains stored food (Option A).

As the embryo grows, the wall of the ovule grows and becomes the seed coat (Option C), while the ovary enlarges around the ovule and becomes the fruit (Option B). Both the seed coat and the fruit protect the embryo from both predators and moisture loss. The carpel (Option E) is the female reproductive structure which includes the stigma, style, and ovary.

30. **(D)**

The primary targets of B-cells are bacterial infections. All other options are the targets of T-cells.

31. **(C)**

Normal body temperature does not provide enough energy of activation to start reactions. A catalyst (such as an enzyme) lowers the energy of activation needed to bring reacting molecules together to cause a chemical reaction. The amount of free energy change, G, from the initial state to the final state is not changed by the presence of the catalyst. Only the activation energy necessary to start the reactions is different for catalyzed and uncatalyzed reactions.

32.   **(D)**

A codon consists of three nucleotides, and this triplet forms the code for a specific amino acid. The twenty amino acids are coded for by 61 (not 64) triplet codons. The three additional codons are the "stop" signals to terminate protein synthesis.

33.   **(A)**

Humans (mammals) and birds use negative pressure breathing whereby air is drawn into the lungs. This process involves raising of the rib cage and the downward movement of the diaphragm during inhalation. The volume of the chest cavity is increased, reducing the internal air pressure, resulting in air being drawn into the lungs to equalize the pressure. In contrast, positive-pressure breathing occurs when air is <u>forced</u> into the lungs. For example, a frog closes its nostrils and raises the floor of its mouth, thus reducing the volume of the mouth cavity and forcing air into the lungs. Active transport of air does not occur in humans. The presence of air sacs in birds allows for a unidirectional flow of air through a bird's lungs.

34.   **(D)**

In an open circulatory system, blood goes through sinuses (open spaces) and has contact with the organs and cells. In insects, the blood does not carry oxygen; the tracheae do. An open circulatory system is characteristic of most molluscs and arthropods. In contrast, in a closed circulatory system the blood flows in well-defined vessels. Closed circulatory systems are characteristic of earthworms and all vertebrates.

35.   **(C)**

Three-chambered hearts are characteristic of all amphibians and most reptiles (except crocodilians). These animals are all poikilotherms. Poikilotherms are cold-blooded animals. They do not maintain constant body temperatures and do not need to break down as much glucose to heat their bodies. Thus, they do not need as much oxygen for the respiratory process.

36.   **(D)**

Oxygen diffuses from the water into the blood. The circulatory structures are arranged in the gills so that the blood is pumped into them in a direction that is opposite to that of the direction of the water with its load of oxygen. The blood vessels can then extract a larger percentage of oxygen from the water, because the water will always contain a higher concentration of oxygen than the blood will.

37.   **(D)**

In fish, the blood returns to the atrium after passing through both the respiratory (gill) and systemic (body tissues) circulatory system. A fish's heart consists of one atrium and one ventricle. No mixing of oxygenated and deoxygenated blood occurs.

38.   **(A)**

At the arterial end of the capillaries the blood pressure is higher than the pressure of the tissue fluid outside the capillaries. This differential causes fluid to leave the capillaries and go into the tissue. At the same time the concentration of proteins in the tissue fluid is less than the concentration of proteins in the blood because the large protein molecules cannot easily diffuse through the capillary walls. Thus, water tends to move into the capillaries by osmosis to equalize the osmotic pressure; this occurs at the venous end. Approximately 99% of the water that exits capillaries at the arterial ends due to the net force of blood pressure, re-enters the capillaries at their venous ends due to the net force of osmotic pressure.

39.   **(C)**

A cofactor is a nonprotein substance that helps an enzyme to catalyze a reaction. Ions, such as manganese ions (Mn^{2+}) (Option A), can be cofactors for certain enzymes. A coenzyme is a type of cofactor, and more specifically, is a nonprotein organic molecule that can function as an electron acceptor. NAD^+ (Option B), FAD (Option D), and ascorbic acid (vitamin C, Option E), are electron acceptors and are bound to enzymes.

40.   **(D)**

Glycolysis occurs in the cytoplasm of the cells. The Krebs cycle, which occurs after glycolysis in aerobic respiration, takes place in the mitochondria of animal cells.

41.   **(E)**

Guard cells can generate turgor pressure by converting starch to sugar in daylight resulting in an increased concentration of solute within the cells. Water then moves into the guard cell by diffusion. Recent research indicates that the level of potassium in the guard cells is related to their opening and closing (Option C). The potassium ions are actively transported between the guard cells and the surrounding fluid using ATP as the energy source. Potassium levels are shown to rise when the stomata open and fall when the stomata close. The changing solute-solvent concentration causes water to diffuse into the stomata by osmosis when the level of potassium ions is up, causing the stomata to open.

42.   **(C)**

The Phylum Nematoda are pseudocoelomates, which have a more complex body plan than the acoelomates.

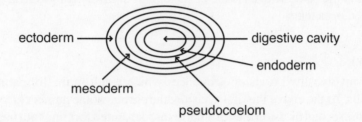

The pseudocoelom, located between the endoderm and the mesoderm, does not have the epithelial lining of a true coelom — a cavity located within the mesoderm in which are suspended the digestive tract and other internal organs.

43.   **(D)**

Euchromatin is a loosely packed or unfolded form of DNA. Euchromatic regions in the chromosomes contain active genes, and are the sites of active RNA transcription.

44.   **(E)**

The nucleolus, located in the nucleus of eukaryotic cells contains DNA, RNA, and protein. The RNA that is part of the structure of the newly-forming ribosomes is directly transcribed from the DNA in the nucleolus.

45.   **(A)**

At the end of Telophase II of meiosis, there are four cells that are derived from the original diploid cell. Each nucleus has a haploid (n) number of chromosomes.

46.   **(E)**

Cytokinesis, the dividing of cytoplasm, occurs in both mitosis and meiosis. In mitosis during Telophase, chromosomes, identical to those in the original nucleus, group around poles of the spindle. The nuclear envelope reforms and the cell cytoplasm divides.

In meiosis, there are two cytoplasmic divisions. During Telophase I, homologous chromosomes (chromosomes that have replicated and are connected by a centromere) separate from their homologues and move toward opposite poles of the spindle. The cytoplasm then divides; for many types of cells, Metaphase II starts immediately. In Telophase II, four haploid nuclei are formed, each with one member of each pair of chromosomes from the original nucleus.

47.   **(B)**

The products that result from mitosis are diploid; they have two sets of chromosomes. The number of chromosomes is thus maintained from one generation to the next. Mitosis is the basis for cell division (for physical growth) in many-celled organisms.

48.   **(A)**

Meiosis involves two division sequences which result in the formation of four haploid cells. At the end of the first division, the chromosome number is reduced. At the end of the second division the chromatids are separated forming four haploid cells with single stranded chromosomes. Option (C) is part of the second division sequence of meiosis.

49.   **(C)**

Salivary amylase, a digestive enzyme found in the mouth, begins the breakdown of starch to form maltose.

50.   **(B)**

Pepsin, a secretion of the stomach, breaks apart the peptide bonds that link the amino acids which form the proteins. The protein is not completely digested; the peptide bonds linking a few amino acids are broken.

51.   **(D)**

Lipase is an enzyme that is secreted by the pancreas. It hydrolyzes a small portion of the fats to glycerol and fatty acids.

52.   **(A)**

The hormone glucagon helps in the breakdown of glycogen which, in turn, increases the blood sugar.

53.   **(A)**

Population growth is regulated by these three mechanisms (competition, parasites, and predators). For example, when the population size increases, mechanisms such as competition, parasites, and predators can act on the population to decrease the birth rate, increase the death rate or foster emigration of the population from the affected area.

54.   **(C)**

A J-shaped curve occurs when the birth rate remains above the death rate. The addition of new individuals to the potential reproductive base (without an accompanying increase in the death rate) can lead to unrestrained growth.

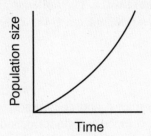

55.   **(D)**

The "S" shaped curve shows logistic growth. At first exponential growth occurs, then the curve reaches a plateau and flattens out as the carrying capacity of the environment is reached.

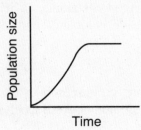

56.   **(B)**

In disruptive selection, the more extreme types in a population increase in number while the intermediate forms are selected against. Two divergent populations can eventually be produced.

57.   **(B)**

After the first application of insecticide, many insects are killed but some in the population may survive because of differences in their bodies that allow them to resist the effects of the insecticide. If the differences are genetic in origin, then these traits can be passed on to subsequent generations, resulting in a strain of individuals resistant to the insecticide because of traits that are not shared by the population as a whole. This type of selection, called disruptive selection, favors extremes in a population rather than those at the midpoint of a distribution. A bimodal (two-humped) distribution results.

58.   **(B)**

The male reproductive structure is called the stamen. The pollen grains (young male gametophytes) develop in the stamen. It is composed of the anther (Option E) and the long filament.

59.   **(D)**

The stigma is the place on which the pollen grains land after being released by the anther of another (or the same) flower. The pollen grains then develop pollen tubes that grow down through the style and reach the ovule in which the egg cells are located.

60.   **(E)**

Acoelomates, pseudocoelomates, and coelomates are triloblastic which means they have three tissue layers: ectoderm, endoderm, and mesoderm (which is located between the ectoderm and the endoderm). The basic arrangement of three-tissue layers that is characteristic of the acoelomates becomes more complex as we shift from acoelomates to pseudocoelomates to coelomates.

61.   **(E)**

The digestive cavity is a food-containing cavity that is surrounded by the endoderm in acoelomates, pseudocoelomates, and coelomates.

62.   **(C)**

Mollusks, annelids, and more complex animals each have a coelom (fluid-filled cavity) which distinguishes these animals from acoelomates and pseudocoelomates.

63.   **(C)**

(A) represents the polarization of the membrane. Negatively charged large organic ions and the leakage of K^+ to the outside set up a negative charge inside the membrane. (B) represents the stimulation of the membrane by an impulse. The membrane becomes permeable to Na^+ which diffuses inward, causing a momentary reversal of membrane poplarity; thus, the inside of the membrane becomes slightly positively charged. This change in the distribution of charges along the neuron is called the action potential. (C), THE CORRECT ANSWER, the membrane becomes permeable to K^+, which rush out of the cell faster than the sodium can move in. This shift starts to repolarize the membrane, setting up a positive charge outside the membrane. (D) the membrane becomes less permeable to Na^+ as the sodium-potassium pump begins to pump three Na^+ out of the cell for every two K^+ it pumps in. The source of energy for the sodium-potassium pump is ATP. (E), the resting potential is again achieved because of the difference of electrical charges inside and outside the membrane. This potential is maintained by the sodium-potassium pump, which pumps Na^+ outside the membrane and pumps K^+ inside the neuron.

64.   **(B)**

(B) represents the stimulation of the membrane by an impulse. The membrane then becomes permeable to Na^+ which diffuses inward causing a momentary reversal of polarity; the inside of the membrane has a positive charge relative to the outside. This change in the distribution of charges along the neuron is called the action potential.

65.   **(D)**

The sodium-potassium pump uses ATP as the energy source. It pumps three Na^+ ions out of the membrane of the motor neuron for every two K^+ ions pumped in, resulting in a charge difference inside and outside the membrane.

66.   **(A)**

In xylem, (both primary and secondary) the movement of water and solutes is upward. This movement results from a combination of the force produced by water that enters the roots (root pressure) and the force produced by water that escapes from the leaves (transpirational force). Water enters by osmosis because the concentration of solutes is greater in the root cells than in the soil water. The primary reason for the movement of water up into the leaves of trees is transpiration. The loss of water due to transpiration at the leaves pulls more water into the leaf cells from the stem and roots. This is due to the cohesiveness of water.

67.   **(B)**

Sugars (carbohydrates) move upward and downward through the plant via the cells of the phloem's sieve tubes due to an osmotic gradient caused by the differing concentrations of sugars in the cells. The turgor pressure in areas of the plant such as the leaves is then greater than that of the regions of lower pressure, such as actively growing areas. This differential results in a mass flow of materials from the area of high turgor pressure (e.g. the leaves) to an area of lower turgor pressure. In this way, translocation of the photosynthetic products to other tissues occurs.

68.   **(E)**

The vascular cambium layer is growing and dividing mitotically. It gives rise to the secondary vascular tissues which include secondary xylem (toward the inside of the cambium) and secondary phloem (toward the outside of the cambium).

69.   **(A)**

Growth rings are made up primarily of secondary xylem. The secondary xylem is produced by the vascular cambium. Secondary growth is the process by which woody plants increase the diameters of their stems, trunks, and roots. This type of growth is different from primary growth which is growth in length.

70.   **(A)**

In C_3 photosynthesis, the fixation of CO_2 by the plant is linked to the reactions of the Calvin Cycle. The enzyme that catalyzes this reaction is RuBP carboxylase (Ribulose Bisphosphate Carboxylase Oxygenase or RuBisCO) which is found in the chloroplast.

71.   **(B)**

In C_4 photosynthesis, CO_2 reacts with phosphoenolpyruvate (PEP) and a cata-lyzing enzyme, forming oxaloacetic acid in the mesophyll cells. Oxaloacetic acid is transported to bundle sheath cells where it is broken down to release CO_2. CO_2 reacts with RuBP through the catalytic properties of RuBisCO. It is in the bundle sheath cells that CO_2 enters into the Calvin Cycle. The speed at which the PEP enzyme works keeps the level of CO_2 lower in the leaf than in the outside environ-ment. Then, when the stomata open, carbon dioxide enters the leaf more rapidly to equalize the concentration gradient of CO_2. Thus, the stomata do not have to be open a long time in the dry climate; this prevents the loss of water.

72.   **(B)**

Carbohydrates are stored for future energy use in the form of glycogen in vertebrates. Lipids in the form of fats and oils function in energy storage in both plants and animals. In fact, fats contain more chemical energy than carbohydrates. Both lipids and carbohydrates are the major reservoirs for energy storage although all organic molecules (including proteins) release energy when they are oxidized.

73.   **(C)**

Steroids and fats, both of which are lipids, contain carbon, hydrogen, and oxygen only. Carbohydrates also contain only those elements. Nucleic acids contain, in addition to the aforementioned elements, phosphorus and nitrogen. Only proteins that contain the amino acids methionine or cysteine contain sulfur.

74.   **(C)**

The rate of most reactions that are catalyzed by enzymes drops off quickly at around $40\,°C$ because the enzyme becomes denatured. The enzymes begin to lose their three-dimensional structure because of the breakdown of hydrogen bonds and other weak bonds by heat.

75.   **(E)**

Enzymes are specific for certain substrate molecules because the shape of the enzyme's active site allows only certain molecules to fit.

76.   **(D)**

Even though the compound added is not the usual substrate for the enzyme, the results for experiment 2 indicate that there is, nonetheless, some activity. If more of this compound were to be added, slightly more color change would occur, indicating greater enzyme activity. With an increase in temperature, the change would be even more pronounced since enzyme activity increases with increased temperature, up until the point of denaturation (usually greater than 40° C). Thus, activity would increase, but it still would not be as pronounced as the activity found with the usual substrate.

77.   **(C)**

"Homozygous" describes a situation in which the alleles for a particular trait are identical. Organism "J" has a BbSs genotype. Organism "O" has a bbSs genotype. The genes assort independently producing the following gametes:

		BS	Bs	bS	bs
	bS	BbSS	BbSs	(bbSS)	bbSs
organism "O"	bs	BbSs	Bbss	bbSs	(bbss)
	bS	BbSS	BbSs	(bbSS)	bbSs
	bs	BbSs	Bbss	bbSs	(bbss)

- organism "J"

78.   **(C)**

"Heterozygous" describes a situation in which the genes for a trait are different.

		BS	Bs	bS	bs
	bS	BbSS	(BbSs)	bbSS	bbSs
organism "O"	bs	(BbSs)	Bbss	bbSs	bbss
	bS	BbSS	(BbSs)	bbSS	bbSs
	bs	(BbSs)	Bbss	bbSs	bbss

- organism "J"

79.   **(B)**

A homozygous recessive male would have the genotype bbss and the heterozygous female would have the genotype BbSs. The following Punnett square shows the offspring.

	bs	bs	bs	bs	- male
Bs	Bbss	Bbss	BbSS	Bbss	
female BS	BbSs	BbSs	BbSs	BbSs	
bS	bbSs	bbSs	bbSs	bbSs	
bs	bbss	bbss	bbss	bbss	

The progeny with brown eyes and curly hair would have the genotype Bbss.

80.   **(B)**

In this type of survivorship curve there is a high productivity early in life coupled with a high mortality rate. Those that survive early on have a good chance of surviving later in life. Examples of this survivorship are insects, fish, and plants.

81.   **(C)**

Curve #1 is representative of long-lived organisms such as mammals that produce a few well-endowed young over their entire life span. Parental investment is high and there is exponential growth, then steep mortality which may be correlated with population density factors (ex. competition, predation, etc.). Curve #2 shows populations with a fairly constant rate of change in mortality at all ages. Examples of curve #2 organisms are birds and small animals.

82.   **(D)**

The carrying capacity of a population is the maximum density of organisms that an area can handle under a certain environmental situation. A population can reach the carrying capacity after undergoing exponential growth. When the carrying capacity is reached, the curve tends to plateau. Unless the environmental conditions change, the population usually hovers around its carrying capacity. When a population exceeds its carrying capacity, it declines; when the population goes below its carrying capacity, it tends to increase. Sometimes a poulation overshoots its carrying capacity, then crashes because the resources of that area (e.g. food) cannot support a population that size. Usually, the population crashes due to starvation and disease until the population size is well below the carrying capacity.

83.   **(A)**

The I^A, I^B, and i are alleles (or forms of a gene) responsible for human ABO blood groups. Mr. Jones' blood group, AB, has the $I^A I^B$ genotype, and Mrs. Jones' blood group B has the $I^B I^B$ or $I^B i$ genotype. The "i" allele is recessive to I^A and I^B. The only phenotypes possible based on these genotype combinations are $I^A I^B$, $I^B I^B$, $I^A i$, or $I^B i$. Baby 1 with blood group A could have the Jones' as parents since the genotype combination making blood group A could be $I^A i$.

84.   **(B)**

If Mr. Jones' blood group was O his genotype would be "ii" which is recessive to I^A and I^B. For baby 2 to have blood group O, both parents must pass on an "i" allele to the Baby. The blood group B of Mrs. Jones can be represented as the $I^B I^B$ genotype or $I^B i$ genotype. Thus, if Mrs. Jones was $I^B i$, both parents could pass the "i" allele to baby 2.

85.   **(A)**

Baby 1 with blood group A could belong to Mr. and Mrs. Jones. The blood group genotype for Mr. Jones is $I^A I^B$ and the blood group genotype for Mrs. Jones is either $I^A I^A$ or $I^A i$. The "i" allele is recessive and would not show up in the blood type unless both parents had that recessive allele, and Mr. Jones does not. Therefore, Baby 2 (B) could not belong to the Jones.

86.   **(C)**

The solid line is the lynx population. It follows the oscillations of the hare population. As the density of the hare population increases, the density of the lynx population increases correspondingly but slightly later in time.

87.   **(A)**

Zero population growth occurs where births and deaths are in balance. The curve becomes more flattened (growth slows down and finally stabilizes). The decline or rise in the curve after the zero population growth has been reached may be due to environmental factors such as food (prey) supply.

88.   **(D)**

Predators are more likely to take the old (A), and those in poor physical condition (B). Predators usually are not dependent on only one species (C) but may adjust their hunting pattern to prey upon the most commonly available species. However, the most limiting factor to the prey (and predator) population is food resources.

89.   **(D)**

As the urine passes through the ascending loop of Henle (#4), the chloride ions are actively pumped out into the tissue surrounding the loop. The sodium ions follow by diffusion. The ascending loop is impermeable to water which then passes to the collecting duct. The chloride ions (and Na^+ ions) then flow to the descending loop (#2) where they are pumped out again. This constant circulation means that the ascending and descending loop of Henle is always surrounded by a salt solution.

90.   **(B)**

The walls of the proximal tubule (#2) are freely permeable to water which is transported out (by osmosis) along with sodium and chloride ions. As the fluid descends the loop of Henle (#3), it becomes concentrated (hypertonic) as water moves out by osmosis into the surrounding fluid which has a higher salt concentration than in the tubule. When the fluid ascends the loop of Henle (#4), sodium and chloride ions move out but water does not because the loop is impermeable to water. When the fluid reaches the distal tubule (#5) it is hypotonic, but the walls of the tubule are again permeable to water as are the walls of the collecting duct (#6). Water then flows out as a result of the zone of high salt concentration into the surrounding tissue. The urine left in the collecting duct is hypertonic.

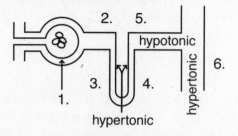

91.   **(A)**

Filtration involves the movement of blood plasma from the glomerulus into the Bowman's capsule (#1). The glomerulus is the convoluted group of thin-walled capillaries surrounded by the Bowman's capsule. Blood plasma and solutes (except protein or blood cells) filter through the walls of the glomerulus into the Bowman's capsule tubule.

92.   **(D)**

That the genes are linked is indicated by the large numbers of progeny with the combination of ebony body and normal wing AND the combination of normal body and curly wings.

93.   **(B)**

Since the genes are linked, the only phenotypes which can be obtained without crossing over are normal body, curly wing and ebony body, normal wing. Crossing over in the female allows for the production of normal body, normal wing and ebony body, curly wing progeny. In this way the genotypes of the female gametes is Ec, eC, EC, ec. In the male, the gametes will always have the genotype ec regardless of whether or not crossing over occurs. Thus crossing over need not occur between the genes for body color and wing type in the male.

94.   **(B)**

In primary succession, the initial substrate is bare rock. The first organisms to grow on bare rock are known as pioneer organisms. Such organisms include lichens and mosses. As time progresses, weathering of the rock and the death of organisms builds up the soil. In secondary succession, soil is already present for the plants to grow on. Abandoned farms and burned areas are sites where secondary succession often occurs. The invading plants are often weeds (herbaceous). In each case of succession, the herbaceous plants give way to larger woody plants.

95.   **(E)**

The most stable stages are often termed climax communities. These communities are still dynamic (changing) rather than static, but in comparison to other communities, the climax community is most stable.

96.   **(E)**

The later stages of succession have communities with greater diversity, not only of plants, but of animals. In the earliest stage, only a few weedy species are present. However, in a climax forest, there are many tree species, shrubs, and herbaceous species.

97.   **(A)**

Communities in succession usually produce more organic matter than they use. In climax communities, an equilibrium is reached between net production and utilization.

98.   **(C)**

Since the virus inserted only radioactive phosphorus (with its DNA) into the host cell, then DNA (not the protein coat) was shown to be the genetic material from which the entire bacteriophage could be replicated. This experiment was done by Hershey and Chase to determine which substance, DNA or protein, was the genetic material.

99.   **(D)**

The *E. coli* bacteriophages reproduce by injecting the DNA core into a bacterial host cell leaving the protein coat outside the host cell. Once inside the host cell, the bacteriophages (with their protein coats) are synthesized by the DNA in the host cell; thus, demonstrating that DNA is the genetic material.

100.   **(B)**

Since only DNA invaded the host cell (as shown by the presence of radioactive phosphorus in the host cell), and since the bacteriophages replicated themselves completely within the host cell, DNA is the material that transmits genetic information.

SECTION II

ESSAY I

Biogeochemical cycles are the movement of inorganic or abiotic matter through an ecosystem, such as nitrogen, phosphorus, and carbon cycles. Broken down, "geo" refers to the environment — the atmosphere, land, and waters of the earth. "Bio" refers to living organisms, both producers and consumers. An important component of this cycle is the detritus feeders, which consume dead organic matter and degrade it to inorganic material, which then is released to cycle through the land and water.

The earth's major supply of nitrogen comes from the atmosphere, where it exists as a gas. However, the movement of nitrogen in the cycle occurs as inorganic matter. Nitrogen is used in physiological systems to form amino acids and other nitrogen-containing compounds that are needed for growth and maintenance.

Nitrogen fixation by bacteria provides much of the usable nitrogen for organisms. In this process, free nitrogen is reduced to organic compounds, such as ammonia (NH_3) or ammonium ions (NH_4+). An example of nitrogen-fixers is the bacteria found at the roots of legumes. The elemental nitrogen they convert is used by the legumes, and any excess is released to the soil.

Detritus feeders decompose the complex nitrogen compounds found in dead organic tissues into simpler amino acid compounds, which they incorporate into their body, releasing any excess into the soil as ammonium compounds. The remainder of the compounds is oxidized by nitrite bacteria to nitrites (NO_2), which is toxic to plants. The nitrites are then oxidized to nitrates by nitrate bacteria, which is the form of nitrogen most commonly utilized by plants. They absorb the nitrogen through the roots and assimilate it into organic nitrogen compounds. This process is called nitrification.

After nitrogen compounds are leached from the soil by plants, animals absorb the nitrogen through digestion of a plant or herbivore. In the process of denitrification, the nitrogen containing compounds are returned to the solid through detritus feeders, which decompose the tissues and dissolve the nitrogen in soil water, which perpetuates the cycle.

Nitrogen can also return to the atmosphere as a gas because denitrifying bacteria can convert ammonia, nitrites, and nitrates to gaseous nitrogen.

Carbon dioxide is the source of inorganic molecules from which organic carbon is derived and is found most frequently in the atmosphere as dissolved carbon dioxide. Plants incorporate extracted carbon which is broken down into respiration. For each turn of the carbon cycle, carbon is released to the atmosphere as CO_2.

Carbon is the building block of life, as it can form covalent bonds with hydrogen, oxygen, nitrogen, or other carbons. It can bond to hydrogen through single, double, or triple bonds, forming hydrocarbons, which produce a great variety of organic molecules forming the basis of compounds essential to living systems. It is found in sugars, carbohydrates, nucleic acids, and lipids, to name a few.

Animal acquire carbon by eating plants and other animals, forming complex molecules from the simple ones absorbed in digestion. Carbon can be excreted as part of animal wastes. Other carbon remains in plant and animal bodies, so upon death, decomposers release the carbon through respiration. If the tissue remains are not completely decomposed, they may be converted into inorganic carbon substances such as coal, or oil, which can be burned as a fuel, releasing carbon dioxide into the atmosphere.

The major supply of phosphorus comes from sedimentary rocks, when they are dissolved by rain. Phosphorus is also released from dead organic matter and animal excretions by detritus feeders, re-entering the soil as phosphates, which the plants absorb and use for growth and maintenance. Animals eat plants and aquatic organisms eat algae, and it becomes incorporated in animal shells, skeletons, and tissues. Excretions of the organisms return phosphates in solution to water. Detritus feeders in the water consume dead organic matter, releasing phosphates in solution. Phosphates in the soil are mixed with water where some phosphates become part of the sedimentary rock at the bottom of the body of water, renewing the phosphorus cycle. Too much phosphate in the water causes excessive algae growth, death of aquatic life as the oxygen is diminished, and eutrophication (aging) of the water body. One important use of phosphorus is that it forms part of the energy molecule adenosine tripsophate (ATP), the energy source for many living organisms.

Humans can cause havoc in these cycles. For example, farmers can leach all of the nitrogen from the soil by continuously growing the same type of crop on their land and not rotating the product with legumes. This leaves the soil nitrogen-starved and makes it very difficult for plants to grow. To combat this, many fertilizers contain nitrogen and phosphorus. This fertilizer often dissolves in rainwater and runs off to a water body, promoting the growth of algae. This kills much of the aquatic life, leaving them limited oxygen and can lead to early eutrophication.

Any machine that burns a carbon-based fuel emits carbon dioxide into the air. As the levels increase beyond the ocean's ability to absorb it for the carbon cycle, CO_2 remains in the air and prevents other gases from escaping to the atmosphere. This increases the basal temperature of the Earth and is known as the greenhouse effect. In addition, pollution causes temperature inversion, which traps cooler air under the hotter polluted air, and toxic chemicals are not released to the atmosphere.

ESSAY II

STRUCTURE OF DNA

A DNA molecule is shaped like a twisted ladder (double helix). The "sides" of the ladder are made up of sugars and phosphates while the "rungs" of the ladder are made up of the nucleotides — adenine, thymine, cytosine, and guanine.

The nucleotides form complementary base pairs. Adenine pairs with thymine and guanine pairs with cytosine. The nucleotides adenine and guanine are purines. The nucleotides thymine and cytosine are pyrimidines. The complementary base pairs are connected by hydrogen bonds. DNA is located in the nucleus. Genetic information in the DNA is in the sequence of bases. The genetic code is a four-lettered alphabet: adenine (A), thymine (T), guanine (G), and cytosine (C).

FUNCTION OF DNA

DNA contains codes for proteins that are synthesized in the cytoplasm of the cell. Condensed DNA and associated histone proteins are collectively referred to as chromosomes.

REPLICATION OF DNA

Replication or duplication of DNA takes place in the nucleus of the cell. Replication takes place before the cell divides mitotically. The strands' hydrogen bonds break and each half of the single strand acts as a template for a new complementary strand. These new strands are built from free nucleotides in the nucleus. These free nucleotides bind to the template bases according to the rules for complementary base pairing.

TRANSCRIPTION

Transcription is the creation of RNA (specifically, messenger RNA) by DNA. Certain sections along the chromosome (condensed DNA) unwind as hydrogen bonds are broken. DNA directs the formation of RNA along these exposed sections. Free nucleotides attach to the open bases, except that uracil is substituted for thymine. RNA (called messenger RNA) forms a complementary strand, using the DNA as a template (pattern). The copy is not identical to DNA, but is complementary. The ribosome attaches to the mRNA and moves along the length of its strand, matching the codons of the mRNA to the anticodons of tRNA. The tRNA with the correct complementary sequence then goes to the correct location on the mRNA. The tRNA attaches to the mRNA codon for a short time. It then leaves, but the amino acid stays behind. It becomes attached to a growing chain of amino acids that were brought to the mRNA in the ribosome by other tRNA molecules. After the mRNA has directed a certain number of amino acid sequences, it breaks apart. The chains of amino acids form proteins. Depending on the mRNA message, these proteins can be structural proteins or enzymes.

ESSAY III

Development in flowering plants begins with a seed, which consists of the embryo, stored food, and the seed coat. The seed is a period of dormancy before the plant germinates, or begins growth. Seeds are important in the dispersal of plants as they can travel long distances and do not have to germinate immediately upon soil contact.

The seed coat protects the embryo against drying out and injury. It permits it to stay in a reduced activity period until conditions are favorable for its growth. Some scientists believe there may be some hormones responsible for a role as germination inhibitors.

The endosperm contains the stored food, which is utilized in the early stages of germination. Plants that do not have endosperms, such as peas, have cotyledons. The stored food is believed to be a starch. To test this postulate, soak the seed overnight in water, then cut it in half with a sharp blade. The Lugol's Iodine test could be used. If it is a starchy material, the iodine will turn black.

The seed is a mature ovule. Its parts include some of the parent plant's genetic material, as well as some of the previous generation. The endosperm actually has 3n cells, two female and one male. The embryo, or the part that will grow, is diploid, one n from the mother and one n from the father. In the early germination stages, the seed coat splits open and falls to the ground. A root then forms to anchor the seed in the ground. It is believed that gibberellins and auxins plant hormones stimulate the growth or combat the germination inhibitors. After the plant has utilized the stored food, the root uses capillary action to obtain water and nutrients such as phosphorus, magnesium and nitrogen from the soil. When the plant breaks the soil surface, then chlorophyll can be used to make energy from the sun.

To determine if seeds contain a substance similar to antibiotics, soak the seeds in water overnight. Cut them with a sharp razor blade. Place the cut seeds onto a nutrient rich agar that has been spread with bacteria. Incubate the agar plates. For controls, use an agar plate with only bacteria and one with seeds that have not been cut. If there is an antimicrobial agent, there should be clear plaques around the seeds that were soaked and cut.

ESSAY IV

1. FIRST LAW OF THERMODYNAMICS

The First Law of Thermodynamics states that energy cannot be created or destroyed, but instead is transformed from one form to another. The potential energy of the reactants equals the sum of the potential energy of the products and the energy that is released as a result of the reaction.

Energy that is released may not be in a form that is usable by organisms. For example, heat, a form of energy, may dissipate into the surrounding environment (to nonliving matter); therefore, it would not be available for use by biological systems. Also, living cells draw primarily on chemical energy derived from complex organic molecules rather than heat energy to do their work. Because not all energy is usable by living system, there must be a source of usable energy outside the organism that would be available for it to use. An example is the use of the sun's energy by plants to form complex organic molecules, such as glucose, that contain potential energy for later use by the cell.

2. THE SECOND LAW OF THERMODYNAMICS

The Second Law of Thermodynamics states that with each energy transformation that takes place, the amount of usable (free) energy at the end of a reaction is less than the amount of usable (free) energy present in the beginning. With each energy transformation, entropy (or randomness) of a system increases. An example of this law in biological systems is the tendency toward disintegration or death.

A source of energy for the system is needed (e.g., the sun). The addition of energy to a system allows the system to achieve a state of decreased entropy, or increased organization. Examples of organization in biological systems are the formation of tissues from cells, the formation of organs from tissues, the formation of systems from organs, resulting in the formation of entire organisms from systems.

3. ANABOLISM

Anabolism is the sum of those chemical reactions in biological systems in which energy is used to synthesize or build structures within the cell or within the organism. Anabolic reactions are referred to as being endergonic reactions because they require an input of energy to start the reaction. The input of energy increases the kinetic energy of the molecules in cells, increasing the likelihood that they will collide with each other with enough force to overcome the repulsion they have for each other and to break the chemical bonds that keep the molecules in their present state. An example of an anabolic process is photosynthesis, which requires energy input from the sun to create complex organic molecules such as glucose and compounds that are synthesized from the glucose. Glucose is an example of a molecule that stores energy to be used later to do work or for growth and maintenance of the organism. ATP is the most widely used, but not the only energy currency unit.

4. CATABOLISM

Catabolism describes those chemical reactions in which larger molecules are broken down into smaller molecules with an accompanying release of energy. This type of reaction, in which heat is released, is called an exergonic reaction. Respiration is an example of a catabolic reaction. In this reaction, energy-rich glucose molecules are broken down. The breaking-down phase allows the cell to synthesize new ATP to be used both for future anabolic reactions and for growth and maintenance of the organism.

5. PHOSPHORYLATION OF ADP TO ATP

In phosphorylation reactions, ATP is synthesized from ADP and inorganic phosphate. Thus, a molecule of ATP, which contains much chemical potential energy, is formed. The energy needed for synthesis of ATP to occur is ultimately derived from the sun in the photosynthetic process. A non-photosynthetic organism can make ATP by using the energy from other energy-rich molecules, but not energy from the sun. Phosphorylation reactions are endergonic because energy must be added to the system when ATP is synthesized from ADP and phosphate.

6. COUPLED REACTIONS

The occurrence of an endergonic reaction (e.g., photosynthesis, phosphorylation) that supplies energy to an exergonic reaction (e.g., respiration, degradation of ATP to ADP with the accompanying release of energy) is called a coupled reaction. The energy released from the exergonic process is used to "drive" the endergonic process.

Coupled reactions allow living systems to produce more complex molecules from less complex ones, despite the seeming violation of the Second Law of Thermodynamics. The Second Law is not violated during synthesis, because although free energy is needed to synthesize molecules, this anabolic process is coupled to a catabolic reaction (e.g., the hydrolysis of ATP).

THE ADVANCED PLACEMENT EXAMINATION IN

BIOLOGY

TEST VI

ADVANCED PLACEMENT
BIOLOGY EXAM VI

SECTION I

100 Questions
80 Minutes

DIRECTIONS: For each question, there are five possible choices. Select the best choice for each question. Blacken the correct space on the answer sheet.

Use the following diagram with the lettered trophic levels to answer questions 1-2:

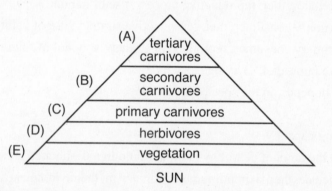

SUN

1.   If the pyramid diagram is a biomass pyramid, where would you find the greatest biomass of organisms?

   (A) At the top

   (B) All would be equal

   (C) At the herbivore level

   (D) Can't tell from the given information

   (E) At the bottom

2.   If the pyramid diagram indicated energy levels, what would be observed if the pyramid ended at trophic level "C" instead of "A"?

   (A) Less usable energy would be lost as you go up the food chain.

   (B) More usable energy would be lost as you go up the food chain.

   (C) No change would occur.

    (D) Usable energy would be generated as you go up the food chain.

    (E) It would be better to feed plants to humans rather than giving them to livestock.

3.   Which of the following statements about the influence of a predator on a prey population is _not_ correct?

    (A) Prey organisms in poor physical condition are taken by predators in higher numbers than healthy ones.

    (B) Predation is a principal cause of determining species diversity in a particular community.

    (C) Predators limit the carrying capacity of a population within a community.

    (D) Food limits the carrying capacity of a population within a community.

    (E) All of the above are true.

4.   The description of a niche includes:

    (A) predator, diet, reproductive process, use of habitat

    (B) primary consumer, diet, reproductive strategy, use of habitat

    (C) primary consumer, reproductive strategy, amount of rainfall

    (D) predator, diet, carrying capacity

    (E) it depends on the species involved.

4.   Carrying capacity:

    (A) is the amount of soil by volume found in a designated area.

    (B) includes the maximum number of organisms the environment can support.

    (C) is used to describe both aquatic and terrestrial ecosystems

    (D) is limited by the resources (food, water, space) available to a species

    (E) both (A) and (D)

6.   RNA polymerase dominates the process of:

    (A) transcription   (D) conjugation

    (B) translation   (E) transference

    (C) transduction

7.   _____ carry amino acids to the ribosomes.

    (A) Messenger RNAs

    (B) Ribosomal RNAs

(C) Transfer RNAs

(D) DNA and messenger RNAs

(E) RNA polymerases

8. Viruses have:

(A) the ability to replicate their genetic material

(B) the ability to make their own energy

(C) their own metabolic machinery

(D) their own enzymes

(E) both (A) and (C)

9. _____ is/are directly associated with anticodon.

(A) Messenger RNA

(B) Transfer RNA

(C) Ribosomal RNA

(D) DNA and messenger RNA

(E) RNA polymerase

10. The cell membrane has the following structure(s):

(A) one outer layer of phospholipids and one layer of proteins inside the phospholipid layer

(B) two layers of phospholipids arranged in bilayers

(C) protein extending through the bilayers

(D) hydrophilic lipids

(E) both (B) and (C)

11. In eukaryotic cells, cilia and flagella are:

(A) a group of microtubules anchored to a point of attachment in the cell membrane called a baseplate

(B) a 9+2 arrangement of microtubules attached to a basal body

(C) a 9+0 arrangement of microtubules attached to a 9+2 basal body under the cilia

(D) attached directly to the centrioles

(E) a chain of proteins not enclosed in the cell membrane

12. An enzyme is a large organic molecule with a surface geometry that is composed of:

(A) amino acids   (D) polysaccharides

(B) monosaccharides   (E) triglycerides

(C) glycerol and fatty acids

13. A coenzyme is

(A) a substance that makes an enzyme less effective

(B) a substance that directly reacts with the substrate

(C) a substance that some enzymes need before they can function

(D) a substance that is a catalyst

(E) All of the above

14. Thylakoids are:

(A) outfoldings of the mitochondrial membrane

(B) sites that trap light for photosynthesis

(C) sites of protein synthesis

(D) sites of transformation of ATP in the mitochondria

(E) small structures of the chlorophyll molecules

15. Oxygen is released by the:

(A) light reaction of photosynthesis

(B) dark reaction of photosynthesis

(C) formation of ATP from ADP

(D) "excited" electrons in the chlorophyll molecule

(E) splitting of the 6-carbon sugar

16. A chemical has been added to the mitochondria that causes H+ ions to be transported through the membrane. What would be the result(s)?

(A) More ATP would be formed

(B) Less ATP would be formed

(C) The electrical gradient is destroyed

(D) Both (A) and (C)

(E) Both (B) and (C)

17. The term "coupled reaction" refers to:

(A) linking endergonic and exergonic processes

(B) linking of two reactions using the same enzyme

(C) linking of ADP and inorganic phosphate group

(D) linking of reactions in a metabolic pathway

(E) the joining of a nucleotide with a five-carbon sugar

18. DNA differs from RNA in that:

(A) RNA has three bases while DNA has four bases

(B) RNA has a single strand and DNA has a double strand

(C) RNA has a base thymine instead of the base uracil as in DNA

(D) DNA contains nucleotides while RNA does not

(E) None of the above

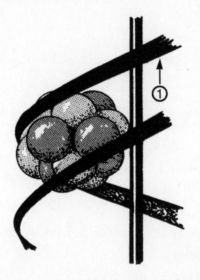

19. Which of the following structures is the one marked 1 likely to be?

(A) DNA   (D) prokaryote

(B) RNA   (E) flagellum

(C) histone protein

20. Bacteriophages are:

(A) composed of a protein core surrounded by a coat of DNA nucleic acid

(B) bacteria that attack viruses

(C) bacteria that feed viruses

(D) bacteria that "take over" the genetic machinery of viruses

(E) viruses that attack bacteria

21.   A restriction enzyme cleaves the following DNA segment between adjacent
       guanine and adenine.

                              G\AATTC
                              CTTAA\G

       Which of the following sequences indicates that sticky ends have formed?
       (A) TTAA----------AATT
       (B) GAAT---------GAAT
       (C) G--------------G
       (D) TC-------------CT
       (E) None of the above

22.   Using the previous example, what complementary base of foreign DNA
       could be inserted?
       (A) GGCC---------CCGG
       (B) TTCC----------AATT
       (C) TTAA----------AATT
       (D) CCGG---------GGCC
       (E) AATT----------TTAA

23.   Which of the following DNA mutations could be deadly?
       (A) Codon substitution
       (B) A nucleotide is added or deleted
       (C) Inversion of part of nucleotide for another
       (D) Change of one nucleotide for another
       (E) Both (C) and (D)

24.   The F_2 generation of a heterozygous dihybrid cross is produced by:
       (A) two distinctly different gametes
       (B) three distinctly different gametes
       (C) four distinctly different gametes
       (D) eight distinctly different gametes
       (E) None of the above

25.   The F_2 generation of a heterozygous dihybrid cross has:
       (A) two distinctly different genotypes

(B) four distinctly different genotypes

(C) five distinctly different genotypes

(D) eight distinctly different genotypes

(E) nine distinctly different genotypes

26. Genes responsible for hemophilia in man are carried:

(A) on the X chromosome not the Y chromosome

(B) on the Y chromosome not the X chromosome

(C) on any chromosome pair except the X and Y chromosomes

(D) on both X and Y chromosomes

(E) on either the X or Y chromosomes depending on whether the individual is male or female

27. The theory of punctuated equilibrium assumes that

(A) there are periods of time of stability in which little evolutionary change occurs

(B) speciation can occur in a very short period of time and is marked by rapid changes

(C) evolution occurs gradually within lineages

(D) Both (A) and (B)

(E) All of the above

28. The basis for the taxonomic and systematic classification of organisms is:

(A) binomial system of nomenclature

(B) grouping by genus

(C) grouping by morphological features

(D) grouping by species

(E) division into plants and animals

29. What traditional criterion(a) is(are) used to differentiate between prokaryotes and protists?

(A) Method of obtaining nutrition

(B) Methods of reproduction and motility

(C) Presence (or absence) of cell wall

(D) Number of cells

(E) Both (A) and (C)

30. All living organisms have a eukaryotic cell structure except:

    (A) Monera   (D) Plants

    (B) Protista   (E) Animals

    (C) Fungi

31. Which of the following is true about the five-kingdom classification system?

    (A) All one celled organisms are grouped in one kingdom.

    (B) All heterotrophs are grouped in one kingdom.

    (C) Organisms are divided into kingdoms based on their evolutionary history.

    (D) Eukaryotes are grouped in one kingdom.

    (E) All prokaryotes are grouped in a single kingdom.

32. Directly after meiosis occurs, what structure is produced in ferns?

    (A) Haploid spores

    (B) Diploid spores

    (C) Haploid sporophyte

    (D) Haploid gametes

    (E) Diploid sporophyte

33. A gametophyte is:

    (A) a plant that produces gametes

    (B) haploid

    (C) diploid

    (D) produced by the fusion of gametes

    (E) Both (A) and (B)

34. In angiosperms, the immature male gametophyte is:

    (A) the megaspore

    (B) the stamen

    (C) the pollen tube

    (D) the pistil

    (E) the pollen grain

35. Germination starts when:

    (A) the seed coat permits water to enter the tissues of the seed

(B) the sporophyte emerges

(C) the seeds are planted

(D) the apical meristems of the root elongate

(E) None of the above

36. Which is a characteristic of a hormone?

    (A) Large quantities are needed to produce a desired effect

    (B) They are produced in the tissue that they affect

    (C) Small quantities can produce effects

    (D) They work interdependently with other hormones

    (E) Both (C) and (D)

37. When a seedling rights itself, this is a _____ response.

    (A) gravitropic

    (B) photoperiodic

    (C) circadian

    (D) phototropic

    (E) None of the above

38. In phyla advanced beyond the level of sponges, embryonic cells aggregate into:

    (A) organs

    (B) organ systems

    (C) gametes and somatic cells

    (D) tissues

    (E) amino acids

39. A nervous impulse starting at the dendrite will next pass through the:

    (A) cell body

    (B) axon

    (C) nodes of Ranvier

    (D) synaptic bouton

    (E) None of the above

40. The process by which blood plasma moves out of the glomerulus capillaries and into Bowman's capsule is called:

(A) reabsorption

(B) secretion

(C) countercurrent exchange

(D) filtration

(E) multiplication

41. The subunit of a kidney that purifies blood and maintains a safe balance of solutes and water in humans is called:

(A) glomerulus

(B) loop of Henle

(C) urethra

(D) Bowman's capsule

(E) nephron

42. Memory cells produced by B-lymphocytes help the organism to respond more quickly to an infection the second time because they:

(A) start a cell-mediated response

(B) have created their own antigens from the first exposure to the infection

(C) rapidly clone antibodies picked up during the first exposure to the infection

(D) directly attack the invaders instead of producing antibodies

(E) are not specific to a particular antigen

43. Which of the following donors would be the best choice for a skin graft?

(A) Identical twin

(B) A sister with the same blood

(C) A non-family donor and the patient will be given a drug to suppress the immune response

(D) A parent

(E) (A), (B) or (C) would be an acceptable donor

44. The formation of eggs and sperm are called:

(A) metamorphosis

(B) gastrulation

(C) ovulation

(D) fertilization

(E) gametogenesis

45.   Which of the following correctly shows the path of blood in the blood vessels?

(A)   arterioles - capillaries - arteries - veins - venules

(B)   arteries - arterioles - capillaries - venules - veins

(C)   capillaries - arterioles - arteries - veins - venules

(D)   venules - capillaries - veins - arteries - venules

(E)   veins - venules - arterioles - capillaries - arteries

46.   The process of cleavage produces a:

(A)   zygote

(B)   blastula

(C)   gastrula

(D)   archenteron

(E)   None of the above

47.   If the blood pressure of a human is 111/80

(A)   the systolic pressure is 80

(B)   the diastolic pressure is 80

(C)   the pulse rate is 80 beats per minute

(D)   the blood pressure during contraction of the heart is 80

(E)   the right atrium moved 111 milliliters of blood per beat and the left atrium moved 80 milliliters of blood per beat

48.   The heart, bones, and blood develop primarily from the:

(A)   endoderm

(B)   ectoderm

(C)   mesoderm

(D)   morula

(E)   blastula

49.   The diversity of animals is chiefly a result of what characteristic?

(A)   The cells are eukaryotic

(B)   Their complex nervous system

(C)   They are multicellular

(D)   Their mode of reproduction

(E)   Their mode of nutrition

50.   Animals are classified into phyla chiefly by:

(A) number of tissue layers

(B) basic body plan

(C) presence or absence of true coelom

(D) pattern of development from embryo

(E) All of the above

51.   In the animal kingdom, bilateral symmetry is related to:

(A) three germ layers

(B) two germ layers

(C) more efficient movement than radial symmetry

(D) Both (A) and (C)

(E) Both (B) and (C)

52.   Which is associated with the movement from radial to bilateral symmetry?

(A) Paired organs

(B) Circulatory system

(C) A coelom

(D) Two - ended digestive system

(E) Two germ layers

53.   Which of the following is not an assumption of the Hardy-Weinberg rule?

(A) random mating

(B) no selection

(C) no mutation

(D) large population size

(E) migration

DIRECTIONS: The following groups of questions have five lettered choices followed by a list of diagrams, numbered phrases, sentences, or words. For each numbered diagram, phrase, sentence, or word choose the heading which most directly applies. Blacken the correct space on the answer sheet. Each heading may be used once, more than once, or not at all.

Questions 54 - 56 refer to the following list of cell organelles:

(A) mitochondrion

(B) lysosome

(C) Golgi Bodies

(D) rough endoplasmic reticulum

(E) plasma membrane

54. The organelle primarily responsible for intracellular digestion.

55. The organelle responsible for cellular respiration.

56. The site where proteins are modified, packaged and secreted from the cell.

Questions 57 - 59 refer to the following list of activities that occur in the cytoplasm of the cell.

(A) phagocytosis

(B) active transport

(C) endocytosis

(D) exocytosis

(E) osmosis

57. The taking in of solid material by white blood cells and unicellular organisms, such as amoebas.

58. The movement of water through a membrane from an area of high concentration of water molecules to one of lower concentration of water molecules.

59. The use of energy to move a substance through a membrane against its concentration gradient.

Questions 60 - 61 refer to the following list of terms relating to populations.

(A) Adaptive Radiation

(B) Allopatric Speciation

(C) Sympatric Speciation

(D) Directional Selection

(E) Disruptive Selection

60. This is the geographic separation of two populations accompanied by gradual divergent evolution between the two populations.

61. This process occurs when populations within the same distribution range reproduce in isolation.

Questions 62 - 63 refer to the following diagram.

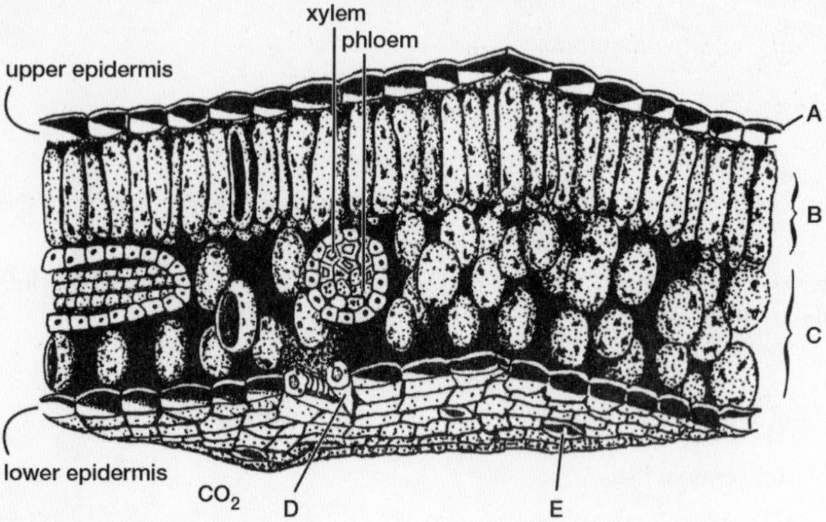

62.   Used for protection against desiccation, disease, insects

63.   Most photosynthesis takes place here

Question 64 refers to characteristics of:

(A) acoelomates

(B) pseudocoelomates

(C) coelomates

(D) acoelomates and pseudocoelomates

(E) acoelomates, pseudocoelomates, and protosome coelomates

64.   Triloblasty is characteristic of which group?

Questions 65 - 66 refer to the following list of processes for functions that occur in digestion.

(A) The absorptive surface of the digestive tract is increased

(B) The food is manipulated and mixed with saliva

(C) Supportive connective tissue

(D) Used to cut food

(E) A thin layer of connective tissue covered by moist epithelium

65.   Which is the function of the microvilli?

66.   What is the function of the peritoneum?

Questions 67 - 68 refer to the lettered structures that are listed below.

    (A) Shoot

    (B) Node

    (C) Rhizome

    (D) Lateral buds

    (E) Apical meristem

67.   Leaves are produced by this structure.

68.   These structures can differentiate to form branches, flowers, and shoots having a special function.

69.   A strand of DNA is a _____ and can generate a new_____ strand of DNA

    (A) copy, identical

    (B) parent, identical

    (C) duplicate, duplicate

    (D) template, complementary

    (E) base, double

70.   The DNA strand has a backbone of alternating:

    (A) sugar and phosphate molecules

    (B) complementary base pairs

    (C) hydrogen bonds

    (D) pyrimidines and purines

    (E) nitrogen - containing bonds

Questions 71 - 72 refer to the following plant hormones:

    (A) Auxins   (D) Ethylene

    (B) Cytokinins   (E) Abscisic Acid

    (C) Gibberellins

71.   You observe that a monocot seed is shrinking. Which hormone is probably present?

72.   You observe that seeds appear to be dormant, and on a dry day, the stomata of the leaves are closed. Which hormone is probably present?

Questions 73 - 75 refer to reproductive structures of a generalized flower that are identified by letters.

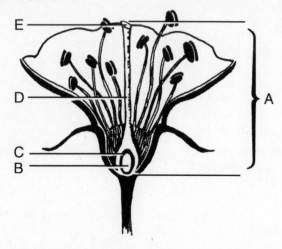

73. Structure in which the female gametophyte (megagametophyte) develops.
74. Structure in which the ovule develops and which becomes the fruit.
75. Structure which becomes the seed.

Questions 76 and 77 refer to the following enzymes of digestion and organs of digestion:

Enzymes	Organs
(A) amylase	(A) liver
(B) lipase	(B) pancreas
(C) pepsin	(C) salivary glands
(D) disaccharidase	(D) intestinal mueasa
(E) trypsin	(E) stomach

76. Which structure secretes <u>all but one</u> of the above enzymes?

77. Which of these enzymes acts first on the proteins in food after it has been ingested and swallowed?

To answer questions 78 - 79 refer to the following diagram and the list of microorganisms:

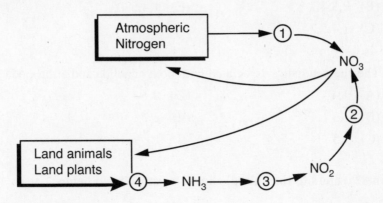

(A) nitrogenfixing bacteria

(B) plankton

(C) nitrifying bacteria

(D) denitrifying bacteria

(E) decomposing bacteria

78.   What group of bacteria belongs in circle 1?

79.   What group of bacteria belongs in circle 4?

DIRECTIONS: The following questions refer to experimental or laboratory situations or data. Read the description of each situation. Then choose the best answer to each question. Blacken the correct space on the answer sheet.

Questions 80 - 81 refer to the list of characteristics of mollusca, annelida, and arthropoda. Some characteristics may refer to more than one group:

1.   Head - foot body type

2.   Segmented body type

3.   One - way digestive tract

4.   Visceral mass containing organs of digestion, excretion, and reproduction.

5.   Jointed exoskeleton

6.   Mantle

7.   Mechanisms for excretion

8.   Closed circulatory system

80. The characteristics associated with mollusca include:

    (A) 1,3,5,8   (D) 2,5,6,8

    (B) 2,3,4,7   (E) 1,4,6,7

    (C) 1,4,5,7

81. The characteristics associated with both annelida and arthropoda include:

    (A) 1,4   (D) 2,6

    (B) 1,3   (E) 2,7

    (C) 2,5

Question 82 refers to the animal characteristics listed below:

1. embryonic development has spiral cleavage pattern
2. embryonic development has radial cleavage pattern
3. mouth development near blastopore
4. anus development near blastopore
5. coelom formation by splitting of mesoderm
6. coelom formatting by out-pocketing of embryonic gut
7. presence of coelom
8. absence of coelom

82. The characteristics associated with protostomes are:

    (A) 1,3,5,7   (D) 2,3,5,8

    (B) 2,4,6,8   (E) 1,3,4,7

    (C) 1,4,6,7

83. Entropy:

    (A) increases in a community that is undergoing primary plant succession

    (B) increases in a community by the action of decaying organisms

    (C) requires an excess of energy to do work

    (D) both (A) and (B)

    (E) both (B) and (C)

Questions 84 - 85 refer to the following situation. A mother with Rh-negative blood had a baby with Rh-positive blood and two years later had another Rh-positive baby.

84.   This situation can be dangerous for the second child because:

(A)   The second baby may make antibodies to a factor in the mother's blood

(B)   The mother may make antibodies to a factor in the first child's blood

(C)   The father has donated a dominant gene to the child

(D)   The father will donate antibodies to the second child

(E)   Both (B) and (D)

85.   To say that the baby has Rh-positive blood means that:

(A)   The baby has an antigen on his red blood cells that the mother's red blood cells do not have.

(B)   The baby lacks an antigen on his red blood cells that the mother has

(C)   The baby has an antigen for blood group 0

(D)   Rh is a multiple allele

(E)   The father has donated antibodies to the child

Questions 86 - 87 refer to the graphs below:

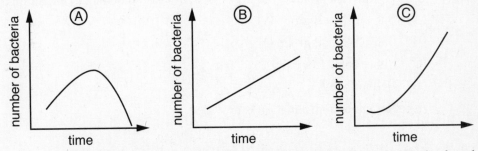

86.   Which graph shows the long-term growth of a population of bacteria placed in a nutrient medium in a covered dish?

(A)   Graph A   (D)   All of the above

(B)   Graph B   (E)   None of the above

(C)   Graph C

87.   Which graph shows the long term growth of a population of bacteria placed in a nutrient medium in which there is plenty of food, space, and other natural resources?

(A)   Graph A   (D)   All of the above

(B)   Graph B   (E)   None of the above

(C)   Graph C

Answer questions 88 - 89 using the following information and chart.

Both the Smith family and Jones family had babies on the same day at the same time. There was a mix-up in the nursery, but the hospital had the blood types of the Smiths and the two babies. The chart below gives that information.

> Mrs. Smith   - Group O
> Mr. Smith   - Group AB
> Baby 1   - Group A
> Baby 2   - Group O

88.   Which of the two babies could belong to the Smiths?

     (A) Baby 1 (blood group A)

     (B) Baby 2 (blood group 0)

     (C) Either baby 1 or baby 2

     (D) Neither baby

     (E) Not enough information

89.   If Mr. Smith had group O blood, which child would belong to the Smiths?

     (A) Baby 1 (blood group A)

     (B) Baby 2 (blood group O)

     (C) Either baby 1 or baby 2

     (D) Neither baby

     (E) Not enough information is provided

90.   A large number of genetically identical mice are randomly put into two groups. The experimental group is fed mouse food mixed with 2% DTT. The control group is fed mouse food only. At the end of six months, the following data were recorded:

	Experimental Group N=40	Control N=39
% of deaths	30%	0%
% of births compared to original number	40%	82%
% diseased but not dead	20%	2%
average weight	190g	220g
food weight eaten in a day	30g	39g

The data indicates that:

(A) The DDT fed mice appeared to be eating more frequently

(B) The control group mice weighed less and ate less

(C) The DDT fed mice died more frequently, reproduced less, had a higher frequency of disease

(D) The control group mice died less frequently, reproduced more, had a lower frequency of disease, and weighed and ate more.

(E) Both (C) and (D)

The diagrams below demonstrate three types of evolutionary trends of a population.

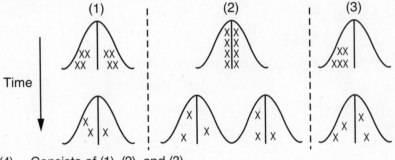

(4) Consists of (1), (2), and (3)

(5) Consists of (1) and (3) only

Answer questions 91 – 93 based on the diagrams above.

91. Adaptations arise from:

(A) 1   (D) 4

(B) 2   (E) 5

(C) 3

92. The optimum birth rate of babies is approximately 7 pounds. What type of natural selection is represented by this fact?

(A) 1   (D) 4

(B) 2   (E) 5

(C) 3

93. Which is an example of directional selection?

(A) 1   (D) 4

(B) 2   (E) 5

(C) 3

Questions 94 - 95 refer to the following listing of characteristics of basic muscle types which are classified either by appearance or location.

		Type 1	Type 2	Type 3
1.	Found in visceral organs		+	
2.	Attached to skeleton	+		
3.	Voluntary	+		
4.	Unstriated		+	
5.	One nucleus per cell		+	+
6.	Branched network of cells			+
7.	Involuntary		+	+
8.	Intercalated discs			+

94.   Which type is classified as smooth muscle tissue?

(A) Type 1   (D) Type 1 or 3

(B) Type 2   (E) Type 2 or 3

(C) Type 3

95.   Which type is classified as cardiac muscle tissue?

(A) Type 1   (D) Type 1 or 3

(B) Type 2   (E) Type 2 or 3

(C) Type 3

96.   Identical plants which are sensitive to light are grown in four pots. Pot 1 is exposed to white light. Pot 2 is exposed to red light. Pot 3 is exposed to blue light, and pot 4 is kept in the dark. The plants growing in the four pots look different from each other. These differing appearances demonstrate that:

(A) A change in environmental condltions influences the process of differentiation

(B) Changes in less important proteins can cause changes in appearance

(C) Organ systems work together in such a way as to change the activity of the genes.

(D) The nucleus controls differentiation in the cell

(E) The cytoplasm controls the expression of genes in cells that differentiate

Question 97 refers to the following experiment.

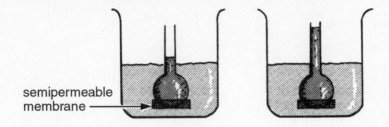

Experiment-

A thistle tube is filled with colored water and starch and immersed in distilled water. Distilled water has a 100% concentration of water molecules. A semipermeable membrane separates the starch solution from the water. The second diagram shows what has happened after time has elapsed.

97.   In what direction does the movement of liquid occur?

   (A) Down the concentration gradient

   (B) Up the concentration gradient

   (C) From an area of low concentration to an area of high concentration

   (D) Both (B) and (C)

   (E) Both (A) and (C)

Questions 98 - 100 refer to the following experiment described below.

Four test tubes are filled with H_2O. Five drops of phenol red, a solution that is pink when basic and yellow when acidic, is put in the test tubes. Carbon dioxide is added to Test Tubes 1 and 3 by blowing across them. The liquid turns yellow indicating the presence of CO_2 as carbonic acid (a weak acid). All four test tubes are put into a beaker with cold water and an Elodea leaf is put in Test Tubes 1 and 2. They are exposed to a bright light source. The results are:

Test Tube 1 (pink)	with leaf
Test Tube 2 (pink)	with leaf
Test Tube 3 (yellow)	without leaf
Test Tube 4 (pink)	without leaf

98.   In which test tube(s) are gas bubbles produced?

   (A) Test Tube 1   (D) Test Tube 4

   (B) Test Tube 2   (E) Test Tubes 1 and 2

   (C) Test Tube 3

99.   The gas referred to in question 118 is:

(A) Carbon monoxide

(B) Oxygen

(C) Carbon dioxide

(D) Hydrogen oxide

(E) ozone

100.   Which test tube(s) changed color upon exposure to the light source?

(A) Test Tube 1   (D) Test Tube 4

(B) Test Tube 2   (E) Test Tubes 1 and 2

(C) Test Tube 3

SECTION II

DIRECTIONS: Answer each of the following four questions in essay format. Each answer should be clear, organized and well-balanced. Diagrams may be used in addition to the discussion, but a diagram alone will not suffice. Suggested writing time per essay is 22 minutes.

1. Mitosis and meiosis use much of the same cellular machinery. There are some important differences, however, between them. Explain the differences according to:

   (A) Chromosomal movements and the action of the spindle apparatus (assume there are 4 chromosomes consisting of two homologous pairs)

   (B) The final result of the process with regard to number of chromosomes and genetic makeup of the cell

2. Explain how the properties of water make the following statement true:

   Water is essential to the sustenance of life.

3. The relationship of the predator and prey populations with each other represents a type of community interaction among species of organisms. In this essay you will focus on the unique interaction among predator and prey.

   Discuss the dependency that predator and prey have on each other with respect to their potential numbers in a given feeding area. Include a definition of predator. Discuss what types of organisms are susceptible to predators. Relate the "carrying capacity" of the predator population to the prey population. Explain why there is a lag of time between the growth of predator numbers and prey. The parasite/host relationship is a special kind of predator/prey relationship. Explain the difference. Include the definition of "parasite."

4. Respiration in aerobic organisms (such as man) is the intake of oxygen and the accompanying release of carbon dioxide. Discuss the respiration process as a four stage process.

   Stage 1 - Discuss how bulk oxygen gets from the external environment to the lungs. Include in your explanation the path taken by the air starting at the nose, the mechanical process of inhaling and exhaling, and the control center for that process.

   Stage 2 - Discuss how the oxygen gets across the membrane of the lungs and into the blood.

Stage 3 -   Discuss how oxygen gets from the blood to the tissues.

Stage 4 -   Discuss how carbon dioxide gets from the tissues to the blood and out the nasal passages.

ADVANCED PLACEMENT BIOLOGY EXAM VI

ANSWER KEY

1.	(E)	26.	(A)	51.	(D)	76.	(B)
2.	(A)	27.	(D)	52.	(A)	77.	(C)
3.	(C)	28.	(D)	53.	(E)	78.	(A)
4.	(A)	29.	(E)	54.	(B)	79.	(E)
5.	(D)	30.	(A)	55.	(A)	80.	(E)
6.	(A)	31.	(E)	56.	(C)	81.	(E)
7.	(C)	32.	(A)	57.	(A)	82.	(A)
8.	(A)	33.	(E)	58.	(E)	83.	(E)
9.	(B)	34.	(E)	59.	(B)	84.	(B)
10.	(E)	35.	(A)	60.	(B)	85.	(A)
11.	(B)	36.	(E)	61.	(C)	86.	(A)
12.	(A)	37.	(A)	62.	(A)	87.	(C)
13.	(C)	38.	(D)	63.	(B)	88.	(A)
14.	(B)	39.	(A)	64.	(E)	89.	(B)
15.	(A)	40.	(D)	65.	(A)	90.	(E)
16.	(E)	41.	(E)	66.	(E)	91.	(D)
17.	(A)	42.	(C)	67.	(E)	92.	(A)
18.	(B)	43.	(A)	68.	(D)	93.	(C)
19.	(A)	44.	(E)	69.	(D)	94.	(B)
20.	(E)	45.	(B)	70.	(A)	95.	(C)
21.	(A)	46.	(B)	71.	(C)	96.	(A)
22.	(E)	47.	(B)	72.	(E)	97.	(A)
23.	(B)	48.	(C)	73.	(B)	98.	(A)
24.	(C)	49.	(D)	74.	(C)	99.	(B)
25.	(E)	50.	(E)	75.	(B)	100.	(A)

ADVANCED PLACEMENT
BIOLOGY EXAM VI

DETAILED EXPLANATIONS
OF ANSWERS

SECTION I

1.　　**(E)**

Normally the biomass (the total dry weight of all living organisms that can be supported at each trophic level in a food chain) decreases with each succeeding trophic level.

2.　　**(A)**

The shorter the food chain, the less the usable energy that is lost. Thus, if plants are fed to livestock and livestock are in turn eaten by humans (with the accompanying energy loss at each trophic level), more energy would be lost than if humans ate plants directly.

3.　　**(C)**

Predation can affect the size, fitness, and evolution in a community, but food resources are often the factor that limits the carrying capacity of a population. It has not been shown that predation limits the carrying capacity of a population.

4.　　**(A)**

To describe the niche of a species, we must know what it eats, what eats it, what environment (weather, temperature, chemicals) it can handle, the type and size of its habitat, how it affects other species and the non-living environment, and how these factors affect it.

5.　　**(D)**

Carrying capacity is the maximum population that a given environment can support indefinitely. No population can grow rapidly indefinitely. Eventually, some resource is used up, and then the death rate will exceed the birth rate. Eventually, the population grows again until the birth rate and the death rate are about equal. The carrying capacity is determined by environmental conditions, and if these conditions do not change, the number of individuals supported remains about the same.

6.　　**(A)**

RNA polymerases are enzymes that catalyze the synthesis and assembly of nucleotide chains called RNA transcripts. These chains are formed using the unzipped area of the DNA double helix, which acts as a template for assembling the complementary base pairs. This process is called transcription.

7.　　**(C)**

The transfer RNA with its amino acid at one end carries that amino acid to the ribosome. There, the three-nucleotide combination of the tRNA (called an anticodon) positions itself at the binding site of a complementary mRNA codon. As a second tRNA moves into a binding site on the ribosomal mRNA, the amino acids from the anticodons align with each other by the formation of a peptide bond. This is the beginning of a growing chain of amino acids that will be linked together by peptide bonds.

8.　　**(A)**

Viruses are parasites in that they cannot multiply outside their host cell. They use the energy sources (B), metabolic machinery (C), and enzymes (D) of the host cell. Viruses do have the ability to replicate their genetic material DNA or RNA). They do so by inserting a copy of their genetic material and using the resources of the host cell to replicate the material and to form their own protein coats. The virus particle then escapes from the host cell and is ready to infect another host cell.

9.　　**(B)**

Transfer RNA is transcribed from the DNA of the cell and is found in the cytoplasm. It is clover-leaf shaped with an amino acid attached at one end and a loop at the other end containing three nucleotides (one of which is usually guanine). This sequence of three nucleotides is called an anticodon. During protein synthesis, the anticodon attaches itself to a complementary mRNA codon located in the ribosome. The amino acid of the tRNA forms a peptide bond with the amino acid of a second tRNA with its particular anticodon which has attached itself to an adjacent mRNA codon in the ribosome.

10.　　**(E)**

The fluid mosaic model of the cell membrane provides a model of the structure of a cell membrane.

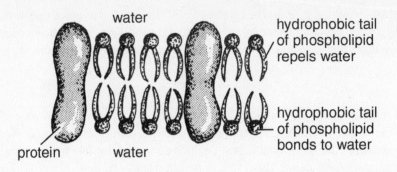

The phospholipids have a hydrophilic (water-loving) and a hydrophobic (water-fearing) tail. The lipids are hydrophobic. The proteins extending through the bilayer have hydrophobic regions where they are in contact with the hydrophobic phospholipid tails, and hydrophilic regions where they are in contact with the cytoplasm or the outer environment.

11. **(B)**

(A) and (E) apply to prokaryotic flagella. The microtubular arrangement in option (C) is the reverse of what it should be. The centrioles referred to in (D) are structurally similar to the basal bodies, but they are distributed differently in the cell and may play a role in the spindle formation that occurs during mitosis. (B) has the correct structure. The basal body from which the cilia and flagella arise has the 9 + 0 arrangement of microtubules.

12. **(A)**

An enzyme is a type of protein which catalyzes biological reactions. The surface geometry plays an important part in its specificity for substance molecules.

13. **(C)**

Coenzymes are small organic molecules that activate enzyme proteins. They are usually derived from water soluble vitamins, such as the B-complex. They are essential for the function of some enzymes. They are not proteins. They do not react directly with the substrate.

14. **(B)**

Photosynthesis occurs in chloroplasts which are located in the main body of the leaf (mesophyll). These chloroplasts are composed of a double outer membrane which surrounds the stroma (a semi-fluid matrix). Inside the stroma is a series of membranes that form a series of disks stacked on one another. Each disk is called a thylakoid, and it is here that the pigments necessary for photosynthesis are found, and where "the light" reactions of photosynthesis take place.

15.   **(A)**

When the water molecule is split (H-OH) by the NADP, the hydrogen ions from the water molecules are picked up by the NADP which becomes $NADPH_2$ and then enters the dark reaction. The OH loses an electron which is eventually recycled back to the chlorophyll molecule. The OH molecules from the splitting of water form O_2 and H_2O. Oxygen is considered a by-product of the light reaction of photosynthesis.

16.   **(E)**

If the H+ ions can be transported through the membrane, no concentration gradient of H+ ions can be established. In order for ATP to be synthesized, there must be an electrochemical gradient (H+ concentration and voltage gradient) to make energy available to power the synthesis.

17.   **(A)**

For a coupled reaction to occur, an exergonic (energy-releasing) reaction such as respiration must occur at the same time as an endergonic (energy-requiring) reaction such as photosynthesis. The energy that results from the exergonic reaction is used to make the endergonic reaction "go". The other options are incorrect.

18.   **(B)**

Both DNA and RNA have four bases. Adenine, guanine and cytosine are found on both. However, where DNA has thymine, RNA has uracil. Both DNA and RNA contain nucleotides (D). Therefore, (B) is the correct answer.

19.   **(A)**

The nucleosome consists of DNA as a connecting "string" that winds around histone proteins. An average gene is made up of three or four nucleosomes.

20.   **(E)**

Bacteriophages are viruses that attack bacteria by attaching themselves to the bacteria cell wall, injecting their genetic material into the cell and parasitizing it.

21.   **(A)**

When the two strands are cleaved between the G and A, the following separation results:

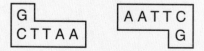

These single strands have complementary bases that protrude, and have sticky ends which are ready to receive a complementary sequence.

22.   **(E)**

The complementary bases for the protruding sticky end TTAA would be AATT, and the complementary bases for sticky end AATT would be TTAA.

23.   **(B)**

A change in a nucleotide of a codon sequence may or may not change the amino acid called for. However, an entire protein may be structurally and functionally altered upon the addition or deletion of a nucleotide.

24.   **(C)**

Use the following P_1 generation as an example of a dihybrid (two - trait) cross:

    B = black hair (dominant)

    b = blonde hair (recessive)

    G = grey eyes (dominant)

    g = blue eyes (recessive)

The P_1 gametes typical of a dihybrid cross (BG and bg) undergo fertilization producing an F_1 generation (BbGg) which then separates into the following gametes-BG, Bg, bG and bg. Each gamete is both male and female. Therefore, there is a total of four distinctly different gametes.

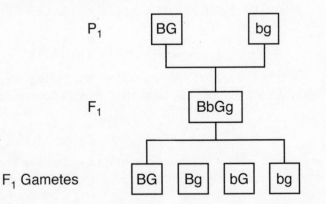

25.   **(E)**

The nine possible genotypes using the example of a dihybrid cross given in the answer to problem 55 are: BBGG, BBGg, BbGG, BbGg, BBgg, Bbgg, bbGG, bbGg and bbgg.

	BG	Bg	bG	bg	- female
BG	**BBGG**	**BBGg**	**BbGG**	**BbGg**	
Bg	BBGg	**BBgg**	BbGg	**Bbgg**	
bG	BbGG	BbGg	**bbGG**	**bbGg**	
bg	BbGg	Bbgg	bbGg	**bbgg**	

(male, on the left side: BG, Bg, bG, bg)

26.   **(A)**

Hemophilia is caused by a recessive gene that is found on the X chromosome. A woman who has this gene usually has a dominant normal gene on the other X chromosome and so doesn't have hemophilia. On the other hand, a man with the gene for hemophilia has no second X chromosome with a normal gene, so he will have hemophilia.

27.   **(D)**

The theory of Punctuated Equilibrium can account for the sudden appearance and disappearance of fossil species. The fossil record shows periods of stability with regard to appearance and disappearance of species as well as periods of sudden change.

28.   **(D)**

Classifying organisms by species is the basis for organizational systems such as the taxonomic, systematic, and evolutionary systems. "Species" is defined as a group of organisms that can interbreed and produce fertile offspring but not with members of other groups. The definition focuses on the biological aspects of organisms. (A), (C), and (E) are ways to classify organisms, but there are also other ways. (B) describes the grouping of species that are related to each other in some ways but distinct from one another in other ways. The fundamental unit is always the species.

29.   **(E)**

Prokaryotes are traditionally classified using absence or presence of cell wall and mode of nutrition. (E) is correct. Their reproductive patterns are not complex, (B), and some patterns (e.g. conjugation) are found in other kingdoms (e.g. Protists). Also, both Prokaryotes and most protists are unicellular (D), so this criterion cannot be used to distinguish one from the other.

30.   **(A)**

The kingdom Monera, (the prokaryotes) consists of two major divisions, the blue-green algae (cyanophyta) and the bacteria (schizophyta). They differ from the eukaryotes in that the DNA is in the form of a large single molecule in the cytoplasm and is not associated with histones (five basic proteins bound to the

DNA in eukaryotic cells). In addition, prokaryotes do not have a membrane-bound nucleus or membrane-bound organelles. Prokaryotic cell membranes do not have cholesterol and other steroids (as eukaryotes do), and the electron transport system is located on the membrane (in eukaryotes. it is found in the mitochondria). Finally, the cell walls of prokaryotes do not contain cellulose and other complex polysaccharides (as do eukaryotes). Instead, the cell walls can contain complex polymers (peptidoglycans), in addition to lipoproteins which are not found in eukaryotic cells.

31.   **(E)**

Prokaryotes (Monera) constitute a separate kingdom because their differences from eukaryotic cells are sufficient to warrant this separation.

32.   **(A)**

In the life cycle of fern, meiosis occurs in the sporangia (the bodies that produce haploid spores). These sporangia are located on the underside of the fronds of the diploid sporophyte. The single celled, haploid spores which result from meiosis undergo many cell divisions to produce a multicellular plant known as the gametophyte. The gametophyte produces gametes. When fertilization occurs, a diploid zygote results. The zygote is a new sporophyte. It undergoes cell division to produce, ultimately, a new adult sporophyte plant.

33.   **(E)**

In the alternation of generations life cycle, the gametophyte grows from the haploid spores released by the mature sporophyte plant. Mature gametophytes produce sperm cells and egg cells which are located in protective structures on the plant. Fertilization occurs when a sperm cell fuses with an egg cell, and the resulting zygote divides mitotically and gives rise to a mature diploid sporophyte.

34.   **(E)**

As plants evolved, the male gametophyte stage that is part of the life cycle of alternation of generations shrank in size. In angiosperms and gymnosperms, the pollen grain is the male gametophyte. The megaspore is the result of meiosis in the female structures. It divides several times and the multicellular structure is the megagametophyte. The remaining choices refer to reproductive structures of a flowering plant.

35.   **(A)**

The seed coat has protected the embryo from water and carbon dioxide until the conditions are favorable for growth and survival. Germination is initiated when water enters the seed coat which has been worn away or weakened by the elements. The seed coat then breaks and the embryo begins to grow into a young sporophyte.

36.   **(E)**

(A) and (B) are incorrect. Hormones of animals are produced in certain tissues but are transported to and affect other tissues. They can exert specific influences using very small quantities.

37.   **(A)**

A gravitropic response refers to the tendency of shoots to grow upward and of roots to grow downward even if the seedling is placed in an unfavorable position. Gravitropism is an important survival response for young plants. Photoperiodicity is a response to the duration and timing of light and dark conditions. Circadian refers to changes in response over a given time period, usually 24 hours. Phototropism is a directional response toward light.

38.   **(D)**

Cells which are similar in structure and function unite into tissues.

39.   **(A)**

The impulse received by the dendrite is then passed to the cell body of the nerve cell which then conducts it to the axon which carries the nerve impulse away from the cell body to other cells and organs. Neurons may vary in size, but they have a basic structure of dendrite, cell body, and axon. The nodes of Ranvier are found at breaks of myelin along the axon. They allow for impulse transmission. The synaptic bouton is found at the end of the axon, and releases neurotransmitters which stimulate the dendrites of the next nerve cell.

40.   **(D)**

Within the nephron and associated capillaries of the kidneys, three processes take place – filtration, secretion (B), and reabsorption (A). After filtration takes place, the filtrate passes into the nephron tubule where most of the water and solute that entered the nephron are returned to the bloodstream. This process is called reabsorption. Some substances such as metabolic wastes are also actively transported from the peritubular capillaries into the nephron tubule and they become part of the urine. This process is called secretion. Countercurrent multiplication (E) and countercurrent exchange (C) are processes that help to keep the osmotic gradient that is necessary for maintaining consistent solute concentrations in the urine. It takes place across the loop of Henle.

41.   **(E)**

The glomerulus (A), the loop of Henle (B) and Bowman's capsule (D) are part of the nephron. The urethra (C) is the structure used to remove urine from the body, but it is not part of the nephron.

42.   **(C)**

The memory cells are part of the secondary immune response. When the B-cells and T-cells initially clone to fight the first infection, some of the clones are not used. Instead they can be activated to clone when they later come in contact with the same antigen. The antigens may then be destroyed before they cause the disease.

43.   **(A)**

The graft will be least likely to be rejected if it comes from the person who approximates the patient's body chemistry as much as possible. An identical twin is the best choice. Drugs can be given to suppress the immune response, but as infection is a potential problem it is best not to suppress the general immune response.

44.   **(E)**

The sperm and the egg form within the parental reproductive system. The sperm grows a tail that will help it move to the egg cell, and the egg cytoplasm gains nutrient.

45.   **(B)**

Arteries carry blood away from the heart. They can expand and recoil thus forcing blood into the arterioles. These structures function in controlling blood flow distribution in the body by contraction and expansion of their diameters. The blood flows from the arterioles to the thin walled capillaries which have a large surface area for materials-exchange between blood and interstitial fluid. Capillaries merge into venules which then become veins that return blood to the heart.

46.   **(B)**

Cleavage occurs after fertilization. It is a time of cell division without a growth in size. As cleavage, proceeds. a blastula forms. The blastula is a hollow sphere with a cavity called the blastocoel, resulting in an embryo with three germinal layers. The archenteron is the primitive digestive cavity of the gastrula.

47.   **(B)**

Blood from the veins fills the atrial chambers then both atria are at rest. As blood fills the atrial chambers, pressure rises and the blood is forced into the ventricles by the contraction of the arteries when the pressure inside the atria becomes greater than the pressure inside the ventricles. The contraction of the atria is called "systole" and the relaxation of the atria is called diastole. When a measure of blood pressure is taken, both the systole and diastole readings are taken at large arteries. The systolic measurement is that of the highest pressure in the artery. The diastolic measurement is taken at the lowest pressure of the artery. Diastolic pressure is usually about 80 millimeters of Hg (Mercury).

48. **(C)**

The endoderm (A) gives rise to the inner lining of the digestive and respiratory tract, as well as the liver and pancreas. The ectoderm (B) gives rise to the epidermis and nervous system. The morula and blastula are early zygotic stages of division.

49. **(D)**

Animal diversity is primarily due to their mode of reproduction: sexual fertilization and meiosis. These patterns increase the chance of diversity in the offspring by the incorporation of crossing over and independent assortment of the chromosome complement of the gametes.

50. **(E)**

Each of these criteria is used in classifying animals.

51. **(D)**

Bilaterally symmetrical animals have three germ layers (ectoderm, mesoderm, and endoderm) and can move more efficiently than animals whose body structures are radially symmetrical. Bilateral symmetry is characteristic of higher level animals starting with the phylum platyhelminthes.

52. **(A)**

Bilateral symmetry means that the body is organized longitudinally having the left and right halves as approximate mirror images of the other. The existence of paired organs fit this criterion. The other options are not associated with bilateral symmetry. As bilateral symmetry evolved, animals developed anterior - posterior ends, dorsal-ventral orientation, and three germ layers-ectoderm, mesoderm, and endoderm.

53. **(E)**

The Hardy-Weinberg rule predicts that in the absence of agents of change (i.e., mutation, migration, natural selection), the frequencies of different alleles and genotypes in a population will remain stable.

54. **(B)**

Lysosomes are located in the cytoplasm. They contain digestive enzymes which break down molecules and malfunctioning cell parts.

55. **(A)**

The mitochondria, located in the cytoplasm, are the place where cellular respiration, which produces energy for activities in the cell, occurs.

56.   **(C)**

Some proteins pass through the endoplasmic reticulum and are enclosed in stacks of membrane which separate from the endoplasmic reticulum. This stacked membrane system is called the Golgi Bodies. Proteins may be changed and stored there until they are needed by the organism. The rough endoplasmic reticulum is the site of protein synthesis. The plasma membrane is the outer membrane of a cell.

57.   **(A)**

Phagocytosis or "cell-eating" refers to the engulfment of solid particles by amoebas and white blood cells of vertebrates. Endocytosis is the uptake of large particles across the cell membrane. It occurs by the invagination of the cell membrane until a membrane enclosed vesicle is pinched off within the cytoplasm. In exocytosis cellular excretions are enclosed in a membrane-bound vesicle which merges with the membrane and releases its contents to the extracellular environment.

58.   **(E)**

For osmosis to occur, there must be both a selectively permeable membrane and a concentration differential between the water solutions on either side of the membrane. The movement is from an area of higher concentration of water molecules (lower concentration of solute) to an area of lower concentration of water molecules.

59.   **(B)**

Active transport in a cell occurs when materials are moved across a membrane from an area of lower concentration (fewer water molecules) to an area of higher concentration (more water molecules). Since this movement is against a concentration gradient, energy is required.

60.   **(B)**

Allopatric speciation can occur when physical barriers between sections of a population prevent interbreeding among offspring.

61.   **(C)**

Sympatric speciation is a type of speciation that occurs without geographic isolation. Adaptive radiation results from the competition between two closely related species which diverge into two distinct and different species niches. Directional selection acts against one extreme characteristic, resulting in a population shift in one direction. Disruptive selection acts against individuals in the mid-part of a distribution, favoring both extremes. This results in a split into two subpopulations.

62.   **(A)**

The cuticle is on the epidermis, and is especially thick on the part closest to the sun.

63.   **(B)**

Most chloroplasts are located in the palisade layer. The chloroplasts are located closer to the leaf surface which puts them closer to the sun. The spongy layer (C) stores starch. The guard cells (D) control the degree to which the stoma (E) are open.

64.   **(E)**

Acoelomates, pseudocoelomates, and protostomes are all triloblastic, which means they have three tissue layers—ectoderm, endoderm, and mesoderm which is located between the ectoderm and the endoderm. The basic body plan of three-tissue layers, the characteristic of the acoelomates, becomes more complex as we shift from acoelomates to pseudocoelomates to protostomes.

65.   **(A)**

The microvillus is a thin extension of the surface of the animal cell that increases cellular absorption and secretion. They are found in great abundance in the small intestine of the human digestive tract.

66.   **(E)**

The peritonium is composed of a thin layer of connective tissue covered by moist epithelial cells which line the abdominal cavity containing the stomach, intestines, pancreas, and liver.

67.   **(E)**

Just as root growth is initiated by cell divisions in the apical meristem of the root. leaves are produced by the primordium apical meristem of the shoot.

68.   **(D)**

Lateral buds can also remain dormant during one stage of growth. They are located in the axil where the leaf joins the stem. The shoot is the stem with leaves. flowers. and other appendages. The node is the point on the stem where a leaf or bud was/is attached. The rhizome is an underground stem.

69.   **(D)**

During self-replication, the DNA unwinds at the weak hydrogen bonds which join the complementary base pairs. Free nucleotides in the environment become attached to the open bases of the parent strands if the proper catalyzing enzymes are present. The attachments follow the principle of complementary base pairing so that the strand produced is complementary, not identical, to the intact parent strand. The original strand acts as a "template" for the generation of a complementary strand.

70.　**(A)**

The sugar phosphate backbones run in opposite directions so that the nucleotide bases can align with and be bonded to their complimentary base in the DNA moecule. (B), (D), and (E) are synonyms for each other. Along with the hydrogen bonds (C), they form the "rungs," not the backbone, of the DNA ladder.

71.　**(C)**

In monocot seeds such as grasses, the hormone gibberellin stimulates the production of enzymes that convert the stored food in the endosperm into sugars and amino acids. These converted foods can be used by the seedling, causing the seed to shrink.

72.　**(E)**

Abscisic acid is a growth-inhibiting hormone. It also affects stomatal closures and plays a role in dormancy. Of the remaining choices, auxins promote cell elongation, cytokinins promote cell division, and ethylene stimulates fruit ripening, a function of the aging process.

73.　**(B)**

The ovule encloses and protects the female gametophyte which has developed from the megaspore.

74.　**(C)**

The ovary contains the ovules and will become the fruit of the angiosperm.

75.　**(B)**

The ovule located in the ovary is the structure from which the female gametophyte develops and which develops into the seed once fertilization occurs.

76.　**(B)**

The pancreas secretes all the enyymes except pepsin which is secreted by the stomach. The pancreas secretes a large number of enzymes which digest a wide range of foods – carbohydrates (amylase and disaecharidase), fats (lipase). proteins (trypsin); and nucleic acid.

77.　**(C)**

The digestion of proteins begins in the stomach which secretes the digestive enzyme pepsin. This enzyme breaks down the peptide bonds holding the proteins together. Further digestion of proteins is accomplished by the enzymes trypsin, chymotrypsin, and carboxypeptidase which are secreted by the pancreas.

78.   **(A)**

The microorganisms in circle 1 are nitrogen-fixing bacteria. They live in the soil and convert (or fix) the gaseous nitrogen into organic nitrogen-containing compounds (called nitrates -NO_3)which dissolve in soil and water and are taken in by plant roots.

79.   **(E)**

When plants and animals die, decomposing bacteria and fungi break down the larger organic nitrogen molecules in the dead bodies into forms of ammonia (NH_3). This process is called ammonification. The bacteria in circle 3 are nitrifyng bacteria which oxidize the forms of ammonia to nitrates (NO_2), a compound that is toxic to plants. The bacteria in circle 2 oxidize the nitrates which then can be used by plants.

80.   **(E)**

The mantle secretes the shell.

81.   **(E)**

Annelids are characterized by a one-way digestive tract, paired nephridia (excretory organs), a closed circulatory system, and a well-defined nervous system. Arthropods, the largest phylum in the animal kingdom, are characterized by a hard exoskeleton made of chitin and a complete digestive and nerve cord with paired ganglia. Characteristics that are common to both annelids and arthropods include a segmented body type and excretory mechanisms (nephridia in annelida and malpighian ducts in arthropods).

82.   **(A)**

Coelomate animals are divided into protostomes and deuterostomes according to the pattern of development by the embryo, but all have a coelom.

83.   **(B)**

When a system converts energy from one form to another, there is a loss of heat energy that cannot be used for useful work. For example, when an organism dies, the ordered pattern of molecules decays (facilitated by decay organisms) into smaller molecules that are spread throughout the environment. This tendency for a system to go to disorder is called entropy. (A) is wrong because it represents an orderly System that begins in an area (e.g., bare rock) that has not been previously occupied by a community of living things and proceeds through a series of growth stages until a climax community is realized. The clue is "orderly" succession, the opposite of entropy.

84. **(B)**

When an Rh-negative woman has an Rh-positive baby, the woman's blood will usually form antibodies at the time of delivery, when the infant's blood enters the mother's bloodstream. In subsequent pregnancies, these antibodies can be passed into the fetal bloodstream during the last month of pregnancy and cause destruction of the red blood cells of an Rh-positive fetus. This is called erythroblastosis fetalis.

85. **(A)**

An Rh-negative women can bear an Rh-positive baby if the father is Rh positive. "Rh positive" describes a genetically determined antigen (antigen D) found on the surface of red blood cells. A person with Rh-negative blood has no antigen D and will produce antibodies when exposed to an Rh-positive fetus.

86. **(A)**

Without subsequent addition of nutrients, the population will accelerate toward maximum growth. As the resources are depleted, fewer numbers can be supported and there is a decrease in the population.

87. **(C)**

The graph shows an ever-increasing number of individuals over a unit of time under ideal conditions. This is called 'exponential' or geometric growth. Graph (B) shows arithmetic growth which is non-characteristic of bacteria.

88. **(A)**

The I^A and I^B and ii are forms or alleles of the gene responsible for human ABO blood groups. The I^A and I^B are co-dominant when they are paired together. The "i" allele is recessive when paired with I^A or I^B. Mr. Smith has blood type AB. Therefore, he has the genotype $I^A I^B$ so he cannot be the father of baby 2 who has blood type O. This blood type has the genotype ii. Therefore the father must have had at least one "i" gene to pass on. Baby 1 has blood group A and could have either I^{Ai} or $I^A I^A$ genotype. Mr. Smith with blood type AB would contribute the I^A allele to Baby 1, while Mrs. Smith with blood type O would contribute the "i" allele resulting in Baby 1 having an $I^A i$ genotype.

89. **(B)**

Both Mr. and Mrs. Smith have blood group O which has the "ii" genotype. That "ii" form is both recessive to both I^A and I^B and would not come out unless both the mother and father contributed an "i" gene.

90. **(E)**

The difference is dramatic. The DDT affects the rats' ability to gain weight, reproduce, and resist disease.

91.   **(D)**

Adaptations arise primarily from natural selection. The diagrams (A), (B), and (C) represent three types of natural selection — stabilizing selection, disruptive selection, and directional selection, respectively.

92.   **(A)**

(A) represents a type of natural selection called "stabilizing selection." In this type, extreme phenotypes (e.g., low birth weight) are eliminated, and the most frequently occurring phenotypes are maintained in the population.

93.   **(C)**

In directional selection, a species adjusts gradually to changes in its environment with the result that a phenotypic character of a population shifts as a whole in a consistent direction. (B) is an example of disruptive selection. It favors extreme phenotypic characters. Such a shift results in two distinct subpopulations.

94.   **(B)**

Smooth muscle tissue is composed of small individual cells each with a single nucleus. The tissue is unstriated (no stripes when seen under the microscope) and is found in the walls of internal organs such as digestive organs. Smooth muscle is categorized as involuntary because contraction is not under the control of the organism. Type 1 represents a skeletal muscle tissue and Type 3 represents cardiac muscle tissue.

95.   **(C)**

Cardiac muscle cells are branched and shorter than skeletal muscle tissue. Cardiac muscle cells are fused end to end at locations called intercalated disks so that when one cell receives a message to contract, the other cells also contract. Both cardiac and smooth muscle tissue (Type 2) are unstriated and involuntary.

96.   **(A)**

Environmental conditions such as declining food supply, light and temperature serve as signals which influence those genes that are necessary for cell differentiation. (B), (D), and (E) can affect gene differentiation, but under different situations.

97.   **(A)**

The movement occurs from an area of high concentration to an area of low concentration. The area of high concentration is the distilled water (100% water molecules) and the area of lower concentration is the starch solution (with a lower percentage of water molecules).

98.   **(A)**

For photosynthesis to occur, carbon dioxide and water are needed as raw materials along with sunlight, an energy source. Carbon dioxide is present in the exhaled air (blown over the test tubes). One end product of photosynthesis is oxygen. The gas bubbles of oxygen were produced in Test Tube 1 because all the raw materials and the energy source were present.

99.   **(B)**

In the photosynthesis reaction, oxygen is produced as a by-product as carbon dioxide is used up.

100.   **(A)**

Test Tube 1 changed color because oxygen was produced as carbon dioxide was used up. The yellow color changed back to pink reflecting the decreased level of carbon dioxide.

SECTION II

ESSAY I

- In mitosis, chromosomes duplicate themselves before mitosis begins. When a chromosome is duplicated, it becomes in time, two chromatids joined by a centromere.
- In meiosis, chromosomes duplicate themselves before meiosis begins. When a chromosome is duplicated, it becomes, for a time, two chromatids joined by a centromere.

PROPHASE

- In mitosis chromosomes become visible, the nuclear envelope and nucleolus disappear and the mitotic spindle is formed.
- In mitosis chromosomes have doubled, forming 2 identical sister chromatids attached at the centromere.
- In meiosis each chromosome pair condenses and lines up with its homologue (One chromosome of a pair containing one of two genes that constitutes a gene pair). This lining up produces four chromosome equivalents apiece.
- In meiosis, crossing over occurs between nonsister chromatids of each homologous chromosome.

METAPHASE

- In mitosis, homologous chromosomes line up on the mitotic spindle on opposite sides of the midplane of the spindle.
- In meiosis four chromosomes, each made up of two identical sister chromatids, attached at the centromere line up on the midplane. The chromosomes line up without pairing.

ANAPHASE

- In mitosis the centromeres divide and each identical chromosome moves to the poles of the cell on the mitotic spindle. There is now a complete set of four chromosomes at each pole identical to the nucleus.
- In meiosis the homologous chromosomes separate and move to opposite poles. The chromosomes have formed two groups, each made up of 2 sister chromatids. Therefore the genetic material is not the same at the poles of the cell.

TELOPHASE

- In mitosis the chromosomes uncoil forming a mass of DNA
- In mitosis the nuclear membrane forms around each set of chromosomes.
- In mitosis the cytoplasm divides when the cell membrane is constricted down the middle and pinches apart. This process is called cytokinesis.
- In mitosis each daughter cell now has chromosomes identical to those in the parent nucleus.
- In meiosis, one of each pair of homologous chromosomes is clustered around each of the two spindle poles. The chromatids are still attached to the centromere. The cell starts to divide and the nuclear membrane reforms. The chromosome number will be haploid (one of each kind of chromosomes) but the centromeres remain. Prophase II begins.

PROPHASE II

- In each daughter cell the chromosomes prepare for the next division.
- The genetic material is not replicated before prophase II

METAPHASE II

- The spindles reform and the replicated chromosome aligns at the midplane of the spindle. The centromere divides and each replicated chromosome becomes two separate chromosomes.

ANAPHASE II

- The separate chromosomes move toward opposite ends of the spindle.
- The cytoplasm divides and the nuclear envelopes form.

TELOPHASE II

- Four daughter cells each with a haploid nucleus are formed. Each of the nuclei has one member of each pair of chromosomes from the original nucleus. From the 4 original chromosomes, each nucleus has two chromosomes.
- All haploid nuclei contain different genetic material due to crossing over and independent assortment.

ESSAY II

Living organisms are dependent on water for their existence. It is the most abundant biomolecule, comprising most of the mass of living cells. The chemical and physical properties of water, which make it so important, are the polarity, specific heat, heat of vaporization, heat of fusion, and the density of the liquid state.

Consisting of an oxygen covalently bonded to two hydrogens, there is polarity, or uneven distribution of charge, throughout the molecule of water. This allows it to form intermolecular bonds, giving water its unusual properties. The oxygen is more electronegative than the hydrogens, thus it tends to attract positive hydrogen atoms from other nearby water molecules, forming hydrogen bonds. As the bonds between water molecules form, a lattice pattern due to the repulsion of like charges is observed.

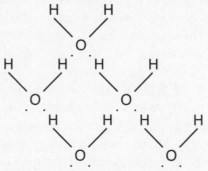

Polarity also affects water's adhesion to other surfaces, and gives rise to capillary action, where water is passively drawn upward. This is most important in plant roots, which use capillary action to obtain water from the soil. It makes water a good solvent for ionic com-pounds, such as salt (NaCl), giving rise to the term "hydrophilic" — water loving. Water's polarity also causes nonpolar substances to become "hydro-phobic" — water fearing — which makes them tend to group together, minimizing surface contact. If a substance is amphipathic, or has both hydrophilic and hydropho-bic tendencies, in water the substance would form a micelle, with the hydrophobic tails inside and hydrophilic heads outside.

This is important in cellular membrane formation.

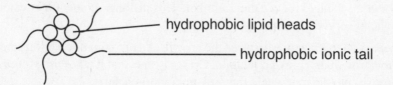

As expected, the cumulative effects of many hydrogen bonds give rise to its unusual properties. Water's specific heat, or the amount of heat required to raise the temperature of one gram of liquid by one degree Celsius, is greater than that of most other liquids because more heat is required to raise the kinetic energy. Since most cellular mass is water, this minimizes temperature fluctuations in the cell. This is important as most biologically significant reaction rates are temperature sensitive.

The heat of vaporization is also greater than that of most liquids. Water requires more heat to evaporate as the intermolecular hydrogen bonds must be broken to permit disassociation of molecules. Because it is an endergonic, or heat-absorbing reaction, this makes perspiration decrease body temperature.

About 80 calories of heat per gram is needed for heat of fusion, which causes a substance to change or go from the solid to the liquid state. This is also due to the number of hydrogen bonds. This moderates body temperatures for living organisms during external temperature fluctuations.

The density of most substances increases upon freezing; however, due to the lattice structure of the hydrogen bonding, this is not so with water. The maximum density of water is at four degrees Celsius. Below this, it expands, which causes it to be less dense than water. If it were more dense than water, it would sink to the bottom, killing the organisms in it. Since it floats on top of water, it sustains life in water bodies by keeping the water temperature below the ice layer relatively constant.

ESSAY III

- A predator is an organism that captures and eats organisms in order to get nutrients for growth and energy. The size of the predator population is dependent on the carrying capacity of the environment of the prey population. If the resources of the environment cannot support a critical mass of prey, the prey population may start to decrease, and eventually the predator population may also be adversely affected

- The prey numbers in a given feeding area may not be as adversely affected if the predator is territorial, and if the numbers of prey are larger than the predator can handle. Fish traveling in schools are an example of strength in numbers, since a predator cannot eat enough of them to decrease their numbers appreciably.

- Concentrations of predators on one part of a population (old, sick, young) can affect the prey population. In this case, the fittest may Survive to perpetuate the special genetic make-up that allowed them to survive to subsequent generations.

- Predators can also affect the actual numbers of a prey population by eating enough of them to reduce their number. This decrease could affect whether the prey can survive as a species or die out.

- There is often a lag time between the growth of a predator population in response to the growth of a prey population. One reason is that it takes time for predators to move into an area where the prey population is larger.

Another reason is that the size of the predator population is dependent on such natural factors as

- Fertility
- Natural catastrophes that may decimate a population
- The activities of man
- The activities of the "predators of the predators" in the food web

Some mechanisms that prey use to escape from predators include:

- mimicry — Some organisms escape from predators by looking or behaving like those prey that may have an offensive taste or behave aggressively enough toward predators that they might be frightened away.

- camouflage — Using protective coloring or behaving like a harmless plant or inanimate object (e.g. grass, rock), a prey organism can actually "hide" in the open.

- display behavior — Some organisms, when cornered, will behave in such a way as to startle or intimidate an attacker.

- Some organisms produce many young in a short period of time so that a predator cannot possibly eat all of them.

- Chemical defenses such as obnoxious odors can be sprayed toward attackers to drive them away.

- Some organisms hibernate, so that they "wake-up" a generation later and hopefully avoid their predators. The 17-year cicada is an example of an organism that hibernates.

- Some organisms burrow into the ground or take to higher ground to escape predators.

- The parasite/host relationship, while it may be a form of a predator/prey relationship, is primarily different in that the parasite gets nourishment from the host but usually does not kill the host outright. The host may die from weakness or infection, but it is not usually eaten by the parasite.

- Another difference is that the parasite is often smaller than the host, while a predator is usually bigger than the prey.

ESSAY IV

STAGE 1

- Air enters through the nose which is lined with cilia and hairs to trap dust.

- The nasal cavity is lined with epithelial cells which secrete mucus that keeps the air moist and warm as it travels to the lungs.

- The air goes to the pharynx or throat cavity.

- The air then goes to the larynx which contains the vocal chords.

- The air then goes to the trachea which branches into two bronchi, which in turn, subdivide into bronchioles that are located in the lungs.

- The exchange of oxygen for carbon dioxide occurs in the alveoli which are grape like clusters located at the ends of the smallest bronchioles.

- Changes in the pressure gradients between the alveoli and the atmosphere causes air to flow into and out of the chest cavity.

- These changes are the result of changes in the volume of the chest cavity which are caused by the contraction and relaxation of the diaphragm and the intercostal muscles.

- During exhalation the diaphragm contracts, moving downward and flattens while the intercostal muscles act to pull the rib cage up and out. Thus, the column of the chest cavity enlarges.

- Air pressure is then lower in the chest cavity than in the outside atmosphere. The pressure differential causes the air to move into the lungs resulting in the lung tissue enlarging.

- During exhalation, the muscles relax, the diaphragm returns to its original position, the volume of the chest cavity decreases, the air is forced out from the lungs, into the air tubes and out into the atmosphere.

- The respiratory center in the brainstem is called the medulla. It controls the rate of breathing and the amount of air that is taken in.

- The brainstem receives signals from parts of the body such as the lungs about the level of substances such as oxygen and carbon dioxide in the lungs and blood vessels. The respiratory center then sends signals to the diaphragm and intercostal muscles and they respond by contracting or relaxing.

STAGE 2

- The air coming into the alveoli has been warmed and made moist to prepare it for diffusion, a process that requires a thin membrane and a concentration differential.

- Oxygen from the air diffuses from the alveoli into the interstitial fluid (a connective tissue separating the alveoli from the capillaries) and into the capillaries.

- The alveoli have a large surface area which brings them into contact with many capillaries.

STAGE 3

- Oxygen transport is increased by the protein hemoglobin in the blood to which oxygen molecules can bind. The amount of oxygen that can bind to hemoglobin is directly proportional to the partial pressure of the oxygen.

- The hemoglobin gives up the oxygen more readily to a tissue which is undergoing increased metabolic activity and producing increased levels of carbon dioxide.

STAGE 4

- Blood flowing into the capillaries has a lower pressure of carbon dioxide compared to the level of carbon dioxide in the tissues. Therefore, the carbon dioxide diffuses from the tissue into the capillaries.

- Most carbon dioxide in the capillaries is carried in the blood in the form of a bicarbonate ion. This ion is formed when carbon dioxide and water form carbonic acid which then can dissociate into bicarbonate ions and hydrogen ions. This process is also reversible.

- The lower concentration of carbon dioxide in the alveoli (compared to that of the capillaries) causes the carbonic acid to dissociate into water and carbon dioxide. The carbon dioxide then diffuses into the alveoli, then into air passageways, and out into the atmosphere.

AP
BIOLOGY
ANSWER SHEETS

AP BIOLOGY
TEST 1

1.	Ⓐ Ⓑ Ⓒ Ⓓ Ⓔ	34.	Ⓐ Ⓑ Ⓒ Ⓓ Ⓔ	67.	Ⓐ Ⓑ Ⓒ Ⓓ Ⓔ
2.	Ⓐ Ⓑ Ⓒ Ⓓ Ⓔ	35.	Ⓐ Ⓑ Ⓒ Ⓓ Ⓔ	68.	Ⓐ Ⓑ Ⓒ Ⓓ Ⓔ
3.	Ⓐ Ⓑ Ⓒ Ⓓ Ⓔ	36.	Ⓐ Ⓑ Ⓒ Ⓓ Ⓔ	69.	Ⓐ Ⓑ Ⓒ Ⓓ Ⓔ
4.	Ⓐ Ⓑ Ⓒ Ⓓ Ⓔ	37.	Ⓐ Ⓑ Ⓒ Ⓓ Ⓔ	70.	Ⓐ Ⓑ Ⓒ Ⓓ Ⓔ
5.	Ⓐ Ⓑ Ⓒ Ⓓ Ⓔ	38.	Ⓐ Ⓑ Ⓒ Ⓓ Ⓔ	71.	Ⓐ Ⓑ Ⓒ Ⓓ Ⓔ
6.	Ⓐ Ⓑ Ⓒ Ⓓ Ⓔ	39.	Ⓐ Ⓑ Ⓒ Ⓓ Ⓔ	72.	Ⓐ Ⓑ Ⓒ Ⓓ Ⓔ
7.	Ⓐ Ⓑ Ⓒ Ⓓ Ⓔ	40.	Ⓐ Ⓑ Ⓒ Ⓓ Ⓔ	73.	Ⓐ Ⓑ Ⓒ Ⓓ Ⓔ
8.	Ⓐ Ⓑ Ⓒ Ⓓ Ⓔ	41.	Ⓐ Ⓑ Ⓒ Ⓓ Ⓔ	74.	Ⓐ Ⓑ Ⓒ Ⓓ Ⓔ
9.	Ⓐ Ⓑ Ⓒ Ⓓ Ⓔ	42.	Ⓐ Ⓑ Ⓒ Ⓓ Ⓔ	75.	Ⓐ Ⓑ Ⓒ Ⓓ Ⓔ
10.	Ⓐ Ⓑ Ⓒ Ⓓ Ⓔ	43.	Ⓐ Ⓑ Ⓒ Ⓓ Ⓔ	76.	Ⓐ Ⓑ Ⓒ Ⓓ Ⓔ
11.	Ⓐ Ⓑ Ⓒ Ⓓ Ⓔ	44.	Ⓐ Ⓑ Ⓒ Ⓓ Ⓔ	77.	Ⓐ Ⓑ Ⓒ Ⓓ Ⓔ
12.	Ⓐ Ⓑ Ⓒ Ⓓ Ⓔ	45.	Ⓐ Ⓑ Ⓒ Ⓓ Ⓔ	78.	Ⓐ Ⓑ Ⓒ Ⓓ Ⓔ
13.	Ⓐ Ⓑ Ⓒ Ⓓ Ⓔ	46.	Ⓐ Ⓑ Ⓒ Ⓓ Ⓔ	79.	Ⓐ Ⓑ Ⓒ Ⓓ Ⓔ
14.	Ⓐ Ⓑ Ⓒ Ⓓ Ⓔ	47.	Ⓐ Ⓑ Ⓒ Ⓓ Ⓔ	80.	Ⓐ Ⓑ Ⓒ Ⓓ Ⓔ
15.	Ⓐ Ⓑ Ⓒ Ⓓ Ⓔ	48.	Ⓐ Ⓑ Ⓒ Ⓓ Ⓔ	81.	Ⓐ Ⓑ Ⓒ Ⓓ Ⓔ
16.	Ⓐ Ⓑ Ⓒ Ⓓ Ⓔ	49.	Ⓐ Ⓑ Ⓒ Ⓓ Ⓔ	82.	Ⓐ Ⓑ Ⓒ Ⓓ Ⓔ
17.	Ⓐ Ⓑ Ⓒ Ⓓ Ⓔ	50.	Ⓐ Ⓑ Ⓒ Ⓓ Ⓔ	83.	Ⓐ Ⓑ Ⓒ Ⓓ Ⓔ
18.	Ⓐ Ⓑ Ⓒ Ⓓ Ⓔ	51.	Ⓐ Ⓑ Ⓒ Ⓓ Ⓔ	84.	Ⓐ Ⓑ Ⓒ Ⓓ Ⓔ
19.	Ⓐ Ⓑ Ⓒ Ⓓ Ⓔ	52.	Ⓐ Ⓑ Ⓒ Ⓓ Ⓔ	85.	Ⓐ Ⓑ Ⓒ Ⓓ Ⓔ
20.	Ⓐ Ⓑ Ⓒ Ⓓ Ⓔ	53.	Ⓐ Ⓑ Ⓒ Ⓓ Ⓔ	86.	Ⓐ Ⓑ Ⓒ Ⓓ Ⓔ
21.	Ⓐ Ⓑ Ⓒ Ⓓ Ⓔ	54.	Ⓐ Ⓑ Ⓒ Ⓓ Ⓔ	87.	Ⓐ Ⓑ Ⓒ Ⓓ Ⓔ
22.	Ⓐ Ⓑ Ⓒ Ⓓ Ⓔ	55.	Ⓐ Ⓑ Ⓒ Ⓓ Ⓔ	88.	Ⓐ Ⓑ Ⓒ Ⓓ Ⓔ
23.	Ⓐ Ⓑ Ⓒ Ⓓ Ⓔ	56.	Ⓐ Ⓑ Ⓒ Ⓓ Ⓔ	89.	Ⓐ Ⓑ Ⓒ Ⓓ Ⓔ
24.	Ⓐ Ⓑ Ⓒ Ⓓ Ⓔ	57.	Ⓐ Ⓑ Ⓒ Ⓓ Ⓔ	90.	Ⓐ Ⓑ Ⓒ Ⓓ Ⓔ
25.	Ⓐ Ⓑ Ⓒ Ⓓ Ⓔ	58.	Ⓐ Ⓑ Ⓒ Ⓓ Ⓔ	91.	Ⓐ Ⓑ Ⓒ Ⓓ Ⓔ
26.	Ⓐ Ⓑ Ⓒ Ⓓ Ⓔ	59.	Ⓐ Ⓑ Ⓒ Ⓓ Ⓔ	92.	Ⓐ Ⓑ Ⓒ Ⓓ Ⓔ
27.	Ⓐ Ⓑ Ⓒ Ⓓ Ⓔ	60.	Ⓐ Ⓑ Ⓒ Ⓓ Ⓔ	93.	Ⓐ Ⓑ Ⓒ Ⓓ Ⓔ
28.	Ⓐ Ⓑ Ⓒ Ⓓ Ⓔ	61.	Ⓐ Ⓑ Ⓒ Ⓓ Ⓔ	94.	Ⓐ Ⓑ Ⓒ Ⓓ Ⓔ
29.	Ⓐ Ⓑ Ⓒ Ⓓ Ⓔ	62.	Ⓐ Ⓑ Ⓒ Ⓓ Ⓔ	95.	Ⓐ Ⓑ Ⓒ Ⓓ Ⓔ
30.	Ⓐ Ⓑ Ⓒ Ⓓ Ⓔ	63.	Ⓐ Ⓑ Ⓒ Ⓓ Ⓔ	96.	Ⓐ Ⓑ Ⓒ Ⓓ Ⓔ
31.	Ⓐ Ⓑ Ⓒ Ⓓ Ⓔ	64.	Ⓐ Ⓑ Ⓒ Ⓓ Ⓔ	97.	Ⓐ Ⓑ Ⓒ Ⓓ Ⓔ
32.	Ⓐ Ⓑ Ⓒ Ⓓ Ⓔ	65.	Ⓐ Ⓑ Ⓒ Ⓓ Ⓔ	98.	Ⓐ Ⓑ Ⓒ Ⓓ Ⓔ
33.	Ⓐ Ⓑ Ⓒ Ⓓ Ⓔ	66.	Ⓐ Ⓑ Ⓒ Ⓓ Ⓔ	99.	Ⓐ Ⓑ Ⓒ Ⓓ Ⓔ
				100.	Ⓐ Ⓑ Ⓒ Ⓓ Ⓔ

AP BIOLOGY
TEST 2

1. Ⓐ Ⓑ Ⓒ Ⓓ Ⓔ	34. Ⓐ Ⓑ Ⓒ Ⓓ Ⓔ	67. Ⓐ Ⓑ Ⓒ Ⓓ Ⓔ
2. Ⓐ Ⓑ Ⓒ Ⓓ Ⓔ	35. Ⓐ Ⓑ Ⓒ Ⓓ Ⓔ	68. Ⓐ Ⓑ Ⓒ Ⓓ Ⓔ
3. Ⓐ Ⓑ Ⓒ Ⓓ Ⓔ	36. Ⓐ Ⓑ Ⓒ Ⓓ Ⓔ	69. Ⓐ Ⓑ Ⓒ Ⓓ Ⓔ
4. Ⓐ Ⓑ Ⓒ Ⓓ Ⓔ	37. Ⓐ Ⓑ Ⓒ Ⓓ Ⓔ	70. Ⓐ Ⓑ Ⓒ Ⓓ Ⓔ
5. Ⓐ Ⓑ Ⓒ Ⓓ Ⓔ	38. Ⓐ Ⓑ Ⓒ Ⓓ Ⓔ	71. Ⓐ Ⓑ Ⓒ Ⓓ Ⓔ
6. Ⓐ Ⓑ Ⓒ Ⓓ Ⓔ	39. Ⓐ Ⓑ Ⓒ Ⓓ Ⓔ	72. Ⓐ Ⓑ Ⓒ Ⓓ Ⓔ
7. Ⓐ Ⓑ Ⓒ Ⓓ Ⓔ	40. Ⓐ Ⓑ Ⓒ Ⓓ Ⓔ	73. Ⓐ Ⓑ Ⓒ Ⓓ Ⓔ
8. Ⓐ Ⓑ Ⓒ Ⓓ Ⓔ	41. Ⓐ Ⓑ Ⓒ Ⓓ Ⓔ	74. Ⓐ Ⓑ Ⓒ Ⓓ Ⓔ
9. Ⓐ Ⓑ Ⓒ Ⓓ Ⓔ	42. Ⓐ Ⓑ Ⓒ Ⓓ Ⓔ	75. Ⓐ Ⓑ Ⓒ Ⓓ Ⓔ
10. Ⓐ Ⓑ Ⓒ Ⓓ Ⓔ	43. Ⓐ Ⓑ Ⓒ Ⓓ Ⓔ	76. Ⓐ Ⓑ Ⓒ Ⓓ Ⓔ
11. Ⓐ Ⓑ Ⓒ Ⓓ Ⓔ	44. Ⓐ Ⓑ Ⓒ Ⓓ Ⓔ	77. Ⓐ Ⓑ Ⓒ Ⓓ Ⓔ
12. Ⓐ Ⓑ Ⓒ Ⓓ Ⓔ	45. Ⓐ Ⓑ Ⓒ Ⓓ Ⓔ	78. Ⓐ Ⓑ Ⓒ Ⓓ Ⓔ
13. Ⓐ Ⓑ Ⓒ Ⓓ Ⓔ	46. Ⓐ Ⓑ Ⓒ Ⓓ Ⓔ	79. Ⓐ Ⓑ Ⓒ Ⓓ Ⓔ
14. Ⓐ Ⓑ Ⓒ Ⓓ Ⓔ	47. Ⓐ Ⓑ Ⓒ Ⓓ Ⓔ	80. Ⓐ Ⓑ Ⓒ Ⓓ Ⓔ
15. Ⓐ Ⓑ Ⓒ Ⓓ Ⓔ	48. Ⓐ Ⓑ Ⓒ Ⓓ Ⓔ	81. Ⓐ Ⓑ Ⓒ Ⓓ Ⓔ
16. Ⓐ Ⓑ Ⓒ Ⓓ Ⓔ	49. Ⓐ Ⓑ Ⓒ Ⓓ Ⓔ	82. Ⓐ Ⓑ Ⓒ Ⓓ Ⓔ
17. Ⓐ Ⓑ Ⓒ Ⓓ Ⓔ	50. Ⓐ Ⓑ Ⓒ Ⓓ Ⓔ	83. Ⓐ Ⓑ Ⓒ Ⓓ Ⓔ
18. Ⓐ Ⓑ Ⓒ Ⓓ Ⓔ	51. Ⓐ Ⓑ Ⓒ Ⓓ Ⓔ	84. Ⓐ Ⓑ Ⓒ Ⓓ Ⓔ
19. Ⓐ Ⓑ Ⓒ Ⓓ Ⓔ	52. Ⓐ Ⓑ Ⓒ Ⓓ Ⓔ	85. Ⓐ Ⓑ Ⓒ Ⓓ Ⓔ
20. Ⓐ Ⓑ Ⓒ Ⓓ Ⓔ	53. Ⓐ Ⓑ Ⓒ Ⓓ Ⓔ	86. Ⓐ Ⓑ Ⓒ Ⓓ Ⓔ
21. Ⓐ Ⓑ Ⓒ Ⓓ Ⓔ	54. Ⓐ Ⓑ Ⓒ Ⓓ Ⓔ	87. Ⓐ Ⓑ Ⓒ Ⓓ Ⓔ
22. Ⓐ Ⓑ Ⓒ Ⓓ Ⓔ	55. Ⓐ Ⓑ Ⓒ Ⓓ Ⓔ	88. Ⓐ Ⓑ Ⓒ Ⓓ Ⓔ
23. Ⓐ Ⓑ Ⓒ Ⓓ Ⓔ	56. Ⓐ Ⓑ Ⓒ Ⓓ Ⓔ	89. Ⓐ Ⓑ Ⓒ Ⓓ Ⓔ
24. Ⓐ Ⓑ Ⓒ Ⓓ Ⓔ	57. Ⓐ Ⓑ Ⓒ Ⓓ Ⓔ	90. Ⓐ Ⓑ Ⓒ Ⓓ Ⓔ
25. Ⓐ Ⓑ Ⓒ Ⓓ Ⓔ	58. Ⓐ Ⓑ Ⓒ Ⓓ Ⓔ	91. Ⓐ Ⓑ Ⓒ Ⓓ Ⓔ
26. Ⓐ Ⓑ Ⓒ Ⓓ Ⓔ	59. Ⓐ Ⓑ Ⓒ Ⓓ Ⓔ	92. Ⓐ Ⓑ Ⓒ Ⓓ Ⓔ
27. Ⓐ Ⓑ Ⓒ Ⓓ Ⓔ	60. Ⓐ Ⓑ Ⓒ Ⓓ Ⓔ	93. Ⓐ Ⓑ Ⓒ Ⓓ Ⓔ
28. Ⓐ Ⓑ Ⓒ Ⓓ Ⓔ	61. Ⓐ Ⓑ Ⓒ Ⓓ Ⓔ	94. Ⓐ Ⓑ Ⓒ Ⓓ Ⓔ
29. Ⓐ Ⓑ Ⓒ Ⓓ Ⓔ	62. Ⓐ Ⓑ Ⓒ Ⓓ Ⓔ	95. Ⓐ Ⓑ Ⓒ Ⓓ Ⓔ
30. Ⓐ Ⓑ Ⓒ Ⓓ Ⓔ	63. Ⓐ Ⓑ Ⓒ Ⓓ Ⓔ	96. Ⓐ Ⓑ Ⓒ Ⓓ Ⓔ
31. Ⓐ Ⓑ Ⓒ Ⓓ Ⓔ	64. Ⓐ Ⓑ Ⓒ Ⓓ Ⓔ	97. Ⓐ Ⓑ Ⓒ Ⓓ Ⓔ
32. Ⓐ Ⓑ Ⓒ Ⓓ Ⓔ	65. Ⓐ Ⓑ Ⓒ Ⓓ Ⓔ	98. Ⓐ Ⓑ Ⓒ Ⓓ Ⓔ
33. Ⓐ Ⓑ Ⓒ Ⓓ Ⓔ	66. Ⓐ Ⓑ Ⓒ Ⓓ Ⓔ	99. Ⓐ Ⓑ Ⓒ Ⓓ Ⓔ
		100. Ⓐ Ⓑ Ⓒ Ⓓ Ⓔ

AP BIOLOGY
TEST 3

1. Ⓐ Ⓑ Ⓒ Ⓓ Ⓔ	34. Ⓐ Ⓑ Ⓒ Ⓓ Ⓔ	67. Ⓐ Ⓑ Ⓒ Ⓓ Ⓔ
2. Ⓐ Ⓑ Ⓒ Ⓓ Ⓔ	35. Ⓐ Ⓑ Ⓒ Ⓓ Ⓔ	68. Ⓐ Ⓑ Ⓒ Ⓓ Ⓔ
3. Ⓐ Ⓑ Ⓒ Ⓓ Ⓔ	36. Ⓐ Ⓑ Ⓒ Ⓓ Ⓔ	69. Ⓐ Ⓑ Ⓒ Ⓓ Ⓔ
4. Ⓐ Ⓑ Ⓒ Ⓓ Ⓔ	37. Ⓐ Ⓑ Ⓒ Ⓓ Ⓔ	70. Ⓐ Ⓑ Ⓒ Ⓓ Ⓔ
5. Ⓐ Ⓑ Ⓒ Ⓓ Ⓔ	38. Ⓐ Ⓑ Ⓒ Ⓓ Ⓔ	71. Ⓐ Ⓑ Ⓒ Ⓓ Ⓔ
6. Ⓐ Ⓑ Ⓒ Ⓓ Ⓔ	39. Ⓐ Ⓑ Ⓒ Ⓓ Ⓔ	72. Ⓐ Ⓑ Ⓒ Ⓓ Ⓔ
7. Ⓐ Ⓑ Ⓒ Ⓓ Ⓔ	40. Ⓐ Ⓑ Ⓒ Ⓓ Ⓔ	73. Ⓐ Ⓑ Ⓒ Ⓓ Ⓔ
8. Ⓐ Ⓑ Ⓒ Ⓓ Ⓔ	41. Ⓐ Ⓑ Ⓒ Ⓓ Ⓔ	74. Ⓐ Ⓑ Ⓒ Ⓓ Ⓔ
9. Ⓐ Ⓑ Ⓒ Ⓓ Ⓔ	42. Ⓐ Ⓑ Ⓒ Ⓓ Ⓔ	75. Ⓐ Ⓑ Ⓒ Ⓓ Ⓔ
10. Ⓐ Ⓑ Ⓒ Ⓓ Ⓔ	43. Ⓐ Ⓑ Ⓒ Ⓓ Ⓔ	76. Ⓐ Ⓑ Ⓒ Ⓓ Ⓔ
11. Ⓐ Ⓑ Ⓒ Ⓓ Ⓔ	44. Ⓐ Ⓑ Ⓒ Ⓓ Ⓔ	77. Ⓐ Ⓑ Ⓒ Ⓓ Ⓔ
12. Ⓐ Ⓑ Ⓒ Ⓓ Ⓔ	45. Ⓐ Ⓑ Ⓒ Ⓓ Ⓔ	78. Ⓐ Ⓑ Ⓒ Ⓓ Ⓔ
13. Ⓐ Ⓑ Ⓒ Ⓓ Ⓔ	46. Ⓐ Ⓑ Ⓒ Ⓓ Ⓔ	79. Ⓐ Ⓑ Ⓒ Ⓓ Ⓔ
14. Ⓐ Ⓑ Ⓒ Ⓓ Ⓔ	47. Ⓐ Ⓑ Ⓒ Ⓓ Ⓔ	80. Ⓐ Ⓑ Ⓒ Ⓓ Ⓔ
15. Ⓐ Ⓑ Ⓒ Ⓓ Ⓔ	48. Ⓐ Ⓑ Ⓒ Ⓓ Ⓔ	81. Ⓐ Ⓑ Ⓒ Ⓓ Ⓔ
16. Ⓐ Ⓑ Ⓒ Ⓓ Ⓔ	49. Ⓐ Ⓑ Ⓒ Ⓓ Ⓔ	82. Ⓐ Ⓑ Ⓒ Ⓓ Ⓔ
17. Ⓐ Ⓑ Ⓒ Ⓓ Ⓔ	50. Ⓐ Ⓑ Ⓒ Ⓓ Ⓔ	83. Ⓐ Ⓑ Ⓒ Ⓓ Ⓔ
18. Ⓐ Ⓑ Ⓒ Ⓓ Ⓔ	51. Ⓐ Ⓑ Ⓒ Ⓓ Ⓔ	84. Ⓐ Ⓑ Ⓒ Ⓓ Ⓔ
19. Ⓐ Ⓑ Ⓒ Ⓓ Ⓔ	52. Ⓐ Ⓑ Ⓒ Ⓓ Ⓔ	85. Ⓐ Ⓑ Ⓒ Ⓓ Ⓔ
20. Ⓐ Ⓑ Ⓒ Ⓓ Ⓔ	53. Ⓐ Ⓑ Ⓒ Ⓓ Ⓔ	86. Ⓐ Ⓑ Ⓒ Ⓓ Ⓔ
21. Ⓐ Ⓑ Ⓒ Ⓓ Ⓔ	54. Ⓐ Ⓑ Ⓒ Ⓓ Ⓔ	87. Ⓐ Ⓑ Ⓒ Ⓓ Ⓔ
22. Ⓐ Ⓑ Ⓒ Ⓓ Ⓔ	55. Ⓐ Ⓑ Ⓒ Ⓓ Ⓔ	88. Ⓐ Ⓑ Ⓒ Ⓓ Ⓔ
23. Ⓐ Ⓑ Ⓒ Ⓓ Ⓔ	56. Ⓐ Ⓑ Ⓒ Ⓓ Ⓔ	89. Ⓐ Ⓑ Ⓒ Ⓓ Ⓔ
24. Ⓐ Ⓑ Ⓒ Ⓓ Ⓔ	57. Ⓐ Ⓑ Ⓒ Ⓓ Ⓔ	90. Ⓐ Ⓑ Ⓒ Ⓓ Ⓔ
25. Ⓐ Ⓑ Ⓒ Ⓓ Ⓔ	58. Ⓐ Ⓑ Ⓒ Ⓓ Ⓔ	91. Ⓐ Ⓑ Ⓒ Ⓓ Ⓔ
26. Ⓐ Ⓑ Ⓒ Ⓓ Ⓔ	59. Ⓐ Ⓑ Ⓒ Ⓓ Ⓔ	92. Ⓐ Ⓑ Ⓒ Ⓓ Ⓔ
27. Ⓐ Ⓑ Ⓒ Ⓓ Ⓔ	60. Ⓐ Ⓑ Ⓒ Ⓓ Ⓔ	93. Ⓐ Ⓑ Ⓒ Ⓓ Ⓔ
28. Ⓐ Ⓑ Ⓒ Ⓓ Ⓔ	61. Ⓐ Ⓑ Ⓒ Ⓓ Ⓔ	94. Ⓐ Ⓑ Ⓒ Ⓓ Ⓔ
29. Ⓐ Ⓑ Ⓒ Ⓓ Ⓔ	62. Ⓐ Ⓑ Ⓒ Ⓓ Ⓔ	95. Ⓐ Ⓑ Ⓒ Ⓓ Ⓔ
30. Ⓐ Ⓑ Ⓒ Ⓓ Ⓔ	63. Ⓐ Ⓑ Ⓒ Ⓓ Ⓔ	96. Ⓐ Ⓑ Ⓒ Ⓓ Ⓔ
31. Ⓐ Ⓑ Ⓒ Ⓓ Ⓔ	64. Ⓐ Ⓑ Ⓒ Ⓓ Ⓔ	97. Ⓐ Ⓑ Ⓒ Ⓓ Ⓔ
32. Ⓐ Ⓑ Ⓒ Ⓓ Ⓔ	65. Ⓐ Ⓑ Ⓒ Ⓓ Ⓔ	98. Ⓐ Ⓑ Ⓒ Ⓓ Ⓔ
33. Ⓐ Ⓑ Ⓒ Ⓓ Ⓔ	66. Ⓐ Ⓑ Ⓒ Ⓓ Ⓔ	99. Ⓐ Ⓑ Ⓒ Ⓓ Ⓔ
		100. Ⓐ Ⓑ Ⓒ Ⓓ Ⓔ

AP BIOLOGY
TEST 4

1. Ⓐ Ⓑ Ⓒ Ⓓ Ⓔ	34. Ⓐ Ⓑ Ⓒ Ⓓ Ⓔ	67. Ⓐ Ⓑ Ⓒ Ⓓ Ⓔ
2. Ⓐ Ⓑ Ⓒ Ⓓ Ⓔ	35. Ⓐ Ⓑ Ⓒ Ⓓ Ⓔ	68. Ⓐ Ⓑ Ⓒ Ⓓ Ⓔ
3. Ⓐ Ⓑ Ⓒ Ⓓ Ⓔ	36. Ⓐ Ⓑ Ⓒ Ⓓ Ⓔ	69. Ⓐ Ⓑ Ⓒ Ⓓ Ⓔ
4. Ⓐ Ⓑ Ⓒ Ⓓ Ⓔ	37. Ⓐ Ⓑ Ⓒ Ⓓ Ⓔ	70. Ⓐ Ⓑ Ⓒ Ⓓ Ⓔ
5. Ⓐ Ⓑ Ⓒ Ⓓ Ⓔ	38. Ⓐ Ⓑ Ⓒ Ⓓ Ⓔ	71. Ⓐ Ⓑ Ⓒ Ⓓ Ⓔ
6. Ⓐ Ⓑ Ⓒ Ⓓ Ⓔ	39. Ⓐ Ⓑ Ⓒ Ⓓ Ⓔ	72. Ⓐ Ⓑ Ⓒ Ⓓ Ⓔ
7. Ⓐ Ⓑ Ⓒ Ⓓ Ⓔ	40. Ⓐ Ⓑ Ⓒ Ⓓ Ⓔ	73. Ⓐ Ⓑ Ⓒ Ⓓ Ⓔ
8. Ⓐ Ⓑ Ⓒ Ⓓ Ⓔ	41. Ⓐ Ⓑ Ⓒ Ⓓ Ⓔ	74. Ⓐ Ⓑ Ⓒ Ⓓ Ⓔ
9. Ⓐ Ⓑ Ⓒ Ⓓ Ⓔ	42. Ⓐ Ⓑ Ⓒ Ⓓ Ⓔ	75. Ⓐ Ⓑ Ⓒ Ⓓ Ⓔ
10. Ⓐ Ⓑ Ⓒ Ⓓ Ⓔ	43. Ⓐ Ⓑ Ⓒ Ⓓ Ⓔ	76. Ⓐ Ⓑ Ⓒ Ⓓ Ⓔ
11. Ⓐ Ⓑ Ⓒ Ⓓ Ⓔ	44. Ⓐ Ⓑ Ⓒ Ⓓ Ⓔ	77. Ⓐ Ⓑ Ⓒ Ⓓ Ⓔ
12. Ⓐ Ⓑ Ⓒ Ⓓ Ⓔ	45. Ⓐ Ⓑ Ⓒ Ⓓ Ⓔ	78. Ⓐ Ⓑ Ⓒ Ⓓ Ⓔ
13. Ⓐ Ⓑ Ⓒ Ⓓ Ⓔ	46. Ⓐ Ⓑ Ⓒ Ⓓ Ⓔ	79. Ⓐ Ⓑ Ⓒ Ⓓ Ⓔ
14. Ⓐ Ⓑ Ⓒ Ⓓ Ⓔ	47. Ⓐ Ⓑ Ⓒ Ⓓ Ⓔ	80. Ⓐ Ⓑ Ⓒ Ⓓ Ⓔ
15. Ⓐ Ⓑ Ⓒ Ⓓ Ⓔ	48. Ⓐ Ⓑ Ⓒ Ⓓ Ⓔ	81. Ⓐ Ⓑ Ⓒ Ⓓ Ⓔ
16. Ⓐ Ⓑ Ⓒ Ⓓ Ⓔ	49. Ⓐ Ⓑ Ⓒ Ⓓ Ⓔ	82. Ⓐ Ⓑ Ⓒ Ⓓ Ⓔ
17. Ⓐ Ⓑ Ⓒ Ⓓ Ⓔ	50. Ⓐ Ⓑ Ⓒ Ⓓ Ⓔ	83. Ⓐ Ⓑ Ⓒ Ⓓ Ⓔ
18. Ⓐ Ⓑ Ⓒ Ⓓ Ⓔ	51. Ⓐ Ⓑ Ⓒ Ⓓ Ⓔ	84. Ⓐ Ⓑ Ⓒ Ⓓ Ⓔ
19. Ⓐ Ⓑ Ⓒ Ⓓ Ⓔ	52. Ⓐ Ⓑ Ⓒ Ⓓ Ⓔ	85. Ⓐ Ⓑ Ⓒ Ⓓ Ⓔ
20. Ⓐ Ⓑ Ⓒ Ⓓ Ⓔ	53. Ⓐ Ⓑ Ⓒ Ⓓ Ⓔ	86. Ⓐ Ⓑ Ⓒ Ⓓ Ⓔ
21. Ⓐ Ⓑ Ⓒ Ⓓ Ⓔ	54. Ⓐ Ⓑ Ⓒ Ⓓ Ⓔ	87. Ⓐ Ⓑ Ⓒ Ⓓ Ⓔ
22. Ⓐ Ⓑ Ⓒ Ⓓ Ⓔ	55. Ⓐ Ⓑ Ⓒ Ⓓ Ⓔ	88. Ⓐ Ⓑ Ⓒ Ⓓ Ⓔ
23. Ⓐ Ⓑ Ⓒ Ⓓ Ⓔ	56. Ⓐ Ⓑ Ⓒ Ⓓ Ⓔ	89. Ⓐ Ⓑ Ⓒ Ⓓ Ⓔ
24. Ⓐ Ⓑ Ⓒ Ⓓ Ⓔ	57. Ⓐ Ⓑ Ⓒ Ⓓ Ⓔ	90. Ⓐ Ⓑ Ⓒ Ⓓ Ⓔ
25. Ⓐ Ⓑ Ⓒ Ⓓ Ⓔ	58. Ⓐ Ⓑ Ⓒ Ⓓ Ⓔ	91. Ⓐ Ⓑ Ⓒ Ⓓ Ⓔ
26. Ⓐ Ⓑ Ⓒ Ⓓ Ⓔ	59. Ⓐ Ⓑ Ⓒ Ⓓ Ⓔ	92. Ⓐ Ⓑ Ⓒ Ⓓ Ⓔ
27. Ⓐ Ⓑ Ⓒ Ⓓ Ⓔ	60. Ⓐ Ⓑ Ⓒ Ⓓ Ⓔ	93. Ⓐ Ⓑ Ⓒ Ⓓ Ⓔ
28. Ⓐ Ⓑ Ⓒ Ⓓ Ⓔ	61. Ⓐ Ⓑ Ⓒ Ⓓ Ⓔ	94. Ⓐ Ⓑ Ⓒ Ⓓ Ⓔ
29. Ⓐ Ⓑ Ⓒ Ⓓ Ⓔ	62. Ⓐ Ⓑ Ⓒ Ⓓ Ⓔ	95. Ⓐ Ⓑ Ⓒ Ⓓ Ⓔ
30. Ⓐ Ⓑ Ⓒ Ⓓ Ⓔ	63. Ⓐ Ⓑ Ⓒ Ⓓ Ⓔ	96. Ⓐ Ⓑ Ⓒ Ⓓ Ⓔ
31. Ⓐ Ⓑ Ⓒ Ⓓ Ⓔ	64. Ⓐ Ⓑ Ⓒ Ⓓ Ⓔ	97. Ⓐ Ⓑ Ⓒ Ⓓ Ⓔ
32. Ⓐ Ⓑ Ⓒ Ⓓ Ⓔ	65. Ⓐ Ⓑ Ⓒ Ⓓ Ⓔ	98. Ⓐ Ⓑ Ⓒ Ⓓ Ⓔ
33. Ⓐ Ⓑ Ⓒ Ⓓ Ⓔ	66. Ⓐ Ⓑ Ⓒ Ⓓ Ⓔ	99. Ⓐ Ⓑ Ⓒ Ⓓ Ⓔ
		100. Ⓐ Ⓑ Ⓒ Ⓓ Ⓔ

AP BIOLOGY
TEST 5

1. (A) (B) (C) (D) (E)	34. (A) (B) (C) (D) (E)	67. (A) (B) (C) (D) (E)
2. (A) (B) (C) (D) (E)	35. (A) (B) (C) (D) (E)	68. (A) (B) (C) (D) (E)
3. (A) (B) (C) (D) (E)	36. (A) (B) (C) (D) (E)	69. (A) (B) (C) (D) (E)
4. (A) (B) (C) (D) (E)	37. (A) (B) (C) (D) (E)	70. (A) (B) (C) (D) (E)
5. (A) (B) (C) (D) (E)	38. (A) (B) (C) (D) (E)	71. (A) (B) (C) (D) (E)
6. (A) (B) (C) (D) (E)	39. (A) (B) (C) (D) (E)	72. (A) (B) (C) (D) (E)
7. (A) (B) (C) (D) (E)	40. (A) (B) (C) (D) (E)	73. (A) (B) (C) (D) (E)
8. (A) (B) (C) (D) (E)	41. (A) (B) (C) (D) (E)	74. (A) (B) (C) (D) (E)
9. (A) (B) (C) (D) (E)	42. (A) (B) (C) (D) (E)	75. (A) (B) (C) (D) (E)
10. (A) (B) (C) (D) (E)	43. (A) (B) (C) (D) (E)	76. (A) (B) (C) (D) (E)
11. (A) (B) (C) (D) (E)	44. (A) (B) (C) (D) (E)	77. (A) (B) (C) (D) (E)
12. (A) (B) (C) (D) (E)	45. (A) (B) (C) (D) (E)	78. (A) (B) (C) (D) (E)
13. (A) (B) (C) (D) (E)	46. (A) (B) (C) (D) (E)	79. (A) (B) (C) (D) (E)
14. (A) (B) (C) (D) (E)	47. (A) (B) (C) (D) (E)	80. (A) (B) (C) (D) (E)
15. (A) (B) (C) (D) (E)	48. (A) (B) (C) (D) (E)	81. (A) (B) (C) (D) (E)
16. (A) (B) (C) (D) (E)	49. (A) (B) (C) (D) (E)	82. (A) (B) (C) (D) (E)
17. (A) (B) (C) (D) (E)	50. (A) (B) (C) (D) (E)	83. (A) (B) (C) (D) (E)
18. (A) (B) (C) (D) (E)	51. (A) (B) (C) (D) (E)	84. (A) (B) (C) (D) (E)
19. (A) (B) (C) (D) (E)	52. (A) (B) (C) (D) (E)	85. (A) (B) (C) (D) (E)
20. (A) (B) (C) (D) (E)	53. (A) (B) (C) (D) (E)	86. (A) (B) (C) (D) (E)
21. (A) (B) (C) (D) (E)	54. (A) (B) (C) (D) (E)	87. (A) (B) (C) (D) (E)
22. (A) (B) (C) (D) (E)	55. (A) (B) (C) (D) (E)	88. (A) (B) (C) (D) (E)
23. (A) (B) (C) (D) (E)	56. (A) (B) (C) (D) (E)	89. (A) (B) (C) (D) (E)
24. (A) (B) (C) (D) (E)	57. (A) (B) (C) (D) (E)	90. (A) (B) (C) (D) (E)
25. (A) (B) (C) (D) (E)	58. (A) (B) (C) (D) (E)	91. (A) (B) (C) (D) (E)
26. (A) (B) (C) (D) (E)	59. (A) (B) (C) (D) (E)	92. (A) (B) (C) (D) (E)
27. (A) (B) (C) (D) (E)	60. (A) (B) (C) (D) (E)	93. (A) (B) (C) (D) (E)
28. (A) (B) (C) (D) (E)	61. (A) (B) (C) (D) (E)	94. (A) (B) (C) (D) (E)
29. (A) (B) (C) (D) (E)	62. (A) (B) (C) (D) (E)	95. (A) (B) (C) (D) (E)
30. (A) (B) (C) (D) (E)	63. (A) (B) (C) (D) (E)	96. (A) (B) (C) (D) (E)
31. (A) (B) (C) (D) (E)	64. (A) (B) (C) (D) (E)	97. (A) (B) (C) (D) (E)
32. (A) (B) (C) (D) (E)	65. (A) (B) (C) (D) (E)	98. (A) (B) (C) (D) (E)
33. (A) (B) (C) (D) (E)	66. (A) (B) (C) (D) (E)	99. (A) (B) (C) (D) (E)
		100. (A) (B) (C) (D) (E)

AP BIOLOGY
TEST 6

1. Ⓐ Ⓑ Ⓒ Ⓓ Ⓔ	34. Ⓐ Ⓑ Ⓒ Ⓓ Ⓔ	67. Ⓐ Ⓑ Ⓒ Ⓓ Ⓔ
2. Ⓐ Ⓑ Ⓒ Ⓓ Ⓔ	35. Ⓐ Ⓑ Ⓒ Ⓓ Ⓔ	68. Ⓐ Ⓑ Ⓒ Ⓓ Ⓔ
3. Ⓐ Ⓑ Ⓒ Ⓓ Ⓔ	36. Ⓐ Ⓑ Ⓒ Ⓓ Ⓔ	69. Ⓐ Ⓑ Ⓒ Ⓓ Ⓔ
4. Ⓐ Ⓑ Ⓒ Ⓓ Ⓔ	37. Ⓐ Ⓑ Ⓒ Ⓓ Ⓔ	70. Ⓐ Ⓑ Ⓒ Ⓓ Ⓔ
5. Ⓐ Ⓑ Ⓒ Ⓓ Ⓔ	38. Ⓐ Ⓑ Ⓒ Ⓓ Ⓔ	71. Ⓐ Ⓑ Ⓒ Ⓓ Ⓔ
6. Ⓐ Ⓑ Ⓒ Ⓓ Ⓔ	39. Ⓐ Ⓑ Ⓒ Ⓓ Ⓔ	72. Ⓐ Ⓑ Ⓒ Ⓓ Ⓔ
7. Ⓐ Ⓑ Ⓒ Ⓓ Ⓔ	40. Ⓐ Ⓑ Ⓒ Ⓓ Ⓔ	73. Ⓐ Ⓑ Ⓒ Ⓓ Ⓔ
8. Ⓐ Ⓑ Ⓒ Ⓓ Ⓔ	41. Ⓐ Ⓑ Ⓒ Ⓓ Ⓔ	74. Ⓐ Ⓑ Ⓒ Ⓓ Ⓔ
9. Ⓐ Ⓑ Ⓒ Ⓓ Ⓔ	42. Ⓐ Ⓑ Ⓒ Ⓓ Ⓔ	75. Ⓐ Ⓑ Ⓒ Ⓓ Ⓔ
10. Ⓐ Ⓑ Ⓒ Ⓓ Ⓔ	43. Ⓐ Ⓑ Ⓒ Ⓓ Ⓔ	76. Ⓐ Ⓑ Ⓒ Ⓓ Ⓔ
11. Ⓐ Ⓑ Ⓒ Ⓓ Ⓔ	44. Ⓐ Ⓑ Ⓒ Ⓓ Ⓔ	77. Ⓐ Ⓑ Ⓒ Ⓓ Ⓔ
12. Ⓐ Ⓑ Ⓒ Ⓓ Ⓔ	45. Ⓐ Ⓑ Ⓒ Ⓓ Ⓔ	78. Ⓐ Ⓑ Ⓒ Ⓓ Ⓔ
13. Ⓐ Ⓑ Ⓒ Ⓓ Ⓔ	46. Ⓐ Ⓑ Ⓒ Ⓓ Ⓔ	79. Ⓐ Ⓑ Ⓒ Ⓓ Ⓔ
14. Ⓐ Ⓑ Ⓒ Ⓓ Ⓔ	47. Ⓐ Ⓑ Ⓒ Ⓓ Ⓔ	80. Ⓐ Ⓑ Ⓒ Ⓓ Ⓔ
15. Ⓐ Ⓑ Ⓒ Ⓓ Ⓔ	48. Ⓐ Ⓑ Ⓒ Ⓓ Ⓔ	81. Ⓐ Ⓑ Ⓒ Ⓓ Ⓔ
16. Ⓐ Ⓑ Ⓒ Ⓓ Ⓔ	49. Ⓐ Ⓑ Ⓒ Ⓓ Ⓔ	82. Ⓐ Ⓑ Ⓒ Ⓓ Ⓔ
17. Ⓐ Ⓑ Ⓒ Ⓓ Ⓔ	50. Ⓐ Ⓑ Ⓒ Ⓓ Ⓔ	83. Ⓐ Ⓑ Ⓒ Ⓓ Ⓔ
18. Ⓐ Ⓑ Ⓒ Ⓓ Ⓔ	51. Ⓐ Ⓑ Ⓒ Ⓓ Ⓔ	84. Ⓐ Ⓑ Ⓒ Ⓓ Ⓔ
19. Ⓐ Ⓑ Ⓒ Ⓓ Ⓔ	52. Ⓐ Ⓑ Ⓒ Ⓓ Ⓔ	85. Ⓐ Ⓑ Ⓒ Ⓓ Ⓔ
20. Ⓐ Ⓑ Ⓒ Ⓓ Ⓔ	53. Ⓐ Ⓑ Ⓒ Ⓓ Ⓔ	86. Ⓐ Ⓑ Ⓒ Ⓓ Ⓔ
21. Ⓐ Ⓑ Ⓒ Ⓓ Ⓔ	54. Ⓐ Ⓑ Ⓒ Ⓓ Ⓔ	87. Ⓐ Ⓑ Ⓒ Ⓓ Ⓔ
22. Ⓐ Ⓑ Ⓒ Ⓓ Ⓔ	55. Ⓐ Ⓑ Ⓒ Ⓓ Ⓔ	88. Ⓐ Ⓑ Ⓒ Ⓓ Ⓔ
23. Ⓐ Ⓑ Ⓒ Ⓓ Ⓔ	56. Ⓐ Ⓑ Ⓒ Ⓓ Ⓔ	89. Ⓐ Ⓑ Ⓒ Ⓓ Ⓔ
24. Ⓐ Ⓑ Ⓒ Ⓓ Ⓔ	57. Ⓐ Ⓑ Ⓒ Ⓓ Ⓔ	90. Ⓐ Ⓑ Ⓒ Ⓓ Ⓔ
25. Ⓐ Ⓑ Ⓒ Ⓓ Ⓔ	58. Ⓐ Ⓑ Ⓒ Ⓓ Ⓔ	91. Ⓐ Ⓑ Ⓒ Ⓓ Ⓔ
26. Ⓐ Ⓑ Ⓒ Ⓓ Ⓔ	59. Ⓐ Ⓑ Ⓒ Ⓓ Ⓔ	92. Ⓐ Ⓑ Ⓒ Ⓓ Ⓔ
27. Ⓐ Ⓑ Ⓒ Ⓓ Ⓔ	60. Ⓐ Ⓑ Ⓒ Ⓓ Ⓔ	93. Ⓐ Ⓑ Ⓒ Ⓓ Ⓔ
28. Ⓐ Ⓑ Ⓒ Ⓓ Ⓔ	61. Ⓐ Ⓑ Ⓒ Ⓓ Ⓔ	94. Ⓐ Ⓑ Ⓒ Ⓓ Ⓔ
29. Ⓐ Ⓑ Ⓒ Ⓓ Ⓔ	62. Ⓐ Ⓑ Ⓒ Ⓓ Ⓔ	95. Ⓐ Ⓑ Ⓒ Ⓓ Ⓔ
30. Ⓐ Ⓑ Ⓒ Ⓓ Ⓔ	63. Ⓐ Ⓑ Ⓒ Ⓓ Ⓔ	96. Ⓐ Ⓑ Ⓒ Ⓓ Ⓔ
31. Ⓐ Ⓑ Ⓒ Ⓓ Ⓔ	64. Ⓐ Ⓑ Ⓒ Ⓓ Ⓔ	97. Ⓐ Ⓑ Ⓒ Ⓓ Ⓔ
32. Ⓐ Ⓑ Ⓒ Ⓓ Ⓔ	65. Ⓐ Ⓑ Ⓒ Ⓓ Ⓔ	98. Ⓐ Ⓑ Ⓒ Ⓓ Ⓔ
33. Ⓐ Ⓑ Ⓒ Ⓓ Ⓔ	66. Ⓐ Ⓑ Ⓒ Ⓓ Ⓔ	99. Ⓐ Ⓑ Ⓒ Ⓓ Ⓔ
		100. Ⓐ Ⓑ Ⓒ Ⓓ Ⓔ

THE ADVANCED PLACEMENT
EXAMINATION IN
BIOLOGY
LAB REVIEWS

Our Lab Reviews are adapted from the acclaimed Web site of James M. Buckley, Jr., an AP Biology teacher at Edwards-Knox Central School in Russell, New York. Mr. Buckley has been a high school science teacher for over 20 years, and was the recipient of the 2003 Outstanding Biology Teacher Award – New York presented by the National Association of Biology Teachers (NABT). He has also been cited as Educator of the Week by WWNY-TV, Watertown, N.Y.

For a Web-based version of this Lab Review and additional information, please visit http://www.ekcsk12.org/science/aplabreview/

The quality of his Web pages has been recognized by SciLinks (National Science Teachers Association) and the Biology Mentor Network.

DIFFUSION & OSMOSIS (LAB 1)

KEY CONCEPTS

Diffusion

Molecules, which are in constant motion, tend to move from regions of higher concentrations to lesser concentrations. Diffusion is defined as the net movement of molecules down their concentration gradient.

Osmosis

Osmosis is the passive transport (diffusion) of water. In osmosis, water moves through a semi-permeable membrane from a region of higher concentration to a region of lower concentration.

Solutions

The terms hypotonic, hypertonic, and isotonic are used to compare solutions relative to their solute concentrations. The hypotonic side is the side with the larger water percentage and a lower solute concentration. The hypertonic side is the side with the smaller water percentage and a higher solute concentration. It is isotonic when both sides have equal concentrations of solute and water percentages.

LAB DESIGN

Exercise 1: Diffusion

Fill a dialysis bag with a sugar/starch solution and immerse the bag in a dilute iodine solution. Water, sugar, starch, and iodine molecules will all be in motion, and each molecule will move to a region of lower concentration, unless the molecule is too large to pass through the membrane. Your task is to determine the relative size of the various molecules and gather evidence of molecular movement.

Note: When iodine comes in contact with starch, it changes from an orange-brown color to blue-black.

Exercise 2: Osmosis

Investigate the relationship between solute concentration and water movement by filling six different dialysis bags with increasing concentrations of sucrose and placing the bags into distilled water. After the time for the experiment has elapsed, compare the initial weight of each bag with its final weight, calculate the percent change in mass, pool your data with that of your classmates, and graph your results.

Exercise 3: Water Potential & Potato Core

This exercise is similar to Exercise 2, except that you use cores from potatoes instead of dialysis bags. Submerge the cores in solutions of varying sucrose concentrations. When calculating the percent change in mass, you will notice some of the cores have gained weight while others have lost weight, depending on the movement of water. Graph this data and determine which concentration of the sucrose solution is in equilibrium with the cores. Since you know that the pressure potential of the surrounding solution in an open beaker is zero, you can now calculate the water potential.

Exercise 4: Water Potential

Use the value for the molar concentration of the potato cores that you obtain in Exercise 3 to determine the water potential for the potato cells.

Exercise 5: Plasmolysis

Watch the effect of placing a living cell into a solution that has a lower or higher concentration of water than the cell.

ANALYSIS OF RESULTS

Solute potential $(\Psi_s) = -iCRT$

i = The number of particles the molecule will make in water; for NaCl this is 2; for sucrose or glucose, this number is 1

C = Molar concentration (from your experimental data)

R = Pressure constant = 0.0831 liter bar/mole K

T = Temperature in degrees Kelvin = 273 + °C of solution

ENZYME CATALYSIS (LAB 2)

KEY CONCEPTS

Enzymes

Enzymes lower the activation energy necessary for a reaction to occur. The molecule that an enzyme acts on is called the substrate. In an enzyme reaction, substrate molecules are changed and a product is formed. The enzyme molecule is unchanged after the reaction, and it can continue to catalyze the same type of reaction over and over. Each enzyme is specific to the reaction it will catalyze.

Note: In this lab, catalase is the enzyme. It will react with hydrogen peroxide (H_2O_2), the substate. The products formed should be water and oxygen.

$$H_2O_2 \text{ --catalase--> } H_2O + O_2$$

Enzyme Structure

Enzymes are globular proteins. Their folded conformation creates an area known as the active site. The nature and arrangement of amino acids in the active site make it specific for only one type of substrate.

Even when different substrate molecules are present, only those that have the specific shape complementary to the active site are able to bind with the enzyme's active site.

When an enzyme binds to the appropriate substrate, subtle changes in the active site occur. This alteration of the active site is known as an induced fit. Induced fit enhances catalysis, as the enzyme converts substrate to product.

Factors Influencing Enzyme Function

Two important influences are pH and temperature. When an enzyme's conformation is significantly altered because of pH or temperature variation, the enzyme may no longer catalyze reactions. An enzyme is said to be denatured when it loses its functional shape.

LAB DESIGN

Overview & Adding Substances

Investigate the rate at which the enzyme catalase converts substrate to product by allowing catalase to react with hydrogen peroxide for varying amounts of time and then stop the reactions by adding H_2SO_4.

To determine the amount of hydrogen peroxide that remains after the reaction, you will do a titration with $KMnO_4$. In such a titration, you slowly add a chemical ($KMnO_4$) that will cause a color change until a target color is achieved.

Add 10 ml of H_2O_2 to 7 different beakers. Label the 7 beakers: 0 sec (control), 10 sec, 30 sec, 60 sec, 120 sec, 180 sec, and 360 sec. Add 1 ml of catalase to each of the beakers. Allow the reaction to occur for the time labeled on each of the beakers. After the time has elapsed, add 10 ml of H_2SO_4 to stop the reaction.

Titration

To determine how much hydrogen peroxide (substrate) has been broken down by catalase at varying times, measure the amount of peroxide remaining in each flask.

To do so, slowly add $KMnO_4$, which is purple, to the flask. The peroxide in the flask causes the $KMnO_4$ to lose color when the solution is mixed thoroughly. When all the peroxide has reacted with $KMnO_4$, any additional $KMnO_4$ will remain light brown or pinkish even after you swirl the mixture. This is the endpoint. Record the amount of $KMnO_4$ you have used. (The more $KMnO_4$ you use, the more peroxide is in the flask.)

ANALYSIS OF RESULTS

We can calculate the rate of a reaction by measuring, over time, either the disappearance of substrate or the appearance of product.

$$\text{Rate} = \frac{\Delta y}{\Delta x}$$

MITOSIS & MEIOSIS (LAB 3)

KEY CONCEPTS

Mitosis

Mitosis is the division involved in the development of an adult organism from a single fertilized egg, in growth and repair of tissues, in regeneration of body parts, and in asexual reproduction. The parent cell produces two genetically identical "daughter cells." Mitosis can occur in both diploid (2n) and haploid (n) cells.

Meiosis

Meiosis is the division of diploid (2n) parent cells to produce the gametes or spores that give rise to new individuals. The process includes two divisions, unlike Mitosis, in which cells divide only once. The parent cell will produce four haploid (n) daughter cells, each with one half of the chromosomes as the parent cell.

In spermogenesis (male), the four cells will be equal in size. In oogenesis (female), there will be one large cell and three smaller cells.

Crossing Over (Meiosis)

Each parent cell has pairs of homologous chromosomes, one from the father and one from the mother. In meiosis, the maternal and paternal chromosomes are put into the daughter cells in many different combinations (in humans there are 2^{23} possible combinations). This ensures genetic variation in sexually reproducing organisms. Further genetic variation comes from crossing over, which may occur during prophase I of meiosis.

LAB DESIGN

Part I: Mitosis

Sketch the events of cell division in either plant or animal cells using a microscope slide of cells at various stages in the process of division.

Interphase (the resting phase): The nucleolus and the nuclear envelope are distinct and the chromosomes are in the form of threadlike chromatin.

Prophase: The chromosomes appear condensed, and the nuclear envelope is not apparent.

Metaphase: Thick, coiled chromosomes, each with two chromatids, are lined up on the metaphase plate.

Anaphase: The chromatids of each chromosome have separated and are moving toward the poles.

Telophase: The chromosomes are at the poles, and are becoming more diffuse. The nuclear envelope is reforming. The cytoplasm may be dividing.

Cytokinesis: Division into two daughter cells is complete.

Part II: Meiosis

In this exercise you observe the results of crossing over in a fungus, *Sordaria*. A cross between two haploid strains of *Sordaria* produces spores of different colors.

Where the growing filaments of the two strains meet, fertilization occurs and zygotes form. Meiosis occurs within fruiting bodies to form haploid ascospores, spores contained in asci (special sacs). Then one mitotic division doubles the number of ascospores to eight.

ANALYSIS OF RESULTS

Part I: Mitosis

Once the approximate duration of a particular cell cycle is known, it's possible to calculate the amount of time the cell spends in each phase. To do so you need to (1) Determine the approximate duration of the entire cycle for the cells you are studying. This information should be provided. (2) Looking at the slide, count and record the number of cells in the field of view that are in each phase. (3) Determine the *total* number of cells counted. (4) Determine the percent of cells in each stage. (5) Calculate the time (in minutes) for each phase by multiplying the percent of cells in that phase by the number of minutes for the whole cycle.

Part II: Meiosis

If the ascospores are arranged 4 dark/4 light, count the ascus as "no crossing over." If the arrangement of ascospores is in any other combination, count it as "crossing over."

PLANT PIGMENTS & PHOTOSYNTHESIS (LAB 4)

KEY CONCEPTS

In photosynthesis, plant cells convert light energy into chemical energy that is stored in sugars and other organic compounds. Critical to the process is chlorophyll, the primary photosynthetic pigment in chloroplasts.

Chromatography

Paper chromatography is a technique used to separate a mixture into its component molecules. The molecules migrate, or move up the paper, at different rates because of differences in solubility, molecular mass, and hydrogen bonding with the paper.

Photosynthesis

In the light reactions of photosynthesis, light energy excites electrons in plant pigments such as chlorophyll, and boosts them to a higher energy level. These high-energy electrons reduce compounds (electron acceptors) in the thylakoid membrane, and the energy is eventually captured in the chemical bonds of NADPH and ATP.

LAB DESIGN

Chromatography

In paper chromatography, the pigments are dissolved in a solvent that carries them up the paper. To separate the pigments of the chloroplasts, an organic solvent must be used.

In this experiment, a drop of leaf extract is placed near the bottom of chromatography paper. This paper is then placed in a solvent, which moves up the paper by capillary action.

Photosynthesis

The rate of photosynthesis in chloroplasts is measured using a dye called DPIP. DPIP changes color when it accepts electrons that would normally be accepted by NADP, the electron acceptor of the light-dependent reaction of photosynthesis. As DPIP accepts electrons, it changes from blue to clear.

A spectrophotometer is used to measure the color change, which gives an indication of the rate of the light reactions of photosynthesis under various conditions.

ANALYSIS OF RESULTS

Chromatography

As the solvent touches the pigment extract, each pigment within the extract moves at a different rate. In the end, there should be four spots on the paper, each representing one of the four pigments (chlorophyll *a*, chlorophyll *b*, xanthrophylls, and carotenoids).

Pigments move at different rates according to their ability to dissolve in the solvent. The pigment that dissolves the best moves up the paper the fastest.

The rate of migration can be calculated.

Photosynthesis

Three things can affect photosynthesis: light intensity, light wavelength, and temperature.

In experimental design, you can vary these three variables to determine their effects on photosynthesis.

Note: Only change one variable at a time.

CELL RESPIRATION (LAB 5)

KEY CONCEPTS

Cellular respiration occurs in most cells of both plants and animals. It takes place in the mitochondria, where energy from nutrients converts ADP to ATP. ATP is used for all cellular activities that require energy.

The equation for cellular respiration is:

$$glucose + oxygen + ADP = carbon\ dioxide + water + ATP$$

LAB DESIGN

Observe evidence of respiration in pea seeds and investigate the effect of temperature on the rate of respiration. To do so, you can measure (1) the amount of glucose consumed, (2) the amount of oxygen consumed, and (3) the amount of carbon dioxide produced.

In this lab we are going to measure the amount of oxygen consumed by using a respirometer. By submerging the respirometer underwater, we know that no air will enter the respirometer. The amount of water that enters the respirometer is directly proportional to the amount of oxygen used up by the organism in the respirometer.

ANALYSIS OF RESULTS

After you have collected data for the amount of oxygen consumed over time by germinating and nongerminating peas at two different temperatures, you can compare the rates of respiration. Let's review how to calculate rate.

$$\text{Rate} = \text{slope of the line, or } \frac{\Delta y}{\Delta x}$$

In this case, Δy is the change in volume, and Δx is the change in time (10 min).

You will find that germinating plants have a high respiratory rate, while non-germinating plants have a low respiratory rate.

MOLECULAR BIOLOGY (LAB 6)

OVERVIEW

In the first part of the lab, you will use antibiotic-resistant plasmids to transform *Escherichia coli* by introducing the gene for resistance to the antibiotic ampicillin from the plasmids into *E. coli* (*E. coli* is killed by ampicillin). If the *E. coli* incorporate the foreign DNA, they will become ampicillin resistant.

In the second part, you will use gel electrophoresis to separate fragments of DNA for further analysis. Then you will compare fragments of unknown size to fragments of a known size to calculate the unknown fragment sizes.

KEY CONCEPTS

Bacterial Transformation

Genetic transformation occurs when a host organism takes in foreign DNA and expresses the foreign gene.

Electrophoresis

Bacteria have enzymes that cut, or "digest," the DNA of foreign organisms and thereby protect the cells from invaders such as viruses. These enzymes are known as restriction enzymes. Each is able to recognize and cut at a specific DNA sequence, known as a recognition sequence.

The discovery of restriction enzymes made genetic engineering possible because researchers could use them to cut DNA into fragments that could be analyzed and used in a variety of procedures.

Restriction Enzymes

Like all enzymes, restriction enzymes are highly specific. They cut DNA only within very precise recognition sequences.

Gel Electrophoresis

Gel electrophoresis is a procedure that separates molecules on the basis of their rate of movement through a gel under the influence of an electrical field. The direction of movement is affected by the charge of the molecules, and the rate of movement is affected by their size and shape, the density of the gel, and the strength of the electrical field.

DNA is a negatively charged molecule, so it will move toward the positive pole of the gel when a current is applied. When DNA has been cut by restriction enzymes, the different-sized fragments will migrate at different rates. Because the smallest fragments move the most quickly, they will migrate the farthest during the time the current is on. Keep in mind that the length of each fragment is measured in number of DNA base pairs.

LAB DESIGN

Part I: Transformation

In this lab, you use plasmids that carry the amp^R gene to transform *E. coli* cells that lack this gene. Also prepare a second group of *E. coli* cells as a control to verify that *E. coli* will not grow on agar with ampicillin unless it is transformed.

The Process: (1) Transfer ampicillin sensitive *E. coli* cells in their log phase of growth to cold $CaCl_2$ solution. (2) Add amp^R plasmids to the experimental cells only (not to control). (3) Heat-shock cells at 42 degrees C. (Some of the competent cells will take up the amp^R plasmid and will be transformed). (4) Spread the treated cells on an agar plate containing ampicillin. (5) Incubate cells for 24 hours. (6) Experiment is finished. You should see that only colonies of *E. coli* that have been transformed by the amp^R gene grow.

The procedure is the same for the control group except in step 2, where you add amp^R plasmids to the experimental cells but not to the control cells.

Part II: DNA Electrophoresis

Three samples of DNA from a virus, the bacteriophage lambda. One sample will be uncut DNA, one will be incubated with the restriction enzyme HindIII, and one will be incubated with EcoRI. By separating the fragments of DNA by electrophoresis and staining the DNA for visualization, you can determine the fragment sizes formed in the EcoRI digest.

ANALYSIS OF RESULTS

Bacterial Transformation

Control 1: No amp^R plasmids added, No ampicillin – *tons of growth*
Control 2: No amp^R plasmids added, Ampicillin – *no growth*
Experiment 1: Amp^R plasmids added, No ampicillin – *tons of growth*
Experiment 2: Amp^R plasmids added, Ampicillin – *little growth*

DNA Electrophoresis

Run the unknown DNA alongside DNA with known fragment sizes. The known DNA acts as a marker. In your laboratory, the DNA that has been cut with HindIII is the marker; you will use it to help you determine the fragment sizes in the EcoRI digest.

Make a standard curve for the known sample, DNA plus HindIII. Measure the distance each HindIII fragment migrated on the gel.

GENETICS OF ORGANISMS (LAB 7)

KEY CONCEPTS

Mendelian Genetics

In the nineteenth century, Gregor Mendel discovered the principles of inheritance through a series of careful experiments with peas. We know now that physical characteristics are transmitted from generation to generation according to some general patterns. When we have sufficient information about the parents, we can predict the occurrence of traits in offspring. By analyzing the offspring, we can discern the mode of transmission—monohybrid or dihybrid, sex-linked or autosomal.

Distinguishing Sexes

Adult Female: long pointy abdomen with stripes

Adult Male: blunt, darker abdomen

LAB DESIGN

By breeding fruit flies (*Drosophila melanogaster*) of unknown genetic composition and studying the traits and ratios seen in their offspring, you will determine whether a trait follows a monohybrid or dihybrid pattern of inheritance and whether it is sex-linked or autosomal. You will use statistical analysis to support your conclusions.

Over a period of four weeks, you will study three generations of flies. You begin with a parental (P) generation that has already mated. Check every generation for the following characteristics and record the numbers.

Males vs. Females
Ebony Body vs. Wingless
White Eyes vs. Sepia Eyes

Note: When eggs and larvae appear, remove the adult flies from the vial so that you don't get generations confused.

ANALYSIS OF RESULTS

The chi-square (x^2) test. This analytical tool tests the validity of a null hypothesis, which states that there is no statistically significant difference between the observed results of your experiment and the expected results. When there is little difference between the observed results and the expected results, you obtain a very low chi-square value; your hypothesis is supported.

The formula for chi-square is:

$$x^2 = \text{the sum of } \frac{(o - e)^2}{e}$$

where:

o = observed number of individuals

e = expected number of individuals

POPULATION GENETICS & EVOLUTION (LAB 8)

KEY CONCEPTS

Hardy-Weinberg Law of Genetic Equilibrium

In 1908, G. Hardy and W. Weinberg independently proposed that the frequency of alleles and genotypes in a population will remain constant from generation to generation if the population is stable and in genetic equilibrium. Five conditions are required in order for a population to remain at Hardy-Weinberg equilibrium:

1. Large Population

2. Random Mating

3. No Mutations

4. No Natural Selection

5. No Immigration

Equations:

$p + q = 1$

$p^2 + 2pq + q^2 = 1$

p = dominate allele

q = recessive allele

LAB DESIGN

The experiment in this laboratory is a test of Hardy-Weinberg equilibrium in a "mating population," represented by you and your classmates. Your instructor will assign each class member a genotype (*AA, Aa,* or *aa*). The initial allelic frequency of the population will be 0.5 *A* and 0.5 *a*. Your population will simulate several different conditions that might alter allelic frequency, and you will determine the allelic frequencies over several generations.

ANALYSIS OF RESULTS

Combine data.

TRANSPIRATION (LAB 9)

KEY CONCEPTS

Movement of Water in Plants

Water enters a plant through the root hairs, passes through the tissues of the root into the xylem, and travels up through the xylem vessels into the leaves. Transpiration, the evaporation of water from the leaves, is the major factor that pulls the water up through the plant.

Transpiration

There are hundreds of stomata in the epidermis of a leaf. Most are located in the lower epidermis. This reduces water loss because the lower surface receives less solar radiation than the upper surface. Each stoma allows the carbon dioxide necessary for photosynthesis to enter, while water evaporates through each one in transpiration.

Guard Cells

Guard cells are cells surrounding each stoma. They help to regulate the rate of transpiration by opening and closing the stomata.

LAB DESIGN

In this lab, you use a potometer. A potometer is a device that measures the rate at which a plant draws up water. Since the plant draws up water as it loses it by transpiration, you are able to measure the rate of transpiration.

Set up four potometers to measure the rate of transpiration in four different scenarios. The four different situations are room temperature (control), mist, wind, and bright light.

Measure the water loss in each of the potometers every three minutes for thirty minutes.

You will also need to measure the surface of the leaf.

In the other part of the lab, you will need to be able to recognize the following plant structures: xylem, phloem, parenchyma, and epidermis.

ANALYSIS OF RESULTS

With the data, calculate the water loss per minute by taking the final amount of water loss (ml) and dividing it by the leaf's surface area.

PHYSIOLOGY OF THE CIRCULATORY SYSTEM (LAB 10)

KEY CONCEPTS

Factors Influencing Heart Rate

Your heart rate changes with your body position. Your heart rate increases when you exercise.

Blood Pressure

A blood pressure reading consists of two numbers: a systolic pressure and a diastolic pressure. Normal blood pressure for a healthy adult is about 120/80. The numerator is the systolic pressure and the denominator is the diastolic pressure.

The Movement of Blood

Blood moving through the blood vessels exerts pressure against the vessel walls. This blood pressure is highest in the aorta. It decreases as the blood moves through the arterioles, capillaries, venules, and veins.

With each contraction of the heart, you can feel the expansion and recoil of the elastic arteries where they pass near the surface of the skin. This is the pulse. When you take your pulse, you measure heart rate—the number of times the heart contracts per minute.

Concept of Q_{10}

Q_{10} measures the increase in metabolic activity resulting from an increase in body temperature. *Daphnia* can adjust their temperature to the environment; as the temperature in the environment increases, their body temperature also increases. This, in turn, increases their heartbeat rate per minute.

Cold Blooded Animals

Heat generated can increase the body temperature and heart rate of cold blooded animals.

LAB DESIGN

Part I: Cardiovascular Activity

In your laboratory you will do five different tests of cardiovascular fitness and assign fitness points based on the results of each test.

Part II: Heart Rate in *Daphnia*

Observe *Daphnia* in a petri dish of water at three different temperatures. Time their heart rate with a stop watch, counting the contractions of their diaphragm.

ANALYSIS OF RESULTS

Part I: Cardiovascular Activity

A fit individual's pulse and blood pressure are lower and will return more quickly to the resting condition after exercise than that of a less fit individual.

Part II: Heart Rate in *Daphnia*

Record and graph the data.

ANIMAL BEHAVIOR (LAB 11)

KEY CONCEPTS

Habitat Selection

Predation and nature of the environment can influence an organism's selection of habitat.

Behaviors

Behaviors may be innate or learned. Many behaviors have both genetic and learned components.

LAB DESIGN

Observe the mating behavior of the *Drosophila melanogaster,* which includes six steps: (1) orientation, (2) male song, (3) following, (4) male licking, (5) copulation, and (6) rejection.

During the lab, you will also observe pillbug behaviors.

ANALYSIS OF RESULTS

You need to set a control in order to be sure that certain factors are influencing behavior. Also, be sure to watch more than one individual's behavior.

DISSOLVED OXYGEN & AQUATIC PRIMARY PRODUCTIVITY (LAB 12)

KEY CONCEPTS

Dissolved Oxygen Availability

Factors that influence the amount of oxygen dissolved in water are: (1) *Temperature:* As water becomes warmer, its ability to hold oxygen decreases. (2) *Photosynthetic activity:* In bright light, aquatic plants are able to produce more oxygen. (3) *Decomposition activity:* As organic material decays, microbial processes consume oxygen. (4) *Mixing and turbulence:* Wave action, waterfalls, and rapids all aerate water and increase the oxygen concentration. (5) *Salinity:* As water becomes more salty, its ability to hold oxygen decreases.

Primary Productivity

Primary productivity is the rate at which plants and other photosynthetic organisms produce organic compounds in an ecosystem.

Gross Productivity

Gross productivity is the entire photosynthetic production of organic compounds in an ecosystem.

Net Productivity

Net productivity is the organic materials that remain after photosynthetic organisms in the ecosystem have used some of these compounds for their cellular energy needs.

LAB DESIGN

In the first part of the laboratory, you measure dissolved oxygen in water at different temperatures. Many kits and testing procedures are available for measuring dissolved oxygen.

A nomograph is used to measure how much oxygen water can hold (saturation levels).

In the next part of the laboratory, you monitor the effect of varying light levels on dissolved oxygen in an algae-rich water culture.

The amount of light available for photosynthesis drops off sharply with increasing depth in an aquatic environment. You model this condition by wrapping water-sample bottles with increasing layers of screen.

The last part of the lab occurs after 24 hours. Measure the amount of oxygen present under the light conditions in each bottle.

ANALYSIS OF RESULTS

You will prove the six factors that influence the amount of oxygen dissolved in water. Refer to the Key Concepts.

THE ADVANCED PLACEMENT
EXAMINATION IN
BIOLOGY
INDEX